Press comments on
The Rough Guide to the Internet

"Brilliant ... MUST HAVE ... provides refreshingly blunt advice on the net ... brilliant hints and tips ... the unmatched leader in its field"
Sunday Times, London

"Well researched, well sourced and well written ... highly recommended"
What PC

"Über-hip. Smarter than *Dummies*. Now even idiots can become Internet savants"
Newsweek

"Anyone who isn't ordering and selling this by the lorry-load shouldn't be running a bookshop"
The Bookseller

"A seriously good book. The best, in fact"
Sun Herald, Sydne

"If knowle

"Cuts through the hype and makes all others look like nerdy textbooks"
The Australian

"Concise enough for the novice, but doesn't patronise the more advanced, if there's anything this book won't help you find, I haven't found it yet"
Evening Standard, London

"A model of brevity and clarity"
Courier Mail, Brisbane

"Written in the plain English that made Rough Guides indispensable for travelers"
MacWorld

"The only Internet book we recommend to friends"
Internet Magazine

"A pocket miracle"
Personal Computer World

"Hip and compelling ... reflects all the latest changes and fads ... a perfect balance of serious, tech-heavy background tutorial and cutting edge yellow-page guide for the 21st century"
Amazon.com

The Rough Guide to

The Internet

There are more than 150 Rough Guide travel, phrasebook, and music titles, covering destinations from Amsterdam to Zimbabwe, languages from Czech to Vietnamese, and musics from World to Opera and Jazz.

To find out more about Rough Guides, and to check out our coverage of more than 10,000 destinations, get connected to the Internet with this guide and find us on the Web at:

www.roughguides.com

This book is dedicated to the memory of my mother

Acknowledgements

I'd like to thank my agent Lesley Shaw and everyone at the Rough Guides and Penguin, especially Orla Duane, Mark Ellingham, Jonathan Buckley, Richard Trillo and Niki Smith.

The Rough Guide to

The Internet

by Angus J. Kennedy

Rough Guide to the Internet Credits

Text editor: Orla Duane
Series editor: Mark Ellingham
Production: Julia Bovis, Michelle Draycott, Susanne Hillen, Katie Pringle, Helen Prior
Design: Helen Prior
Proofreading: Orla Duane, Susanne Hillen

Publishing Information

This seventh edition published October 2001 by Rough Guides Ltd, 62–70 Shorts Gardens, London WC2H 9AH, 375 Hudson Street, New York 10014
Email: *mail@roughguides.co.uk*

Distributed by the Penguin Group

Penguin Books Ltd, 80 The Strand, London WC2R ORL
Penguin Putnam USA Inc., 375 Hudson Street, New York 10014, Penguin Books Canada Ltd, 10 Alcorn Avenue, Toronto, Ontario MV4 1E4, Penguin Books Australia Ltd, PO Box 257, Ringwood, Victoria 3134, Penguin Books (NZ) Ltd, 182–190 Wairau Road, Auckland 10

Printed in the United Kingdom by Omnia Books Ltd

552 pages; includes index

A catalogue record for this book is available from the British Library
ISBN 1-85828-739-1

Contents

Part Two: The Guide

Part Three: Contexts

Read me

Hooking up to the Internet isn't such a big deal these days. So why do you need a book to get online? Or more to the point, why do you need one once you're already online?

You don't, of course. In fact, most people just install some Internet software, start clicking, and worry about the consequences later. That's why they catch viruses (p.142), get scammed (p.178), unwittingly install "spyware" (p.262) and wonder why their computers keep crashing (p.98 and p.336). It's why so few know how to get the best from a search engine (p.157), take part in online discussions (p.197), collect their email on the road (p.134), set up a second account (p.112), maintain their privacy (p.92 and p.138), and stop junk email (p.131). And why most of their time is spent sifting through rubbish Web sites instead of going straight to the best (p.317). You can do it the hard way too, if you don't mind wasting half your life.

Or, you can do it the smart way and leave the hard work to me. I've spent the best part of the last decade test-driving software, sorting through sites, torturing search engines, and figuring out what works best. You'll find the latest results distilled in this small book. Everything from scoring a free email address (p.105) to building an online photo gallery (p.292).

If you only read one chapter, make that "Find It" (p.152). Know it back to front and you'll have the Net around your little finger. You'll be surprised at how quickly you become an expert.

The fact that I find myself flipping through this guide from time to time suggests to me that it's as much a desktop reference for old timers as a beginner's guide. If I've done my job properly, I'm hoping you'll buy the next edition, and maybe even keep a dog-eared copy by your computer for many years to come.

Best wishes and bon voyage!

Angus Kennedy
angus@easynet.co.uk

part one

basics

1

FAQs

Frequently asked questions

Before we get into the nitty-gritty of what you can do on the Internet – and what it can do for you – let's answer a few of the most **F**requently **A**sked **Q**uestions, or **FAQs** as they're called online. You'll find more detail on these subjects throughout the book.

The big picture

Okay, what's this Internet good for?

The Internet, or the **Net** as it's more often called, is a real bag of tricks. You can send documents worldwide in a flash, find an answer to any question, shop the globe, hear new music, dabble in the stock market, visit art galleries, read books, play games, chat, catch up on your latest hometown news, make new friends with similar interests, grab free software, manage your bank account, or just fritter away your spare time surfing the Web.

That's not to say the Internet is merely something to play on when you get home from work. Far from it. It's well entrenched in the workplace. Millions of companies already use it to promote their products, take orders, and support their customers. More communication is done by email than the phone, fax and printed letter combined.

Sounds like fun, but what is it exactly?

Strictly speaking, the Internet is an **international network of computers** linked up to exchange information. The word Internet is a contraction of **inter**national and **net**work.

The core of this international network consists of computers permanently joined through high-speed connections. To get on the Net, you simply connect your computer to any of these networked computers via an **Internet Service Provider (ISP)**. Once you're **online** (connected to the Net) your computer can talk to any other computer on the Internet whether it's next door or in Antarctica.

That's plain enough, but if you want a more picky definition you have to consider what it's used for as well. Mostly, that's the transfer of **electronic mail (email)** and digital publishing on the **World Wide Web**. So when people say they found something on the "Internet", they didn't find it by randomly zipping around the wires hooking up the computers, they either retrieved it from where it was stored on a computer connected to this international network, or someone sent it to them by electronic mail.

Most importantly, the Net is not about computers or the fancy phone lines that string them together. **It's about people, communication, and sharing knowledge**. It's about overcoming physical boundaries so like minds can meet. And that's why you want it.

The Internet and the Web are the same thing, right?

No, but don't be embarrassed. Not too many reporters seem to know the difference either. The **World Wide Web** (or Web) is the popular face of the Internet. It provides a simple way to navigate the vast troves of information stored online. In practice, it works a bit like flicking through a huge magazine by clicking on links with your mouse. But, the Internet is much more than just the Web. See p.69.

What's email?

Electronic mail or **email** is a way of sending messages from one computer to another. An electronic letter can cross the world in under a second.

What are newsgroups, mailing lists, and chat?

Usenet – the Net's prime discussion area – comprises over 85,000 **newsgroups**, each dedicated to a specific topic. So if you have a question, this is the place to raise it. Usenet messages are stored online for a matter of days or weeks, a bit like an online notice board.

Mailing lists perform a similar function, but the messages aren't stored online. The discussions are carried out by email. Each list has a central email address. Everything sent to that address goes to everyone on the list.

Chat, on the other hand, is instant, like a conversation. It's typically more of a social medium. For more on discussions, see (p.197).

What's the difference between the Internet, AOL and CompuServe?

AOL Anywhere

CompuServe and AOL are classed as **Online Services**. They plug in to the Internet, and thus form part of the Internet, but each also has exclusive services and content available only to their members and not to the general Internet public. See p.36.

How many are online and who are they?

Surveys estimate almost one in ten worldwide regularly access the Net. That's about 400 million people, with more than a third of them living in the USA. For in-depth demographics, market research, and statistics, see the following Web sites:

CyberAtlas **http://www.cyberatlas.internet.com**
InternetStats **http://www.internetstats.com**
NUA Internet Surveys **http://www.nua.org/surveys/**
Research Buzz **http://www.researchbuzz.com**
Web Characterization Project **http://wcp.oclc.org**

Which is better: the Net or an encyclopedia?

They don't really compare. You can look something up in an encyclopedia and get a concise answer instantly. Encyclopedias are generally well researched and reliable, and the answer is probably correct. They're also expensive, bulky, date quickly, parochial, conservative, and might not provide enough, or any, information. The Net, on the other hand, isn't edited by a single publisher. So you can find a diverse range of factoids and opinions on even the most obscure subjects. That means you're more likely to get a rounded view, but the process might take longer. Of course, the Net has the best of both worlds as most of the major encyclopedias have their very latest editions online. And what's more, they're mostly free! See (p.418)

Can I shop online?

Of course, that's why we've dedicated a whole chapter to it (p.177).

Is there a lot of really weird stuff?

Yes, lots. Just like in real life, except easier to find. See (p.460).

So is it basically a geek hangout?

It's about as geek as you want it to be, which can vary between twin hip-slung logic probes with a matching pocket protector, to not in the slightest. They say if you're bored with the Net, you're bored with life itself.

But isn't it yet another male-dominated bastion?

No, those days are well behind us. In the USA, **women actually outnumber men online**. And the rest of the world isn't far behind.

Will I make friends on the Internet?

It's easy to meet people with common interests by joining in **Usenet (newsgroup) or mailing list discussions**. And being able to discuss sensitive issues with strangers while retaining a comfortable degree of anonymity often makes for startlingly intimate communication.

Translating email pen pals into the real world of human contact, or even romance, is another matter.

So who's in charge?

No-one actually "runs" the entire Internet but there are several major players who exert unquestionable influence. To illustrate how it works in practice let's separate it into levels.

There are various bodies involved in the **theoretical and administrative levels**, such as **ICANN** which co-ordinates domain names; the **Internet Society** which, amongst other things, acts as a clearing house for technical standards; and the World Wide Web Consortium (**W3C**), which mulls over the

Web's future. You're unlikely to ever encounter any of these groups directly.

At the **practical level**, such aspects as software, network routing, and wiring are controlled by corporations such as Microsoft, Cisco, AOL, and the world's cable providers. Each element is an independent product. So if you have a problem with a program, for example, you'd have to complain to the shop that sold it to you, or the software developers. Or if you had connection problems, you'd need to call your ISP. **There is no official body responsible for tying it all together**.

The **legal level** is governed by local authorities. What's okay in one territory may be an offence in another. That means if you break a local law, you're liable to prosecution, irrespective of whether you're accessing something that's legal, or overlooked, at the source. So just because you can download a pirate copy of Photoshop from a Russian Web server doesn't make you immune to copyright laws at home. And conversely, while you might have the freedom to express your views about a foreign government, nationals of that state may not be so free to read it.

But isn't it run by the Pentagon?

When the Internet was first conceived thirty-odd years ago, as a network for the American Defense Department, its purpose was to act as a nuclear-attack-resistant method of exchanging scientific information and intelligence. But that was then. In the 1970s and 1980s several other networks, such as the **National Science Foundation Network** (NSFNET), joined, linking the

Internet to research agencies and universities. It was probably no coincidence that as the Cold War petered out, the Internet became more publicly accessible. These days, **Intelligence agencies** have the same access to the Internet as everyone else. The extent to which they use it to monitor insurgence and crime is simply a matter for speculation.

Can I make money out of it?

Possibly, but perhaps it's better to ask, "Can I continue to make money without the Internet?" The last few years have seen a gold rush in the computer hardware, software, training, and publishing industries. Some who got in early made a killing getting businesses on the Web – the Net's "commercial zone". Today, it's settled down somewhat. Web page designers are commonplace, and can no longer charge extortionate rates unless they're tied in with a major agency. However, those with serious technical and programming skills are always in big demand.

PROGRAMMER

Thousands of jobs waiting!

There are at least 50,000 openings today for men and women who can write the instructions that make computers work. For the vast majority of good jobs, a high school education, a logical mind and the right preparation are all that are required. Even newcomers earn good pay, and with experience can rise to supervisory positions at salaries of \$12,000 to \$15,000 – often much more.

LaSalle, a world leader in home education, will train you in your spare time. Tuition cost is low. Mail coupon or write to LaSalle, 417 S. Dearborn Street, Chicago, Illinois, 60605.

If you're wondering whether to throw a Web site into your existing **marketing mix** to help boost sales, the answer's probably yes. But rather than use it to try to attract customers, it's better to think of the Net as a place to post in-depth product literature, provide customer support, and canvass feedback. Not too many firms make big money from **direct sales** – though that's improving, particularly for hard-to-get products, or deep-catalog items such as CDs, books, and computer parts.

Another way to profit is to charge others to **advertise on your Web page**. You'll either need to run a very popular site or attract a certain type of customer, and you are usually paid according to the number of times visitors pursue links from your site to your sponsor's. Alternatively, if your site generates heavy traffic and looks promising, someone may want to buy you outright.

Can I make money by bulk emailing?

Advertising on the World Wide Web is perfectly acceptable but emailing protocols are more delicate. **Never, ever, ever, send bulk email** other than to people you know or who've requested information. And never post an advertisement in Usenet or to a mailing list. **Junk email is called "spam", and those who send it (spammers) are universally detested.** Try it and you'll be flooded with hate mail, and kicked offline. On the other hand, email is by far the most efficient direct response device you'll find. For instance, you could set up an **autoresponder** to send out product details upon receipt of a blank message. No dictating over the phone, no data entry from a coupon. It's instant and informal. Plus, you'll have their email address on record to follow up later. So next time you place an advertisement or Yellow Pages listing, add your email address too, and compare response rates.

What is "new media"?

Advertising suits and recruitment agencies use the term **new media** mainly to differentiate between the **old** media world of print, radio, and television and the **new** media world of audio, video, print, and software publishing on the Internet and other digital formats such as CD-ROM.

Getting online

What do I need to get started?

Although you can access the Net through all kinds of gadgets from mobile phones to televisions, to get the full Internet experience, you'll need a **personal computer** (PC), equipped with the appropriate **network device** for the type of access you're seeking. Unless you're willing to pay extra for high speed (**broadband**), you'll most likely be connecting via a **modem** hooked into your normal **telephone line**. Most computers come with modems today, as almost everyone wants to go online. So if you have a PC, modem, and telephone line, all you need next is an **Internet access account**, and possibly some **extra software** to get rolling. For more details, see (p.26).

What's an Internet access account?

You can access the Internet through any **Internet Service Provider (ISP)**. They normally offer a range of accounts, which may include standard **modem dial-up**, **ISDN**, **ADSL** and **cable.** There might also be a selection of pricing plans and added extras. Regardless of the type of Internet access you choose, you should able to do the same things, though perhaps at different speeds. For help choosing an ISP, see (p.35) and (p.467)

What about free Internet access – is it really free?

Of course not. Internet access is a costly business to run, so revenue has to come from somewhere. In the UK, where free ISPs have flourished to the point of becoming the norm, they survive by pocketing a slice of your phone bill, both while you're online and through premium-rate support lines. This scam only exists due to the UK's extortionate timed local call charges.

In other parts of the world, where local calls are unmetered or free, such deals must be subsidized by bombarding customers with advertising, tracking their movements, or by locking them within their sponsor's sites. As yet, these aren't wildly successful or attractive.

Where do I get an email address?

You should get at least one email address thrown in by your ISP with your access account. Many providers supply five or more addresses – enough for the whole family. The only problem with these addresses is that they tie you to that provider. If you want to switch providers, you'll either have to negotiate a mail-only account or obtain an address you can take on the road with you (see p.134). It's a hassle either way, so choose your provider carefully.

If you already have an email address, say at work or college, but want something **more personal or funky**, you can ask any ISP for a POP3 mail-only account, try a mail specialist such as Net Identity (http://www.netidentity.com) or sign up with a Webmail or redirection service. That way you can choose an address and use it over any connection. To score a free email address, see (p.105).

How can I find someone's email address?

The best way is to ask them. See (p.124).

Who pays for the international calls?

The Internet is barely affected by political boundaries and distance. For example, suppose you're in Boston, and you want to buzz someone in Bangkok. Provided you both have Net access, it's as quick, easy, and cheap as sending a message across the street. You compose your message, connect to your local ISP, upload your mail and then, if you're finished, disconnect.

Your **mail server** examines the message's address to determine where it has to go, and then passes it on to its appropriate neighbor, which will do the same. This usually entails routing it toward the **backbone** – the chain of high-speed links that carry the bulk of the Net's long-haul traffic. Each subsequent link will ensure that the message heads towards Bangkok rather than Bogotá or Brisbane. The whole process should take no more than a few seconds.

Apart from your Internet access subscription, **you pay only for the local phone call**. Your data will scuttle through many different networks, each with its own methods of recouping the communication costs – but adding to your phone bill isn't one of them.

Then how does the pricing model work?

Once you're on the Net, most of what's there is free. But unless you have free access through work or study, you'll probably need to pay for the privilege of being connected. That means paying an **ISP** to allow you to hook into its network. Depending on where you live, that could be a set price per month or year, an hourly rate, or a tariff based on how much you download. Then on top of that, you might have some sort of **telephone, ISDN or cable charge**. It's possible – indeed probable – that none of this money will ever go to the people who supply the content you'll be viewing. It simply goes toward maintaining the network. This imbalance is unlikely to continue. In the future you'd expect many publications (or sites) might charge a subscription. As yet, that's still rare, other than for technical and financial publications, so enjoy it while it lasts.

What's bandwidth and broadband?

Bandwidth, which is expressed in bits per second (bps), describes Internet connection capacity. It measures the speed at which you can download material from the Net. Modems are only capable of achieving a relatively **low bandwidth** connection. **Cable**, **satellite**, and **ADSL** fall into the so-called **broadband** category, meaning that they're much **faster than modems**. Strictly speaking, though, the bits and bytes don't move any faster as they're limited by the speed of light. A faster connection simply means you can move more of those bits and bytes across the wires at a time.

What if?

What if I want to cancel an email I've sent?

You can't. So, you'd better think before you click "send".

What if my email doesn't arrive?

In general Internet **email** is considerably more reliable than the postal service. If a message doesn't get through immediately, it should bounce back to you telling you what went wrong. For example, the recipients mail server might be overloaded or down for maintenance. In which case, your mail might be delayed for minutes, hours, or even a weekend. Although it's highly unlikely, it's not impossible for an email to go astray - so if someone says they didn't receive your mail, you'll have to give them the benefit of the doubt. If you don't get a reply within a few days, you could send your message again. At worst, it will act as a reminder. If you find your mail regularly takes more than a few minutes to arrive, consider switching providers.

What if I get loads of junk email?

Unfortunately, once the serious junk starts to arrive, you can't do much about it. You might have to change your address, and keep it a bit more private. See (p.131)

What if I'm harassed online?

It's not easy to harass someone seriously via the Net and get away with it. After all, it generates evidence in writing. There have already been convictions for relatively mild threats posted to Usenet newsgroups. Apart from the nature of the harassment, whether you have a case for action will depend on where you're both based. Across US State lines, it becomes an FBI matter, while internationally you might have no recourse other than to appeal to their ISP.

If you're being harassed by email; in a newsgroup, mailing list or chat channel; or on a Web page, you needn't put up with it. Though, to start with maybe you should. If you simply ignore them they'll probably go away. Most of the time, this is the best defense. If you don't put up a fight, you're no fun. And if you're being harassed unfairly in a public forum, others will usually come to your aid. But if it persists, or the harassment becomes serious you may have to react.

Your first action should be to contact them personally and politely ask them to desist. If that doesn't work, you'll have to decide whether reporting them to their ISP, and getting them booted offline will start an ongoing vendetta. Whether you have their email address or not, you can find out their ISP by tracing their IP address. That's where a Traceroute/WHOIS tool such as **NeoTrace** (http://www.neoworks.com) comes in handy. Even if they've forged their email address, you should be able to figure out where it's come from by picking through the headers for the originating IP address. Once you have the domain responsible, try an email to: abuse@ that domain. If this sounds too technical, call your ISP support for help, or turn the matter entirely over to them. For more, see: http://www.cyberangels.org and http://www.getnetwise.org

What if my children discover pornography or drugs?

If you're at all prudish, you'll get a nasty shock when you hit the Web. You only need type **the merest hint of innuendo** into a search engine to come face to face with a porno advert. In fact, what once wasn't much more than schoolboys trading Big & Busty scans has become the Net's prime cash cow. Most perfectly normal kids will search on a swearword the first chance they get – after all, children are pretty childish. Consequently, if they're the slightest bit curious about sex, it won't be long before they end up at a porno merchant. That's the truth, if you can handle it.

To be blunt, the Net isn't meant for kids, and furthermore, it's not a babysitter. If your children are at a sensitive age, and you leave them online unsupervised, you are a bad parent. While there are plenty of online activities that are perfectly suitable for all ages, risky material is never more than a few clicks away.

What can you do about it? Well, that depends whether you'd rather shield or prepare them. There are **censoring programs** that attempt to filter out questionable material, either by letting only known sites through, banning certain sites, or withholding pages containing shady words. Internet Explorer and Netscape, for example, can restrict access according to a rating system. Bear in mind that a smart kid – and no doubt that's what you're trying to raise – will find a way to veto these filters. Whatever the case, if you're worried about your kids, the Net, and sex, then talk to them about it.

As for **drugs**, there's no way to get them from the Net. In fact, they're likely to find out the dangers of abusing them. So when they come across them in real life they'll be informed. And that can't be such a bad thing.

If you'd like to spy on their online activities, simply click on their browser's History (p.80) button. Should they be smart enough to work out how to cover their tracks, they're probably smart enough to know how to handle what they find.

What about bomb plans?

While the thought of your teenage son locked in his bedroom stacking his hard drive with porn might make you feel a bit uneasy, at least you know it won't kill him. Unfortunately, the same can't be said of the advice contained in the **Anarchist's Cookbook** and similar titles. Again, like porn, it's mostly a boy thing, and you'll have to assume he'll find it. Not that you can get mad at him for being interested. Things that go bang have been the focus of teenage fascination long before the Internet arrived.

As fun as they might make it all sound, it's vital for him to know he can't trust their recipes. These guides are ill researched, entirely irresponsible and downright dangerous. And, of course, about as against the law as it gets. The sooner you discuss the subject the better.

Will being on the Internet put me at risk?

Unless you go out of your way to invite trouble, the Internet should impose no added risk on your **personal safety**. However, you should still take a few precautions.

Don't put your home address or phone number in: your email or Usenet signature; your mail program's address book; an online email address register; or your chat profile. And, it goes without saying to bring a friend along if you decide to meet up with someone from a chat room.

On the other hand, **going online suddenly exposes your computer to all sorts of new risks**, particularly with Windows. To protect your computer against viruses and hackers, see (p.142).

Couldn't someone steal my credit card number?

Believe it or not, your credit details are actually safer online than when you pass your card over in a shop. However, you could still be ripped off. Before entering into any online transaction, read the advice on (p.178).

Should I forward virus warnings?

Except for the odd petition, any email that insists you **forward it on to everyone you know** is almost certainly a **hoax**, or at best a **chain letter**. While the hysterical virus warnings might seem vaguely credible, there is absolutely no excuse to fall for any email that suggests you might be **rewarded in some way** for forwarding it. If you get such a message, do not forward it to everyone you know. Instead flaunt your superiority by directing the forwarding peabrain to:

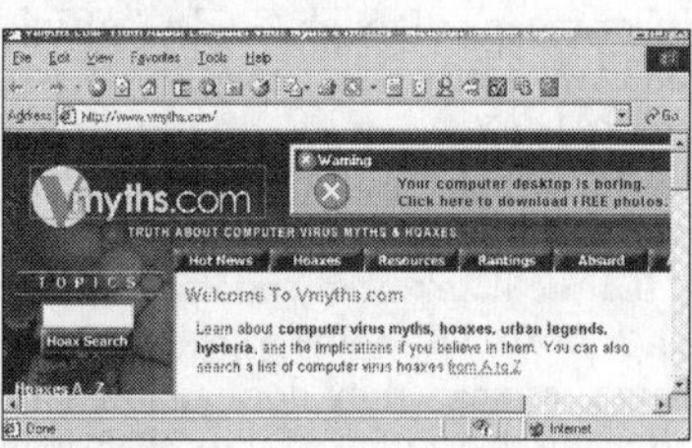

http://urbanlegends.about.com
http://www.breakthechain.org
http://www.chainletters.org/gallery.shtml
http://www.cs.rutgers.edu/~watrous/chain-letters.html
http://www.vmyths.com

Getting technical

What's the difference between a home page and a Web site?

On the World Wide Web, **home page** has two meanings. One refers to the page that appears when you start your browser and acts as your home base for exploring the Web. Whenever you get lost or want to return to somewhere familiar, just click on your "**Home**" button and back you go. The other usage refers to the front door to a set of documents that represents someone or something on the Web. This set of interconnected documents is called a **Web site**.

For instance, Rough Guides' "**official**" home page – found at: http://www.roughguides.com – acts as the publishing company's site index. You can access every page in the Rough Guides site by following links from the home page. Play your cards right and you'll end up at this book's home page.

If a site hasn't been endorsed by whom it represents it's called an "**unofficial**" home page. This is typical of the celebrity worship sites erected by doting fans. Some film and pop stars have so many they're linked into 'Webrings" (http://www.webring.org).

What are hosts, servers, and clients?

In Net-speak, any computer that's open to external online access is known as a **server** or **host**. The software you use to perform online operations such as transfer files, read mail, surf the Web, or post articles to Usenet, is called a **client**. A **Web server** is a machine where Web pages are stored and made available for outside access.

I have a fast connection so why are some sites still slow?

The speed at which you connect to your ISP can make a huge difference to the speed at which you can cruise the Web, listen to audio, and download files, but it's not the final word. Once you start accessing material stored outside your ISP's server – often everything except your mail – you're at the mercy of the bandwidth of all the links in between you and the external server. It's not unlike driving across town. At peak hours, when there are lots of other cars on the road, it's going to take longer. So if a site is painfully slow, try again later and hopefully the traffic will have subsided.

How do I read an email address?

Internet email addresses might look odd at first glance but they're really quite logical. They all take the form someone@somewhere. As soon as you read that aloud, it should begin to make sense. For example, take the email address angus@roughguides.com The "@" sign says it's an email address and means "at", so the address reads "angus at Rough Guides dot com". From that alone you could deduce that the sender's name is "Angus" and he's somehow associated with "Rough Guides". It's not always that obvious but the format never changes.

The somewhere part is the **domain name** of the Internet **host** that handles someone's mail – often their Internet Service Provider or workplace. Anyone who uses someone's provider or works with them could also share the same **domain name** in their email address, but they wouldn't be called someone. That's because the someone part identifies who, or what, they are at that host address. It's usually a name or nickname they choose themselves, or, with companies, a function like "help" or "info".

What's a domain name?

A **domain name** identifies and locates a host computer or service on the Internet. It often relates to the name of a business, organization, or service and must be registered in much the same way as a company name. It breaks down further into the subdomain, domain type, and country code. Look at: sophie@thehub.com.au The subdomain is **thehub** (an Internet Service Provider), its domain type **com** suggests it's a company or commercial site, and the country code **au** indicates it's in Australia.

Every country has its own distinct code, even if it's not always used. These include:

au	Australia
ca	Canada
cc	Cocos Islands
de	Germany
es	Spain
fr	France
jp	Japan
nl	Netherlands
no	Norway
uk	United Kingdom

If an address doesn't specify a country code, it's more than likely, but not necessarily, in the USA. At present, domain types are usually one of the following; however, the range will expand dramatically as recent changes to the domain registration system filter through:

ac	Academic (UK)
com	Company or commercial organization
co	Company or commercial organization (UK, NZ)
edu	Educational institution
gov	Government
mil	Military
net	Internet gateway or administrative host*
org	Non-profit organization

For more on the way domains work, see:
http://www.internic.net/faq.html

* Because of the domain name shortage, it's now become acceptable for commercial sites to use .net

What's an IP address?

Every computer on the Net has its unique numerical IP (Internet Protocol) address. A typical address is four numbers separated by dots and looks like: **149.174.211.5** This is its official location on the Internet.

Your computer will be assigned an IP address when you log on. If it's **dynamically**, or **server**, **allocated**, the last few digits could vary each time you connect.

Internet traffic control relies on these numbers. For example, a router might send all addresses beginning with **213** in one direction, and the rest in another. Eventually, through a process of elimination, everything ends up in the right place.

Thankfully, you don't have to use these numbers. Humans are numerically dim so we use domain names instead, by matching up the names and numbers in a table. Isn't it easier to remember **"roughguides"** than **204.52.130.112**?

Not all IP addresses have attached domain names, but a domain name will not become active until it's matched to an IP address. The table is co-ordinated across a network of **Domain Name Servers** (DNS). Before you can send a message to someone@somewhere.com, your mail program has to ask your Domain Name Server to convert somewhere.com into an IP address. This process is called a **DNS lookup**.

How can I get my own Web page?

Putting a page on the Web is a two-step process. First, you have to prepare it in **HTML**, the Web's mark-up language. Even a word processor can do a basic job by saving a document as HTML. To prepare something more elaborate, you need to use a dedicated HTML editing tool, or to learn HTML code – which isn't too hard for a computer language. Once you have an HTML document ready to go, you need to transfer it to your own special reserved **Web space**. For more on this, flip to p.303.

What's a portal?

The tools for searching the Net have improved exponentially over the last few years, but the methodologies have barely changed. Despite that, they now cluster under a variety of new names courtesy of those very smart people with MBAs. And you can bet those names will continue morphing into even more marketing-friendly nonsense.

You'll almost certainly come across the term **portal**. A site can be classed as a portal if you go there to be directed elsewhere. All search engines and directories (see p.153) are portals. If it concentrates on a specific subject, it's classed as a **vortal** (vertical portal). A site is a **hub** if you would go there regularly for news or information contained within the site. But if they make a concerted effort to attract repeat visitors by setting up bulletin boards, discussion lists, chat forums, or free Web space for members, they might prefer to call themselves a **community**.

What's an Intranet?

The mechanism that passes information between computers on the Internet can be used in exactly the same way over a local network such as in an office. When this isn't publicly accessible, it's called an **Intranet**. Many companies use Intranets to distribute internal documents – in effect publishing Web pages for their own private use.

How does the data know where to go?

For a surprisingly entertaining explanation of how networks, routers, switches, and firewalls shunt data in the right direction, download this movie: http://www.warriorsofthe.net

2

Get online

Or get left behind

By now, you should've seen the Internet in action. After all, it's infiltrated almost every office, every school, and even every shopping center. No matter where you live, there's bound to be somewhere nearby where you can rent time online. Or if you'd like to set it up at home, you needn't wait. It's possible to get everything you need to be up and running in a day or two. The good news is it's not unreasonably expensive or complicated, and it's becoming cheaper and easier by the day.

You don't need to be a computer geek

Perhaps you're not already hooked up because you find the whole computing world a bit off-putting. Well, this is the perfect opportunity to get over it. The rewards of being online far outweigh the effort involved in learning to use a computer.

Although there's ample information in this guide to get you started on the Net, if you're entirely new to computers ask someone computer literate to baby-sit you through a session or two. If you don't know anyone suitable, drop into a **cybercafé** or **Internet center** (p.28) and ask an attendant to kickstart you onto the World Wide Web. Helping out newbies is a big part of their business, so don't be afraid to admit you're green. Getting started is surprisingly simple. You should be able to figure out how to surf the Web within a matter of minutes. Finding your way around is another matter, but you're at an advantage – you have this guide.

If you do strike problems remember that the **online community** – other folks on the Net – is always on tap for help as long as you direct your queries to the right area. Just wait and see; before long you'll be sharing your newfound expertise with others.

Public internet access

Even if you don't own a computer, or use one at work, you can still get online through a range of **public Internet facilities**. These can also be handy if you're **away from home** and need to **collect your mail** or, say, tap the Web for some last minute **shopping research** (see p.182). Public access most commonly comes in the form of so-called **cybercafés**, which are basically coffee shops or bars, with a few Net-connected terminals up for public use.

Lately, though, the concept of mixing cakes, coffee, and computers is giving way to **communication centers** complete with fax, discount phones, printing and network ports to plug in your laptop computer. On top of these, you'll also come across isolated access points in the form of Net-enabled public telephones and coin operated Netbooths in places like airports, major hotels, or shopping malls. Singapore's Changi Airport, for example, boasts free access via video public phones and infrared docking ports. The biggest drawback of all these options, however, is that **they can be very slow**, especially when busy. It's not unknown to be unable to log into Hotmail (p.105) without timing out.

Whatever the case, you should be able to buy **blocks of Net time** at a very reasonable price. If you hunt around you might even find free access offered somewhere, such as your local public library.

Finding public access

You shouldn't have any trouble finding a cybercafé. There's sure to be at least one close to the main street, or tourist district, in any town. If not, try asking at a hotel, backpacker's guesthouse, post office, public library or computer store. Failing that, consult Yahoo (http://www.yahoo.com) or the following directories:

Cybercafé Guide http://www.netcafes.com
Cybercafé Search Engine http://www.cybercaptive.com
Cybercafés of Europe http://www.kiosek.com/eurocybercafes/
easyEverything http://www.easyeverything.com
Internet Café Guide http://www.netcafeguide.com

Collect your mail from any computer

You can send and receive your mail from any computer connected to the Internet. That means if you can get to a cybercafé or Net terminal, you can stay in touch, no matter where you are in the world. To find out how, see (p.134).

Connecting from home

Public access points are fine for light duties like collecting your mail or playing networked computer games (see p.285), but nothing beats having your own PC. Sure, they're expensive, confusing and often troublesome, but it's the only way to experience the Net at full tilt.

To get connected you'll need three things: a **computer** with enough grunt to drive a **Web browser** (p.54), an account with an **Internet Service Provider** (p.35), and a modem, or similar piece of hardware, to connect your computer to the Internet. How you connect can make the difference between pleasure and frustration. You won't necessarily need state-of-the-art computer gadgetry, but no matter what you have, you'll find a way to push it to the limit.

Computer firepower

While it's possible to access the Net with almost any machine you could call a computer, if you can't run your Web browsing and mail software together without a lot of chugging noises coming from your hard drive, you'll get frustrated fast.

Sure, you can squeeze online with an old **486 IBM-compatible PC** or **Macintosh 68030** series by sticking to old software, but it won't be much fun. Things don't start to get bearable until you hit the Pentium II 200 MHz or Apple G3, and they'll behave better with 64 megabytes of RAM or more. Ideally, though, you'll want something much faster.

Unless all your friends own **Macs**, or you intend to pursue a career in design or publishing, think carefully before locking yourself in the Apple closet. You can certainly get by with a Mac, but the Internet is overwhelmingly geared towards PC users. Drop by any software archive and compare the offerings available for Mac and Windows, for example. You'll soon find joining a minority interest group in the computing world won't make you elite. It will make you seem less important.

Your mouse matters

A certain way to boost your computing productivity – especially online where pointing and clicking is your mode of transport – is to equip yourself with a **sturdy wheel mouse**. If your computer came with a no-name mouse that doesn't feel right, or anything with less than two buttons and a wheel, it's time to upgrade. Once you've used a wheel to scroll pages, and explored the context sensitive (differs according to what your click) right-click menus, you'll feel handicapped with anything less. Macs especially will benefit from the upgrade, as apart from the obvious navigation enhancements, the mouse software will override Apple's sluggish interface and practically transform it into a whole new machine. You'll wonder why Apple made you suffer. Anything from Logitech or Microsoft will be top quality, especially the newer USB optical series.

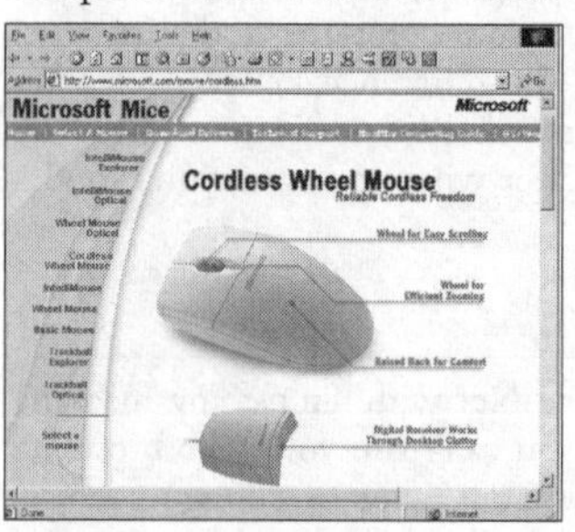

If you have one of the old-fashioned roller ball mice, make sure you remove the ball and clean out the lint at least once a week.

Laptops – connect on the move

Anyone serious about work mobility has a **laptop (notebook) computer**, often as a desktop replacement. After all, almost any-

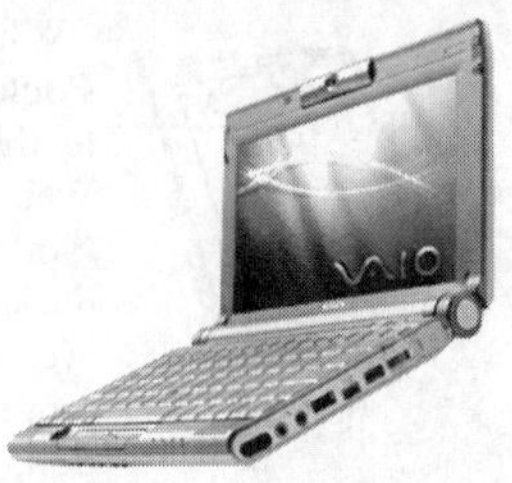

thing you can do on a desktop you can do on a portable – albeit on a smaller screen, at a much higher price. Whatever you buy, ensure it's thin, light, has long battery life, supports dual voltage (100-240 V and 50/60 HZ) and comes with a healthy **international warranty**. Having a notebook go down with all your mail and data on board is one of life's least rewarding experiences. If you can have a replacement shipped to you anywhere in the world the minute you have problems you'll never regret having paid a bit extra.

A **built-in modem** is an added bonus, but PCMCIA and USB models (see p.32) sometimes have better specs, plus you can swap them between machines. There are even cards that combine a cellular phone and modem, if that sounds useful.

Modems are convenient but nowhere near as fast or as cheap as hooking into a corporate network though a **Network card** or **USB to Ethernet adapter**. If you're on business, visiting a branch office, ask the IT manager to fill in your network settings.

Pocket gadgets

You can go even smaller and lighter, without losing too many features, by moving towards sub-notebooks and palmtops that can run Windows programs. Don't expect big savings though. You'll pay a premium for miniaturization. For a lot less money in return for a lot less features, you could try something pocket-sized such as the Psion Organiser, Palm Pilot, Handspring Visor, HP Jornada or Cassiopeia. These combine basic office programs with Net connectivity, and can upload later to your main machine.

While many of these **PDAs** and **Pocket PCs** are capable of connecting to the Net, don't expect to browse the Web on a matchbox-sized screen. Nothing small enough to fit in your pocket, or lacking a decent keyboard, will ever replace your computer. They can prove useful, though, if used in conjunction, or for simple tasks when you're away from your desk. For example, you could download an online newspaper with your desktop computer using AvantGo (http://www.avantgo.com), transfer it to your Pocket PC and read it on the train; send a short email from your phone; check your stock prices under the boardroom table; or more likely, pull it out in a bar to impress your friends.

WAP phones feed close to the bottom of the Internet gadget pool. If you're patient and dexterous, you can tap into the Net to collect and send email, and browse online information in a very limited way. Keep your expectations low, and you won't be disappointed.

Buying a modem

Unless you're hooked up through a network, you'll need a device to connect your computer to the telephone line or cable. There'll be a similar device at your ISP's end. The device you'll need will depend on your Internet account. Most home users connect to the Internet through a **modem hooked into the standard telephone system**. This is called a "**dial-up connection**". If your computer came with a modem, then you should be ready to "dial up." Otherwise, unless you're planning to connect to a broadband (high speed) service (see p.38), you'll need to hit the shops. Modems come in three flavors: internal, external, and PCMCIA. Here's what to look out for:

Internal modems are the cheapest. They plug into a slot inside your computer called a bus. Installation isn't difficult, but you do have to open your computer and follow the instructions carefully (or have your computer store do it). Because they're hidden inside your computer, internal modems don't take up desk space, clutter the back of your computer with extra cables, or require an external power source. On the downside, they lack the little lights to tell you how your call is going, require an empty slot, and can't be swapped between computers without removing the case. If your PC isn't cutting edge, avoid Soft Modems (eg Winmodems). These cut costs by using your PC's processor to do some of their work. If your PC is not up to it, you can experience all sorts of problems, such as frequent dropped connections. Best to spend a little more to be safe.

An **external modem** is easier to install. Depending on the model, it will simply plug straight into your computer's serial or USB port, making it easy to swap between machines (and simple to upgrade). USB is preferable, if your computer supports it (check first!), as they usually don't require an external power supply. All serial (RS232) modems, however, will.

The credit-card-sized **PCMCIA** modems are a mixture of the two. They fit internally into the PC card slots common in most modern notebooks and remove easily to free the slot for something else. Being small makes them portable, which is of supreme importance when you're traveling. They don't require an external power source, but are expensive and you can't use them with a desktop. You can, however, use any external modem with a notebook simply by plugging it into an available serial or USB port.

Something most travelers don't consider, is whether their modem is **approved internationally**. Technically, you could be breaking the law if you're caught using a non-approved modem. If you're trotting the globe, check out 3Com's Global Modem PC cards. They have built-in digital line guards, tax impulse filtering, widespread approval, and software to tweak your modem to the tastes of almost every country's telephone network. See: http://www.3com.com

All the way with 56K

Whichever type of modem you choose, the major issue is speed. Data transfer speed is expressed in bits (not bytes!) per second or **bps**. It can take up to ten bits to transfer a character. So a modem operating at 2400 bps (2.4 Kbps) would transfer roughly 240 characters per second. That's about a page of text every eight seconds. At 28.8 Kbps, you could send the same page of text in two-thirds of a second.

A 14.4 Kbps (V.32) modem can browse the Web, but only just. A faster modem might cost a little more, but it will reduce your online charges, and give you more for your money. The modem standard has now reached **56K (V.90)**, which can theoretically download at up to 56 Kbps, and upload at up to 33.6 Kbps. **Don't waste your money on anything less**.

An emerging slightly faster standard, V.92, is also being tested but isn't supported by many ISPs yet. Still, if you have the option, favor a new modem that supports, or can be upgraded to, V.92. See http://www.v92.com

Unfortunately, though, because of phone line dynamics, **you will never actually connect at 56K**, but you should still be able to get well above 33.6 Kbps, the previous speed barrier. If you have an **X2** or **K56flex** modem, upgrade to V.90, if possible. See: http://www.56k.com

Finally, **make sure whatever you buy will work with your computer**. And if you need help, see: http://808hi.com/56k/

http://www.modemhelp.com
http://www.modemhelp.org
http://www.modemhelp.net

Computer, check. Modem, check. Now what?

To connect to the Internet, you'll need someone to allow you to connect into their computer, which in turn is connected to another computer, which in turn ... that's how the Internet works. But unless you have a working relationship with whoever controls access to the computer that gets you online, you'll have to pay for the privilege. Enter the **Internet Service Provider**.

Internet Service Providers (ISPs)

Companies in the business of providing Internet access are known as **ISPs (Internet Service Providers)**. The industry has matured steadily over the last few years to the point that most established ISPs deliver reasonable performance and service. However, all providers aren't equal, and it's difficult to tell a good one from a bad one, until you've used them over time. Try a few before settling, as poor access will jade your online experience. Some, for example, try to squeeze too many folk online, resulting in frequent busy tones when you dial, and slow transfer rates once you're online.

Ask around for recommendations, or check local **Internet and computer magazines** (who are forever doing comparative tests of speed, service, and so forth). An added bonus with the computer press is that they often carry cover-mounted disks with plenty of Net software to mess up your system.

To help with your quest, there's an ISP listing at the end of this book (p.467), along with a **checklist of questions** – some of which will be important to you, others not, depending on circumstances.

Online Services

CompuServe and its new parent, **AOL**, are the last major players standing in the special class known as Online Services. What sets them apart from normal ISPs is that they value their exclusive online offerings more than their Internet access. They are, to a certain extent, a relic of the past. The Internet now offers far more than any Online Service could ever hope to produce in-house. Indeed, much of their content either comes from the Net or directs you to material located on the Net.

AOL is more of a family orientated service with the emphasis squarely on entertainment, whereas **CompuServe** fancies itself as a content provider for young professionals without kids. The one thing they have in common is that their access software is very much **dumbed down** for the new user. While you might find this an appealing prospect, it will soon become a shackle that will hinder your progress online.

But if you travel abroad regularly, a CompuServe account can get you connected in some 150 countries. The only catch is it will attract a premium charge over your regular access bill. Call for rates and access details before you set off, otherwise you could be up for a nasty credit card shock on your return.

If you feel like giving them a whirl, you'll find their disks on the cover of every second computer magazine, and probably in your mailbox once in a while. By all means try the free trials, but if you're not absolutely delighted, be sure to cancel your account. Otherwise you'll be billed a minimum monthly charge whether or not you use the service. And be sure to **completely uninstall their software once you've finished with them**, as it's known to cause problems.

Before committing yourself to either, compare their network speed, software standards (particularly email), pricing, line availability, and telephone support with a regular ISP.

Connecting away from home

If you often travel with a portable computer, you'll soon appreciate an account that offers instant local call access in the cities you visit. As mentioned, the Online Services are one option, but you might find better value if you shop around. For a range of choices, see Global Roaming (p.476).

Wireless access and WAP

Going cordless seems the way of the future, but right now the offerings are often more suited to gadgeteers than everyday use. You can hook a GSM-ready PC card modem to a cellular phone and dial your ISP, but it's slow and usually prohibitively expensive. A better option is to connect your portable to a dedicated wireless ISP such as **GoAmerica** (http://www.goamerica.net) or **AirWave** (http://www.airwave.com) using one of the new high-speed wireless PC card standards. Rates and services vary, but it's not hard to find unlimited access for an affordable monthly charge. Well, in the USA anyway. The rest of the world hasn't quite caught on yet. For more on wireless connectivity, see:

Yahoo http://mobile.yahoo.com
Wireless.com http://www.wireless.com
Wireless Advisor http://www.wirelessadvisor.com

WAP, on the other hand, is almost everywhere, accompanied by hearty hype but few applications. Drop into any phone sales shop to hear the spiel. For more on Wap, see: http://wap.wapaw.com and http://www.wap.com

Choosing an ISP

For more on choosing an ISP, see p.467.

Broadband – high speed access

What's good about modems is that they are the right-here right-now accepted standard worldwide and work over the regular telephone system without any excess charges. But, once you try the Net at full steam over a **broadband** connection, you'll find it hard to go back. If you're fortunate enough to live somewhere where broadband is available and affordable, it might be worth checking out. However, if you already have a modem, and you're new to the Net, stick to dial up access until you know your demands. Most importantly, don't put money down on a year's subscription if you don't know what you're getting into. **One thing is certain over the next few years: speeds will go up and prices will come down.**

Doubling up modems

It's possible to bind two or more modems together using multiple telephone lines in parallel. This should give you a bandwidth equal to the sum of the combined modems, which often works out cheaper than ISDN. It's simple to set up in Windows 98 or later versions: just right-click on your provider's Dial-up Networking entry, choose "Properties", and add another device under **Multilink**.

The hardest part is finding an ISP that supports it.

ISDN

We should've all been using ISDN's superior line handling and speed for the best part of the last decade, but overpricing put it **out of most home users' reach**. And now, with much faster alternatives available, it's not so appealing. It provides three channels (1x16Kbps and 2x64Kbps) that can be used and billed in various ways. ISDN Internet accounts don't usually cost more but, depending on where you live, the line connection, rental and calls can cost anywhere from slightly to outrageously more than standard telephone charges. One bonus is that instantaneous connections mean you'll only be charged while you're transferring data.

Cable

If you can get cable TV, chances are you can also get cable Internet as a sideline. Cable access offers mega-speed rates (potentially up to 10Mbps, though more likely considerably less than 1Mbps) without call charges. So, if you have cable in your street, make some calls. For rates, availability and local operators, try:

Australia

Optus@home **http://www.optushome.com.au**

Telstra **http://www.bigpond.com/broadband/**

North America

@Home **http://www.home.com**

High Speed Access **http://www.hsacorp.net**

Road Runner **http://www.hsacorp.net**

UK

NTL (UK) **http://www.askntl.com/broadband/**

Telewest (UK) **http://www.blueyonder.co.uk**

DSL

If you haven't already heard of **DSL**, or its most common form **ADSL** (Asymmetric Digital Subscriber Line), you soon will. Although it's been commercially available across much of the USA for a few years, the rest of the world has been slow to catch on. ADSL is potentially capable of download speeds up to 6Mbps, and uploads up to 640Kbps via the normal telephone system without interfering with your voice service. That means you can surf the Net and talk on the phone at the same time over one line. Like cable, it's rarely offered at its full potential. For instance, in the UK, consumer access goes out at a mere 512Kbps downstream and 128Kbps upstream. Because the technology uses the phone system, and requires upgraded exchanges, the main providers of ADSL are the phone companies, and their resellers. To see if it's available and affordable, make your first enquiry to your local phone companies, and then try the larger ISPs in your area. Such as:

Australia

iPrimus **http://www.iprimus.com.au**

Telstra **http://www.bigpond.com.au/broadband/**

North America

AT&T **http://www.att.net**

Bellsouth **http://www.fastaccess.com**

Earthlink **http://www.earthlink.com**

Qwest **http://www.qwest.com/dsl/**

UK

BT Openworld **http://www.btopenworld.co.uk**

ClaraNET **http://www.clara.net**

Demon **http://www.demon.net**

Freeserve **http://www.freeserve.co.uk**

Cable or DSL – which one?

Until you've tried both in your own home there's no way to tell which is better. Although the technologies have their own distinct advantages, in practice the speed and reliability differs between installations. Theoretically, DSL should be superior because you get your own dedicated line. With cable, you have to share your bandwidth with your neighbors. So if everyone on your street is downloading MP3s at once, you'd expect it to slow down. On the other hand, DSL degrades as you move further from the exchange. If it stretches to more than 3.5kms (2.2 miles), you may find yourself disadvantaged. That's if you can get it at all. In practice, it's even more complicated and reliant on other factors such as the individual provider's equipment and the number of existing subscribers. The best you can do is ask around your local area for advice. Be prepared for some horror stories.

Read the fine print

Although broadband deals are typically "**always on**" or "**unlimited access**", they're not always "**all you can eat**". Check the fine print carefully, and beware of **download limits** (caps). If you're charged by the megabyte, once you go over your limit, you could get a nasty shock on your first bill. Unless you're a light user, if it's not "all you can eat", it's probably worth avoiding. And if it mentions something about an "**acceptable use policy**", find out exactly what that means before proceeding.

Can't get DSL or cable?

The catch with cable and DSL is that you need the right wire coming into your house. As DSL is only good for a couple of miles, if you live outside a metro area, you have Buckley's chance of seeing it in a hurry, if ever. Your best chance of getting broadband will probably be from the air – via satellite, microwave cable or some other form of wireless link. Although there's talk of rolling broadband out along rural power lines, it hasn't yet seen commercial fruition.

Satellite access is typically capped at around 400Kbps downstream, but it's capable of being much faster. The upstream speed depends on whether it's a one-way or two-way system. In a one-way system, you have to connect to a regular ISP to complete the return leg, thus restricting the upstream speed to that of a modem (33.6Kbps). Up to 256Kbps is possible through the two-way system. While that's fast in theory, it suffers from fairly savage latency, making it useless for online gaming (p.285). Because the downstream leg is shorter, microwave cable and other tower-based wireless systems have lower latency. However, any one-way system will introduce an undesirable lag. **Don't sign up until you've seen it in action**. For availability and pricing of satellite access, compare:

Chello (INT) http://www.chello.com
DirecPC (INT) http://www.direcpc.com
Starband (US) http://www.starband.com
Telstra (AUS) http://www.bigpond.com/broadband/

High speed wireless access

There's little doubt the future of broadband Internet access is **wireless**. We already have the technology, but as yet, it's only sparsely available. Though mark our words, it's on its way…

Installation

As cable, ADSL and satellite (downfeed) services are "always on" – you won't have to dial, but you'll still need a special modem-like device to connect between your computer and the line. Depending on the service provider this might work like a cable TV contract, where they rent you the box, and charge you some kind of once-off installation fee. As these speeds are in excess of serial card capacity, you'll either need to hook in through a network card, USB port, or their own special card. Whichever way, it shouldn't be a drama if you have a recent PC. Mac support is relatively thin on the ground.

Help – tweak it better

Broadband is pitched at the power user and enthusiast, so a little research mightn't hurt. You'll almost certainly get better results if you tweak your MTU settings. See the following sites for tips, reviews and news:

http://www.adsl.com
http://www.broadband-help.com
http://www.dsllife.com
http://www.cable-modem.net
http://www.cablemodemhelp.com
http://www.cable-modems.org
http://www.cable-modem-internet-access.com
http://www.speedguide.net
http://www.tweak3d.net/tweak/cable/
http://www.whirlpool.net.au

What's it cost?

Ever shopped for a mobile phone? Well, that was easy compared to trying to get the best deal on Internet access. And the range of pricing plans and varieties will get even more confusing as broadband goes mainstream.

Dial up plans

The simplest, and most ideal, access plan is an "all you can eat" account that allows you to stay online for as long as you like for a set fee per month. This commonly goes for around $20 per month in the US with no hidden charges. As local calls are usually free in the **US**, that's all you should have to pay. To shop for the cheapest deal across the USA, try: http://www.getconnected.com

Most **Australian** ISPs offer an assortment of plans, though few offer unlimited hours or unlimited downloads on their fastest network. Expect to pay around $25 per month, or between $1–2 per hour.

The **UK** remains the world's most bewildering market thanks to the ongoing **tyranny of timed local phone calls**. Light users have the choice of myriad timed and fixed monthly plans, the most popular being the "free" services that take a cut from the phone bill. Flat monthly fee, **unlimited access inclusive of phone charges**, is also finally available at a reasonable price. Public enemy BT offers "all you can eat" plans capped at £15 per month for 24/7 access, and £4 per month for off-peak, plus 2p per minute during the day. For a list of unmetered flat rate plans, along with the assorted strings attached, see: http://unmetered.cream.org

Broadband plans

Broadband access should be somewhat more expensive everywhere, but that's not a rule. Sometimes **cable**, for example, can be just as cheap if you subtract the phone line rental. For instance, the US Internet cable provider, **@Home** (http://www.home.com), charges between $40-50 flat per month depending on the cable reseller. In Australia, they offer unmetered cable access with no download limits through the Optus (http://www.optushome.com.au) network, for $70-75 per month. **DSL (ADSL)** is generally tiered into speed levels, and offered around the same price as cable. **Earthlink** (http://www.earthlink.com), for example, charges about $50 for unlimited access across the USA. Pricing in the UK varies from around £30-50 per month.

Installation fee

Most ISPs also charge a **once-off setup fee**. This might include a startup software kit, but if you have Windows 98, Mac OS 8.0, or later, you're much better off asking for instructions to set it up manually (p.49). Broadband setup fees are much higher, as they usually include hardware rental and a physical installation, as with cable TV.

Other providers, especially the Online Services, might offer a **free trial period**, but if you check their pricing for an average year it mightn't work out cheaper overall.

Watch your phone bill

If you intend to connect through a telephone line, ensure your ISP has a **local dial-up number**. And, if you travel, favor one with national access numbers, otherwise you might run up some serious phone bills.

These dial-up numbers are called **Points Of Presence (POPs)**. In the US, if you need to call your provider from interstate, it may offer a free 1-800 number that could carry a surcharge of up to $10 per hour. If you have free local call access, then make sure your provider has a POP in your local zone.

Local calls in Australia are flat rate, which means it's cheaper to stay online all day than to dial up for a few minutes each hour to pick up mail. Check if you'd save money by switching to a telco with cheaper local calls.

While local calls remain metered in the UK, capped monthly plans that include both access and phone charges would seem the wisest option for all but light users. Be wary, however, of ISPs that offer support through an expensive premium rate number. You're sure to call support at some point, so calculate that into your costs.

Some telcos offer a discount to your choice of frequently

called "**Friends and Family**" numbers. Put your provider on this list, as it's sure to become your most called number. Also ask about the possibility of capped monthly charges to certain numbers. This is sometimes offered with timed ISDN.

3

Let's connect

Get ready to dial

Before you can dial into your newly acquired Internet account, you'll need to fill in a few blanks. Unless you're running a very old operating system (Windows 3.1 or pre-System 8.0 Mac), you already have all the software you need to get started. The aim of this section is to **get you online for the first time.**

Which operating system?

The process involved in connecting to the Internet has become progressively easier over the last few years with each new release of Windows and the Mac OS. Of

course, this also means the steps involved differ slightly between say, Windows 95 and ME. So, before you call your ISP for setup instructions you'll need to know which system you're running.

If that turns out to be Windows 3.1, 95a, or a pre-System 8.0

Mac, it's more complex. You'll need to either upgrade your operating system or install some extra connection software. Ask your ISP to send you an installation disk for your system, along with the necessary instructions. If they can't help, keep trying ISPs until you find one that's more receptive. Bear in mind you won't be able to run the latest Internet software on an old computer.

Preparing Windows

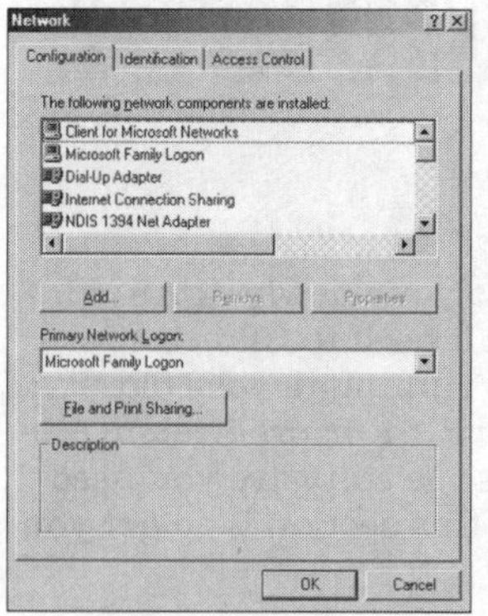

Before you start, ensure Windows has what it takes to establish a dial up connection. Right-click on **Network Neighborhood** or **My Network Places** (on your Desktop) and check you've installed the Client for Microsoft Networks, TCP/IP protocol and Dial-up Adapter. If not, click "Add" and install each in turn. Microsoft is the manufacturer in all cases. Then choose Client for Microsoft Networks or Microsoft Family Logon as your Primary Network Logon. Do not enable File or Printer sharing unless you want to let outsiders from the Net into your computer. If the network icon isn't on your Desktop, open the Control Panel, go to Windows Setup in Add/Remove Programs, and add Dial-up Networking under Communications.

Ask your ISP

Setting up isn't difficult, but it's confusing for newcomers. That's why we suggest asking your ISP for guidance on your first time.

After all, it's in their best interest to assist – the sooner you get online, the sooner they see your money. Most ISPs provide a set-up disk that installs their own custom software and automates the signup process. If possible, rather than install from a disk, ask for step by step instructions to configure it yourself, or have them walk you through it over the phone. Try to avoid dial-up ISPs that insist you need to use their software in order to connect. The less you let them meddle with your system, the better it will run, especially if you switch ISPs later down the track.

If you'd like to know how to set it up yourself, or install a second connection, read on. Otherwise, just follow your ISP's instructions, skip over the next few pages and prepare to arm yourself with the latest Web browser (p.54).

Set it up yourself

You can set up as many ISP connections as you like under Windows or Mac OS 8+, and as many email and Usenet accounts as you like in any version of Outlook Express. Although the various Internet Connection Wizards can set them up in one swoop, connecting to the Internet and collecting your mail are completely independent processes. That means if you're doing it manually, you'll need to set them up in two parts. First, set up your connection (TCP/IP and dialing), and then your mail and news. Before you can start, however, you'll need all the details from your ISP. Once you have the all the numbers and addresses, enter them

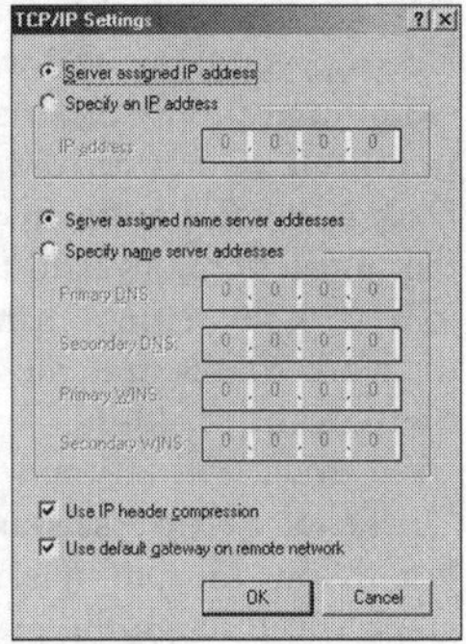

into the **Internet Connection Wizard**, or follow the instructions under **Setting it up manually** – preferably the latter, as it will give you a better understanding of your system. Either way, it should take no more than a few minutes.

The Internet Connection Wizard

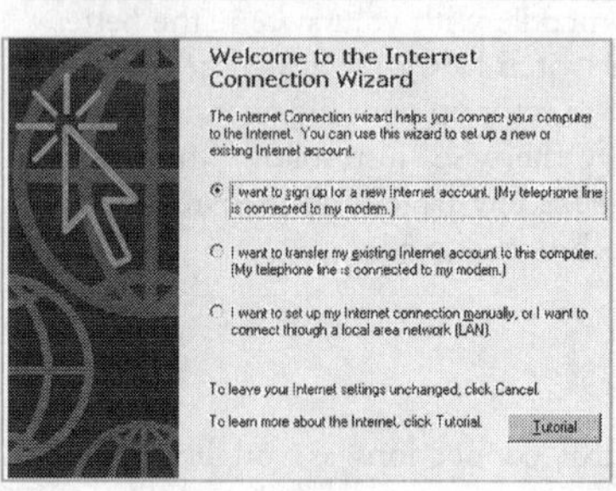

When you install or upgrade Windows (98 onwards), or Internet Explorer, it will place a shortcut (icon) on your Desktop called "**Connect to the Internet**". Clicking on this icon will start the **Internet Connection Wizard**, which will guide you through the process of setting up an Internet connection, followed by your mail and news accounts. It can even find you an ISP if you don't already have one. If the icon isn't on the Desktop, you'll find the wizard in the Start menu, usually under Communications or Internet Tools. Alternatively, opening Internet Explorer for the first time (click on the big E on the Desktop) will also usually start the wizard. As long as you follow the instructions, it's hard to go wrong. All the same, it's simple to rework the settings manually, or repeat the exercise, if it doesn't work. You'll find the entry it created inside the **Dial-up Networking folder**.

The Mac (OS 8.0 and later) has a similar wizard called the "**Internet Setup Assistant**", under Assistants in the hard drive. Just follow the prompts. The iMac's Setup Assistant can also guide you through the process painlessly.

Setting it up manually – Dial-up Networking

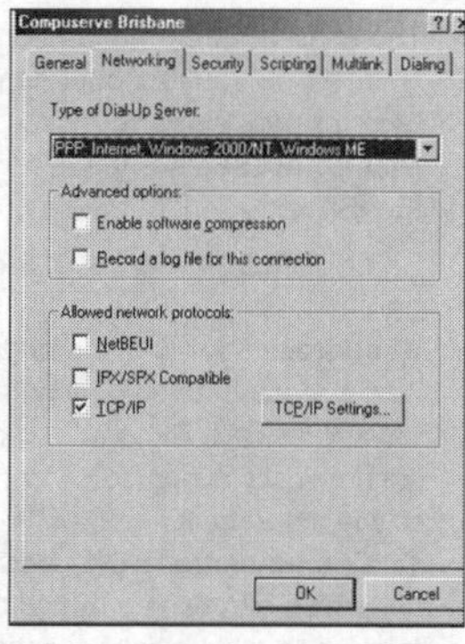

Setting up your **TCP/IP connection** directly through **Dial-up Networking** is a little more involved, but gives you greater control over the configuration. Again, the process will differ between versions of Windows, but not enough to spoil your day.

To start, open the Dial-up Networking folder under My Computer (Windows 95/98) or Control Panel (Windows ME/2000) and click on "Make new connection." **Name the connection** (after your ISP makes sense) and select your modem from the drop down box. Clicking on the Configure button will lead you to your **modem settings**, but leave them be for now.You can adjust them later if needed. Click Next, enter your **ISP's phone number** and then Finish.Your new connection should now appear in the Dial-up Networking folder.

If your ISP has given you an **IP address** or any **name server (DNS) addresses**, you'll now need to configure the **TCP/IP**. Right-click on your new connection and choose Properties. You'll find everything you'll need to configure your connection under the tabs and buttons before you. Add your IP and/or name server addresses within TCP/IP under the Network tab. Go through the tabs and make sure the only protocols allowed are TCP/IP (not Netbui or IPX) and that "Log onto network" is unchecked. Enabling any of these options will delay your log on. Unless instructed otherwise, leave the type of **Dial-Up Server** set to **PPP, enable software compression,** and uncheck **encrypted password**.

What you'll need from your ISP

The minimum information you'll need to onto your ISP is your:

User name Your account name with the ISP.

Dial-up password Your secret access code.

Dial-up access number The number your modem dials to access the ISP.

Some ISPs also require you to configure these **TCP/IP** parameters:

IP address Your location on the Internet. Most ISPs allocate a new one each time you log in. If so, you won't be given a numerical address, you'll be told to choose "server assigned" or "dynamically allocated". In which case you can forget about it, as this is the default setting.

Two name server (DNS) addresses These servers convert friendly domain names into numerical Internet addresses. Again, the trend is to dynamically allocate the addresses, so you mightn't have to touch anything. If not, they'll be numerical, in the form 123.345.123.12

Script It's rare to need extra commands to log in. If the occasion arises, your ISP will need to instruct you how to set it up as a script.

If you're being supplied with a **POP3 email address** (p.107), you'll

Once that's complete, all you'll need to add is your **User Name** and **Password**. Fill these in when you first connect (p.60). To connect, just double-click on the new connection.

The process is much the same on a **Mac**. Just open **Remote Access** from under the Control Panel, click on Setup, then Options, and fill in your details.

Setting up Mail & News

You'll be prompted to enter your email and Usenet account

need the following to set up your email program:
Email address: The address where you'll receive your mail. Will be in the form **someone@somewhere** where the **somewhere** part is a domain name.
Mail login The name you choose as the someone part of your email address.
Mail password The secret code used to pick up your mail.
Outgoing mail server (SMTP) The server that will handle all mail you send. It will be a domain name, eg: **mail.somewhere.com**
Incoming mail server (POP/IMAP) Where your mail is stored. Also a domain name.

In order to access **Usenet newsgroups**, you'll need to know the:
News server address (NNTP) Most ISPs maintain a Usenet server. Enter its domain name into your newsreader, such as Outlook Express (see p.109).

And finally, you might be given an optional, or compulsory, address:
Proxy server Some ISPs use a proxy server to manage traffic flow, and possibly speed up your connection. If so, you'll need to enter this address into your browser's options (p.90) as instructed by your ISP. It might also affect other programs so be sure to ask. Proxies sometimes play up. Try surfing with and without and see which you prefer.

details the first time you open Outlook Express. So, if you already have them, just click on the Outlook Express icon on your Desktop; on your Quick Launch bar; or under the Programs menu. Once that's done, you can fine tune, change them, or add more addresses under Accounts in the Tools menu in Outlook Express. For more on setting up Outlook Express, see p.111.

To set up the Mac version of Outlook Express, add the same details under Internet in the Control Panel, or under Accounts in the Tools menu.

Adding another ISP account

Once your dial-up connection is set, you should be able to forget about it, unless you have to **dial a different provider**. You can add as many ISP accounts as you wish, in the same way as the first. However, if you want one to be your main (default) account, you'll need to tell Internet Explorer. See p.112.

The same goes for Macs. Open Configurations under the File menu in Remote Access, duplicate your connection, and then edit the details. Or in **FreePPP, MacPPP**, and **OT-PPP**, just look for the option "New" to start a new account.

The Web browser

Almost everything you do on the Internet will rotate around one program. It will provide the buttons, bars, and menus to help you navigate through the billions of pages stored online. It will act as the window through which you view the World Wide Web, look after your downloads, and shuttle off activities to other programs such as media players. This program is called a Web browser, and it's likely to be the most useful piece of software you'll ever install.

Choosing a Web browser

A few years back, choosing a Web browser was something of an issue. First Mosaic, and then Netscape, dominated the market with browsing software that was closer to the cutting edge, than reliable. Today, whether you like it or not, the choice has pretty much been made for you. Although Netscape, and several other companies, still make browsers, Microsoft's Internet Explorer commands more than 90 percent of the market share, and there's little incentive for you to buck the trend. Not only is it the fastest, sturdiest, and most functional browser you can get, it's free – and you probably already have it.

Internet Explorer (IE)

If you're running **Windows 98, 2000, or later**, you won't need to download Internet Explorer (also called **IE**) as it's built into the operating system. However, you will need to update it (p.58). Microsoft's policy has been to integrate the browsing experience into the Desktop, so **Windows Explorer and IE share the same interface** – whether you're surfing the Web or ferreting through your hard drive. Installing Internet Explorer over Windows 95 achieves almost the same effect.

Internet Explorer is also on the Desktop of every iMac, and Apple running MacOS 8.5 and later. If it's not on the Desktop, you'll find it in the system installation CD. Internet Explorer's **Macintosh versions** are written entirely afresh for the Mac OS, so expect quite a few differences if you move between the two platforms.

Playing by numbers

Internet Explorer comes in various flavors, catering to Windows 95/98/ME, Windows NT/2000, Windows 3.1, Windows CE, Power Mac, Mac 68k, Mac OS X and Unix. On top of that, each version has several releases.

You can pick the **latest release of any program** by its number. For example, IE5.01 is newer than IE5.0. The first number is the series: these are both "5.x" series browsers (as you'd expect, the "5.x" series came after the "4.x" series). The second number, after the decimal point, tells you if it is the **original release** (.0) or an **interim upgrade** (0.1, 0.2, etc) within the series. Such upgrades generally fix problems and add on a few minor features. In doing so, the previous release in that series becomes obsolete, and in the case of betas and previews (test programs), expires.

A **new series release** – which at present happens about once a year – usually heralds major changes, new features and bug fixes, but also often adds extra system demands. Thus, if your computer resources are low, you may find an earlier series more suitable.

To make matters a bit more confusing, developers sometimes release **a new build** of the same program. So you and a friend can both have IE5.5 but if you downloaded it later, you might have a later build that's fixed a few minor bugs. To see a program's build number, choose **About** from the **Help menu**.

System requirements – PCs

Browsers consume a lot of **disk space**, especially if you choose to load all the added accessories. They also appreciate plenty of RAM and a reasonably fast processor. These demands tend to increase slightly with each new version.

PC users will need at least a 486 DX66 PC, with **16MB of RAM** to get **Internet Explorer** to function under Windows 95/98/3.x, and 24-32MB to run other programs at the same time. Windows NT, 2000 and ME demand at least 32MB of RAM, depending on which optional components you install. A full installation will require at least 80MB of disk space, but you can cut this down to about 27MB by only installing the browser. Furthermore, new releases normally write over the old files. So if you're simply upgrading to a newer version, for example, installing IE6 over Windows ME, then the increase in disk space will only be marginal, say 12MB.

They're the official minimum specifications as supplied by Microsoft, but frankly, if you're running IE5 or later on anything **less than a Pentium 200 with 64 MB of RAM, it's going to hurt.**

System requirements – Macs

All versions of Internet Explorer for the Mac since IE4.5 require at least a **PowerPC processor**, with 12 MB of RAM, and **MacOS 7.5.3 or later**.

Again, while these are the official specs, realistically you'll be happier with a faster machine and more RAM. If you have an earlier **iMac with only 32 MB of RAM**, you should chock it up to at least 64 MB, so you can browse and read mail with a modicum of dignity.

Humble computers

The best choice for older machines running **Windows 3.1** is **Internet Explorer 3.03**. It can get by (just about) on 4 MB of RAM and as little as 7 MB of disk space for a browser-only installation, plus it also includes the TCP/IP dialing software that Windows 3.1 omits.

Mac 68K machines can run IE4, though IE3 requires less RAM and disk space, so it might be preferable. If it's still too heavy, **Netscape 2.0x** is better than no browser at all. Whatever the machine, browser or version number, Macs work best with Virtual Memory switched on.

Alternatively, if you don't mind being served ads, investigate **Opera** (http://www.opera.com), which packs a browser, mail sender, and newsreader into only a couple of MB – and it's even slightly quicker than the 4.0x series browsers.

If you're after an early release of Internet Explorer, you won't find it on Microsoft's Web site. That goes for most other browsers as well. Not to worry, you'll find just about every browser ever released across all systems, including **Amiga, OS/2,** and **BeOS**, for free download at: http://browsers.evolt.org

Important – get the latest version of IE

Although you might have Internet Explorer, you're unlikely to have the latest version. It's very **important to keep it up to date**, not so much to gain new features, but to **fix bugs** and protect you against **security threats**. As Internet Explorer is part of Windows 98 and later, you can update it to the latest version through **Windows Update**. Once you're online, you can reach Windows Update through several channels. You'll find an entry under the Windows Start menu; the Tools menu in IE5 (and later); under Product Updates in the Help menu in IE3 or IE4; or by entering this address in your browser:

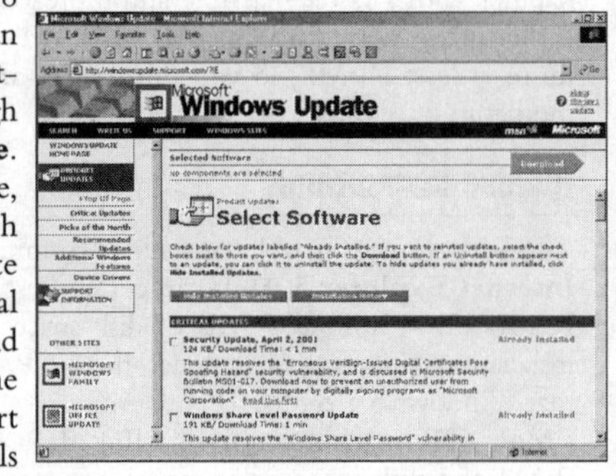

Windows Update **http://www.windowsupdate.com**

Once the page has loaded, click on "**Produce Updates**". The server will automatically interrogate your system to determine which components you need to bring yourself up to date. Then it's just a matter of picking what you want. It should be obvious what's important. If you want to use email, you should download Outlook Express. You can safely avoid MSN Messenger (p.238) for the time being.

If Windows Update won't work, drop into Internet Explorer's home, download the latest setup file, and then call back into Windows Update to top up with critical updates:

Microsoft IE Home http://www.microsoft.com/ie/

To update the **Mac versions** of Internet Explorer and Outlook Express download the separate installation files from:

Mactopia http://www.mactopia.com/ie/

Before you start downloading, beware that it could **take an hour or more** – depending on which options you pick, how busy the sites are, and at what speed you connect. If conditions are normal, you should be able to download well over 10MB per hour with a 56Kbps modem. It's preferable to download it from the Net rather than install it from a magazine CD, or an ISP installation disk. That way you can be sure it's the latest version and free from unwelcome branding. If you'd like **remove the branding,** such as your ISP's logo, see p.89.

Netscape

Netscape is in such a mess it's very hard to recommend even trying the browser, let alone basing your Internet existence around it. Its 4.7 series are slower, less stable and technologically behind IE5 and IE6 on both the PC and Mac. Although the 6 series (forget about 5.0), has been dramatically revamped by the general programming public at Mozilla.org and embellished by parent company AOL, it's still too slow, chronically buggy and cluttered. That's if you can get it to load at all. Despite Netscape's shortcomings, some people still prefer its way of doing things, most notably the Linux community who as a rule oppose anything made by Microsoft. Of course, Microsoft does have a case to answer (literally) and Internet Explorer is a long way from perfect. If you're curious to see whether Netscape plays more to your tune, and are prepared to risk the

after effects, you can download it from:

Netscape http://www.netscape.com

Want more information?

For the latest on browsers, reviews, tests, comparisons, tips, and downloads for a wide range of brands and platforms see:

Browsers.com http://www.browsers.com

Browser News http://www.upsdell.com/BrowserNews/

For discussion of the latest beta releases, see:

BetaNews http://www.betanews.com

For help with Internet Explorer problems:

IE Info Site http://www.ieinfosite.co.uk

More Internet Software

Now you've installed a browser, you can surf the Web looking for other software. For a guide to plundering the world's greatest software mother lode, see p.244.

Your first time

Once you've configured your dial-up networking and mail software to your ISP's specifications, you should be ready to hit the Net. Ideally, you're already armed with a Web browser, as the perfect exercise for your very first connection would be to get straight onto the World Wide Web. If not, install any version of any browser you can find, as you can always get a new one once you're online.

Connecting...

Plug your modem into the phone line and **click on the icon that connects you to the Net**. Which icon? Well that depends on the way you've set it up. Most ISP installations place a shortcut on your Desktop or under the Windows Start menu. If it's not obvious, ask your ISP.

Irrespective of how you've set it up, there will always be a few ways to kickstart your dialer. The best way, especially if you've set it up yourself, is to go straight to the connection entries in the **Dial-Up Networking folder**. You'll find it under My Computer in **Windows 95/98**, and under the Control Panel in **ME** and **2000**. Rather than open the folder every time you want to connect, drag a shortcut from the individual connection onto your Desktop or even better, your Quick Launch Toolbar (just right of the Start button). That way it's easy to get to in future.

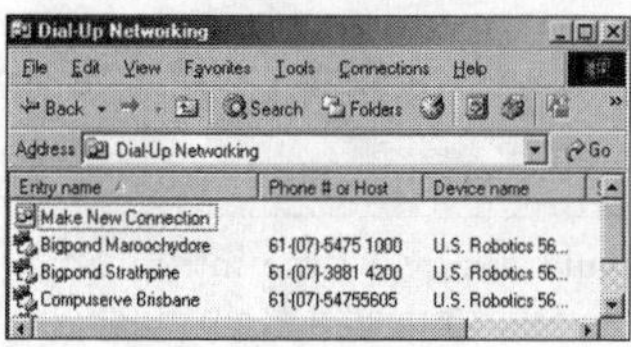

The process is similar on the **Mac** but differs between system versions. It won't take you long to work it out. In OS 8.0x and later, the dial-up networking aspect is called "**Remote Access**". Again, like Windows, you can approach it from several angles, depending on the system. For example, you'll find it under the Apple Menu, in the Control Panel and along the Control Strip. To dial, click on Remote Access and then the "**Connect**" Button.

Negotiating

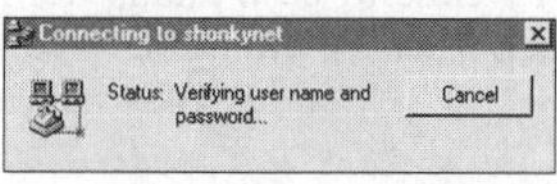

If your modem speaker volume is turned up (look under your modem properties), it will make all kinds of mating noises while connecting, like a fax machine. These sounds will cease once the connection's negotiated. At this point your provider's server will need to identify you as a customer, so if you haven't already entered your **user name and password**, you'll have to now. Once that's done, **click the box that says "Save Password"**, otherwise you'll have to enter it every time you log in. Make sure you keep this password private – anyone could use it to rack up your bill or, perhaps worse, read your mail (although you should be issued with a separate password to retrieve mail). If you fail to connect, try again. If it keeps failing, you'll need to work out what's going wrong. See p.63.

Online

Once you're in, Windows should display a large intrusive box telling you you're connected. You won't need it again, so choose to "never see this box again." You'll then see a smaller box which will tell you your connection speed, how long you've been connected, and how many bytes you've sent and received. Click on OK, to dismiss it. To bring it back, double-click on the twin computers icon in the System Tray (left bottom corner next to the clock). If you're charged by the minute or megabyte to be connected, you might find this information handy. It works similarly in Apple's Remote Access.

Testing, testing

Congratulations, you're online! Now **start your Web browser** and enter a few of the addresses from the Web guide (p.317). You'll find instructions on how to browse the Web starting on p.69. If you can access the Web, it's close to plain sailing from now on. If not, you'll need to find out what's wrong. See p.63.

Disconnecting ...

To finish your session, either right-click on the twin computers icon in the System Tray and choose disconnect, or double-click on it, and click on the disconnect button. On the Mac, re-enter Remote Access and click on disconnect.

Troubleshooting

Rest assured, you'll eventually have problems with your connection, and it won't necessarily be your fault. It happens to everyone. But before you bellow down the phone line at your ISP's support staff, make sure it's not something obvious you can fix yourself.

Getting to the settings

To access all the **connection settings** in **Windows** (modem, scripting, TCP/IP, phone, and dialer), open Dial-Up Networking (under My Computer or Control Panel), right-click on the connection, and choose **Properties**. To change the log-in settings, simply double-click as if dialing.

If you are using a **Mac with Free PPP** (or equivalent), you can access the settings by opening the **Free PPP** window and clicking on "General", "Accounts", or "Locations". You may also need to adjust the settings in your **TCP/IP file**, which you access through the Control Panel under the Apple symbol (top left-hand corner of the screen). **In later Macs**, look under **Remote Access, TCP/IP,** and **Modem** under the Apple menu Control Panel folder.

If you didn't get through

If you **didn't succeed in connecting to your provider**, there's probably something wrong with your Dial-Up Networking or modem configuration. The most common errors are:

No modem detected: Is your modem installed, plugged into

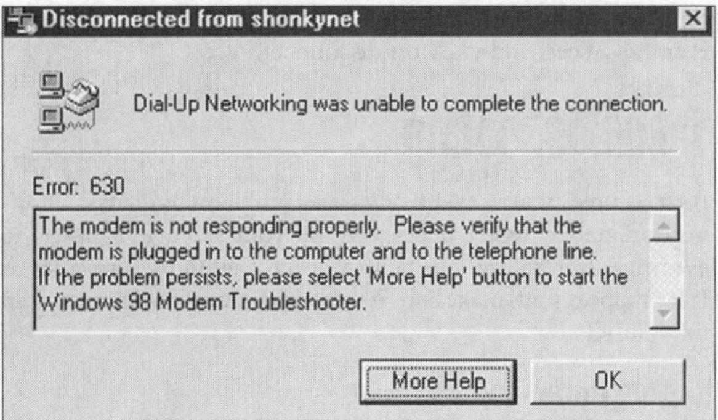

the right port, and switched on? To install or diagnose a modem in Windows, click on the Modem applet in the Control Panel.

Dial tone not detected: Is your phone line plugged in? If this isn't the problem, try disabling Dial Tone Detect or Wait for Dial Tone under the modem settings. If the option's grayed out in Windows, you'll either need to re-install the modem with its correct driver (preferable) or manually enter the initialization string X1 into Extra Settings under the modem's Advanced Connection Settings. Do this in the Modem properties for the connection through Dial-Up Networking, not through Control Panel as this only affects new connections.

No answer: Do you have the right phone number? You can verify your modem's working by dialing a friend. If their phone rings you'll know your Dial-up Networking is talking to your modem.

Busy/engaged: Access providers' lines sometimes fill up at peak hours such as the end of the working day. Keep trying until you get in: even though you dial a single number, there are several modems at the other end. If it happens often, complain, or get a new provider with a **lower user to modem ratio**.

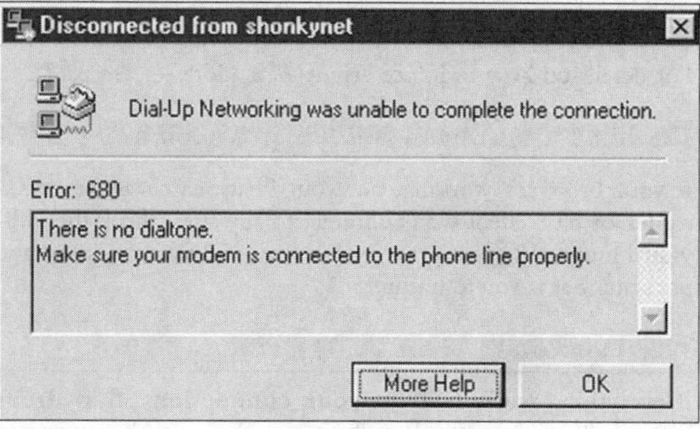

You got through but were refused entry

If you **succeeded in connecting** but were **refused entry**, check your user name, password, and script (if used). If it **failed to negotiate network protocols**, verify your TCP/IP settings. You might need your ISP's help on this one. Keep the settings on screen and phone them.

You're online but not on the Web

If you've **managed to stay connected, but can't access any Web sites**, either your DNS settings are incorrect, you've failed to establish an IP connection, you haven't specified your ISP's proxy properly, or there's a temporary outage. Log off, verify your TCP/IP and proxy settings, and try again. DNS servers go down occasionally, so (unless yours are server-assigned) make sure you specify more than one. Again, call your ISP and ask if there are network problems.

You can't access one or more Web sites

For details on how to locate errant Web addresses, see p.172.

You're on the Web but another program won't work

If your browser's working, but your chat, search agent, newsreader, or FTP client won't connect to any sites, check the individual program's proxy settings. Ask your ISP for the address and port number if you're unsure.

Your connection keeps going down

If everything works fine but **your connection often drops out**, you'll need to check each link in the chain between you and your provider. Unfortunately, there are a lot of links, so it's down to a matter of elimination.

❑ **Does it happen only after an extended period of inactivity?** Then it could be an automatic defense mechanism in your Dial-up Networking or at your provider's end.

❑ **Do you have telephone Call Waiting?** If it's enabled, and you're called while online, those little beeps will knock out your connection.

❑ **Pick up your phone. Does it sound clear?** Crackling sounds indicate a poor connection somewhere. Modems like a nice clean line.

❑ **Do you share a line?** Picking up an extension will drop your connection.

❑ **Do you have the latest modem driver and firmware revision?** Check your modem manufacturer's home page.

As a **last resort** try a different ISP, phone line, and modem. For more troubleshooting advice, contact your ISP or see: http://php.iupui.edu/~aamjohns/

Okay, it works – but it's very slow

When the **Net gets overloaded**, transfer rates slow down: it can happen to the whole Internet backbone at peak hours, particularly with transoceanic routes. If transfers are slow from everywhere, however, it usually means the problem lies closer to home. It could be that your **provider or office network** has too many users competing online, or too much traffic accessing its Web area from outside. In this case your provider or office needs to increase its bandwidth to the Net.

ISPs tend to go through cycles of difficult traffic periods. If they have the resources and the foresight to cope with demand, you won't notice. But as it's such a low-margin business, they're more likely to stretch things. Always call your provider when you have complaints with its service. If you're not treated with respect, no matter how trivial your inquiry, take your money elsewhere.

Finding the bottleneck

If you'd really like to know what's slowing things down, arm yourself with some network diagnostic tools. The staples are: **Ping**, which works like a radar to measure how long it takes a data packet to reach a server and return; and **TraceRoute**, which pings each router along the path to see which one's causing the holdup.

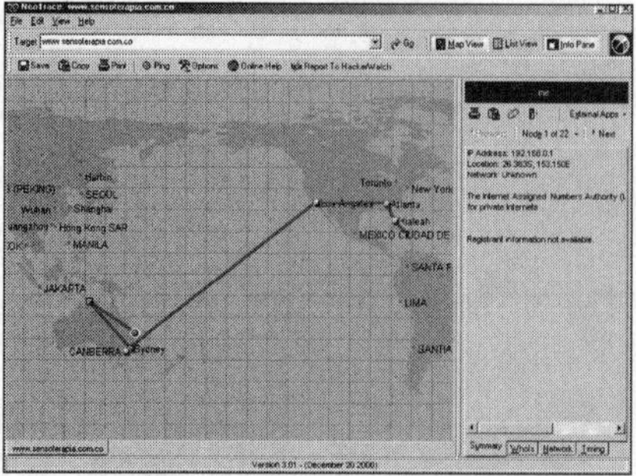

The single best piece of advice

If you know someone who's a bit of an Internet whiz, coax them over to help you hook up for the first time. Throw in enough pizza, beer, and compliments about their technical prowess, and you'll have an auxiliary support unit for life.

Windows users have plenty of choices for obtaining these programs. **NetScan Tools** (http://www.nwpsw.com) has Ping, TraceRoute and loads more. **MyVital Agent** (http://www.vitalsigns.com) can tell you exactly where it's breaking down, whether your provider is falling short, monitor trends, and send off a complaint report. **NeoTrace** (http://www.neoworx.com) adds another level to TraceRoute by identifying who owns the routers, and then maps it all out in Hollywood style.

For Macs, try **WhatRoute** (http://crash.ihug.co.nz/~bryanc/) for tracing routers, and **CyberGauge** (http://www.neon.com) to monitor bandwidth.

4

Surf the Web

The world at your fingertips

When you see something like www.come.and.get.me on an ad, business card, or news story, you're being invited to visit an address on the World Wide Web (the Web), the biggest breakthrough in communications since TV. You'll have no trouble finding such addresses online – all you have to do is type them into your Web browser.

In fact, you'll find all sorts of interesting stuff once you get started. The Web is so cheap and easy to use that it has sparked off more publishing, both professional and DIY, than at any time in history.

Although getting about the Web is undeniably simple, you'll still need a little help to get off the ground. As preparation, we've dedicated this section to explaining **how to set up your Web browser** and point it in the right direction; there's another section on **how to find things** once you're there (see p.152); and most of the back half of this book (see p.317) consists of reviews of **interesting and useful sites**.

What to expect

The Web is the Internet's glossy, glamorous, point-and-click front door: a colorful assault of shopping, investment services, music, magazines, art, books, museums, travel, games, job agencies, movie previews, radio broadcasts, self-promotion, and much, much more. It has information on more than twenty million companies and is accessed by more than four hundred million users in every corner of the globe from Antarctica to Iceland. It will bring the world to the keyboard of your computer. It's better than the best encyclopedia, and for the most part, it's free. **There's no doubt, if you're not on the World Wide Web, you're missing out**.

How to read a Web address (URL)

In tech-speak **a Web address is also called a URL** (Uniform Resource Locator). Every Web page has a unique URL that can be broken into three parts. Reading from left to right they are: the **protocol** (such as http:// ftp:// or news:); the **host name (domain)** (everything before the first single forward slash); and the **file path** (everything after and including the first single forward slash). Consider the address: http://www.star.com.hk/~Chow/Yun/fat.html The http:// tells us it's a HyperText file located on the World Wide Web, the domain www.star.com.hk tells us it's in Hong Kong, and the file path indicates that the file fat.html is located in the folder (directory) /~Chow/Yun/

Anyone who's serious about their presence on the Web has their own domain name. Typically, a company will choose an address that relates to its business name or activity. It's also common, but **certainly not a rule**, for such addresses to start with http://www. For example, you'll find: Apple computers at http://www.apple.com; the BBC at http://www.bbc.co.uk; and assorted spells and potions at: http://www.sorcerers-shop.com

So what do you do with the address? Enter it into your browser, of course. Read on, to find out how ...

Starting out

When you enter a **Web address** into your browser it will retrieve the corresponding page from wherever it's stored on the Internet and display it on your screen. The page is likely to contain a mixture of text and images, laid out like a magazine. But what makes a Web page special is that it can contain **links** (also called hyperlinks). When you **click on a link, something happens**. Generally, it brings up another page, but it might do something else like launch a Net radio broadcast, or start a file download.

How to start Internet Explorer

The most convenient way to open Internet Explorer is to click on the shortcut in the Windows Quick Launch toolbar (beside the Start button). The icon looks like a big blue letter "e". You'll also find one on the Desktop, as well as in the Start menu, under Programs. Don't click on it (for the first time) until you're connected to the Net, otherwise it will probably return an error. Once you've removed the **annoying start page** (p.88), however, you can click on it any time you like.

How to enter an address

To visit a Web site, you have to submit its address to your browser, either by keying it in, or clicking on a link. However, you'll need to be connected to the Internet for it to work, so go online before trying out an address.

Once you're online, open Internet Explorer. It will probably try to access a start (home) page. Let it go about its course and ignore whatever comes up. See the bar running horizontally above the browser pane that says Address on the left hand side? That's the **Address bar**. Click inside it, type www.yahoo.com and hit enter – or click on the Go button at the far right of the bar.

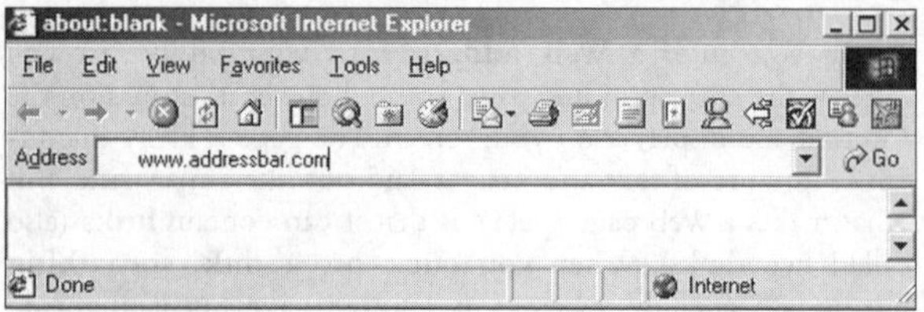

Your browser will examine the address and work out what to do next. If you've submitted a legitimate Web address, it will contact your DNS server to convert the host name into an IP address. You'll see this process happening in the lower left corner of your screen. Once it's converted, the browser will contact the Web site's server and request the page.

It rarely takes more than a minute or two to locate and load Web pages. Over a 56K modem, the average time is around 30 seconds, but if you've a broadband connection, it can be almost instant. If all works well, your browser will retrieve the page and display it on your screen. In this case, you'll arrive at Yahoo, the Web's biggest directory (see p.160).

If you receive an error message, try again. If that fails, see (p.63) and (p.172) for help troubleshooting.

Other ways to enter an address

There are dozens of less convenient ways to enter a Web address, especially in Windows. For example, through Open under the File menu in Internet Explorer; in Run under the Start menu; or directly into the address bar in Windows Explorer (click on

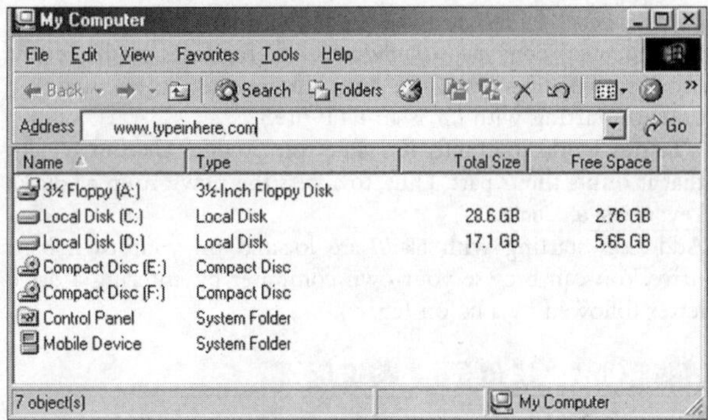

My Computer). In all cases, you simply need to type in the address, and click on OK or hit your Enter key.

What about the http:// bit of the address?

Although the formal way to write a Web address is to start it with http:// for example, http://www.yahoo.com **you don't need to enter the http:// part** into your browser. For that reason, you'll often see Web addresses expressed without it, for example: www.yahoo.com

It won't make any difference which way you enter the address, as your browser will automatically add it on if you omit it. This will only cause problems if the address isn't a Web address. That is, it starts with something other than http://

Other addresses (non http)

You can also access **FTP** (see p.249), **Telnet**, and **Usenet** (see p.197) from the helm of your Web browser.

To **use FTP**, you just add ftp:// to the file's location. So, to retrieve duck.txt located in the directory /yellow/fluffy from the anonymous FTP site **ftp.quack.com** you should enter: **ftp://ftp.quack.com/yellow/fluffy/duck.txt** (In fact, with recent browsers you can omit the **ftp://** part as they know that any domain starting with **ftp.** is an FTP site.)

Telnet works in exactly the same way. So does **Usenet**, except that it omits the // part. Thus, to access the newsgroup **alt.ducks** key: **news: alt.ducks**

Addresses starting with **file:///** are located on your own hard drive. You can browse your own computer by entering a drive letter followed by a colon (eg, c:).

Important – take care with capitals

Note that Web address path names are **case sensitive**. So, key them carefully, taking note of capitals as well as their bizarre punctuation. Host names are almost always written in lower case, but are actually case insensitive. In other words entering: **www.BigStick.com** is the same as **www.bigstick.com**, but **www.bigstick.com/Bigstick/** isn't the same as **www.bigstick.com/bigstick/**.

Address guessing – helpful

Once you've been online for a short time you'll notice Internet Explorer will start trying to guess the address you're entering. It will present a drop-down list of all the sites it knows that so far match your keystrokes. You can either complete the address or click on one of the selections. These are supplied by the History file (p.80).

Address guessing – not so helpful

In a case of trying to be smart, without being useful, if you enter a word or phrase rather than a properly formed address, your browser will also try to guess or search for the site. If that sounds like it might save you time, just try it. You probably won't both-

er again. The various permutations can be set below "Search in Address bar" under the Advanced tab in Internet Options (p.88). You'd be better off using a search engine (p.153).

Clicking on links

You rarely have to enter addresses to get around the Web, because most of the time you'll simply be **clicking on links**. Web pages are written in **HTML** (HyperText Markup Language), which lets documents **link** to other documents. Clicking on such a link effectively turns the page. This creates a sort of third dimension.

Unless you've changed the settings (p.80), **text that contains links** to other documents (or another part of the same document) will usually be highlighted in blue and underlined. Apart from text, images, and movies can also contain links – and not just one either. Pictures might contain links that relate to what's in the picture. For example, clicking on a town's name on a map might send you to a site about that town. In Webspeak, this type of picture is called an "**image map**".

When you pass over a link **your mouse cursor will change from an arrow to a pointing hand** and the target address should appear in a bar at the bottom of your browser. It's easy for site programmers to override this and **place alternate text in the bottom bar**, or **make your mouse do funny things like leave trails**, so don't be alarmed if it doesn't always work the same way.

To pursue the link, simply **click on the highlighted text or**

image. A link is only a **one-way connection**, like a signpost. So when you get to the new page, there won't necessarily be a link back. You might imagine that once you've been clicking for a while you could easily get lost. You won't, because there are some simple ways to retrace your steps, as we'll explain soon.

Surf the web

All the main **navigation buttons** are located on the toolbar above the main browser window. Displaying them is optional, but they're hard to live without.

You'll use the **Back** and **Forward** buttons most. To **go back to a page** you previously visited, click the Back button until you find it. To **return to where you were**, keep pressing Forward. And to go back to your start-up page (p.88) hit **Home**.

You can go back and forward through pages pretty much instantly once you've visited them during a session, as your computer stores the documents in memory. How much material you can click through in this fashion, however, depends on the amount of storage space allocated to **Temporary Internet Files** in your settings. For more, see "Browse Offline" (p.81).

Two other important buttons are **Stop** and **Refresh**. To **cancel a page request**, because it's taking too long to load a site, or you've made a mistake, just hit the Stop button. Occasionally, you might have to hit Stop before Back will work. Alternatively, if a page doesn't load properly, you can hit **Refresh** to load it again. You'd also do this if a page changes regularly, and you want to load a new version rather than one that's stored in your Temporary Internet Files, or on your ISP's proxy server (p.90).

The **Mac versions are laid out slightly differently** with a toolbar located vertically on the left hand side. You can also move the top toolbar to the left by clicking on the arrow in the upper right.

Change the buttons

You can customize the way the buttons and bars appear, which is handy because they take up too much screen real estate in the default state. So, once you're familiar with the buttons, choose to display them **small and without text**. To access the settings, right-click on the toolbar and choose **Customize**, or look under Toolbars in the View menu.

Move the bars

You can also move the bars around to your liking. Just left-click on the bar, hold down with the mouse, move it to your preferred spot, and release the mouse. If you're running IE6.0 or later, you'll need to right-click on the toolbar and unlock the bars first.

Use your mouse

The next most important navigation controls are in your **right mouse button**. Just hold it down and try them all out. The menu will change depending upon what you click. For instance, if you click on a link, you'll have the option of opening the target page in a new window. Click on an image and you'll see the option to save it to disk. You'll also find Back, Forward, Refresh and Print in there.

Although it's **preferable to upgrade your Apple mouse** (p.30) to get the wheel and extra buttons, you can access the same "right mouse" menus by **holding down the Control key** as you click. The Mac versions don't have as many options under the mouse menus but what's there is still useful.

Find a page later – save it to Favorites

Whenever you find a page that's worth another visit, file it into your "**Favorites**" for later reference. **Internet Explorer** stores each address as an individual "**Internet Shortcut**" in the same way it makes shortcuts to programs in Windows. To **arrange your Favorites** into logical folders, choose **Organize Favorites** from the Favorites menu. To move them, click on the entries and drag and drop them into place. Alternatively, right-click on the tree and choose explore. Then you can delete or move the shortcuts around like any other Windows file.

When you add an address to your Favorites, it will ask if you'd like to **make it available offline**. If you agree, it will check the page at whatever intervals you specify to see if it's changed. At the same time, it can also download the page, and others linked to it, so that you can browse the site offline later (see "Browse Offline" – p.81).

You can also **save an address as a shortcut or alias** on your Desktop. Drag and drop the page icon to the left of the address or choose **Send Shortcut to Desktop** from under the File menu.

The links bar – add your favorite sites

You're sure to visit a few sites often, such as your favorite newspaper and search engines. Rather than type in the address every time, or click through your Favorites, you'll find it's quicker to put a link to them in your **Links bar**. The Links toolbar is usually located below the Address bar – or wherever you choose to put it. If it's not there, right-click on the top toolbar in IE and put a tick beside "Links."

While it might look like any old toolbar, the Links bar is actually a special Favorites folder. That means you can add to it, or organize just like any other Favorites folder. You can also drag and drop links directly from the Address bar onto the Links bar, on into a folder on the Address bar. But before you put it to use, clear out all the junk supplied by Microsoft, Apple or whoever provided the browser. Rather than stack it with individual links, create a few folders and drop the links into them.

Make the most of your session

Nothing happens instantly on the Net, so **make sure you're always doing at least three things at once**. You might as well download news, mail, and the latest software releases while you browse several sites at once. If you're reading with nothing happening in the background, you're wasting time online.

It's simple to open multiple sites. While you wait for one page to load, open a **New Window** or **New Browser**, and look elsewhere while you wait. For instance, when reading an online newspaper, scan for interesting stories, and then quickly fire them all open in separate windows. Just click each link in turn while **holding down the Shift key** (Apple key on the Mac) or by selecting **Open in a New Window** from your **mouse menu**. Then you can read it all instantly, perhaps even offline.

Bear in mind, however, that each process is competing for **computer resources** and bandwidth, so the more you attempt, the higher the likelihood that each will take longer – and that your machine might crash. Mac users will need to allocate extra memory to the browser otherwise it won't be able to open more than three or four windows.

Opera (http://www.opera.com) is a browser specifically designed to encourage this practice. It can easily open forty or more site windows within the main window, at a fraction of the resources needed in IE or Netscape. The only catch is you'll have thirty windows open, and Opera will crash, losing the lot. So, it's best to experiment first and see how much your setup can take.

Retrace your steps

During a session browsing the Web, you can **return to recently visited sites** through the drop-down menus found by either holding down the Back and Forward buttons or clicking on the adjacent down arrows. And you can return to the sites you visit most by scrolling through the drop-down menu where you enter addresses. These, however, only keep track of the current session in that window. If you want to retrace through previous sessions, go straight to the **History file**.

Find it again – through your history file

Whenever you visit a site, its name and address go into your **History file**. Clicking on the History button will toggle a window on the left-hand side. You can sort the sites by date, name, order of visits, or number of visits. To revisit a site, either click through the links, or search through the contents. We'll discuss the latter in more detail ahead in "Browse Offline" (p.81).

How to tell where you've been

An **unvisited link** is like a signpost to a new page. You click on the link to go there. It's then called a **visited link**.

You can customize links by displaying them as **underlined** and/or in a **special color**. The setting is in Internet Options (p.88) under Colors in the General tab. The default is usually underlined blue for unvisited links and either black, purple or red for visited links. However, individual sites can override these settings and display their own custom colors.

See how this works for yourself. Look at any page. Links you haven't followed should appear blue and underlined. Now click one and load the page. Next, click "Back" and return to the previous page. The link will have changed color.

What's more, **visited links will appear in the new color wherever they crop up**, even on a completely different page that you are visiting for the first time. This can be useful if you're viewing directories and lists, as you can instantly see what you seen before.

Visited links eventually expire and revert to their old color. You can set the **expiration** period under Internet Options. It's wise to keep the expiry time short (no more than 20 days). A big **History file** can dramatically slow things down, especially if you surf a lot. After a month or so, click on **Clear History** under the General tab in Internet Options see if it speeds things up. If it does, reduce your expiry period.

Browse offline

If you're subject to timed charges, consider **gathering pages** rather than reading. Any pages you load go onto your hard drive, and are available for reading offline later. That means you can run back through your session after you hang up. You can prevent Internet Explorer from trying to go online by choosing "Work Offline" from under the File menu.

Once in this mode, you can **call up sites** by typing in their addresses, following links as if you were online, or by clicking on their entries in your History file. The contents of the pages are stored temporarily in a folder called **the Temporary Internet Files**. Their primary purpose, however, is to speed up browsing. When

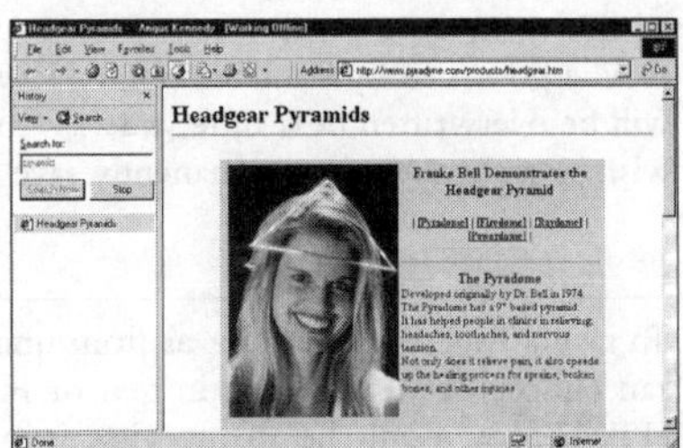

you return to a page, your browser will check this folder first rather than download its components again from the Net.

Clear your Temporary Internet Files

The Temporary Internet Files settings are under the General tab in **Internet Options** (p.88).You can change their location, how much disk space to allocate, and when to check for newer versions. This is also the proper place to delete all the stored pages. **If you try to do it manually, it will cause problems.**

It's best to select the **option to check for newer versions** just once per session. Then if you suspect the document's changed during a session revisit, just hit Refresh. Unless you plan to read offline, it's wise to **delete these files every week or two** as, like the History file, if it gets too big, it can slow things right down.

If your **browser is playing up** and not loading pages properly, try clearing them out. It's often an instant fix.

Search your History

As mentioned earlier, the History file makes it very easy to backtrack your session. But even better, you can **search the contents of the pages stored in your Temporary Internet Files**. It's just like having your own search engine.

Mind you, these pages won't sit on your hard drive forever – they're governed by your Temporary Internet Files settings and will be overwritten next time you visit that same address. If you wish to archive a page permanently, save it.

Save a page

To save a page, choose **Save as** from under the File menu. You can choose between saving in text or HTML. If you **Save as HTML**, you'll only be able to view it in programs that understand HTML such as Web browsers. Save it as text and you can read or edit it in any text viewer or word processor.

The problem with this method is that you'll save the text, but not the images. If you want the images as well, you'll need to save as a **complete Web page** or **Web archive**. The first option automatically saves the images into a separate folder. The latter combines all the elements into a single, transportable file that can only be viewed in IE5 or later.

Save an image, movie, or sound file

Web pages often display reduced images. In Web art galleries especially, such images often have links to another with higher resolution. To save an image, right-click on it, and choose **Save as** or **Save Image as** from the mouse button menu. You can also save images as **desktop wallpaper**. To save a movie or sound clip, click on the link to it and choose **Save Target as** from the mouse menu.

In IE6 and later when you pass your mouse cursor over an image that doesn't contain a link, a toolbar pops up offering shortcuts to save, print and email the image. You'll find right-clicking is quicker, though.

Mass Downloader (http://www.metaproducts.com) integrates into your browser's mouse menu giving you the option of sending files its way instead. Which is ideal for large files as it's faster and can resume broken downloads. It can also scan a page and download all links of your chosen type – handy if you come across a movie archive.

Print a page

To print a page, simply choose **Print** from under the File menu. Note the various layout selections on the pop-up print window. To alter the margins, headers and footers, and other details select

Page Setup. To view how it will look on a page, select **Print Preview**.

Download entire sites while you sleep

If you'd like to read an online newspaper offline – for example on the train to work – you can set up Internet Explorer to go online while you sleep and download as much of the site as you want. (Handy if your access or phone charges are less late at night and you'd like to browse a large site during working hours). Just save the site to **Favorites**, choose **make available offline**, and then click on "Customize" to set how many pages to download and when to grab them. To edit or delete your deliveries, choose **Synchronize** from under the Tools menu. The process is called "**Subscribe**" in earlier versions of IE and IE5+ on the Mac.

But if you're serious about ripping the contents from a site, look no further than **Offline Explorer** (http://www.metaproducts.com). You can set it up to extract only certain types and sizes of files, and configure all manner of keyword restrictions in the server and directory names. For example, you could visit a music site before you retire, right-click on the page, choose "download page with offline explorer", set the parameters, and wake up to a folder full of MP3s.

Know your browser

Rummage through the far reaches of your menus, buttons, and options, and you might think you have a long way to go before you can understand your browser. Well, thankfully, that's not true. Most of the obscure settings can, and should, be left in the default state, and few of the auxiliary features will change your life for the better. Still, it won't do you any harm to gradually investigate the extra powers of your browser, even if only to find out its limitations.

Find something on a page

To search for a word or phrase within a Web page, choose Find under Edit menu, or use the shortcut Ctrl F.

AutoComplete

Apart from suggesting addresses from your History file, Internet Explorer can also **suggest form entries** (such as search engine terms, user names, and passwords) if you choose to enable **AutoComplete**. You'll find various settings, and the option to delete the current data, by clicking the AutoComplete button under the Content tab in Options. To remove an individual entry, select it and hit the delete key.

Change the text size

To change the size of the text on a Web page, take your pick under Text Size in the View menu. Alternatively, try holding down Ctrl as you roll the mouse wheel.

Copy and paste

To copy text from Web pages, highlight the section, choose **Copy** from the Edit or right-click mouse menu (or use the usual shortcut keys), then switch to your word processor, text editor, or mail program and choose **Paste**.

Send addresses to a friend

One of the first things you'll want to do online is **share your discoveries** with friends. The simplest way is to copy the site's address into a mail message, along with a note, or perhaps a section copied and pasted from the page as described above. Alternatively, you can send a link or **whole page**, by choosing **Send** from under the **File menu** in Internet Explorer. However, if you send a whole page to someone who uses a kludgy mail system that doesn't understand HTML mail (eg Lotus Notes), it will come through as mumbo jumbo.

That's straightforward but what if you want to **send a whole list**? This is one area where Internet Explorer and Netscape differ markedly. Both browsers file addresses into folders for later retrieval, but approach the task from very different angles. Netscape stores them in an HTML file – it's actually a Web page in itself which means you can **put it on the Web**, specify it as your home page, or **attach it to mail** as a single file. Internet Explorer saves each address individually as a shortcut, which makes them less convenient to transfer. To send in bulk, **export** a single folder or the whole list as a Netscape Bookmark file with the **Import/Export Wizard** under the File menu in IE. Then drag and drop the result into an email message like any other attachment. (See p.126)

Send email from a Web page

You'll often come across an invitation to **email someone from a Web page**. It mightn't look like an email address – it might be just a name that contains a link. Whatever, it will be obvious from the context that if you want to contact that person you should click on the link. If you pass your mouse over this link it will read something like: mailto: someone@somewhere.com. And then when you click on it, it will call up your mail program, addressing a new message to someone@somewhere.com Just type your message and send it. Any replies will arrive through the normal channels.

If it doesn't work, your **browser/mail combination** isn't set up properly. Before you can send email, you have to complete your email details. You can use any mail program with Internet Explorer. Just choose it from the list under Programs in Internet Options. For instructions on setting up mail, see p.111.

Join a newsgroup from the Web

A Web page might **refer you to a newsgroup** for more information. When you click on the link, your newsreader should open in a separate window. You can continue browsing as you wait for the newsgroup subjects to arrive. Again you'll need to be set up for Usenet. With Internet Explorer, if you're using any Usenet program other than Outlook Express or Internet Mail and News, you'll have to specify it in Internet Explorer under Programs. For more on newsgroups, see p.197.

Download files

Most, if not all, your future **file downloads** and **software upgrades** will be initiated by a link from a Web page. Whether the object is stored on a Web or FTP server makes little difference. The file transfer operation can be completely handled by your Web browser. For more on file transfer, see p.244.

Uncover the source

The smartest way to **learn Web design** is to peek at the raw HTML coding on pages you like. Choose **Source** from the View or right-click mouse menu. For more on Web page design, see p.291.

What's related

If you're bored, Internet Explorer can offer you a list of related sites courtesy of **Alexa** (http://www.alexa.com). Click on **Show Related Links** under the Tools menu. It looks impressive at first, but power users will get better value by going straight to the search engines and directories (p.152).

Internet options

Internet Explorer's main settings lurk under a selection of tabs and buttons in **Internet Options**.You'll find it under the Tools menu in Internet Explorer; by clicking on "Internet Options or Internet" in the Windows Control Panel; or by right-clicking the desktop Internet icon (the big E) and selecting "Properties". Again, the settings are **laid out differently on the Mac**, but the functions are much the same. Look under Preferences in the Edit menu. Before you set about changing everything you can find, beware that the default settings are preferable in most cases. There is one thing you'll definitely need to change, and that's your "home page". Preset home pages are **a nuisance you really can do without**.

Lose the home page

Tired of waiting for a useless page to load every time your open your browser, or browser window? Annoyed that whenever you open Internet Explorer it tries to go online and retrieve this page? If your answer's yes, it's time to get rid of the home (start) page. Don't worry, you don't need it now, and you won't need it ever again.

You'll find the solution under the General tab in Internet Options.You can change the home page to any address you like, even one located on your own hard drive. However, **it's better**

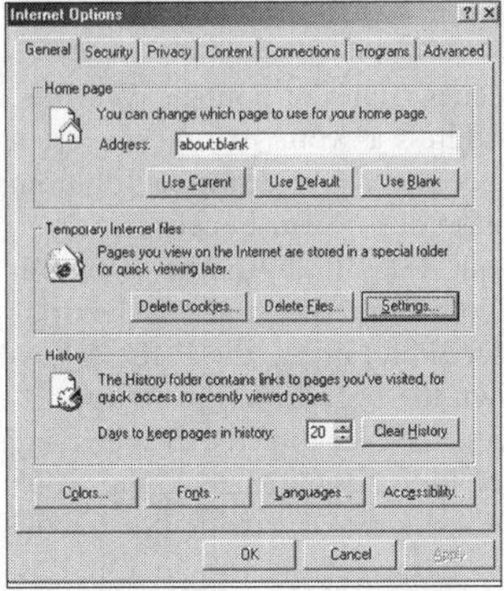

to start with a blank page. That way you don't have to wait for anything to load before you start a Web session and it won't cause problems when you open your browser whilst offline.

Remove the branding

If your browser came from anywhere but Windows, Apple or Microsoft's Web site, it's highly probable the middle party will have added their own touches. Apart from bludgeoning you with their own home page, Links (p.78) and Favorites (p.78), they could also have **plastered their name and logo** in various places. Never mind, it's easy to restore IE and Outlook Express (p.109) to their virgin states. Close all programs and at the Run command, in the Start menu, type this line and click OK:
rundll32.exe iedkcs32.dll,Clear

If you'd like to slap your own brand on either program, try the **Internet Appearance Wizards** on X-Setup: http://www.xteq.com

Stop it trying to connect all the time

If you find your machine trying to connect at inopportune times, such as when you're reading your mail offline, go to the Connections tab in Options and choose to "**Never dial a connection**". Repairing or reinstalling Internet Explorer (p.100) can sometimes reset this, and other options, so be prepared to change it again one day.

Proxy settings

Many ISPs run a server that caches copies of popular Web sites. If you specify this machine's address as your **proxy server,** it might make browsing faster – because you're downloading from closer to you. The real purpose is not for your benefit, however, it's to reduce traffic across your ISP's links to the Net. But because you're downloading a copy of the site, and not the original, it might not be the latest version. Hitting the Refresh button, however, should bring down the page from the source.

Some ISPs won't let you access the Net directly, so specifying the proxy address is compulsory. If you don't enter it, you won't be able to browse at all. If this is the case, ask your ISP for the address and enter it under the **Connection tab** in Options. Select the connection and click on the settings button. If you have a choice, experiment with or without the proxy to see which is faster and more reliable. Proxies tend to get in the road more than they help.

Cookies

A **cookie** is a small file, placed on your computer by a Web server, as a sort of ID card. Then, next time you drop by, it will know you. Actually, it doesn't quite know it's "you", it only recognizes your individual browser. If you were to visit on another machine or with a different browser on the same machine, it would see you as a different visitor. Or conversely, if someone else were to use your browser, it couldn't tell the difference.

Most Web sites routinely **log your visit**. They can tell a few harmless things like what browser you're using, which pages you've requested and the last site you've seen. This is recorded against your IP address. However, because most dial-up users are issued a different IP address each time they log on, this information isn't useful for building individual profiles. If analysts can log this data against a cookie ID instead, they have a better chance of recognizing repeat visitors. Amongst other things, this makes their lives easier when it comes to looking for sponsorship, which means the site has a better chance of staying afloat.

On the next level, if you **voluntarily submit further details**, they can store it in a database against your cookie, and use it to do things like tailor the site to your preferences, or save you entering the same data each time you check in. This won't be stored on your computer, so other sites can't access it. And most importantly, they won't know anything personal about you – not even your email address – unless you tell them.

Under IE5, you can choose to block, or be warned before accepting, cookies. Look under the Security tab in Options. You'd need a good reason, though, as it will end up driving you nuts. IE6 has introduced more control over cookies, through the **Privacy tab**, which is usually best left in the default (medium) state. It also lets you delete them under the General tab. For more on cookies, see:

Cookie Central http://www.cookiecentral.com

Censor Web material from kids

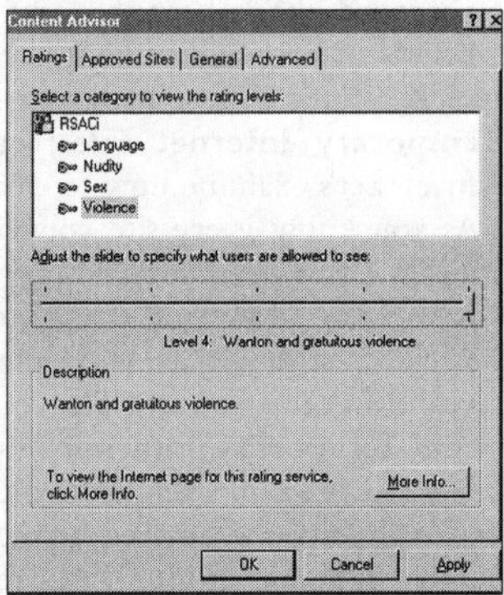

It's possible to **bar access to certain sites** that might be on the wrong side of educational. Internet Explorer employs the **PICS** (Platform for Internet Content Selection) system. You can set ratings for language, nudity, sex, and violence. Look under the **Content Advisor**

settings, within the Content tab in Internet Options. If you **forget your password**, you'll need to delete a registry key to restore full use of the browser. For instructions, see:
http://www.ieinfosite.co.uk/tip_view.asp?id=16

There are several third-party programs such as Surf-Watch, ImageCensor, Cybersitter, and NetNanny, which can impose all sorts of restrictions. None, however, is foolproof or particularly satisfactory. See:

http://www.peacefire.org
http://www.censorware.org
http://www.rsac.org

If you're really concerned about what your children are viewing on the Web, you might do better spending a few hours each week surfing the Web with them. After all, banning something will only make them want it more.

Hide your tracks

Because your browser records all your online activities, it's easy for someone to find out where you've been spending your time. So, if you'd like to keep that area of your life private you'd better find out how to hide your tracks. Traces of your online activities are stored in five areas: your **History file; Address Bar; Temporary Internet Files; cookies;** and **AutoComplete** entries. Let's examine how to clear them out.

As you know, every site you visit is stored in your **History file**. So if you open your History file you'll instantly see where you've been. More evidence is stored under the **Address Bar**. Just click the down-arrow on the right-hand side of the bar to reveal a list of recent sites. The contents of those pages are stored in the **Temporary Internet Files**, and it's very likely the sites deposited their own telltale **cookies** in the special cookie folder. Finally, if you've entered anything into a form such as a search engine, double-clicking in that form will reveal a list of previous entries courtesy of **AutoComplete**. So, how do you cover your tracks? You must either delete all these files and records, or ensure they're not recorded in the first place.

You can **delete your Temporary Internet Files, History and Cookies (IE6 only)**, from under the General tab in Internet Options. Deleting History will also clear the entries from your **Address Bar**.

To **clear the Address Bar but leave your History intact**, right-click on a blank section of the taskbar at the bottom of your screen and choose Properties. In Windows ME, go to the Advanced tab, and click the clear button. In Windows 98, the Clear button is in the Documents menu section. If you'd prefer your browser didn't prompt you with addresses from the History file, enforce your preference by clicking the **AutoComplete** button under the Contents tab in Internet Options.

While you're there, you can clear, or disable, your **AutoComplete** entries. Alternatively, to remove individual AutoComplete entries, double-click in the form, move your mouse down to select the item and hit the Delete key. Hold the delete key down to wipe the entire list.

To **delete individual sites from your History**, click on the History button, right-click on the entry and choose "delete" from the pop-up menu. To **disable History**, set the "**number of days to keep pages in History**" to zero.

Rather than **disable the saving of Temporary Internet Files**, it's wiser to check the box to "**Empty Temporary Internet Files folder when browser is closed**" under the Advanced tab. Bear in mind this will prevent you from browsing offline, or searching through the contents of your past sessions.

Turn off your multimedia

The drawback of the Web's sights and sounds is the time it takes to download them. If your connection is very slow, there is an option of **not showing images and** other **multimedia**. Look under the Advanced tab in Options.

While declining images might load pages faster, some pages contain nothing but images with links behind them. If you strike such a page, select the broken image, and choose **Show Image** from your mouse menu on Explorer, or change your settings and refresh the page.

Installing IE's **Web Accessories pack** will lob an **image toggle switch** on your toolbar. Clicking it will turn images on or off.

Plug-ins and ActiveX

Although your browser can recognize a mind-boggling array of multimedia and other file formats, you'll occasionally come across something it can't deal with. Generally, there'll be an icon nearby suggesting you grab a **plug-in** or an **ActiveX control.** If not, you'll see a broken image which when clicked on will tell you what you need and where to get it.

A **plug-in** is an auxiliary program that works alongside your browser. You download this program, install it, and your browser will call on it when need be. **ActiveX controls** work similarly, but their scope is far greater. When you arrive at a site that relies on an ActiveX control, it checks to see if you already have it, and if not, installs it automatically after you approve the publisher's certificate. As a rule, **don't accept certificates unless you're satisfied the publisher is reputable**. ActiveX currently only works in Internet Explorer for Windows. While you can change all manner of permissions under Security tab in Options, they're best left set to "Medium".

Java and JavaScript

When **Java** – Sun Microsystems' vision of a platform-independent programming language – arrived, it was instantly pounced upon by the Web community. What once was a static environment quickly sprang to life with all sorts of "animated" applications thanks to its simple HTML adjunct, **JavaScript**. Java involves downloading and running a small program (called an applet) whereas JavaScript is interpreted by your browser.

Designers can create some cool effects using Java and JavaScript, but if it's not implemented properly it might work inconsistently or even crash your browser. Scripts only tested on Netscape might cause Internet Explorer to crash, and vice versa. It's worse with earlier versions. If scripts frequently cause problems, you probably need to update or repair your browser (p.100). Alternatively, you could experiment with the settings. Click on the Custom button under the Security tab in Options. To revert to the default settings, reset it to "medium".

Shockwave and RealAudio

There are two plug-in/ActiveX controls you'll definitely need: the **RealPlayer** (which includes **RealAudio** and **RealVideo**) for Internet music and video broadcasts; and the **Shockwave and Flash Players** for multimedia effects. Whether or not they came with your browser download the latest versions from:

http://www.real.com and http://www.shockwave.com

Shockwave Flash appears to have replaced Java as the defacto standard for producing high impact sites. When it's used properly it's welcome, but mostly it gets in the way, particularly when you strike it on a site's front page. If you're not interested in viewing a tedious animated billboard, hit the "skip intro" link. With a bit of luck you'll get to the next page without crashing.

Once you have RealAudio, you can **sample CDs** before you buy at online music stores, listen to Internet concerts, and tune into live and archived radio broadcasts from all over the world. Although Microsoft's **Media Player** is capable of playing Real media, it supports only the older standards. So, when you install the **RealPlayer**, make sure it takes over as your default viewer for all Real media. You'll find the option under the RealPlayer's Preferences.

Meanwhile Microsoft is busy pushing its own streaming media standard, which is starting to gain ground. You'll find it on show at: http://www.windowsmedia.com

Media Player also supports the infamous **MP3** audio standard. For an introduction to online Music and live Internet broadcasts, see p.268 and p.279.

Help

Don't buy into the dream that we're living it up in the cyberspace age. We're still struggling in the computing equivalent of the pre-transistor black and white TV era. These are very much the early days of mass-market Internet programs. So, if you can run your browser for more than a few hours without some kind of strange error, you should consider yourself fortunate. If the glitches are minor or infrequent, don't bust your gut trying to solve them. Life is too short. But, if you're unable to browse, or can't get something to work, turn to the Net for assistance.

Helpful sites

For step-by-step instructions on using or configuring your browser, **refer to the Help menu**. Microsoft provides excellent help, including all manner of troubleshooting wizards. Netscape's is adequate for basic instructions. If you're experiencing frequent errors search on the error code in:

Microsoft's Knowledge Base http://support.microsoft.com

Unofficial FAQ sites, however, are often more useful. For example, try:

ActiveWin http://www.activewin.com/faq/

IE Security Center http://www.nwnetworks.com/iesc.html

IE Infosite http://www.ieinfosite.co.uk

And for tips, news and general troubleshooting try:

C|Net http://www.browsers.com

ZDNet http://www.zdnet.com/zdhelp/

Peer support newsgroups

The very best place to seek advice on Internet Explorer, however, is in Microsoft's peer support newsgroups (p.212). You'll find the full set on Microsoft's own public news server: msnews.microsoft.com

Just start a new account in Outlook Express, or your preferred newsreader, and join any of the groups that look appropriate. You can also browse and post through this Web interface, but it will be slower: http://communities.microsoft.com/newsgroups/

Before you post a question, first search the Usenet archive at **Google Groups** (http://groups.google.com) to see if it's already been answered. Try coining a unique term from the error code, or your problem.

While you might strike the odd Microsoft employee in these groups, most participants are volunteers, so be polite and appreciative. You'll no doubt encounter the MVP gang (Microsoft

Valued Professionals) in your travels. They don't work (officially, anyway) for Microsoft, but come with the Microsoft seal of approval. While you might find their cult-like loyalty to Microsoft irksome, you can usually trust their advice. Their personal sites are also good sources of FAQs on Internet Explorer, Windows, and other Microsoft products:

MVPs.org **http://www.mvps.org/links.html**

For help with Netscape, try:

Netscape NUGgies **http://help.netscape.com/nuggies/**

UFAQ **http://www.ufaq.org**

Crashes and lockups in Windows

Because Internet Explorer is so tightly woven into Windows, problems with one can affect the other. You'll soon discover that when a browser crash takes out your System tray or freezes your system. It's impossible to give a blanket solution for Internet Explorer's misbehavior, but it's usually possible to recover when it stops responding to your mouse clicks. Just give Windows the **three fingered salute** – hold down the **Ctrl-Alt-Del** keys. If the Close Window dialog box appears, you should be able to restore sanity without rebooting. Select the Internet Explorer entry, click on "End task" and wait a few seconds. Either a window will appear asking if you'd like to close the program, or it will close automatically. If that doesn't help, or you have a phantom screen that won't go away, do the same with the Explorer entry. This normally restores everything to normal – except when Explorer reboots, you'll notice some icons missing from the System tray – including the one to disconnect.

Disconnecting when the icon's missing

To disconnect after an Explorer reboot has removed the icon from the System tray, double-click on your connection shortcut to bring up the connection dialog box. If that doesn't work, open Outlook Express and choose Work Offline from the File menu. When it asks if you'd like to hang up your modem, answer, "Yes."

Common culprits

The most common cause of Internet Explorer problems is **bad programming** within the browser itself. There's not much you can do about that except keep it up to date. Unfortunately, problems often arise from the layering of version upon version. This is particularly the case with installing Windows ME over Windows 98. Not only is it preferable to install Windows ME onto a cleanly formatted hard drive, if you install a lot of software your system will run better if you format once a year or so and reinstall everything from scratch. Don't forget to back up first (see p.100).

Next in the line-up is so-called "spyware" – software sponsored by advertisements, such as the dreaded Comet Cursor and Netsonic. See p.262 for advice on how to avoid and remove these bugs. But commercial software can be just as meddlesome, and sometimes harder to troubleshoot. Worst of all, are the programs that run in the background and promise to accelerate your connection, remove pop-up banners, or save passwords, followed by the "crashguard", disk cleanup, and speed utilities. Steer clear, and disable your virus scanner from launching at startup (p.147).

Finally, make sure your video and sound card drivers (check the manufacturer's Web site) are up to date, and uninstall any software you don't need – through Add/Remove Programs in Control Panel only.

AOL and CompuServe browsers

Although AOL's software is Internet Explorer underneath, what it adds over the top tends to get in the road. If its software is playing up on your system, call AOL support for assistance – or switch to a normal ISP. Don't forget to **completely uninstall AOL**, otherwise it could still interfere whether or not you use its service.

Upgrade, repair and reinstall

If you already have the latest release, updating it won't solve anything. Instead, try "**repairing**" or "**reinstalling**" it. If any of the installation files are corrupt, that could involve going online and picking up a few pieces. Prepare to log on, if prompted.

Close all running programs. Open Add/Remove Programs in Control Panel, highlight Microsoft Internet Explorer and Internet Tools, and hit the button. You'll see three options. Choose "Repair".

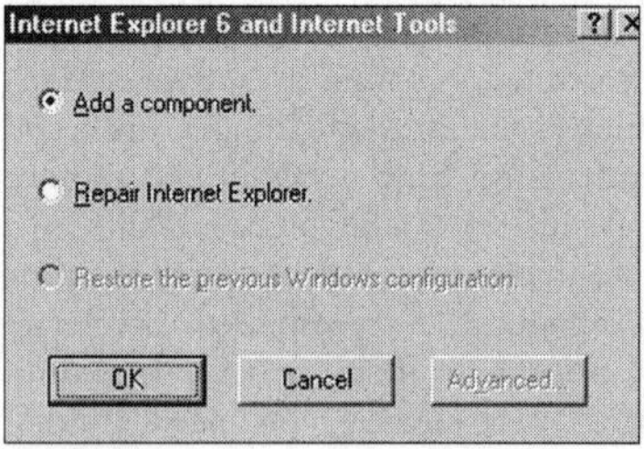

Reboot your computer. Open Add/Remove programs again, and this time uninstall Outlook Express. Reboot again, when asked.

Next, go back to the Internet Explorer and Tools entry in Add/Remove Programs, and this time rather than "Repair" choose: "Add a component." Add Outlook Express. Reboot.

If that didn't solve anything, try the "Reinstall" option.

Backing up and transferring your data

If you're moving machines, formatting your hard drive to reinstall Windows, or just worried about losing data, you'll need to find all the bits and pieces you've created so that you can restore them. Microsoft, unfortunately, hasn't made this task simple. The most important files and settings to locate are your **Favorites, Address Book, mail store,** and **mail account settings**. Here's how:

To **save your Favorites**, choose Import/Export from under the File menu in Explorer. Follow the prompts to export them to a Bookmark file on your Desktop, and then move them to a floppy disk or email them to yourself for later. To import them later, follow the same procedure, except this time, import. You can export your cookies under the same process but it's easy to live without them. It will only mean logging into a couple of sites again so they recognize you.

To **export the Address book**, choose Export from under the File menu in Outlook Express and follow the prompts. To import it, choose Import in the same way.

The **mail store** could be very large – unlikely to fit on a floppy – so you'll need to transfer it to a CD burner, second hard drive, or a networked machine, somehow. To find where it's stored, go to the Maintenance tab under Outlook Express's options, and click on the Store folder button. You'll need to move this entire folder. To restore your mail store, move it into place and assign it as the mail store when you install Outlook Express (or later using the Store folder button), or import the messages through the Import under the File menu in Outlook Express.

Your **mail account settings** aren't so important as you can always enter them again. Nonetheless, you can export and import them under Accounts in the Tools menu.

A much easier way to automate this procedure, catch other data such as your Mail rules and preferences, and export it all as a single file, is to use **Express Assist**: http://www.ajsystems.com

For more information on **backing up and restoring mail**, see: http://www.tomsterdam.com/insideoe5/

5

Email

Like regular mail only better

If you only need one good reason to justify getting online, email should do the trick. Once you get used to corresponding by email, you'll wonder how you lived without it. You'll write more and respond faster – which might make you more productive. But watch out, because email is as time-consuming as it is addictive. At first you might rediscover the joy of old-fashioned letter-writing, but because it's so easy to copy (cc) a message to everyone in your address book you might invite more mail than you can handle.

Why email will change your life

Email is such an improvement on the postal system it will revolutionize the way and the amount you communicate. You can send a message to anyone with an email address anywhere in the world – instantly. In fact, it's so quick they could receive your message sooner than you could print it.

All you need to do is **type an address**, or choose it from your **email address book**, write a brief note, and click **Send**. No letterheads, layout, printing, envelopes, stamps, or visiting the post office. And once you're online your mail program can automatically check in at whatever interval you like. You needn't wait for the postie to arrive. Email arrives 24 hrs a day, seven days a week, every day of the year.

Email is also better than faxing. It's always **a local call to anywhere, at any time**. No busy signals, paper jams, or failed attempts. Plus you receive the actual text and not a photocopy, or an actual image file and not a scan. So that means you can send **high-resolution color** and **long documents**. As a matter of fact, each edition of this book has been submitted and edited via email.

Email even **beats the phone** at times. You can send a message to a part of the world that's asleep and have a reply first thing in the morning. No need to synchronize phone calls, be put on hold, speak to voicemail, or tell some busybody who's calling. With email, you take the red carpet route straight through to the top. And you don't have to make small talk, unless that's the purpose of the message.

Replacing the post and fax is not email's only strength. You can also **attach any computer file to a message**. That means you can forward things like advertising layout, scanned images, spreadsheets, assignments, tracks from your latest CD, links to Web pages, or even programs. And your accompanying message need only be as brief as a Post-it note.

What's more, with email **everything you send and receive can be filed** in a relatively small amount of disk space. No filing cabinets, no taped phone calls, and no yellowing fax paper. All in writing, and instantly searchable for later reference.

Brief, yet intimate

Out with stuffy business letters, and in with email. As email messages are (for the most part) simply text files, there's no need to worry about fonts, letterheads, logos, typesetting, justification, signatures, print resolution, or fancy paper. It distills correspondence down to its essence – words.

And what's more, it's encouraging people to get to the point. Which means you'll be able to punch out more letters, and deal with more people than ever before.

Conversely, email is also putting personal correspondence back into letters rather than phone calls. Most new users remark on this – and the way it often seems to spark off a **surprising intimacy**.

Avoiding viruses

If you've updated Windows with the latest security patches (p.58), the only way you'll catch a virus from email is by clicking on an attachment. For a rundown on the precautions you should take, see p.142.

What you'll need

If you can get online, even through a public terminal (p.27), you can set yourself up with a **free email address** in a matter of minutes (p.105). As soon as you've done that you can send and receive email immediately – you don't even need an Internet account or your own computer. You simply log in through a Web browser on any machine connected to the Internet. Although this sounds convenient, there are some disadvantages to this type of account (p.106).

If you do sign up with an ISP, however, you should automatically get at least one **email address**, which you can **access through your own mail program (p.109), or through the Web (see below), when you're not at home (p.134)**. This is the superior option.

Your new address

Before you can become a card-carrying member of the Internet generation, you'll need to get yourself an email address. That's no problem, as they're very easy to find. However, before you grab the first one that comes your way, determine which type would suit you best. The main types of accounts you'll strike are: **Webmail, POP3, IMAP4**, and **mail forwarding**.

Webmail – usually free and easy, but slow

As the name suggests, **Webmail** accounts work through the Web. Rather than use an email program, you simply log into a

> **One is never enough – get a second free**
>
> Need an email address that you can keep for as long as you like without paying a penny, or signing up for Internet access? Perhaps you already have one through work, but you'd like an alternative for personal mail – one that your boss can't read. Or you need a second one for junk mail. Or to take on vacation. No problem. You can score one (or more) online within minutes and it needn't cost you a thing, though you might have to suffer a little advertising. For thousands of free email providers, see:
> http://www.fepg.net
> http://www.emailaddresses.com
> http://www.internetemaillist.com

Web site to collect, write and send your mail. Your messages are stored on the remote server until you decide to delete them. That means you can access all your email, past and present, from any computer with a Web browser.

No matter what computer you're on, you won't need to change any settings; you just log into your account using a Web browser. Plus, you can scan through your headers first and retrieve only what interests you. Of course, you need reasonable Web access, so collecting your mail can be tiresome, and even impossible over low bandwidth or congested cybercafé connections. Webmail addresses also carry **zero prestige** – if that's an issue – so try not to use one as your **permanent business address.**

Webmail accounts are everywhere, and **usually free**. Just about every major site will give you one in an attempt to get you to return. **Hotmail** (http://www.hotmail.com) is the most popular and heavily featured with junk mail detection and automatic virus scanning. It's hard to go wrong, as there's nothing to configure. You simply follow the instructions on the screen. Just log in, give a few details and you'll have a mail account in seconds. You can even do it through a menu entry in Outlook Express. **PlanetAccess** (http://www.planetaccess.com) is another with a good reputation for its speed. You might find it better for traveling. Or if you'd rather a more distinct address, try **Another.com** (http://www.another.com).

As you can give any details you like, you can **stay anonymous** – though abusers can still be traced by their IP address.

While you can collect Webmail with Outlook Express 5+ and Netscape 6+, you'll find it tediously slow to send and receive compared to a POP3 account from an ISP. **If you have your own computer and ISP account, POP3 is the way to go**.

POP3

Without getting into the superior technical aspects of the **Post Office Protocol (POP3)**, the main distinction as far as you're concerned is that POP3 email is normally handled by a mail program (eg Outlook Express), rather than a browser. Dedicated email programs give you far more power, especially for filing, handling attachments, and dealing with large quantities of mail. Still, if you prefer to use a browser, you can also send and receive your POP3 mail through the Web, on any computer without having to set up, through **Mail2Web** (http://www.mail2web.com).

Most ISPs will provide at least one **POP3 email account** with your Internet access. If not, you shouldn't sign up with them. A Webmail account is no substitute either, as they're commonly given away free. You can also buy a POP3 mail-only account, which isn't a bad idea as it leaves you free to switch ISPs without sacrificing your email address. Ask any ISP, or try a mail specialist such as **NetIdentity** (http://www.netidentity.com).

You can get free POP3 accounts, but they're not as common. **Yahoo Mail** (http://mail.yahoo.com) is probably the best of the

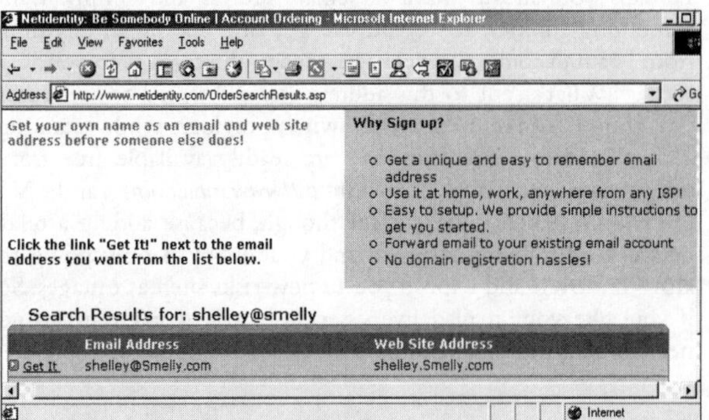

bunch (and least likely to fold). Apart from being slower and less reliable, free POP3 accounts usually aren't as convenient either, as you normally have to check your mail before you can send – Outlook Express likes to do it in the opposite order. The ideal solution is to specify your ISP's SMTP server as the outgoing mail server.

IMAP4

If you like the idea of organizing your mail into folders on a remote server, rather than storing it locally, IMAP4 might be for you. When you log onto the server with your mail program it will synchronize your computer with the server, and download all the new mail headers. Clicking on the message will download the body, but not delete it from the remote server. The most obvious advantage is you can access your mail archives from different machines. The disadvantage is it might become a bit cumbersome over a dial-up connection. Ask your ISP if it's available.

Mail forwarding

Perhaps you already have an email address and simply want something funkier. If so, you can get one ending in anything from @struth.com to @donkeylover.com through a forwarding service. What's sent to this address gets redirected to wherever you choose. You're then free to switch providers while retaining a fixed address. Such addresses are readily available free from such sites as **Mail.com** (http://www.mail.com) and **V3** (http://www.v3.com). Be careful, though, because adding a relay between your incoming mail and your inbox is only going to **slow it down** and expose you to new risks such as outages. So if you take your mail delivery seriously, you won't want to go near these types of accounts.

Your email program

As your **email program** will become the workhorse of your Net kit, you should choose it as carefully as your browser. Still, that need only be one decision, as Internet Explorer's **Outlook Express** and Netscape's **Messenger** lead the pack by a length and a half. Outlook Express acts like an independent mail program, whereas Messenger clings closely to Navigator, and is every bit as buggy.

If it comes down to nitpicking between the two, **Outlook Express** starts quicker, is more stable, and handles multiple mail accounts superbly. It even supports Hotmail, treating it like an IMAP server. In fact, if you don't have an email address you can start a Hotmail account on the spot through the Tools menu. Not surprising if you consider that Microsoft owns Hotmail.

Messenger concentrates more on getting the basics perfect than trying to be clever. That means there's never a hitch carrying out simple everyday tasks such as replying to a message, or forwarding it to someone else. It also gives you greater hands-on control of your formatting. Outlook Express isn't quite as well polished in this regard as we'll explain later. It does have some annoying quirks of its own though, as you'll soon find out. Going online to pick up ads isn't its most endearing aspect. Support for multiple accounts, including AOL mail and Netscape Webmail has been added in version 6.

It's not worth trying to mix the browser suites as neither Outlook Express nor Messenger can be installed without their respective browsers. **So ultimately, if you're browsing with Internet Explorer, use Outlook Express**. Simple as that.

Other mail programs

Microsoft has put out some real email stinkers over the years such as **Exchange** (built into Windows 95) and **Outlook 97** (part of Office 97). Exchange should be avoided at any cost, but Outlook 97 can be improved by installing the Office 97 upgrades at http://officeupdate.microsoft.com

Outlook 98 was touted as the next step up from Outlook Express. Although it adds contact, calendar, and task-management tools along with some neat features such as mapping and return receipt, you can safely get by without them. And unless you're using it for internal office mail, ensure you choose the **Internet mail only** installation – it loads faster. Its successor **Outlook 2000** adds more bulk that you can safely do without.

Internet Mail & News, which accompanies IE3, however, is simple, elegant, and ample for the task if you're strapped for disk space.

If you'd prefer a custom-built email program, Eudora (http://www.eudora.com) remains the choice option. You can have it free, but you'll have to view a few ads.

Where to get email programs and tools

If these options can't satisfy your email appetite, you'll find plenty of alternative mail programs and tools at:

DaveCentral http://www.davecentral.com

Download.com http://www.download.com (Mac and PC)

Hotfiles http://www.hotfiles.com (Mac and PC)

Winfiles http://www.winfiles.com

This includes utilities for polling your accounts and downloading just the headers, selectively deleting mail from your server, and attaching all sorts of multimedia such as video and voice. You're unlikely to need them though.

And for dozens of AppleScripts to enhance **Outlook Express** and **Entourage** on the Mac, see:

AppleScript Central http://www.applescriptcentral.com/paul/

Setting up

Before you can start sending and receiving email, you'll need to fill in a few **configuration details** for whoever supplied your email account (usually your ISP). Even if this process is automated by a wizard or your ISP's software, take some time to understand your email profile so you can enter it on other machines. For more on email addresses, see p.21.

You might also like to **change a few of the default settings**, as they're not always the best for everyone.

Starting a new account

You cannot even open Outlook Express 5+ without an account. It won't let you. So at some stage, either during the Internet Setup Wizard routine, or when you first try to open the mail program, you'll have to fill in the blanks. Of course, you'll need all the details first. To **start a new account in Outlook Express**, open **Accounts** under the Tools menu, choose "Add Mail" and follow the prompts. To change the settings select the account and choose Properties. Even if you set it up through a wizard, it wouldn't hurt to go in and check the details.

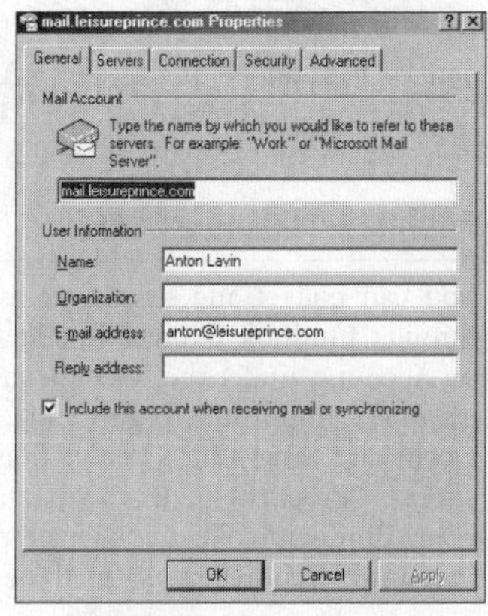

Let's say you're Anton Lavin and your email address is **anton@leisureprince.com**

Open your settings in any

mail program and here's what you'll strike: **Name**: Anton Lavin (Who or what will appear as the sender of your mail.) **Email Address**: anton@leisureprince.com (Where mail you send will appear to come from.) **Return Address**: anton@leisureprince.com (Where replies to your mail will go. Most users opt for their regular email address but you could divert it to a work account, for example.) **Outgoing Mail (SMTP)**: mail.leisureprince.com (The server to handle your outgoing mail – usually your own provider.) **Incoming Mail (POP3)**: mail.leisurepince.com (Where your mail is stored. This should be the same as the last part of your email address, though often with pop. or mail. added at the start.) **Account Name**: anton (The first part of your email address.) **Password**: ****** (Careful, don't let anyone see you enter this one.)

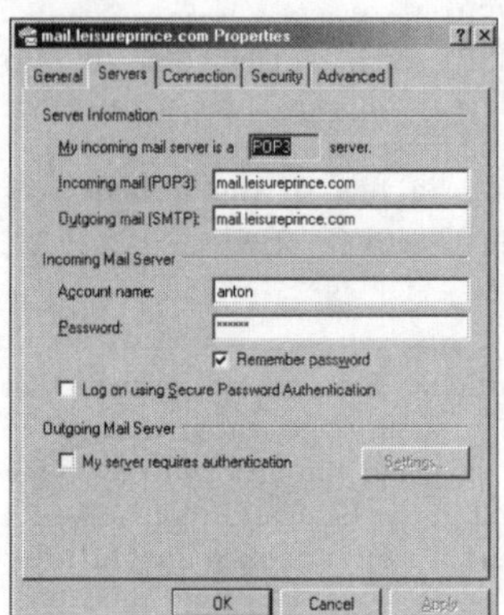

Adding a second account

You can collect and send from as many accounts as you like through Outlook Express. To add another account, simply click on Accounts under the Tools menu, and then "Add mail". While it's almost impossible to go wrong, there are a couple of options worth checking. Once you've finished, select the account, and choose "Properties". If you'd rather not check this account every time you collect your mail uncheck the box "include this account when receiving mail or synchronizing". Under the

Servers tab, make sure you have the right **outgoing mail server**. This should **match your ISP**, not the provider of the mail account. If you have **more than one ISP account**, under the Connection tab, uncheck the box "always connect to this account using". Otherwise it might drop your connection if you try to collect on the other account.

Options – change the default settings

If you leave Outlook Express in its default settings, a couple of features might annoy you. We won't go through all the settings here as the meanings should be obvious, once you see them. You should go through them, though, checking each option and deciding what you'd prefer.

Let's go through each tab in turn. Open Options from under the Tools menu and start at the **General tab**. For a brief explanation of each item, right-click on the text and click on "**What's This**?" Clear any boxes you accidentally check in the process. It's sure to happen. As ever, **the Mac versions are completely different**, and somewhat cut back on features. The settings are located under **Preferences in the Edit menu**.

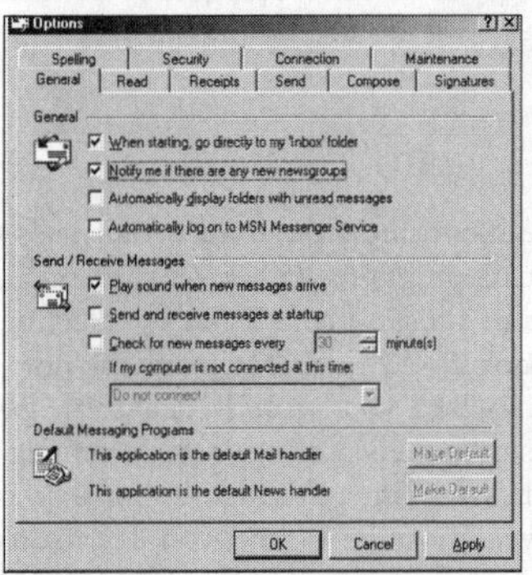

The options that cause the most problems are under the Send/Receive section. If you're dialing in, it's best to clear "**Send and Receive messages at Startup**" and "**Check for new messages every x minutes**". Otherwise it will try to go online whenever you have the program open. Instead, send and receive manually (p.114). It's not a big inconvience. And unless you use MSN instant messenger (p.239), clear the box "**Automatically log on to MSN**".

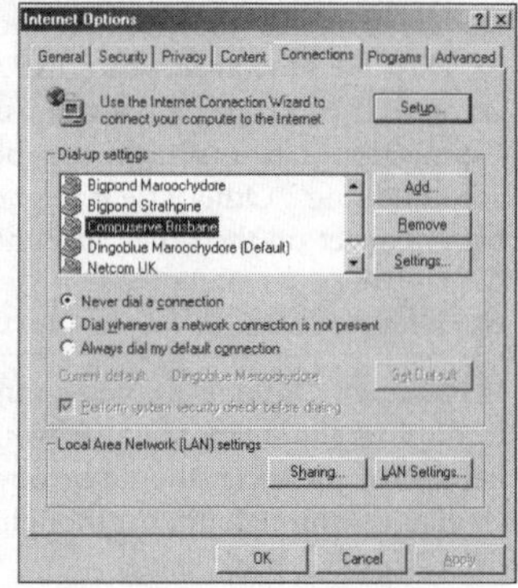

Next the **Send tab**. Clear the box "Automatically put people I reply to in my address book" unless you think it would suit you. It probably won't. Clear "**send messages immediately**" or it will try to connect when you compose offline.

Finally, under the **Connections tab**, check the box to "**ask before switching connections**" and uncheck the box "**hang up after sending and receiving**". Click on the Change button under the Internet Connection settings to reach Internet Explorer's connection options. "**Never dial a connection**" is preferable, as otherwise you'll find it trying to go online at inopportune moments such as when you're reading HTML mail (p.112) offline.

Email basics

You don't have to be on the Net to **compose an email message**. Simply open your mail program, start a new message, address it either by entering an address manually or by selecting a name from your **address book**, add a **subject**, write the note, and then click **Send**. Then when you want it delivered, **go online and send**. Sending is usually tied in with receiving. Normally you do both at the same time, although it's possible if necessary to separate the two. If you're offline, you'll want to

Send Later. This is automatic in Outlook Express, but you'll have to choose it from the new message's File menu in Messenger. Then once you're online, you'd choose **Send Unsent Messages** from the File menu.

Outlook Express stores **unsent mail** in a folder called the **Outbox. In Netscape Messenger** it's called **Unsent Messages**. Once the message is dispatched, it moves into the **Sent** folder.

Incoming mail arrives in the **Inbox** or wherever your filters (Message Rules) dump it. When it arrives, you'll hear a sound, get a message and/or see a little envelope in your system tray. That depends on what you configure in your options (p.113). You can **change the new mail sound** in Windows under Sounds in the Control Panel.

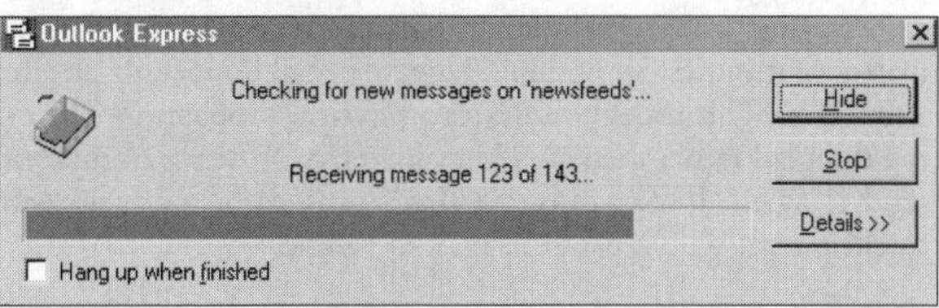

Outlook Express and Messenger both let you **read mail as it arrives**, as well as preview messages in a separate window. You can tell which **messages are new as they'll be bold** and the **little envelopes next to them will be closed**. Outlook Express displays a number beside each folder to tell you how many unread messages it contains.

Check your other accounts

If you've set up more than one account and opted not to check it every time, you'll need to collect it manually. Click on the account under Send and Receive in the Tools menu. This is also the way to **check for mail without sending** from your Outbox queue.

How to start a new email

Open your mail program. Click on the **New Message icon** on the taskbar, or choose New Mail Message under the File menu. You'll see a line starting with **To:** That's where you type in your **recipient's address**. Internet email addresses should be along the lines of someone@somewhere where someone is the recipient's account name and somewhere identifies the server where they collect their mail. It will end in .com, co.uk, .com.au, .net or another domain (p.22).

If you submit a wrongly constructed or a non-existent address, your message should bounce back to you with an **error message** saying what went wrong. This tends to happen within a matter of minutes. Sometimes, however, mail bounces back after a few days. This usually indicates a physical problem in delivering the mail rather than an addressing error. When it occurs, just send it again. If it's your end that's caused the problem, you might have a whole batch of mail to resend.

The address book

Despite first appearances, Internet email addresses aren't so hard to recall. Their name-based components are stacks easier to remember than telephone numbers and street addresses. However, there's no real need to memorize them, nor do you have to type in the whole address every time. Not when you have an **address book**.

Start your address book by putting yourself in. Open it in Outlook Express from under the Tools menu or by clicking on the book icon. In Messenger it's under the Communicator menu. Choose **New Card** or **New Contact** and fill in the blanks.

To **add an address from a message** simply right-click (or click in Macs) on the sender's name and choose **Add to Address Book** from your mouse menu. If the address is already there, it will tell you.

You can **send a message to someone in your address book** in several ways, from within the Address Book or the New Message window. Start off by adding every email address you know, and click on all the options until you know it inside out. With most email programs you can **click** or **double-click** on addresses in your address book to create new mail, or with Netscape **drag and drop addresses** into the **To**: or **CC** fields of a new message.

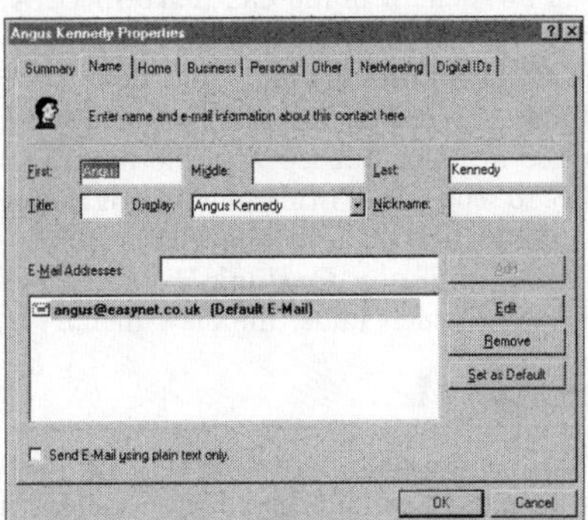

You can also **assign nicknames** to act as shortcuts – and even if you don't the programs are smart enough to help you out. For example, you might only have to enter a few letters of a name, an address or a nickname and it will search the address book for the closest matches. Just be careful it does enter the right address – otherwise it could prove embarrassing.

It's worthwhile experimenting to see which way you prefer. Understanding your address book's capabilities will save you time and tedium in the long run. But the simplest way to address a message is by replying to a previous one.

Sending to more than one

If you want to send two or more people the same message, you have two options.

When you don't mind if recipients know who else is receiving it, one address will have to go in the **To**: field, and the other addresses can also go in this field or in the **CC** (**carbon copy**) field.

Put recipients in the **BCC** (**blind carbon copy**) field if you want their names and addresses masked from all others. However, everyone, including those in BCC, can see who the message is addressed and copied to. To send a bulk mailer without disclosing the list, put yourself in the To: field and everyone else in BCC.

If you don't see a BCC option in Outlook Express, open a new message and tick All Headers under the View menu.

Send from another account

To send a message from an account other than your main (default) account, simply start a new message, click on the down arrow at the end of the **From:** bar, and select your other account.

The subject

Let your email recipients know what your message is about. Put something meaningful in the **Subject:** heading. It's not so important when they first receive it – they'll probably open it even if it's blank. However, if you send someone your résumé and you title it "Hi dude", two months down the track when they're looking for talent, they'll have a hard time weeding you out of the pile.

Filling in the subject is optional when replying. If you don't enter anything, it will retain the original subject and insert **Re:** before the original subject title to indicate it's a reply.

Replying

Yet another great thing about email is how you can quote received mail. To **reply to a message**, simply select it, and click on the **Reply** button or choose **Reply** from under the Message or mouse button menu. This will automatically copy the original message and address it back to the sender.

Depending on your settings (check your Help file or experiment), this new message will contain the original, with **quote tags** (>) prior to each line, or underneath a dotted line perhaps with a bar down the side. It will also contain the **header** of the original message detailing the sender, subject, and delivery date.

To change the **quote style** in **Outlook Express** go to the Send tab in Options, and play with the Mail Sending Formats. Start with the **Send format set to Text** as not all mail programs understand HTML. Then you can select to send HTML on a per message basis under the Format menu in the New Message window. Messenger gives a far greater depth of control over reply formatting. Its settings are within Preferences under the **Messages** and **Formatting** tabs in Mail & Newsgroups.

Unfortunately, formatting and wrapping replies is **Outlook Express' biggest shortcoming**. Six generations into the program and it still creates orphans (single word lines) throughout the message, making it look very messy indeed. It also has difficulty indenting some formats of replies with quote tags. It's not an issue with Netscape, nor any other mail program – except MS Outlook, of course.

You can **keep parts or the entire original message**, including the subject – or delete the lot. So when someone asks you a question or raises a point, you're able to include that section and answer it directly underneath or above. This saves them having to refer back and forth between their message and your answer. It also saves keying their address.

Don't fall into the habit of including the **entire contents of the original letter** in your reply. It wastes time for the receiver and its logical outcome (letters comprising the whole history of your correspondence) hardly bears thinking about.

Note also that the **Reply all** option addresses your message not only to the sender but also to all recipients of the original. That's not something you'll always want to do.

You can normally tell if a message is a reply because the **subject will start with Re:**

Forward a message

If you'd like to share an email with someone, just **forward it on**. Forwarded messages are like replies except they're not addressed to the original sender. You'll have to add the addresses manually. Unfortunately, Outlook Express treats forwarded messages under the same rules as replies. That means if your replies come with quote tags, your forwarded messages will follow suit. It's better to forward them **inline**, that is, **beneath a dotted line**. The only way to switch over in Outlook Express is to re-enter Options. That's quite a pain. Alternatively, you could **forward the message as an attachment**. This isn't a bad option.

To forward in Outlook Express, select the message and either select **Forward** or **Forward as an attachment** from the mouse menu, toolbar, or under the Message menu. The same for Messenger, except it differentiates between Forward Quoted and Forward Inline (three cheers!)

You can tell if a message has been forwarded to you because the subject line will start with **Fwd:** or **Fw:**

Resend a message

There isn't a menu option to resend a message in either Outlook Express or Messenger, so the easiest way is to right-click on the message, choose "select all", then copy and paste the text into a new message and reenter the subject and recipients.

Signatures and vCards

All mailers let you add your personal touch at the end of your composition in the form of a **signature file**. This appears automatically on the bottom of your email, like headed notepaper. It's common practice to put your address, phone number, title, and perhaps round off with a recycled witticism. There's nothing to stop you adding a monstrous picture, frame, or your initials in ASCII art. Except you have more taste than that.

To create and manage your signature(s) click on the "**Signatures**" tab in Outlook Express's Options, or under Identity in Messenger's Mail & Newsgroups' Preferences. In Messenger, you have to create the signature in a separate text file, say in Windows Notepad, and then locate it with the Choose button. You can do the same in Outlook Express, or simply create one in the box provided.

A **vCard** is an address book entry with as much contact details as you care to disclose. You might like to attach a copy to your mail so your recipients can add it to their address books. To set it up in Outlook Express, edit the Business card section under the Compose tab in Options. In Messenger, choose Edit Card under Mail & Newsgroups' Preferences.

```
 ////\\      //||\\      //\|\\      ///||\
/`O-O'      ` @ @\     //o o//       a a
   ]           >        ) | (         _)
   -           -          -            ~
 John        Paul      George       Ringo
```

Return receipts

If you'd like to know if your mail has been delivered and/or opened, you could try requesting a "**delivery receipt**" and/or "**read receipt**". Delivery receipts verify that your message has arrived safely on your recipient's mail server, but only if it supports the Delivery Service Notification (DSN) standard. If it doesn't support it, you'll get no reply. Read receipts notify your message has been opened. But again, the recipient must be using a mail program that supports the Message Disposition Notification (MDN) standard. Not only that, even if their mail program supports it, when they receive your message, a box will pop up asking whether they'd like to acknowledge receipt. If they say no, you'll get no receipt. In other words, it's not a reliable system and really **not worth the bother**.

Still, if you feel like experimenting with it, you can easily enable either or both types in Messenger, on a per message, or per recipient, basis. Outlook Express only supports read receipts. For instructions, search on the keyword "receipt" in your help file.

If you're serious about confirmation, you should ask them to reply, send a follow up, make a phone call, or use a third party confirmation service such as: http://www.itraceyou.com

Rich Text (HTML) and sending Web pages

Not long ago, email was a strictly plain text affair. Microsoft Exchange introduced formatting, but it didn't really make an impact until Netscape introduced **HTML mail** as a new standard. Today, if your mail program lacks HTML support you'll feel a bit backward. Surprisingly, some still do, so you might get the odd complaint if you habitually send in **Rich Text** (HTML).

HTML mail blurs the distinction between email and the World Wide Web, bringing Web pages right into your email.

This means Web publishers, particularly magazines and news broadcasters, can send you regular bulletins formatted as Web pages complete with links to further information. It also means you can send Web pages by email. Either drag and drop them into a message or choose Send Page from under the File menu. Just make sure your recipient also has an HTML compliant email program, otherwise they'll get all the formatting as a useless and time-wasting attachment.

To **change the font, size or color of your message** text or add a **background color, picture or sound**, choose Rich Text (HTML) under the format menu of a new message, and experiment with the various options along the toolbar and under the Format menu.

Although the concept of fancying up your email with **stationery** and a business logo might seem more professional, it's unnecessary, and perhaps even inappropriate. It actually detracts from one of email's strongest features – simplicity. So don't spend too much time worrying about the appearance of your email. Just get the words right.

For lessons on using Outlook Express HTML mail and stationery, see: http://lettermanstationery.tripod.com

Your first email

So, you're online and ready to send your first email? OK, let's go. The best way to start is to **send yourself some email**. That way you'll get to both send and receive something. If you're dialing in, start this exercise offline with your mail program in **offline mode**.

1. To set up **Outlook Express**, open Options, then General and choose not to send and receive messages at Startup, not to check mail regularly, and not to **Send mail immediately** under the Send tab.

In **Messenger**, open Preferences, then Offline, and choose **Ask me**. Restart the program, and choose **Offline**. Open the Mail Servers tab in the Mail & Newsgroup Preferences, click on the Incoming Mail server and choose Edit. Uncheck the box to check the mail every 10 (or so) minutes.

You can alter all these settings later when you know what you want.

2. Presuming you've completed your server details (p.111), the first step is to put yourself into the address book (p.116). Next, open up a new message, choose yourself from the address book, give the message a subject, enter something in the body and click **Send** in the **New Message** window. If you're **in offline mode**, that will place your message in a queue to be sent once you go online. Otherwise, it might try to send it immediately. That depends on your Connection tab settings (p.89).

3. Now click on your connection shortcut (p.60) and connect to the Net. Once you're online (and not before) click on the Send and Receive icon on the taskbar to first send your mail queue, and then check your server for mail. Outlook Express will pop up a progress window to tell you what's going on, except on the Mac where it reports the activity in the bottom right hand corner.

4. Once you've sent yourself the message keep checking every 30 seconds until you receive it. It shouldn't take more than a few minutes. Now repeat this exercise until you're confident to face the rest of the wired world.

Find an email address

By far the best way to find out someone's email address is to **ring up and ask.** Don't know their phone number? Then try one of the online phone directories (p.167). Alternatively, if you know where they work, look up their company's Web page. However, if they fall into the long-lost category, it might be possible to trace them though the Web. You could start by searching **Google** (p.155) for leads. It will help if their name is reasonably unique. You might find their name mentioned somewhere on the Web, and perhaps even their personal Web site. If not, you could try the people finding services.

People finders

Your email address should be private unless you instruct someone to list it in a directory or make it public in some other way. Unlike the telephone networks, there are no official public email registries. There are, however, a few independent **people search services** that boast huge email address databases – sometimes combined with street addresses and phone numbers. Unfortunately, you'll find most of the email addresses are out of date. Still, if you're trying every angle to locate a long-lost childhood sweetheart, they might be worth a look as a last resort. It mightn't hurt to list yourself either, that way they might find you!

Bigfoot **http://www.bigfoot.com**

Classmates **http://www.classmates.com**

ICQ Email directory **http://www.icq.com/search/email.html**

InfoSpace **http://www.infospace.com**

Internet Address Finder **http://www.iaf.net**

Switchboard **http://www.switchboard.com**

WhoWhere **http://www.whowhere.com**

Yahoo PeopleSearch **http://people.yahoo.com**

The people finding features built into Windows, the Mac OS, Outlook Express, and Netscape Messenger are supposed to tap into these databases, but rarely work well, if at all. Instead, to query several at once, try:

Copernic **http://www.copernic.com**

Help

Need to brush up your Net detective skills? See: **FAQ on finding email addresses**: http://www.qucis.queensu.ca/FAQs/email/finding.html **Yahoo's email search directory**: http://dir.yahoo.com/Reference/Phone_Numbers_and_Addresses/Email_Addresses/

Attachments

Suppose you want to email something other than just a text message – such as a **word processor document, spreadsheet, or an image**. It's a piece of cake. In **Outlook Express,** simply address a new message, click on the paperclip icon (or choose File attachment from the Insert menu), locate the file and click "attach". Or, even simpler, drag and drop the file (or files) from its location, into the New Message window. It will normally work without a second thought from you.

Well, it's almost that simple. Both parties' mail software needs to support a common encoding standard, otherwise it will appear in gibberish. The most used methods are **MIME** and **UUencode**. It doesn't really matter which you use as long as it works every time, so try a practice run first.

If you have problems getting a file to someone, refer to your Help file on how to specify an encoding method, as it varies between packages. MIME is gaining acceptance across all platforms (it's all that Netscape's older mailers recognize), so if you have the option, set it as the default. Eudora for Macs includes **Binhex**, Apple Single and Apple Double. Always choose Apple Double.

If your mail program doesn't automatically decode attachments, ditch it for one that does. It's not worth the bother. Old office systems like early Microsoft Mail, and AOL mail are notoriously fussy. If you're not allowed to use an email program that handles attachments with grace, consider a new job.

Opening attachments – beware viruses

Before you click on that attachment, consider that it might contain a virus. Ignore the advice on (p.142) at your own peril.

When it bounces

Servers at both ends can strip or bounce messages, if the size of the attachment exceeds the server's relay limit, or storing it would exceed the mailbox's size limit. If the mail server rejects the attachment, it will normally bounce an error message back to you. You can usually get around mail server restrictions by splitting your messages into smaller chunks. Open Accounts under the Tools menu in Outlook Express, and click on the Advanced tab. Check the box to "Break apart messages larger than", and specify an arbitrary size, say 1000 KB.

To compress or not compress?

If you're sending something large, you can reduce the byte size by **compressing it first**. Smaller files take less time to download, so the other end might be thankful. Or, if you're sending a lot of small files, you could bundle them all into one, using an archive program. How you'd go about it depends on the type of file and where it's going. The most commonly used archive format on the PC is ZIP, and on the Mac, Stuffit (.SIT). As a rule, **don't send Stuffit files to PC users** as they won't be able to

* Don't ever send an attachment of more than a few hundred kilobytes without prior warning or agreement. Large attachments can take ages to download and even crash meager machines. It's no way to make friends.

open them without downloading Stuffit Expander, a program they wouldn't otherwise need. Stuffit for the Mac, however, can unzip ZIP files. For more on archiving, see p.256.

There's nothing to be gained, however, by archiving JPG images, MP3 audio files, or any movie formats. They're already compressed. If you're sending an image over about 500KBs, you might consider reducing it by either converting it to a JPG, resizing it, or reducing the quality. It depends whether quality is more important than speed. See p.293 for more on **compressing images for the Web**.

Funny programs that end in .EXE

Before you send that "funny" program or circulated greeting card to a friend, are you sure it's not a virus? Don't forward it on unless you're certain, and don't open one sent to you. Checking it with a virus scanner isn't enough. See p.142.

How to send a CD track

If you'd like to share a tune from your new CD, try encoding it as an MP3 or Windows Media Format file and attaching it to a message. All your friend will need is an MP3, or Windows Media, player. For instructions, see p.270.

Faxes and Voicemail

Although, thanks to email, the fax's days are clearly numbered, not everyone is quite up to speed. So what do you do if your fax is in Houston, and you're in Hochow? **Efax** (http://www.efax.com) and **J2** (http://www.j2.com) have the answer. They can allocate you a free phone number in the US or UK, or an inexpensive number in about a hundred cities worldwide. Faxes sent to these numbers are converted to email attachments, redirected to your email address or online mailbox, and can be converted to text by OCR. Callers can also leave voice messages, which are forwarded as compressed audio files. Sending faxes from your desktop is also a breeze, and the whole thing can even integrate with your mobile Internet toyphone. **So forget fooling around with faxmodem software, this is the way to go.**

Managing your mail

If your provider or phone company charges by the minute to stay connected, it's best to **compose and read your mail offline** (ie, when you are not connected by phone). That way, while connected you're actually busy transferring data, and getting your money's worth. All email programs allow you to send your messages immediately or place them in a queue, as well as to collect mail at regular intervals or on request.

Unless you're always online, you should choose: **not to send mail immediately; to check manually (not every x minutes)**; and **to not check for messages at startup**. Otherwise your software will try to send and collect when you're offline. It's best to go online, collect your mail, upload your unsent mail, reply to anything urgent, log off, deal with the rest, and send your new bag of letters next time you go online.

If you have **unsent messages** it will ask you if you wish to send them whenever you open or close the program. Choose **No** if you're offline.

Filing

Just as you keep your work desk tidy, and deal with paper as it arrives, try to keep your email neat. Most programs can organize your correspondence into **mailboxes** or **folders** of some sort and offer you the option of automatically filing sent mail into a **Sent Mail** folder.

It's good discipline to use several folders for filing and to transfer your sent mail into periodic archives. Otherwise you'll create unwieldy folders containing thousands of messages that are possibly hard to open. Similarly, when you have dealt with mail, either delete it (and empty this folder regularly) or put it into a topic folder.

Sorting

To **sort your messages** by date, sender, size or subject, click on the bar at the top of each column. Click again to sort in a different way. Sorting by date makes the most sense so you can instantly see what's most recent.

Filtering – message rules

Your mail program can **filter** incoming mail into designated mailboxes, either as it arrives or afterwards. It looks for a common phrase in the incoming message, such as the address or subject, and transfers it to somewhere other than the default inbox. This is indispensable if you subscribe to a lot of mailing lists (see p.209) or get a ton of junk office email.

To set up your filters in Outlook Express, open **Message Rules** under the Tools menu. In Messenger, the **Message Filters** are located under the Edit menu.

Tracking replies

Transfer email that needs attention into a special folder until it's dealt with so you can instantly see what's urgent. Do the same with your Sent box. Transfer the mail that's awaiting replies.

Alternatively, "**flag**" it for attention. Clicking in the flag column to the left of the sender in the mail folder, will toggle a red flag on and off. Click on the top of the flag column to sort the folder, and instantly see what's outstanding.

As email is quick, and people tend to deal with it immediately, if you don't get a reply within a few days you'll know what to follow up. Once you've received your reply, you can either archive or delete your original outgoing message.

Stop the junk!

If you start receiving piles of unsolicited mail (commonly called **spam**), contrary to popular advice, **there's not a lot you can do about it**. You can set up Message Rules (filters) to shuffle them into folders, but it won't save you any time. It's just as quick to delete them directly from your inbox.

What's spam?

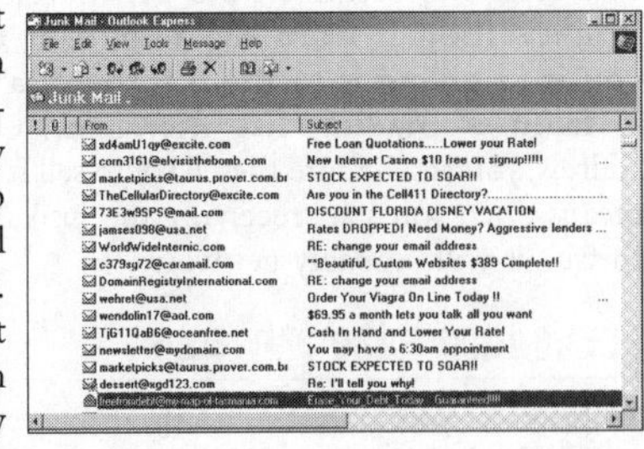

Unlike most Internet slang, "**spam**" isn't an acronym or abbreviation, nor is there any logical relationship between junk email and spiced meat. According to Net folklore, the non sequitur probably came from a Monty Python sketch. On the Internet, "to spam" means to send bulk email to a list gathered by unscrupulous means, or post (usually commercial) messages across multiple inappropriate newsgroups (p.212). The messages themselves are also called "spam".

What's not spam?

Although some of the mail you receive might be delivered in

bulk or seem irrelevant to you, it's not spam if you've granted permission for someone to mail you. For example, you might've given your email address when you registered with a Web site and checked a box to keep you informed of special deals, or given the OK for them to pass your details onto their partners. This is known as **opt-in** or **permission-based** email. The difference between this and spam is you should be able to get off the list by "**unsubscribing**". If there isn't an unsubscribe instruction within the email, contact the site's support address and demand to get off the list. With genuine spam, however, you can't get off the list, even if you try to unsubscribe as the return addresses are almost always bogus.

How spammers get your address

The main way spammers can get your address is by: **guessing it; harvesting it from the Web, chat or Usenet; tricking you into giving it to them through a Web site**; or **buying it from a mailing list merchant**. Once they have your address, you can be sure they'll try to sell it to someone else. That means once you start receiving the junk, it's not likely to stop. In fact, it will probably get worse.

Prevention – the only cure

So how do you stop it? The short answer is you can't once it starts. The best you can do is prevent them from getting your address in the first place.

Guessing is surprisingly common. They simply take a dictionary of given names, append it to a list of domains, run a test mailing, and, perhaps cull any that bounce. So if your address is john@ a major ISP, there's not much you can do to stop them. You can, however, prevent them from getting your address through **Usenet, chat** and on the **Web**. Here's how:

1. **Set up a secondary email address** for registering with Web sites. Never give your main address to any Web site, unless you're making a credit card purchase, or you're sure they're reputable. If you do give your main address, ask **not** to be sent any occasional offers from their "associates".
2. **Never post** messages to Usenet, or in a chat forum **under your main address**. Either use a fictitious alias, your secondary account, or mask your real address (see p.215).
3. Don't enter your main email address in **competitions** or hand it out at **trade shows**. Use your secondary account.
4. Don't use your main email address when logging into **FTP sites**.
5. Don't **register software** under your main address. Use your secondary account.

Setting filters

If you feel like trying to beat them at their game, make a new mail folder called Junk Mail, and experiment with filters (Message Rules under the Tools menu) to redirect emails containing typical spam words within the message or address. It won't take you long to spot them but you'll find it impossible to catch them all.

Complaining

Spammers know they're **detested**, but that doesn't bother them. It's a numbers game. They know there'll always be **someone stupid enough to send them money**. There's no point

replying or asking to be taken off their list. They rarely use a valid email address, and if they do, it's normally shut down almost instantly. Few ISPs will tolerate people spamming from their services. For that reason, the normal course of recall is to complain to their ISP, and the owners of any of the open mail relays involved. Don't expect them to thank you, though. You won't be alone in complaining. The easiest way is through **SpamCop** (http://www.spamcop.net) which can automatically pick through the fake headers and send off the complaint on your behalf. For more on the war against spam, see:

Cauce **http://www.cauce.org**

Spamfree **http://www.spamfree.org**

Whew **http://www.whew.com**

Email on the run

Once you have an **email address**, no matter where you roam, people can reach you. You might shift house, business, city, or country, but your email address need never change. Whether you're **at home, at work, out shopping**, or **on vacation**, if you can get online, you can get your mail. So, take care when choosing your address, as it might become your virtual home for years to come. Here's how to collect your mail, wherever you are today:

Get online – any way you can

The first thing you should know is **your email address does not tie you to your ISP**. While your mail may be stored on your ISP's server, you needn't dial into your ISP to access it. All you need to do is get online through any means, and access the server through the Net. So, get yourself in front of a public access terminal (p.27) such as a **cybercafé, friend's comput-**

er, Wap phone or anything with a screen that's connected to the Net.

Through the Web

The simplest way to collect and receive your mail on someone else's machine, is to use a Web interface. That means you won't have to go near their email program or configure anything. Of course, this is how you always use Webmail accounts such as Hotmail, so nothing changes there.

The quickest way to your POP3 or IMAP mail is through **Mail2Web:** Mail2Web http://www.mail2web.com

Just enter your ***long email address** and password to **collect** and **send** your mail on the fly. No need to set up an account.

Unless you choose to delete messages, they'll still be there next time you collect. That means you'll have to download your entire mailbox (headers only) afresh whenever you collect. If you like to keep a record of your outgoing mail, don't forget to CC (p.118) yourself, so you can file it later when you get back to your own machine. Just move the message from your Inbox to your Sent folder.

---

* Your long email address is your mail account name @ your incoming mail server name. For example, the long email email address of angus@easynet.co.uk is angus@mail.easynet.co.uk (mail.easynet.co.uk is the incoming mail server address).

You can also configure Hotmail to collect your POP3 mail and retain the headers in your mailbox. You can choose, when setting up, whether to delete the messages from the server at the point of collection. It will also store your outgoing mail in the Sent folder. When you return to your machine, you can synchronize the Hotmail account with Outlook Express and file the messages into your usual archives. If you like the sound of that, you could set up a dummy account just for this purpose, and forget about it until you need it. Keep in mind that Hotmail is a much slower interface than Mail2Web. Of course, if you have temporary problems with HotMail, you can always switch to Mail2Web. The messages will still be there next time you check in with Hotmail.

Through a Wap phone

Your phone dealer should be able to show you how to send and receive email through your Wap phone. For example, you can read and reply to your POP3 mail though Mail2Wap:

Mail2Wap **http://www.mail2wap.com**

Use someone else's mail program

To collect mail using an email program on **another computer**, you need to set up a new account with your details (p.111). Enter your **user name**, your **incoming mail server** address, and your **password**, when prompted. To send email you also need to enter your **identity** (who you want your mail to appear it's come from) and your **return address** (your email address). Although you can sometimes use your regular **outgoing mail server** address **if you collect your mail first**, you'll get a faster response if you use the one maintained by the ISP through whom you're dialing. So if the machine you're using has one set, leave it be. Don't forget to delete your mail from both the Inbox and Sent items folder when you're finished, otherwise someone else might read it.

Through a portable

If you're taking **your computer** with you, it's doubly easy to collect your POP3 mail.You mightn't even have to change your mail settings – only your dial-up configuration and perhaps your outgoing mail server. If your connection's slow or difficult, you can **configure your mail program** to download the first 1 KB or so of each message and then select which you want to read. Alternatively, if your mail server supports **IMAP4** (a superior form of POP mail which allows you to manage mail on the server – ask your provider), you can download just the headers. So, when you're up in a plane paying 14¢ per second to download at 2400 bps, you can leave all those massive mail list digests for later. One day, you'll also be thankful that you **maintain an alternative address for priority mail**. For tips on **connecting your computer away from home**, see p.476.

Through Telnet

Some universities and workplaces don't maintain POP3 mail accounts. If that applies to you, you might have to use **Telnet** to log in. Once you get over the indignity of not being able to point and click, it's not so bad.You can access Telnet in Windows by opening **Run** on the **Start** menu and typing telnet. Collecting this way will involve logging into your mail server over the Net, supplying identification, then typing commands into a UNIX mail program. **You can also read your POP3 email by Telnetting to your mail server** on port 110 (you'll have to add this in manually in Windows), entering user then your user name, pass then your password, and list to list your messages. To read messages selectively, type retr followed by the message's number. This is also the best way to collect mail when you're operating over a **very low bandwidth**, under poor conditions, or limited by software, for example with a palmtop. Ask your ISP or systems manager for further instructions.

AOL Netmail

You can collect your AOL mail from any computer by firing up your Web browser and pointing it at: http://www.aol.com/netmail/

Privacy

Occasionally, when sending mail or joining a discussion (p.197), you might prefer to **conceal your identity** – for example, to avoid embarrassment in health issues. There are three main ways to send mail anonymously. As mentioned earlier (p.105), **Webmail** is one.

The second might seem less ethical. You can **change your configuration** so that it looks like it's coming from somebody else, either real or fictitious. However, if anyone tries to reply, their mail will attempt to go to that alias, not you. But, be warned, it's possible to trace the header details back to your server, if someone's eager – and your national law enforcement agency might be if you're up to no good.

The third way is to have your IP address masked by a third party, such as an anonymous remailer. This can be almost impossible to trace. See:

http://www.anonymizer.com
http://anon.xg.nu
http://www.andrebacard.com/remail.html

Snoopers – your boss could be one

Although there's been a lot of fuss about hacking and Net security, in practice email is potentially more secure than your phone or post. In fact, most new-generation email programs (including Messenger and Outlook Express) have some kind of **encryption** built in. But it's not hackers who are most likely to read your mail – it's whoever has access to your incoming mail server and, of course, anyone with access to your computer. If it happens to be at work, then you can **assume your boss can read your mail**. In some companies it's standard practice, so don't use your work mail for correspondence that could land you in hot water. Instead, set up a private account and don't store your messages on your work machine. You can collect and send your POP3 mail from a Web interface such as Mail2Web (**http://www.mail2web.com**), or from within HotMail. Alternatively, set up a free Webmail account, the most private being **HushMail** (**http://www.hushmail.com**), which offers secure storage and encrypted messaging between users.

If you're serious about privacy, you may want to investigate **PGP (Pretty Good Privacy)**, a powerful method of encryption, which generates a set of public and private "keys" from a passphrase. You distribute the public key and keep the private key secure. When someone wants to send you a private message, they scramble it using your public key. You then use the private key, or your secret passphrase, to decode it. For more about PGP and other security add-ons, see: **http://www.pgpi.org** and **http://www.slipstick.com/addins/security.htm**

Find out who's having an affair in your office

Want the hot gossip on who's seeing who in your workplace; who's looking for a new job; or who's talking about you behind your back? Get drunk with your office's mail server administrator. It'll make you think twice about what you send in future.

Digital signing and encryption

Internet Explorer, Netscape Communicator, and their associated mailers already support emerging encryption and digital signing standards but few use them.

Digital signing proves your identity via a third party certificate. Here's how to get yours. First up, fetch a personal certificate from Verisign (http://www.verisign.com). You can't go wrong if you follow the instructions. Once it's installed, open your mail security settings and see that the certificate is activated. You may choose to sign all your messages digitally by default, or individually. Then send a secure message to all your regular email partners, telling them to install your certificate. Those with secure mailers can add your certificate against your entry in their address books. From then on, they'll be able to verify that mail that says it's from you is indeed from you. Don't use it flippantly, though, because **it's a pain for your recipients**.

Encryption works similarly, though you'll also need your email partners' certificates to encrypt messages to them. Also, as each certificate only works on one installation, you'll need a different one for work and home. This makes it a bit cumbersome if you're collecting mail on the road. It also means anyone with access to your machine could pretend they're you.

Yes, it's all a bit flaky at this stage. So spend a few minutes in your Help file figuring out the finer details, try it with your friends, and decide amongst yourselves whether it's worth the bother.

If you're frustrated with Outlook Express, or Netscape Messenger, you'll find help on the same Web and Newsgroup circuits as their respective browsers (see p.96). Just follow the links. Again, the best place to find help with Outlook Express and Outlook is on the Microsoft support groups. For tutorials, bug fixes, and FAQs, on Outlook Express and Outlook, try the:

Outlook FAQ http://www.slipstick.com/outlook/faq.htm

Outlook Express FAQ http://www.tomsterdam.com/insideoe5/faqs/

Outlook Express Knowledgebase http://members.home.net/jlpick99/oe.htm

For instructions on how to **backup and restore your email**, address book and mail rules, see p.100.

6

Play it safe

Now not later

Picture this: you receive an email from your best friend, with an attachment demanding "You have to see this!" Because you trust them, you open it without a second thought. Nothing unusual happens. A few days later you notice that all is not well, and some of your documents won't open. Your friend says they had the same problem, which turned out to be caused by a virus – a new strain that your virus software didn't detect. After many frustrating hours, you manage to update your virus software, and remove the infection. The damage, however, has already been done, and your computer can't be restored without technical knowledge. The easiest solution is to wipe your hard drive and reinstall everything from scratch.

Sounds extreme doesn't it? Regrettably, it's not, and if you don't understand how viruses spread **you stand a very high**

chance of being infected. The first thing to know is that anti-virus programs might not protect you. In fact, they often cause more problems than they solve. However, as long as you adhere to the few simple rules laid out in this following section, it shouldn't be an issue.

The bad guys

Let's start by examining the various threats lurking beyond your network connection, and then set out a strategy to protect yourself.

Viruses

A **virus** is a program that infects other program files, or floppy disk boot sectors, so that it can spread from machine to machine. In order to catch a virus you must either run an infected program (possibly without your knowledge), or boot your machine with an infected floppy disk inserted fully into the drive. There are thousands of strains, most of which are no more than a nuisance, but potentially capable of setting off a time bomb that could destroy the contents of your hard drive. A **macro virus** spreads by infecting Microsoft Word or Excel documents.

Worms

Worms, like viruses, are designed to spread. But rather than wait for an earthling to transfer the infected file or disk, they actively replicate themselves over a network such as the Internet. For example, they might send themselves to all the contacts in your email address book. That means worms can spread much faster than viruses. The "**email viruses**" that made world news recently were strictly speaking, worms, not viruses.

Trojans

A Trojan (horse) is a program with a hidden agenda. When you run the program it will do something unexpected, usually without your knowledge. While viruses are designed to spread, Trojans are usually (though not always) designed to deliver a once-off pay packet. There are dozens of known Trojans circulating the Net, most with the express purpose of opening a back door to your computer to allow hackers into your system while you're online. A custom-built Trojan can be bound to any program, so that when you install it, the Trojan will also install in the background. For a sobering insight into the power they can hand over to even the most inexperienced hackers, see: **http://www.sub7files.com**

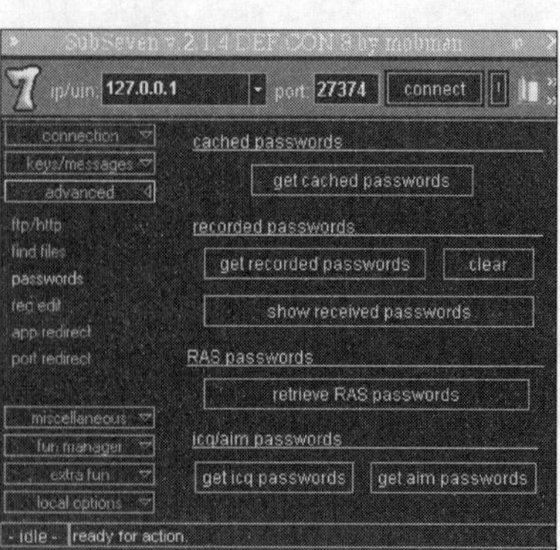

Hackers

While the term **hacker** is something of a fuzzy expression amongst the computerati (**http://www.happyhacker.org/define.shtml**), the popular definition is the one that concerns us here. That is, someone who wants to break into, or meddle with, your computer. They might be a professional out to steal your secrets or a "script kiddy" playing with a prefab Trojan. They might be a vandal, a spy, a thief, or simply just exploring. As far as you're concerned it doesn't matter, you don't want them, or their handiwork inside your computer.

Marketeers

People who want to sell you something – or sell information about you – might be more annoying than threatening, but it won't take long before they get on your goat. Unless you keep your contact details to yourself, your inbox will receive an unstoppable flood of junk mail, and you can never be sure what information is being gathered about you by programs that "**phone home**" (see spyware p.261).

Get protected

Contrary to popular belief, antivirus software isn't the answer. While you should still install a virus scanner, it's more important to understand how viruses work, and use caution (and an up to date system) as your first line of defense. Here's how:

Rule one – think before opening attachments

Assuming your system is presently clean and up to date, the only way you can be attacked by a virus or hacker, is to introduce a program onto your computer. The obvious points of entry are floppy disks and installation CDs, but these are far less of a risk than in previous times.

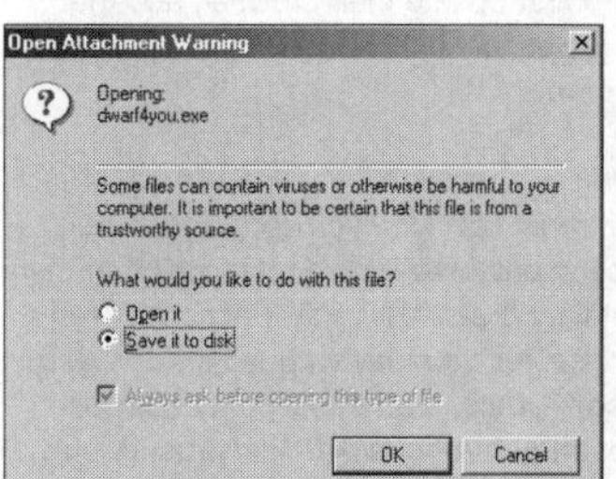

The single most risky thing you can do is to open files attached to emails (p.126). The same, of course, applies to files attached to other forms of communication such as Instant Messaging, Chat and Usenet. **Unless you're 100 percent certain that an attachment is safe, even if it's from your best friend: DON'T OPEN IT!** Instead, save it to your Desktop or a quarantine folder, and examine it carefully before proceeding. (See p.149).

Treat the **gag programs** and **animated cards** that tend to circulate around the festive season with utmost caution. These are some of the favorite vehicles of Trojan distributors.

If everyone followed this basic rule, it would stop almost all viruses, worms, and Trojans in their tracks.

Rule two – stay up to date

Rather than perfect their products before release, Microsoft and other software publishers prefer to rush out their programs and fight the ensuing security fires in the form of "patches" and "service releases". If you don't apply these minor software upgrades, you're prone to whatever blunder they've puttied over. For example, the version of Outlook Express (5.0) that shipped with Windows 98 Second Edition can be infected by the KAK worm, an email borne virus that spreads simply by highlighting the message. But if you upgrade Outlook Express, or apply the appropriate security release from Windows Update, you'll be safe. For instructions on how to stay up to date, see p.58.

Incidentally, if you receive a message that **contains an Active X control**, tell the sender they probably have the **KAK worm**. Scanning and cleaning isn't enough, as they could easily reinfect themselves. They'll need to first update their browser, and then run a virus scanner or KAK cleaner such as:
http://www.getvirushelp.com

Rule three – don't run Office macros

The "macros" used to automate tasks in Microsoft Word and Excel are programs that can contain viruses. And more often than not, that's all they do contain. So as a rule, never accept to run a **macro** unless the creator assures you they've put it in for a good reason. If you use **Microsoft Office**, read the security advice at:
http://officeupdate.microsoft.com/Focus/Articles/virusres.htm

Rule four – go to the source

If someone sends you a program, script or registry patch (.REG or .INF) by email, ditch it, and ask them to send you a link to the source instead. Only download directly from the software publisher or through a reputable file repository, such as those listed on (p.265). If the source looks unprofessional, tread carefully.

Rule five – scan, as a last resort

Before you open any incoming file, whether or not it looks safe, scan it with a virus checker (look under the right-click menu). It will only take a few seconds. However, don't put too much faith in the results, especially if it's out of date. Most scanners will pick up viruses but their record with Trojan horses isn't so hot. Naturally, you'll need to install a virus scanner first. Try **AVG** (http://www.grisoft.com). It's as good as any, and free. New PCs typically come with McAfee's VirusScan or Norton AntiVirus. They're supposedly the best in the field, but often cause more problems than they solve, especially when left to run in the background (real-time protection). Instead, switch them off and simply scan all new arrivals. Most importantly, though, **don't forget to keep the signature file up to date**. Check in every week or two. Refer to the help file for instructions.

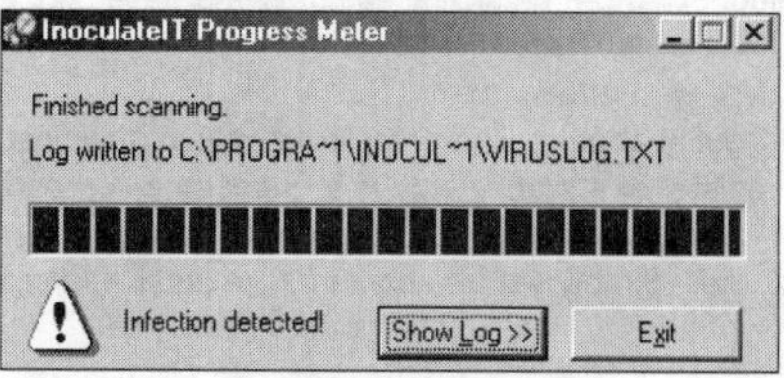

If you suspect a program might contain a Trojan, try scanning it with **The Cleaner**: (http://www.moosoft.com)

Rule six – become invisible with a firewall

As a line of defense against hackers, install a security firewall. For PCs you need look no further than the excellent, and free,

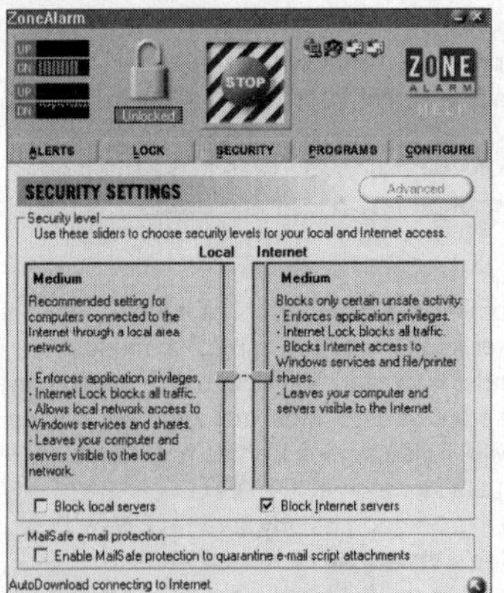

ZoneAlarm (**http://www.zonelabs.com**). It will let you choose which programs can access the Net, and effectively make your PC invisible to outsiders, thus protecting you against inquisitive hackers, and Trojans that open remote control backdoors into your computer. Don't stop to think about it. Just do it.

Rule seven – beware "spyware"

Protect your privacy and prevent crashes, by avoiding software that is supported by advertisements or tracks your movements. ZoneAlarm (above) can help by telling you if a program is trying to "phone home". **Ad-aware** (**http://www.lavasoft.de**) can remove the bugs left behind after uninstalling. For more on so-called "Spyware", see p.261.

Rule eight – go undercover

Don't feel guilty about giving an alias when you download software or register at a Web site. It won't upset the company's statistical records, but it will offer you a buffer of privacy and reduce your junk mail. Simply set up an alternative email address. (See p.105).

Rule nine – don't forward virus warnings

Although there are plenty of real concerns out there, any email that insists you forward it on to "everyone you know" is almost certainly a hoax. Do us all a favor and break the chain. See: **http://www.vmyths.com** & **http://www.urbanlegends.com**

How to examine an attachment

Any program entering your computer is a risk until proven otherwise. So to protect yourself, you'll need to learn how to recognize danger.

Windows uses "**file extensions**" to distinguish between various types of files. These come at the end of the file name. For example, Microsoft Word creates documents that end in .DOC A file ending in .JPG is a JPEG image, while one ending in .EXE is an executable, the most common type of program file. You should be able to tell whether a file is a program simply by looking at its file extension.

To make computing seem simpler for newbies, Windows hides file extensions by default. It would be wise to change this, however. Set all your folders to "Details view" and unhide all the hidden files and extensions as follows:

Double-click on My Computer. Choose "Details" under the View menu. Go to the View tab under Folder Options in the Tools menu. Tick "Show hidden files and folders" and clear the tick from "Hide file extensions for known file types". Then click on button to set all folders: "Like Current Folder".

Alternatively, if you'd like to hide the extensions, create a new folder on the Desktop to quarantine incoming files, and apply these changes to it alone.

Good attachments, bad attachments

Most attachments aren't capable of carrying viruses. The trouble is you have to be able to pick the odd one that can. The following, most commonly attached, file types are always safe:
Plain text (.TXT)
Images (.JPG, .GIF, BMP, .TIF, .WMF)
Movies (.AVI, .MPG, .MOV, .WMV)
Portable Documents (.PDF)

Audio (.MP3, .WAV, .WMF)
Internet Shortcuts (.URL)
Email and Web pages (.EML, .HTM, .HTML) are normally safe. Though it's possible to wreak havoc with scripts, it's not something to worry about.

The following file types are **highly suspect and should never be opened** unless you're certain they're safe: .BAT, .COM, .EXE, .INF, .JS, .JSE, .PIF, .REG, .SCR, SHS, .VBE, .VBS, .WSF, and WSH.

Warning – don't be fooled by fake extensions
Before you click on that attachment that appears to be a safe music, movie, image, or document file, **check the icon** that comes with it. Is it the right one for that type of file? If not, you might find a long series of spaces inserted between the fake extension and the real one, for example:
Read this message.TXT .PIF (The real extension is PIF).

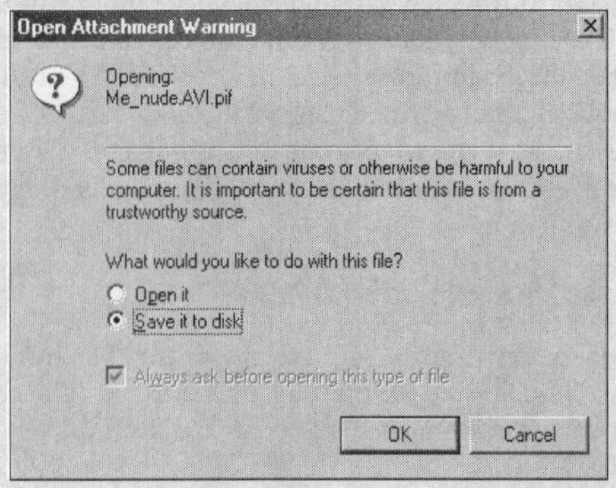

Always double check: it's the way most viruses spread.

More on viruses:

Some ISPs automatically scan your mail attachments for viruses. It's another factor to consider when shopping around for a provider. To see what's presently top of the virus pops, check the scanning stats at: http://www.star.net.uk

You'll find everything you need to know about viruses at:

About.com http://antivirus.about.com

Alt.comp.virus FAQs http://www.faqs.org/faqs/computer-virus/

Symantec http://www.symantec.com/avcenter/

Computer Associates http://www.cai.com/virusinfo/

7

Find it

Without losing your mind

The art of **finding something** pinned up on the world's biggest scrapboard is, without doubt, **the most valuable skill** you can glean from your time online. If you know how to use the Net to find an answer to almost anything quickly and comprehensively, you'd have to consider yourself not only useful, but pretty saleable too. Most people, including many Net veterans, simply **bumble their way around**. Yet, it's a remarkably basic skill to master. So read this section, then get online and start investigating. Within an hour or two you'll be milking the Net for what it's worth. It might turn out to be the best investment you'll ever make!

How it works

The Net is massive. Just the Web alone houses well over two billion pages of text, and many millions more are added daily. So you'll need some serious help if you want to find something. Thankfully, there's a wide selection of search tools to make the task relatively painless. The job usually entails keying your **search terms** into a form on a Web page and waiting a few seconds for the results.

Over the next few pages, we'll introduce you to **search tools** that can locate almost anything: on the Web; linked to from the Web; or archived into an online Web database, such as email addresses, phone numbers, program locations, newsgroup articles, and news clippings. Of course, first it has to be put online, and granted public access. So just because you can access US government servers doesn't mean you'll find a file on DEA Operative Presley's whereabouts.

Your weapons

There are three main types of Web search tools: **search engines, hand-built subject directories** and **search agents**. Apart from the odd newspaper archive, they're usually free. Because they're so useful and popular, there was a trend towards tacking other services onto the side and building themselves into so-called **portals, communities**, and **hubs**. More recently, that trend has begun to reverse with the launch of several skeletal search tools free of fancy overheads. Irrespective of which you use, ignore the quantity of froufrou and concentrate on the quality of the results. The next few pages discuss each category in detail, and show you how to torture them for answers.

Search engines

The best way to find just about anything online is to start with a **search engine**. The good thing about search engines is they can search through the **actual contents** of Web pages (and file servers), and not just descriptions. The better search engines can rifle through **billions of Web pages** in a fraction of a second. You simply go to the search engine's Web site and submit **keywords**, or search terms, into a simple form. It will query its database and, almost instantly, return a list of results or "**hits**". For example, if you were to search on the expression "Rough Guide to the Internet", here's what might come up on top:

1. Welcome to the Rough Guide to the Internet
The Rough Guide to the Internet is the ultimate guide to the Web, complete with a 2500+ site directory.
www.roughguides.com/internet/index.html

In this case the top line tells us the name of the page or site. Followed by a description excerpted from the page, and then the page's address. If it suits, click on the link to visit the site.

Tip: Don't just click on a result, and then hit the Back button if it's no good. Instead, run down the list and open the most promising candidates in new browser windows. It will save you tons of time. Do this by holding down the **Shift key** as you click.

The reason it's so quick is **you're not searching the Web live**. **You're merely searching a database** of Web page extracts stored on the search engine's server. This database is compiled by a program that periodically "crawls" around the Web looking for new or changed pages. Because of the sheer size of the Net, and a few factors relating to site design, it's not possible for the crawlers to find every site, let alone every word on every page. Nor is it possible to keep the database completely up to date. That means you can't literally "search the Web", you can only search a snapshot taken by a search engine. So naturally, different search engines will give you different results depending on how much of the Web they've found, how often they update, how much text they extract from each page and how well they actually work.

So, which search engine?

There are dozens of search engines, but only a few worth trying. In fact, you'll rarely need more than one. But since you'll be using it often, make sure it's up to speed. You'll want the **biggest, freshest, database**. You'll want to **fine-tune your search** with extra commands. And you'll want the most hits you can get on one page with the most **relevant results on top**. Right now, that's **Google:**

Google **http://www.google.com**

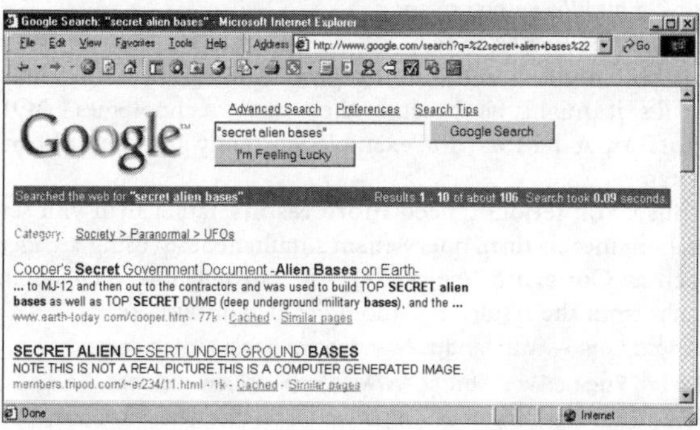

This completely free service has an uncanny knack of getting it right in the first few hits, both from within its search engine database and its association with the **Open Directory** (see p.162). It also provides local cache access to pages that have disappeared since its crawl, or are otherwise unavailable. Click on "cached" to see how this works. Use it when you can't get a link to load.

If Google falls short, try **All the Web** and **AltaVista**. They're also big, fast, clutter free, and can deliver a long page of relevant hits. Next up, **Northern Light** is worth a shot. It's also big, but not so fast or user-friendly despite its curious system of organizing hits into folders.

All the Web **http://www.alltheweb.com**

AltaVista **http://www.av.com**

Northern Light **http://www.nlsearch.com**

As for the rest? Just because an engine isn't the biggest or best, doesn't mean it's worthless. Even the smallest engines can find unique hits. Still, unless you're after extra hits, you're unlikely to need them. Of course, they might improve:

Excite **http://www.excite.com**

HotBot **http://www.hotbot.com**

Lycos **http://www.lycos.com**

If you notice some engines give identical, or very similar, results it might be because they share technologies. **AOL, HotBot**, and **MSN**, for example, currently use the **Inktomi** system.

But if you seriously need **more results**, rather than visit several engines in turn, query them simultaneously using an agent such as **Copernic** (see p.164). You can tell how each engine ranks from the results. For more detailed analysis, see:

Search Engine Watch **http://www.searchenginewatch.com**

Search Engine World **http://www.searchengineworld.com**

Search Engine Showdown **http://www.searchengineshowdown.com**

Search Lore **http://www.searchlore.org**

They keep tabs on all the finer details such as who owns what, how they tick, and who's currently biggest. Essential reading for budding Webmasters.

Limitations

Search engines aren't the be all and end all of what's on the Web. **They're only as good as their most recent findings**, which might be just a small proportion of what's actually there and, possibly, months old. So just because you can't find it through a Web search doesn't mean it's not there. If you're after something brand new, they're not always the best choice. You might be better off searching **Usenet** (see p.168) or a news service.

How to use a search engine

Okay, get this right and you'll find anything. The trick is to think up a **search term** that's unique enough to get rid of junk results, but broad enough not to miss anything useful. It will depend entirely on the subject, so be prepared to think laterally!

One search won't fit all – read the instructions

Although most search forms look alike, the mechanisms behind them differ. That means you might have to adjust your search terms slightly, depending on the engine, to get the best results. The same applies to online stores, encyclopedias, newspaper archives, and anything else you can search. It also means some engines work better than others.

While the easiest way to learn is to dive straight in, at some point, pause and read the instructions. You should find a link to an FAQ, Search Tips, or Help section on the front page. The main things to glean are how to **create a phrase**, how to **search on multiple phrases**, and how to **exclude certain words.** A few minutes' study could save hours of weeding through poor results.

A typical search

Let's start with a complex example. Suppose we want to search for something on the esteemed author, Angus Kennedy. Let's see how you'd do it in **All the Web**.

If you were to enter: angus kennedy it would return all pages that contain "angus" **or** "kennedy" **or both**. That means there'd be lots of pages about Angus cattle and JFK. We don't want to sift through those so let's make sure the pages contain **both words**. In Raging Search, and most other search engines, you can use a **plus sign (+)** to state that the page **must contain a word**. So let's try: +angus +kennedy

That's better. All the pages now contain both words. Unfortunately, though, there's no guarantee that they'll be next to each other. What we really want is to **treat them as a phrase**. A simple way to do this is to enclose the words within quotes, like this: "angus kennedy"

Now we've captured all instances of Angus Kennedy as a phrase, but since it's **a person's name**, we should look for Kennedy, Angus as well. So let's try: "angus kennedy" "kennedy, angus"

As with the first example we now catch pages with **either or both phrases**. Now suppose we want to narrow it down further and exclude some irrelevant results, for example, others with the same name. Our target writes books about French literature, so let's start by getting rid of that pesky Rough Guide author. To **exclude a term**, place a minus sign (-) in front. So let's ditch him: "angus kennedy" "kennedy, angus" -"rough guide"

That's about all you need to know in most instances. These rules should work in most engines, as well as the search forms on individual sites. However, there are exceptions.

Variations – such as Google

Google makes searching easier by including all the search terms. Which means you don't have to add the + sign. So searching on: angus kennedy would search for pages containing "angus" **AND** "kennedy." If you want to search for pages containing either, do two separate searches or use the Boolean operator "OR": angus OR kennedy

Many engines also have a **drop down menu** with the options of "any of the words", "all the words", or "the exact phrase". If the meaning of that isn't instantly obvious, try it.

To tune your searches further, look for an "advanced search option", or refer to the instructions. Observe how the engine interprets **capitals**, dashes between words, brackets, wild cards, truncations, and the **Boolean** operators such as AND, OR, NEAR, and NOT.

In particular, watch out for "**stop words**". These are words that are normally ignored. In Google, for example, single letters are ignored unless you place a "+" sign in front of them. So to search for Angus J Kennedy, you'd enter: **"angus +j kennedy"**

Translations

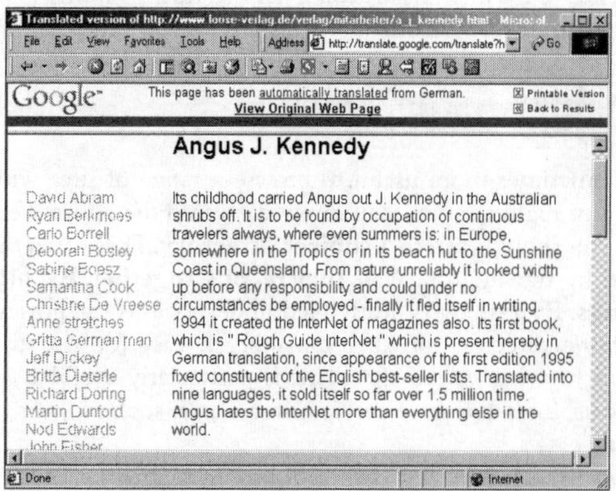

If your results include foreign language sites, Google and Altavista can roughly translate them into English, or another preference. Just click on "translate."

Tip: You'll be using your favorite engines often, so drop their addresses onto your browser Links bar. But rather than save the front page, favor the one with advanced options. At All the Web, for example, click on "Advanced search" to bring up an assortment of tuning boxes, including the friendlier 100 hits per page option. At Google and Raging Search, click on "Preferences" and "Customize" respectively to increase the default number of hits per page. You can then save the front page, as your preferences will be stored in your cookies.

Can't find it?

Just because search engines can't find something, doesn't mean it's not on the Web. It just means their trawlers haven't visited that site yet. Which means you'll have to turn to another, maybe fresher source. Read on.

Subject directories

It's sometimes more useful to browse a range of sites within a topic or region, rather than throw darts into the entire Web. For this you should turn to a **subject directory**. These aren't compiled by trawling the Web, **they're put together by human beings**. Everything is neatly filed under various categories, like a phone directory or library, making it easy for you to drill down to what you're after. This is particularly useful if you're looking for a listing of services in an area, such as your home town.

You usually have the choice of browsing directories by **subject group** and sometimes by other criteria such as **entry date or rating**. Often you can search the directory itself through a form, rather like a search engine. Unlike search engines, directories don't keep the contents of Web pages but instead record titles, categories, and sometimes comments or reviews, so adjust your search strategy accordingly. Start with broad terms and work down until you hit the reviews.

General directories

The Internet doesn't have an official directory, but it does have several broad focused directories that will help you on your way to most subject areas. The best **general directories** are:

About.com **http://www.about.com**

Open Directory **http://dmoz.org**

Yahoo **http://www.yahoo.com**

Yahoo is the closest the Net has to a central directory. If the Web has seven wonders, it would probably be the first. Apart from the massive site directory, it also has loads of added extras such as national and metropolitan directories, regional TV listings, weather reports, kids' guides, seniors' guides, yellow pages, sport scores, plus outstanding news and financial services. You should spend at least one session online exploring its reaches. Chances are, you'll be back there every day.

If you're located outside the USA, or looking for country specific information, then switch to the relevant regional guide, if available. For example:

Yahoo Asia **http://asia.yahoo.com**

Yahoo Australia & NZ **http://www.yahoo.com.au**

Yahoo Canada **http://www.yahoo.ca**

Yahoo UK & Ireland **http://www.yahoo.co.uk**

The Open Directory is a relatively recent project, that's compiled by about 37,000 volunteers and served through several sites including Google. While it lacks Yahoo's armada of added services, its directory is better maintained in many areas. It pays to look at both.

About.com deserves a special mention, because unlike most broad directories, its topics are presented by expert guides. This makes it an excellent jumping off point if you need a helping hand. If you like this approach, **Suite101** (http://www.suite101.com) attempts the same tack.

There's no shortage of alternatives, which might prove useful if the above fail, such as:

AltaVista http://www.av.com
Excite http://www.excite.com
LookSmart http://www.looksmart.com
Lycos http://www.lycos.com

But broad subject directories aren't always the best at digging up everything within a category, or giving you expert guidance. For that you need a specialist directory – or as the suits call them, vortals.

Specialists

Whatever your interest, you can bet your favorite finger it will have several dedicated sites and another that keeps track of them all. Such **specialized directories** are a boon for finding new, esoteric or local interest pages – ones that the major directories overlook. How do you find a specialist directory? You could go straight to Google with a very specific search, but in this case it would make more sense to seek a helping hand. Try **About.com** first. It maintains specialist directories on most common interests. Next, try Yahoo and the Open Directory. If there's more than a couple of Web directories on the subject, they'll put them in their own section. You might also glean something from consulting a directory that specializes in listing specialist directories such as:

Complete Planet http://www.completeplanet.com

Directory Guide http://www.directoryguide.com

GoGettem http://www.gogettem.com

Search Bug http://www.searchbug.com

Search Engine Guide http://www.searchengineguide.com

Search IQ http://www.searchiq.com

Webdata http://www.webdata.com

Specialist sites often maintain a **mailing list** to keep you posted with news and, in some cases, run **discussion lists** or **bulletin boards** so you can discuss issues with other visitors. If you feel you can contribute to the site, email the Webmaster. That's how the Web community works. You'll find hundreds of specialist sites all through our Web guide.

Search agents

Search agents, or **searchbots**, gather information live from a limited number of sites. For example, to find new information, to compare prices or stock, or combine the results from several search engines. **Shopping agents** (p.195), like Shopper.com scan online stores for the best deals.

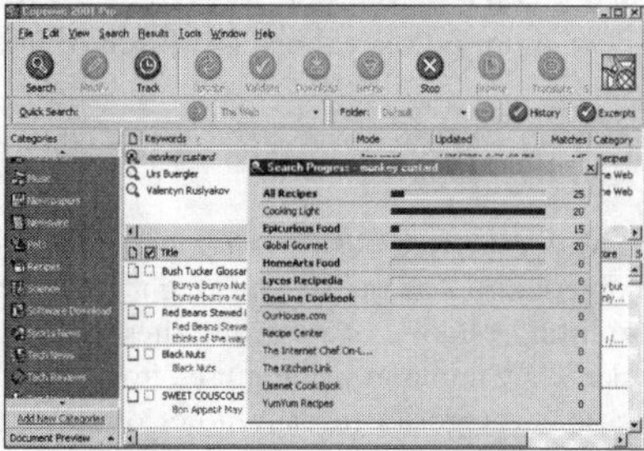

"**Metasearch**" sites that query multiple search engines and directories simultaneously, such as Metacrawler, Vivisimo, Dogpile, Mamma and

Ixquick are close to useless. You will get better results, faster, by going directly to Google.

You'll find the same goes for the bewildering layers of **search aids built into Internet Explorer** and **Windows**. Click on IE's Search button, or "Search (Find) on the Internet" from Windows' Start menu, and a search form will appear on the left-hand side of your browser. Click **Customize** to choose from an impressive array of search engines, directories, email databases, maps, and more. It looks promising but again you'll probably get better value at the source. Only use Apple's metasearch agent, **Sherlock** if you feel you need a handicap.

But all is not lost. For serious research, try **Copernic** (http://www.copernic.com). It's a standalone program that can query hundreds of search engines, directories, Usenet archives, shops, and email databases, at once. It filters out the duplicates, displays the results on a single page in your browser and even retrieves them automatically for offline browsing.

There are also dozens of ways to monitor search engines, individual sites, and newsgroups for changes. For example, **Spyonit** (http://www.spyonit.com) can notify you by email, pager, SMS or ICQ, whenever your search term comes up on an auction, TV listing, directory or search engine. And **Tracerlock** (http://www.tracerlock.com) will let you know when your keywords come up on AltaVista, Usenet or the online personals.

For more on searchbots, see: BotSpot (http://bots.internet.com)

Lists, picks and weblogs

If you're merely browsing for pleasure, rather than looking for something in particular, you might like to try the sites dedicated to listing, ranking or reporting sites that are new, "cool", or popular. They come in many guises, from the top 100 busiest sites in various categories to daily doses of extreme weirdness. Weblogs

(blogs) are generally kept like diaries, with daily postings on whatever's attracted the author's interest over the last 24 hours. To find hundreds, run a search on "Weblog" at Dmoz.org. For some light entertainment, shuffle through the following selection:

100 Hot Websites

http://www.100hot.com
http://www.hitwise.com
Attempts to rank the hundred most visited Web sites each week, overall or by category, in several countries.

Cruel Site of the Day

http://www.cruel.com
Something horrid daily.

Losers.org

http://www.losers.org
A list you don't want to make.

MemePool

http://www.memepool.com
Daily Weblog from multiple authors, archived by subject. A great source of interesting links.

Netsurfer Digest

http://www.netsurf.com/nsd/
Subscribe to receive weekly site updates and reviews.

Portal of Evil

http://www.portalofevil.com
At least three guaranteed jaw-droppers from the Web's outer limits daily. Not for the squeamish.

Useless Pages

http://www.go2net.com/useless/
http://www.worstoftheweb.com
The sludge festering at the bottom of the Net.

Yahoo's picks

http://www.yahoo.com/picks/
http://dir.yahoo.com/new/
What's new and cool, according to the staff of the world's biggest Web directory.

Finding stuff

Although a general search engine or directory might not instantly strike gold, they'll often point you in the right direction. As you get more familiar with the run of the Net, you'll gravitate toward specialist sites and directories that index more than just Web pages, add their own content, and shine in specific areas. What's best depends largely on what you're after. When you find a useful site, **store it in your Favorites or Bookmarks**, so you can return. Here's how to:

Find someone's email address

Not as simple as you might think. See (p.124).

Find local information

You'll sometimes want to find sites that cater to a very specific region. Say, for example, you want to look up film screenings across your city, or select a honeymoon suite in Tamanrasset. Although it might seem logical to use a local search engine to find local sites or information, it's often not the most efficient method. Always start your searches with Google and then move on if that fails. Most small local search engines simply aren't very good. Directories, however, can be another matter. Try Yahoo and the Open Directory and see what's listed in the region. Don't make it too narrow as it might be filed under the country, state or province rather than the town or suburb. Then drill down from the broad region into your area of interest. These should lead you to the major specialist directories in your area of interest. For a directory of regional directories, see:

Search Engine Colossus http://www.searchenginecolossus.com

Find a local business or phone number

While online residential and business telephone directories can be kept more current than their paper equivalents, they're not usually as easy to browse. Apart from the phone companies offerings you'll also find a raft of private directories in competition. Some even deliver a book as well. If you haven't been exposed to their advertising, don't expect too much. Investigate

Australia

CitySearch http://www.citysearch.com.au
White Pages http://www.whitepages.com.au
Yellow pages http://www.yellowpages.com.au

United Kingdom

192 Enquiries http://www.192enquiries.com
192.com http://www.192.com
BT PhoneNet http://www.bt.com/phonenetuk/
Scoot http://www.scoot.co.uk
Yellow Pages http://www.yell.co.uk

USA & Canada

Anywho http://www.anywho.com
CitySearch http://www.citysearch.com
Infospace http://www.infospace.com
SuperPages.com http://www.superpages.com
Switchboard http://www.switchboard.com

To find a phone number in almost any country:

World Pages International Directories
http://www.worldpages.com/global/

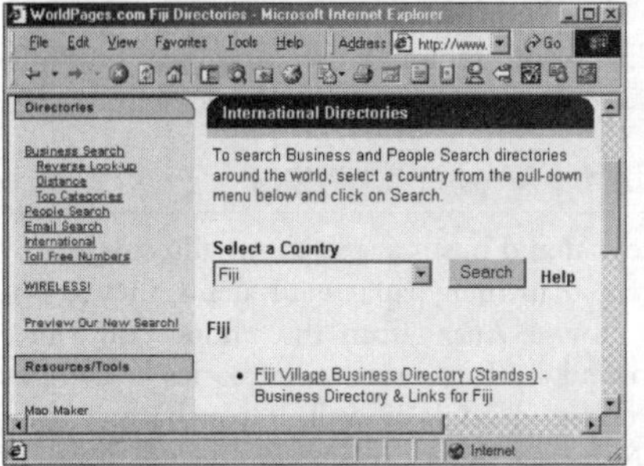

a few of the following major services and see what they offer in your area, and keep your eye out for advertisements in your local press. They should come looking for you, not vice versa.

Find answers to the most common questions

Where else would you look for answers to the most Frequently Asked Questions than the repository for Usenet FAQs? If the answer's not in http://www.faqs.org try Usenet (p.212) itself.

Find out what others think on Usenet

You want to, but you don't know how. You want one, but you don't know which one. You have one, but you can't get it to work. You want more than just a second opinion. You want a forum on the subject. That's Usenet (see p.212).

There's no better place to find opinions and personal experiences than Usenet, but it's a lot of text to scan. Although it's sorted into subject bundles, if you had to find every instance of discussion about something, it could take you days. And if it was tossed around more than a couple of weeks ago, the thread might have expired.

With **Google Groups** (http://groups.google.com), however, not only can you scan close to all Usenet now, but a fair chunk of its history as well. You can pursue entire threads and profile each contributor. Which means you can follow a whole discussion, as well as check out who's who and how well they're respected. And on top of that, you can identify which groups are most likely to discuss something and then join the group. You'll get to the bottom of even the most obscure subject.

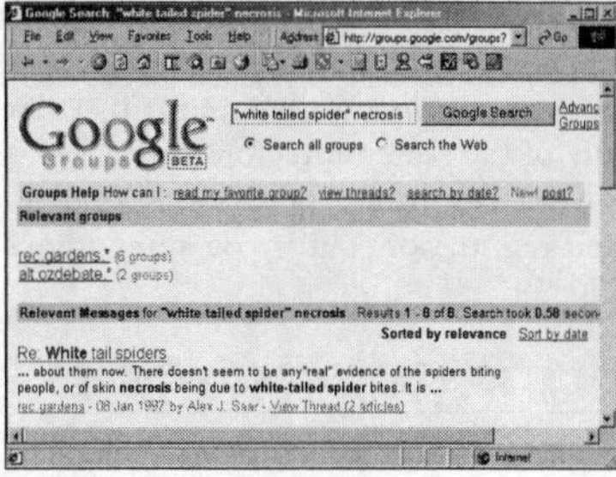

However, since moving over from Deja.com, the archive has become a little less friendly to navigate. It would pay to read the Help page.

Find computer help

Enter a couple of unique phrases from your error or computer problem into Google Groups. Try both the Usenet and Web searches. If your question isn't answered in the archives, join a relevant newsgroup and post it there. See also Web guide computer section p.334.

Find games, hints, and cheats

Try one of the big games sites such as the **Games Domain, Gamespot**, or **Happy Puppy**, or search through Usenet as explained above. Stuck on a level? Look for a walkthrough, or ask in Usenet.

Find a product review or an online shop

See Shopping (p.182).

Find product support

Whenever you buy anything substantial, see if the company has a Web site offering **follow-up support** and **product news**. If it's not on the accompanying literature, try putting its name between www and .com and if that doesn't work, look it up in any of the search directories.

Most companies offer some kind of online product support and registration, but if you want advice from other users, go to Usenet.

Find the latest news, weather, finance, sport, etc

Apart from hundreds of newspapers and magazines, the Net carries several large **news-clipping archives** assembled from all sorts of sources. Naturally, there's an overwhelming amount of technology news, but also an increasing amount of services dedicated to what you would normally find on the newsstands – and often fresher on the Net. They occasionally charge, though usually only for the archives. For pointers, check the Web guide under News, Fashion, Finance, Weather, and so forth. The best place to start would be **Moreover** (http://www.moreover.com), where you can search or browse headlines from over 1500 newsfeeds and then link to the story. **Yahoo Daily News** (http://dailynews.yahoo.com) is also good.

Find out about a film or TV show

See Film & TV (p.347) or try the entertainment section of any major directory for leads to specialist sites. The **Internet Movie Database**, for example, is exceptionally comprehensive and linked to Amazon in case you're tempted to order the video.

Find the latest software

See Downloading Software (p.244).

Find health support

Start by searching the Web. Try Yahoo for listings of organizations and so forth, and then Google for mentions on Web pages. Chances are they'll refer you to useful mailing lists and discussion groups. If not, try Google Groups to see if, and in which groups, it's being discussed on Usenet. Ultimately, though, you'd like to join a mailing list.

Find a mailing list

The best place to find mailing lists is through a well-worded Web search (that includes "mailing list" and the topic), or through the small list directories at:

PAML **http://www.paml.net**

Meta List **http://www.meta-list.net**

List Universe **http://www.list-universe.com**

Liszt **http://www.liszt.com**

If that's not satisfactory, try Google Groups and check the FAQs from groups with hits.

Find something you've forgotten

Don't give up if you can't remember where you saw that hot tip last week. Just open Internet Explorer's History and search the cache. So long as it hasn't been deleted, you should even be able to recall it offline.

Find advice

If all else fails – and that's pretty unlikely – you can always turn to someone else for help. Use Deja.com to find

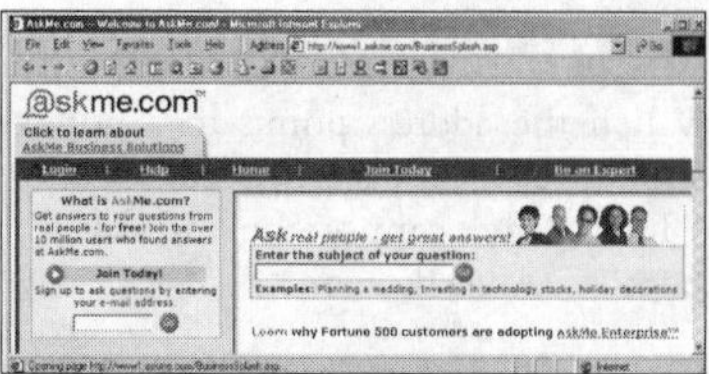

the most appropriate newsgroup(s). Summarize your quest in the subject heading, keep it concise, post, and you should get an answer or three within a few days. Alternatively, try a mailing list or one of the free "expert" advice services such as:

Abuzz http://www.abuzz.com

AllExperts http://www.allexperts.com

AskMe.com http://www.askme.com

Finding the right Web address

You're sure to come across a **Web link or address that won't work**. It's common and usually not too hard to get around. Many of the addresses in this book will be wrong by the time you try them. Not because we're hopeless, they just change. That's the way of the Net. The most useful thing we can do is show you how to find their new homes.

Error codes

When something goes wrong, your browser will **display a page with an error message** – or nothing will happen, no matter what you try. To identify the source of the problem, get familiar with the types of errors. Different browsers and servers will return different error messages, but they'll indicate the same things. As an exercise, identify the following errors:

Incorrect host name

When the address points to a nonexistent host, your browser should return a page headed "Cannot find server" and reading "The page cannot be displayed". Test this by keying: http://www.rufgide.com

Illegal domain name

If you specify an **illegal host name** or **protocol**, your browser should tell you. Try this out by keying http://wwwrufguide and then http:/www.ibm.com (noting the single slash before the www). Internet Explorer should automatically detect the latter error, and correct it.

File not found – 404 error

If the **file has moved, changed name**, or you've overlooked **capitalization**, the server will tell you the file doesn't exist, or send you back to the front page. It differs between servers. Test this by keying a valid address with a bogus path, such as http://www.bbc.com/bogus/ and http://www.cnn.com/bogus/

Busy host or host refuses entry

Occasionally you won't succeed because the server is either **overloaded with traffic**, or it's temporarily or permanently **off-limits**. This sometimes happens when a site is heavily promoted or makes the news. It's a bit hard to test, but you'll come across it sooner or later. You might find foreign sites less busy when the locals are sleeping.

When nothing works

Now that you're on speaking terms with your browser, you're set to troubleshoot that problem address. First check your **connection**. Try another site, like: http://www.yahoo.com

If that works, you know it's not your connection. If you can't connect to any Web site, **close and then reopen your browser**. It might only be a software glitch. Otherwise, it's most likely a problem with your Net connection or proxy server (if you're using one).

Check your mail. If that fails, log off, then back on. Check it again. If your mailer connects and reports your mail status normally, you know that the connection between you and your ISP is okay. But there still could be a problem between it and the Net or with your proxy server. Check you have the right proxy settings and if so, disable them. If it still doesn't work, **ring your ISP** and see if there's a problem at their end or diagnose it yourself.

To do this, test a known host – say www.yahoo.com – with a **network tool** such as **Ping, TraceRoute** or **NetMedic** (see p.67). If this fails, either your provider's connection to the Net is down, or there's a problem with your **Domain Name Server**. Get on the phone and sort it out.

If you've verified that all connections are open but your browser still won't find any addresses, then the problem must lie with your **browser setup**. Check its settings and re-install it if necessary.

When a page won't display

You'll sometimes find a page or frame inside a page instantly comes up blank. You can tell your browser hasn't tried to fetch the page because it happens too quickly. In this case hit the Refresh button. If that doesn't work, reboot your browser, and re-enter the address. Failing that, open your Internet Options and clear your Temporary Internet Files or browser cache. Finally, if you're still having problems and it appears to be related to Internet Explorer security, such as the acceptance of an ActiveX control at an online banking site, check your security settings within Internet Options, disable **Content Advisor**, and consider adding the site to your Trusted sites.

When one address won't work

If only **one address fails**, you know its address is wrong or it has server problems. Now that you're familiar with error messages you can deduce the source and fix that address.

Web addresses disappear and change all the time, often because the address has been simplified, for example from: http://www.netflux.com/~test/New_Book/htm to http://www.newbook.com

Sometimes they'll leave a **link to the new page** from the old address, but that too might be out of date. Since the Web is in a constant state of construction, just about everything is a test site in transit to something bigger and more glorious. Consequently, when a site gets serious, it might change hosts and discard the old address.

If you're convinced the address is fine, then try it later, perhaps even days later. It might be down for maintenance or experiencing local problems. If you can reach it on another machine, but not yours, the problem might lie with your Windows Hosts file – especially if you've ever installed any browser acceleration software. If so, first get rid of the offending program properly through the Add/Remove applet in Windows Control Panel. Then locate the file called Hosts in your Windows folder. It will have no file extension. Open it with Notepad and remove any lines not starting with # except for the localhost entry. Save the file, and exit.

Finding that elusive address

The error messages will provide the most helpful clues for **tracking elusive addresses**. If the problem comes from the host name, try **adding** or **removing the www part**. For example, instead of typing http://roughguides.com try http://www.roughguides.com Other than that you can only guess. It may only be that the host is busy, refusing entry, or not connecting, so **try again later.**

If you **can connect to the host but the file isn't there**, there are a few further tricks to try. Check capitalization, for instance: book.htm instead of Book.htm Or try **changing the file name extension** from .htm to .html or vice versa, if applicable. Then try **removing the file name** and then each subsequent directory up the path until finally you're left with just the host name. For example:

http://www.roughguides.com/old/Book.htm
http://www.roughguides.com/old/book.htm
http://www.roughguides.com/old/book.html
http://www.roughguides.com/old/
http://www.roughguides.com

In each case, if you succeed in connecting, try to locate your page from whatever links appear.

If you haven't succeeded, there's still hope. Try **submitting the main key words** from the site's address or title into **Google**. If Google knows the site, but it's not available, you can still access Google's copy by clicking on "cached". Failing that, try searching on related subjects, or scanning through one of the subject guides like **Yahoo** or the **Open Directory**.

By now, even if you haven't found your original target, you've probably discovered half a dozen similar if not more interesting pages, and in the process figured out how to navigate the Net.

8

Shopping

Have your credit card handy

Welcome to the world's biggest bazaar. Whether you're after a ticket to the **monster trucking safari** (http://www.ticketmaster.com) or a **midget tourist submarine** (http://www.ussubs.com), just step right up and click.

So is it merely catalog mail order made complicated by computers? Sometimes, maybe, but that's only part of the story. The Net hasn't entirely killed off catalogs just yet, but it already blitzes them in many ways. To start with it's interactive not static. That means you can sift large inventories in seconds. And get the latest information, be it new releases, stock levels or recommendations based on your tastes. So, if you're shopping for music, for example, you could plough through a performer's entire back catalog, listening to samples as you read what other customers have to say about each album. Plus you can **visit several stores, in different parts of the world, all at once**, simply by opening multiple browser windows. Or send a search engine to forage for the best prices or availability across hundreds of shops simultaneously. Catalogs don't even come close.

But **you might be concerned that it's unsafe**. Fair enough, but you needn't worry too much. As long as you follow the advice here you'll find it's considerably less risky than the offline world.

Pros and cons

The Net isn't as neatly arranged as your average shopping center, but it does offer some advantages – particularly when you can't find something as cheaply, if at all, locally. Nonetheless, while you can't rule anything out completely, some products are definitely more suited to selling online. **Books** and **CDs**, for example, fit perfectly because you can sample and read reviews before you buy. And if you don't like your purchase, you can return it for a refund. Or if you couldn't be bothered, you haven't blown your life savings. Clothes, on the other hand, are much trickier. You might squeeze by on generics like jeans and t-shirts, but anything that requires trying on will cause problems. While you can always return them if they don't fit, it's a hassle involving extra postage costs and monetary risk.

In essence, the Net isn't suitable if: you need to examine the goods; the weight or size makes shipping too costly; they can't deliver in time; or it costs more without being more convenient. **So just because you're on the Net doesn't mean you'll never have to leave the house again.**

Shop safe

Without wishing to scare you unduly, beware that sharks do lurk out there. Not that many, but certainly enough to keep you on your toes. Contrary to the popular notion, the biggest threat isn't some boy hacker sneaking off with your card number. They mostly only break into sites to show off. In the unlikely chance one does get your number, they probably won't even use it. Besides, **there are easier ways to nab your credit details**. Like getting a part-time job in a shop, for instance.

On the other hand, with **organized online crime** on the rise it's not impossible that your card could fall into the wrong hands, and be used in an unauthorized transaction. Of course, regardless of whether you use credit online you should always reconcile your statement each month and report any discrepancies to your issuer immediately.

Still, you should be more concerned with con artists running seemingly legitimate sites, or approaching you by unsolicited email. Ignore the following warnings at your own peril:

- If anything at all seems fishy, don't shop there.
- If a site hasn't gone to the effort of registering its own domain name, then don't expect it to be professional in any other way. **Merchants using free servers like Geocities should be regarded as classified ads** rather than shops. And regard any business operating out of a collective shopping mall as a **market stall**.
- **Never deal with a site that doesn't give a street address** and phone number. An email address isn't enough. And a free email address, like Hotmail, spells trouble. Mind you, failure to display a phone number doesn't make them instantly dodgy. It's an all too common omission on even the best-known sites. And some, such as Amazon, bury their contact details at the bottom of a help file. **Feel free to abuse them about it**. Tell them we sent you.
- Any site or email that uses **LOADS OF BOLD UPPER CASE TEXT** isn't to be trusted.
- Always **switch to a secure connection** when modifying your account details or checking out. When a connection becomes

secure the beginning of the address will change from http:// to https:// and a closed lock will appear in the bottom bar of your browser. If a shop doesn't offer secure purchasing, it's not serious about its online presence. Shop elsewhere, or phone through your order. **Never send your credit card details by email.**

❑ To make an online purchase you should only need to provide your name, billing address, delivery address, credit card number, account name, expiry date, and shipping preferences. **You should never need any other form of identification** such as your social security, health insurance, driver's license, savings account, or passport number.

❑ The **username/password combination** you choose for a site, applies to that site only. Never give it to another site, or to anyone by email or phone. Avoid using the same combination at every site, and especially don't use your mail or dial-up connection password.

❑ **Don't respond to spam** (unsolicited email, p.131). Those "get paid to surf", "stock tips", "work from home", "recruit new members", "clear your credit rating", and various network-marketing schemes **are** too good to be true. It should go without saying that ringing a number to claim a prize will only cost you money.

❑ Read this government bulletin before following **investment advice** found online, whether on the Web, or through a newsletter: http://www.sec.gov/investor/pubs/cyberfraud.htm

❑ **Don't install free browser or mouse cursor enhancements**, including so-called Web accelerators. Or let any site make itself your "home page". They're only interested in collecting marketing data. Your browser is fine the way it is.

❑ Avoid any site that pops up a new window when you try to leave, or spawns multiple windows. Don't deal with, or download software from, any site that seems to consist of top lists of other sites, which in turn point you to more lists. These are merely trying to milk click-through referrals. It mightn't cost you anything but it wastes your time.

❑ It has to be said: **almost all online scams revolve around porn** sites. More than is let on, because their victims are often too embarrassed to own up. **Don't pass over your credit details to adult sites unless you're prepared to be stung**. And whatever you do, don't download any connection software, picture viewers, or browser add-ons from adult sites. These have been known to drop your line and redial somewhere like Vanuatu, racking up a massive phone bill in the process. If you must delve in porn, go wallow in the binary newsgroups.

❑ Consider giving your money to charity rather than an **online casino**.

❑ Never accept **ActiveX controls** unless you're absolutely positive they're from a reputable firm.

❑ Beware free trials and **subscription services** that require your credit details - such as AOL. You might find it harder to cancel than you anticipated. Or they might bill you whether you use the service or not. Check your bill carefully each month for discrepancies, and make sure the subscription doesn't renew itself automatically.

❑ Don't believe everything you read. As much as the Net is the greatest source of consumer advice, it's also the great source of **misinformation**. Look for a second opinion before you fork out cash on the basis of a recommendation.

❑ And don't forget: **keep a record of your order**, so you can balance it against your bank statement.

Are you covered?

Credit and debit cards provide varying degrees of **protection against fraud**. You'll need to read the fine print on your agreement for specifics, but normally you're only liable for a set amount. You also might be able to pay a yearly surcharge to fully protect your card against fraud. Ask your bank, along with what to do if you suspect you've been wrongly charged. Some sites also offer to pick up the balance if you can show they're at fault.

Help

For more advice and information on online fraud, see:

CyberCrime http://www.cybercrime.gov

Fraud Bureau http://www.fraudbureau.com

Internet Fraud Complaint Ctr https://www.ifccfbi.gov

Scambusters http://www.scambusters.com

Know your product

Whether you're buying online or off, the Net is an invaluable mine of consumer advice. However, consumer written reviews can often be more anecdotal than scientific, and somewhat prone to rigging. So while you can't take it all at face value, the more you know the better your chance of a happy purchase. Usenet (p.212) is often the best place to ask advice, but search **Google Groups** (http://groups.google.com) first to see if it's already been discussed. For buying guides, customer opinions, ratings and product reviews, try:

Amazon http://www.amazon.com

Ciao (UK, EUR) http://www.ciao.com

Consumer Guide http://www.consumerguide.com

Consumer Report http://www.consumerreports.org

Consumer Review http://www.consumerreview.com

Consumer Search http://www.consumersearch.com

Dooyoo (UK, EUR) http://www.dooyoo.com

Epinions http://www.epinions.com

eSmarts http://www.esmarts.com

Rateitall.com http://www.rateitall.com

Review Board http://www.reviewboard.com

Top Ten Buys (UK) http://www.toptenbuys.co.uk

You could also query Yahoo, the Open Directory or a search engine to locate trade magazines or sites that specialize in your desired product category. Such as:

Computers http://www.zdnet.com

Digital Cameras http://www.dpreview.com

Gadgets http://www.the-gadgeteer.com

Hi-Fi http://www.audioreview.com

Or perhaps one of the consumer organizations, like:

Choice http://www.choice.com.au (AUS)

Consumers Int. http://www.cosumersinternational.org (INT)

Which http://www.which.net (UK)

These can also alert you to problem products and recalls, as will:

Recall Announcements (UK, US, INT)
http://www.recallannouncements.com

But if you need hands-on experience you should examine the goods in a shop first, and then check whether you can get a better deal online.

Buying foreign

With the entire Net at your fingertips, you're empowered to shop the world. And placing an order with a foreign store should be no harder than doing it locally, especially if you're paying by credit card. But, it does require a little more effort on the vendor's part, and certain products aren't suitable for export, so many stores, particularly in the US, won't accept foreign orders. You can usually find this out fairly quickly by looking up the store's shipping and handling section.

Before you leap on a bargain, **ensure it will work at home**. Phone or power plugs can be adapted quickly, but if the conversion involves something complex like replacing a power transformer, question if it's worth the effort. Other things that may differ between countries include: DVD region codes; console games; TV and video devices (check whether they're PAL or NTSC); PC keyboard layouts; software editions; and of course, anything where measurements could cause confusion such as recipes, clothing, and space exploration vehicles.

Finally, when applicable, ask if it's covered by an **international warranty**, whether spares are available locally, where you'd have to send it for repairs, and who's responsible for shipping.

But is it really a steal?

Sure, you can save money by shopping abroad, but if saving cash is your primary motive, you'll need to do your figures carefully. To start with you'll need to work out what it costs in your own currency. Call your bank for the going forex rate less transaction charges, and compare it with the wholesale rate at http://quote.yahoo.com. Then you'll be able to work it out in future.

Next, balance the shipping costs against transit time. Heavy items will naturally cost more, and cheaper options will take longer. How long can you wait? If you need it pronto, you'd better check they have the stock at hand.

And not least, the **sticky issue of tax**. The ideal scenario is to buy duty free, and have it arrive untaxed by local customs. That can happen, but it will depend on the countries involved, the nature of the product, what it's worth, and whether anyone could be bothered to chase it up. The US is the most complex due to its state taxes. Technically, you should be able to buy duty free between states as long as the shop doesn't have an office in your home state. If you need more info on your tax laws, call your local post office or customs helpdesk. Or if you live in the UK, US, or Australia, try unpicking some sense from this lot:

Australian Customs **http://www.customs.gov.au**

HM Customs & Excise **http://www.hmce.gov.uk**

US Customs **http://www.customs.ustreas.gov**

Auctions

Whether it's new or used, collectable or disposable, if it can be sold, you can bet it's up for sale, somewhere in an online auction. Unlike much of what's happening online, auctions aren't an overnight fad. With millions of goods in thousands of categories changing hands every day, they're definitely here to stay. You really won't believe what's up for grabs:

Who Would Buy That? **http://www.whowouldbuythat.com**

How they work

You know how auctions work: the sale goes to the highest bidder, as long as it's above the preset reserve price. Or in the case of a Dutch auction, the price keeps dropping until a buyer accepts. Well, it's the same online, but less stressful. Most obviously, you don't have to drive across town and waste a day. You simply set a starting bid, and then an amount to incrementally counterbid until it hits your ceiling. If no-one outbids you, the deal is struck at your highest offer – which could be your starting bid if it's above the reserve and there aren't any other bidders.

Once the deal's been settled, it's up to the buyer and seller to arrange delivery and payment, though both can be arranged via trusted third parties. The auctioneer typically takes a cut of the vendor's taking.

As long as you take the time to read the new user's section, and follow the prompts from there, you should have no problem getting started.

Finding an auction

If you've watched TV in the last year, you've surely heard of eBay. It was the first auction house to take the Net by storm. Since then hundreds more have appeared, but eBay, with branches in Australia, Canada, France, Germany, Japan, the UK and USA, remains the biggest and best known. You should investigate it first:

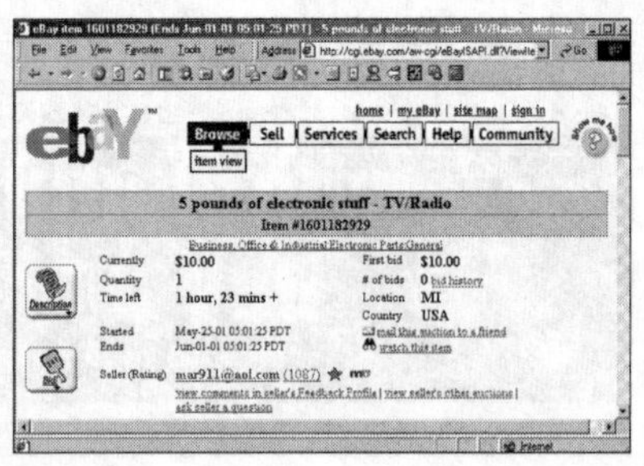

eBay http://www.ebay.com

If you like what you see, but aren't satisfied, try a few more such as:

Amazon http://www.amazon.com (or local branch)

Loot http://auction.loot.com

QXL http://www.qxl.com (US, UK, Europe)

Sold.com.au http://www.sold.com.au (AUS)

Yahoo http://auctions.yahoo.com (or local branch)

While these carry most items, some objects, such as art and antiques, are better suited to a specialist dealer. For a more comprehensive list, try Yahoo, the Open Directory, or a dedicated auctions directory:

Bidfind http://www.bidfind.com

Internet Auction List http://www.internetauctionlist.com

Open Directory http://dmoz.org/Shopping/Auctions/

Tools and twists

To search across hundreds of auctions simultaneously try **Auctionwatch.com, BidXS, GoTo Auctions**, or one of the many auction programs – search for "auction" at Download.com or Tucows (http://www.tucows.com). And check out **Esnipe**, which can help you get a better price at eBay by waiting until the last minute to bid.

The Net has also added a raft of new twists to the bidding game. At **Priceline, eWanted** and **Lastminute.com**, for example, you state how much you'd like to pay and wait to see if anyone accepts. **Ybag, LiquidPrice** and **myGeek** approach merchants on your behalf looking for the best deal. While **LetsBuyIt.com** uses collaborative buying power to clinch lower prices. At **NexTag** you can compare the going prices of new against used, and add yours to the marketplace. **Eppraisals** can also offer you a valuation, but you'll have to pay for the privilege. And at **Webswappers** you can exchange your goods for something other than money.

Ventures like these attract ample press so watch the shopping and Internet sections of your newspaper for further leads. But be warned, although they promise the world, don't be surprised if you end up inconvenienced or lumped with a so-so deal.

Auctionwatch.com http://www.auctionwatch.com

BidXS http://www.bidxs.com

Eppraisals http://www.eppraisals.com

Esnipe http://www.esnipe.com

eWanted http://www.ewanted.com

GoTo Auctions http://search.auctions.goto.com

Lastminute.com http://www.lastminute.com

LetsBuyIt.com http://www.letsbuyit.com

LiquidPrice http://www.buyersedge.com

myGeek http://www.mygeek.com

NexTag http://www.nextag

Priceline http://www.priceline.com

Webswappers http://www.webswappers.com

Ybag http://www.ybag.co.uk

Classified ads

Online classifieds need no explanation. They're like the paper version, but easier to search and possibly more up to date. In fact most papers are moving their classifieds onto the Net, though you might have to pay to see the latest listings. Here's just a small selection, but as they tend to work on a local level check your hometown papers, or regional Yahoo for listings in your area:

Excite Classifieds http://www.classifieds2000.com

Half.com http://www.half.com

Loot http://www.loot.com (UK, NY, IE)

Newsclassifieds http://www.newsclassifieds.com.au (AUS)

Trader.com http://www.trader.com (INT)

Trading Post http://www.tradingpost.com.au (AUS)

Zshops http://www.zshops.com

Let's shop!

Shopping's the same the world over: you collect your booty, head to the checkout, fix the bill and carry it home. As you'd expect, that's also how it works online. While the intricate details might differ between sites, once you've used one, the rest should fall into place. Let's use **Amazon** as an example:

A journey through Amazon.com

Getting online and not visiting Amazon would be like going to Cairo and skipping the pyramids. Although it hasn't yet reported a profit, it's without argument the very model of online shopping excellence. Since launching in 1995 as a not so humble bookstore – allegedly the world's biggest – it's blossomed into a massive department store carrying music, DVD, electronics, furniture, cosmetics, toys, tools, the next biggest auction house after eBay, classifieds, and loads more – even cars. But as you'll soon see, it's not the sheer bulk of stock alone that makes it so special. Amazon has branches in:

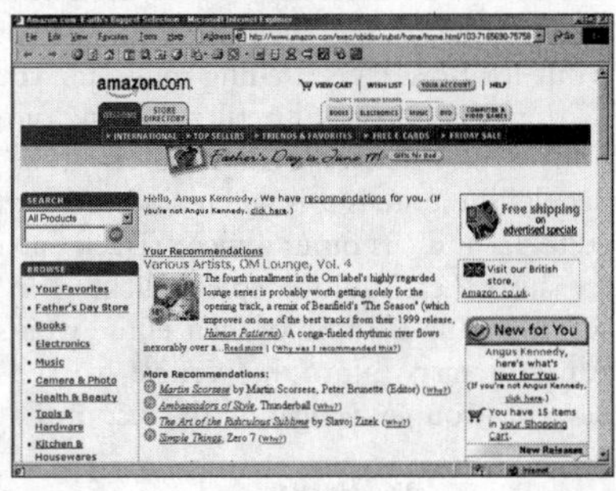

France http://www.amazon.fr

Germany http://www.amazon.de

Japan http://www.amazon.co.jp

UK http://www.amazon.co.uk

US http://www.amazon.com

Although their inventories and editorials overlap, they're all separate outlets, with local stock and distribution hubs. The US operation is ahead of the rest, stocking a wider range of products and features. But, it's worth checking both the UK and US operations, especially if you're after music.

Sifting the inventory

Point your browser at: http://www.amazon.com You'll find no time-wasting intro there. Everything's linked from the front page, so save it into your favorites. Explore the links around the page. You can either search the inventory using the form at the top left, or browse through the categories. Information about the vendor, including shipping and help is located at the bottom of the page. This is standard practice at all well-designed sites. After you've clicked a little, it will soon become clear how it works. But it might take you an hour or two to fully appreciate everything on offer. We'll leave that up to you.

But for now, try searching music for your favorite performer. Within seconds it will return a listing of entries from each section of its inventory. Click on any title to display the album details. Sometimes this will include a full track listing, along with editorial and customer reviews. Track entries that look like links are short RealAudio samples. Clicking on the performer's name will bring up a listing of their entire works, or at least those that Amazon carry. Now that you've worked that out, you should have no trouble navigating the rest of the site.

The shopping basket

Although you can't actually purchase anything until you set up an account, you can add items to your "**shopping basket**". This is just like a shopping basket in the familiar sense. If you see something you like, drop it into your basket by clicking the 'add to basket" button. All good sites use this system. Don't worry about how much you add to your basket. You're not committed to buy until you move the items through the checkout. You can always take items out later, or simply leave them there for another time. To return to shopping, hit your back button or start another search. You can return to your basket at any time by clicking on the basket icon at the top of the screen or on the link at the bottom of the page.

Starting an account

When you're ready to buy, go to your basket and examine its contents. At this point, you can remove items, change the quantities or save them for later. But again, don't worry because you'll be given the chance again. Clicking "**proceed to checkout**" will bring up the "**signing in**" page. If it's your first visit you'll need to create a new account. Just choose "**I am a new customer**" and follow the prompts. You can change your account details later by clicking on "your account" at the top of the page, or when you're checking out. Once you move into the account phase, the server goes into secure mode – the address changes to https:// and a closed lock appears on the bottom bar. If your browser doesn't support secure purchasing, then either download one that does, or don't shop online!

Your privacy

Whenever you give your details to any site it will ask whether you'd like to receive mail from them, or associated parties. **Say no.** You don't need junk mail from them or anyone else.

Checking out

Once you've logged in with your password, checking out is as straightforward as following the prompts. The most difficult part will be deciding between the various shipping options. If you've bought more than one item you'll have to decide whether to ship them all at once, or as they arrive at their warehouse. One item might take weeks to arrive, delaying the rest of the order. You'll see an indication of how long Amazon thinks each item will take to arrive underneath its entry in the basket. The rest should be all self-explanatory. Just read the help files if you're unclear.

Confirmation

Almost all shops send you an instant email confirming your order. Some shops need a reply to confirm acceptance, though Amazon doesn't. Keep all your orders and shipping notices together in a separate folder so you can refer to them later if something goes amiss.

Tracking

To check the status of each item in your order at Amazon, click on "your account", sign in, and look under Order History. Some sites can give you order tracking details right down to the shipping hubs. If your package fails to arrive, report it to customer support. They should send you a replacement without question.

Your next visit

Next time you arrive at Amazon it will welcome you by your name. This will only work if you're using the same computer, though, as it stores your ID in a cookie file. This isn't a bad thing generally as it learns from your purchases and attempts to recommend stuff you might like. It's not a security concern, as you still have to sign in with your password to make a purchase or change your account details.

Find a shop

We listed individual shops in our earlier editions but there are so many now it's no longer practical. So many that there's now a Rough Guide to Shopping Online, and several others like it. But, even these guides are feeling the strain. Soon it will be like trying to replicate the Yellow Pages. Nonetheless, you might find such a guide useful if it's well researched and can save you time.

Otherwise, it's tough to advise you where to start. It depends where you live, what you're after, and of course, what you like. The major search portals like Yahoo, Excite, and AltaVista index shopping sites within their normal directories, but they don't make it obvious. Instead, when you click on 'Shopping" you're shunted towards their own hybrid shopping malls that favor their partnered vendors. Still, if you're looking for a specific product rather than a type of shop, this can be a good way to go. **The Open Directory** (http://dmoz.org), on the other hand, treats shopping like any other category, making it much easier to browse.

Shopping directories

There are also hundreds of specialist shopping directories. None, however, can claim to list every shop, and even with the few they do carry, they make fossicking hard work. Such as:

Buyersguide http://www.buyersguide.to

InternetMall http://www.internetmall.com

Internetshopper http://www.internetshopper.com

InernetShopping (UK) http://www.internetshopping.com

MyTaxi (UK) http://www.mytaxi.co.uk

Ozshopping (AU) http://www.ozshopping.com.au

Premierstores http://www.premierstores.com

ShopSmart (UK) http://www.shopsmart.com

UKShopping (UK) http://www.ukshopping.com

For more, see: http://dmoz.org/Shopping/Directories/

Most directories provide a description, but if you'd rather a rating or review, see:

Bizrate http://www.bizrate.com

Gomez http://www.gomez.com

Planet Feedback (US) http://www.planetfeedback.com

Shopping Sites (UK,US) http://www.shopping-sites.com

Special needs

If your needs are more specialized, try searching the Web with **Google** (p.155). You'll really need to refine your searching skills though, as it's likely to return pages of hits. Your best bet might be to locate the manufacturer's site and work from there. Or, if you need advice, scan **Google Groups** (http://groups.google. com) for an appropriate newsgroup. For example, if you ask about coffee grinders in alt.coffee, you'll get the rundown on various brands and vendors, and be pointed to several FAQs. A shopping directory is less likely to be so helpful.

Given the wealth of information online, this might sound like an odd suggestion, but the best way to keep up with what's hot in online shopping is to follow the regular media, especially the full-page ads in the glossy magazines.

Finally, if you can't find what you're after, try posting your request at **iWant.com** (http://www.iwant.com), and see if someone comes to your rescue.

Prefer it on paper?

Then drive your postie crazy by ordering every catalog in the world:

Buyers Index http://www.buyersindex.com

Catalog Site http://www.catalogsite.com

Try our Web guide

You'll find short guides to buying music, cars, books, travel, financial services, groceries, and more in our Web guide, which starts on p.313.

Find the best deal

Comparing prices across shops is the craze amongst shopping portals. Whether they're called comparison engines, **shopping bots**, or bargain finders, they more or less do the same thing. Which is, you enter a product or keyword and they return a listing of prices and availability across a range of retailers. Sounds great, but unfortunately few seem capable of consistently keeping their databases current. Which kind of defeats the point of the exercise.

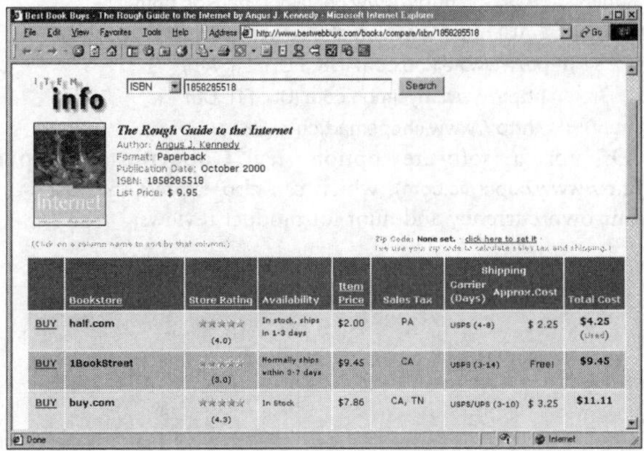

Generally, the bots that specialize in one product group do better than the Swiss army knife variety. Particularly if they scan a lot of shops, including all the big names. Take **Shopper.com** and **Pricewatch.com**, for example. If you're after anything computer related, they're definitely the best place to start.

But it also depends on the shops queried, and whether they're passing out correct information. You'll find some, for example Altavista's **Shopping.com**, query a lot of products but across a very limited and often obscure selection of shops. In the end you might get a better deal at Amazon.

So again, like the shopping directories, it's a hit and miss affair. Try a few and see what works for you:

AddAll! **http://www.addall.com** (books worldwide)
Best Book Buys **http://www.bestbookbuys.com** (books)
Buy.co.uk **http://www.buy.co.uk** (UK utilities)
Deal Time **http://www.dealtime.com** (US, UK, DE, JP)
Egg **http://shopping.egg.com** (UK)
Genial Comparison **http://www.genialcomparison.com**
InfoChoice (AU) **http://www.infochoice.com.au** (Flights, Utilities)
Kelkoo **http://www.kelkoo.com** (UK, EUR, Lat Am)
My Simon **http://www.mysimon.com** (US, FR, DE)
ShopSmart **http://www.shopsmart.com** (UK)

Or, for a software option, try **Copernic Shopper** (**http://www.copernic.com**), which can also express the prices in your own currency and hunt for product reviews.

9

Discussions

Make friends, get answers

Whatever you do, don't think the Net starts and ends with the World Wide Web. If you miss the discussion areas, particularly Usenet, you've barely scratched the surface. In this section, you'll find out how to use the Net to interact with other people, and not just pages.

It's all talk

As outlined earlier (p.5), the main forms of online discussion are Mailing Lists, Usenet, and Chat. **Mailing list** (p.209) discussions are carried out in private by email. In **Usenet** (p.212), your messages form part of an ongoing dialog on a public notice board. Whereas **Chat** (p.228), is instant, like a conversation. You can chat with complete strangers on the **Web** (p.236), or in an **Internet Relay Chat** room (p.231). To natter amongst your friends, you might prefer to use **instant messaging** (p.238). Chat isn't restricted to sending simple text messages either. You can speak by **Internet telephone** (p.241), place a **PC call to**

a normal telephone (p.242) or even set up a **videoconference** (p.243). You'll never feel alone again.

Read the rules, first

However, before you jump headfirst into the rough and tumble of online forums, make sure you're familiar with some of the **accepted codes of conduct**. Read on.

Rules of the game

Apart from your **provider's contract**, the Net has no formal rules. Instead, there are certain established, or developing, codes of conduct known as **Netiquette** (Net-etiquette). These apply mainly to Usenet (p.212).

People who **make complete pigs of themselves** in discussions sometimes get reported to their ISP or news provider, which might result in them losing their account, or even being sued. The address for reporting someone is generally abuse@serviceprovider where *serviceprovider* is the name of their news server or ISP.

But mostly, offenders just get ignored, or **abused**. On the Net, personal abuse is called **flaming**. You don't have to breach netiquette to get flamed – just expressing a contrary or naive opinion should do the trick. When it degenerates into name-calling, it's called a **flame war**. Just about every busy group will have a flame war in progress within one of the threads, and sometimes, for example in the alt.flame.* hierarchy, that's about all that's in there. You'll probably be swinging insults yourself before too long. It's all part of the fun.

But, before you charge in armed with barbs, read the ground rules, so at least you'll know where you stand.

Terms of service

When you sign up with any kind of access provider, whether it's for the complete works, or a Usenet-only account (p.226), you'll have to agree to a few **terms and conditions** in the fine print. These are, needless to say, too boring to read, unless they're someone else's terms and conditions, and you're hoping to get them in trouble. Irrespective of that, these are the **formal rules that apply to your Internet connection**. They're not there to make the Internet a safer place, they're there to protect your provider from being responsible if you run riot. About all you need to know is that if you breach the rules, your provider might cut off your access and force you to look elsewhere. Or worse, if your provider happens to be your office, school or library, you might find yourself out of work, expelled or banned.

The law of the land

Although the Net itself has no law, you're still bound by the laws of your country or state (p.8). So being online doesn't grant you permission to threaten, steal, or libel. **The Net isn't an entirely new country**.

Netiquette – mind your manners

You won't go to jail for breaching the stiff, and often overly proper, codes of conduct that fall under the banner of "**netiquette**" but you'll certainly be lectured. And any protest on your behalf will inevitably lead to a long, heated debate. The first thing to know is as long as you're not breaching your **terms of service**, or **laws of your land**, you can do whatever you like. However, you might find yourself ostracized for exercising your right. On the other hand, if you stick to the following rules, you'll spare yourself the pain and be treated better by the group. It's your choice.

Read the Frequently Asked Questions (FAQs)

Most newsgroups (p.212) have at least one **FAQ** (Frequently Asked Question) document. This should describe the newsgroup's charter, give guidelines for posting, and compile common answers to questions. They should always be your first source of information. FAQs are periodically posted and usually updated every few weeks. You can usually find them by searching **Google Groups** (p.168) or the:

FAQ archive http://www.faqs.org

Post to the right group

It's wise to **get the feel of a newsgroup** before posting. If it's a big group, one session should do, but don't be in a hurry. Read all the **relevant FAQs** first, to ensure your message isn't old hat. Some newsgroupies are not too tolerant of repeats. But that's no rule.

Next, make an effort to **post in the most relevant group**. If you were to ask for advice on fertilizing roses in rec.gardening you might find yourself politely directed to rec.gardening.roses but if you want to tell everyone in talk.serious.socialism about your favorite Chow Yun Fat film, don't expect such a warm response.

Use descriptive subjects

Sum up your Usenet post in the Subject line (p.221) so busy people can instantly see whether they'll want to read or reply. The more detail you can squeeze into the fewest words, the better.

Warn if you might spoil a surprise

If your Usenet message reveals something that might spoil a surprise such as the plot of a film, or the score in a sports match, start the subject line with the word "**Spoiler**", or "**Warning spoiler**".

Mark off-topic posts

When you want to post something that **might interest the group**, but it **doesn't directly relate to the topic** of the group, start the subject with "**OT**" (off-topic).

Be humble

Before you call someone a **retard** or **question their intelligence**, consider that they might indeed have a **mental handicap**, and being able to get it together enough to take part in an online discussion on their favorite sport or hobby might be an achievement in itself.

Bite your tongue

Never post in anger. You'll regret it later, especially when everything you send is archived at Google Groups. And beware of **Trolls**. These are baits left to start arguments or make you look stupid. If someone asks something ludicrous or obvious, says something offensive or inappropriate, or attacks you personally, don't respond. Let it pass. Tread carefully with sarcasm, too, as not everyone will get it, especially those nationalities with no sense of irony. (This is meant to be a joke, but how can you be sure?) As much as you might **frown on smilies** (p.207), they're better than being misunderstood.

Mind your language

Nothing will get you on the wrong side of a discussion faster than **swearing**. You can swear freely (almost) in everyday life, so you might think the same should apply online. You're welcome to try, but it probably won't work in your favor. It's not so much that you'll stand to offend, it's that you'll be set upon by the pious, who'll furthermore delight in complaining to your ISP. Yet if you reduce your 20th century obscenity to an obvious abbreviation, such as F or F★★★, you'll not hear a peep of protest!

Watch your words

Unless you're on a private mailing list, you should consider discussions to be **in the public domain**. That means they could end up archived on the Web. This isn't the case with most mailing lists, and may not even be legal, but it's safer not to test it. Whether or not you appear anonymous, if you threaten or maliciously defame someone, it will be possible to trace and prosecute you under your local laws. Take care not to say anything you wouldn't like to see next to your name on the front page of your local paper.

Don't use all UPPERCASE

NEVER POST IN UPPERCASE (ALL CAPS) unless you're shouting (emphasizing a point in a big way). It makes you look rude and ignorant.

Respect confidentiality

Don't post email you've received from someone else without

their consent. Apart from being rude, it's an illegal **breach of confidence**.

Keep it simple

Express yourself in plain English (or the language of the group). Don't use **acronyms** or **abbreviations** unless they reduce jargon rather than create it. And avoid over-using **smileys** and other **emoticons** (p.207). They spell "newbie". And keep your **signature file** short and subtle. Three to five lines, no ASCII art. Got it?

Don't be a grammar pedant

Everyone makes spelling mistakes and grammatical errors online. Sometimes every time they post. You don't need to point it out, especially when they're not posting in their first language.

Use plain text

Although most email programs and newsreaders can display HTML and Mime Quoted Printable format, expect a lecture if you send a message to a newsgroup or mailing list in anything but plain text. Sometimes it's more appropriate, for example if you're pasting a long URL, but feel the water first.

Posting ads

Having such a massive captive audience pre-qualified by interests is beyond the dreams of many marketeers. Consequently, you will frequently come across **advertisements and product endorsements** crossposted to inappropriate newsgroups.

Spamming (p.131) is the surest way to make yourself unpopular in Usenet. Try and you'll be bombed with hate mail and more than likely reported. In other words, it's not good publicity. As a rule no-one who uses this technique to advertise is reputable, as with those who send mass emails.

If you'd like to make **commercial announcements**, you could try the groups in the .biz hierarchy; after all that's what they're for. The catch is no-one reads them because they're chock-full of the usual network marketing schemes. In other groups, tread more subtly with mentions of your new book, CD, or whatever; otherwise you might come in for a hard time. You can still do it, but only in the right groups and in the right context.

Ironically, nobody minds what you put in your **signature**, so if you put in your Web address it's sure to attract a few visitors.

Chat netiquette

IRC is almost diversity defined. You're as likely to encounter a channel full of Indian expats following a ball-by-ball cricket commentary as a couple of college kids flirting. So long as no-one rocks the boat too much, coexistence can be harmonious. Of course, there's bound to be a little mayhem now and then, but that usually just adds to the fun of the whole event.

However, some actions are generally frowned upon and may get you kicked from channels, or even banned from a server. These include dumping large files or amounts of text, harassment, vulgarity, beeping constantly to get attention, and inviting people into inappropriate channels.

Get in there

These warnings aside – and they're pretty obvious – don't hold back. If you can forward a discussion in any way, contribute. That's what it's all about. **Post positively** and invite discussion rather than make abrasive remarks. For example, posting "Hackers are social misfits" is sure to get you flamed. But: "Do hackers lead healthy social lives?" will get the same point across and invite debate, yet allow you to sidestep the line of fire.

Overall it's a matter of courtesy, common sense and knowing when to contribute. Remember, you're a complete stranger until you post. You'll be known through your words, and how well you construct arguments. So if you want to make a good impression, think before you post, and don't be a loudmouth. If you're a real stickler for rules, read:

Netiquette http://www.etiquette.net

Or if you'd prefer a less conservative approach:

Emily Postnews http://www.psg.com/emily.html

Guide to Flaming http://www.heenan.net/flame/

Usenet Tomfoolery http://www.elsop.com/wrc/humor/usenet.htm

Net language

Before the Internet became a public thoroughfare, it was overrun with academics. The greasy geek types were more likely to be chatting and swapping shareware on the bulletin board networks. Popularizing the Internet brought the two cultures together, along with, more recently, the less digitally versed general public. While the old school types are now in the minority, their culture still kicks on, as witnessed by the continued use of their exclusively online way of expression.

Low transfer speed, poor typing skills, and the need for quick responses were among the pioneers' justifications for keeping things brief. But using Net lingo was also a way of showing you were in the know. These days, it's not so prevalent, though you're sure to encounter acronyms in IRC and, to a lesser extent, Usenet and Mailing Lists. Chat is a snappy medium, messages are short, and responses are fast. Consequently, like CB radio, it's developed its own dialect. Unlike CB, people won't ask your "20" to see where you're from but they might ask your a/s/l – age/sex/location. Acronyms and abbreviations are mixed in with normal speech and range from the innocuous (BTW = by the way) to a whole panoply of blue phrases. But don't be ashamed to stick with plain English, Urdu, or whatever. After all, you'll stand a better chance of being understood.

Shorthand: Net acronyms

AFAIK As far as I know
AOLer AOL member (rarely a compliment)
A/S/L Age/Sex/Location
BOHICA Bend over here it comes again
BBL Be back later
BD or **BFD** Big deal
BFN or **B4N** Bye for now
BRB Be right back
BTW By the way
CUL8R or **L8R** See you later
CYA See ya
F2F (S2S) Face to face (skin to skin)
FWIW For what it's worth
g Grin
GR8 Great
HTH Hope this helps
IM(H)O In my (humble or honest) opinion
IYSWIM If you see what I mean
IAE In any event
IOW In other words
LOL Laughing out loud
MOTD Message of the day
NRN No reply necessary
NW or **NFW** No way
OIC Oh I see
OTOH On the other hand

POV Point of view

RO(T)FL (MAO) Roll on the floor laughing (my ass off)

RTM or **RTFM** Read the manual

SOL Sooner or later

TIA Thanks in advance

TTYL Talk to you later

WRT With respect to

WTH? or **WTF?** What the hell?

YMMV Your mileage may vary

Smileys and emoticons

Back in the old days, potentially contentious remarks could be tempered by tacking **<grins>** on the end in much the same way that a dog wags its tail to show it's harmless. But that wasn't enough for the E-generation, whose trademark smiley icon became the 80's peace sign. From the same honed minds that discovered **71077345** inverted spelled Greenpeace's *bête noire*, came the ASCII smiley. This time, instead of turning it upside-down, you had to look at it sideways to see a smiling face. An expression that words, supposedly, fail to convey. Well, at least in such limited space. Inevitably this grew into a whole family of emoticons (emotional icons).

The odd smiley might have its use in diffusing barbs but whether you'd want to use any of the others is up to your perception of the line between cute and dorky. The nose is optional:

:-) Smiling

:-D Laughing

:-o Shock

:-(Frowning

:'-(Crying

;-) Winking

X= Fingers crossed

:=) Little Hitler

{} Hugging

:* Kissing

$-) Greedy

X-) I see nothing

:-X I'll say nothing

:-L~~ Drooling

:-P Sticking out tongue

(hmm)Ooo.. :-) Happy thoughts

(hmm)Ooo.. :-(Sad thoughts

O:-) Angel

}:> Devil

(_)] Beer

:8 Pig

\o/ Hallelujah

@}-`—,—- Rose

8:)3)= Happy girl

A few others, mostly Japanese anime-derived, work right way up:

@^_^@ Blushing

*^_^* Dazzling grin

^_^; Sweating

T_T Crying

Emphasis

You could also express actions or emotions by adding commentary within < **these signs** >. For example:

<flushed> I've just escaped the clutches of frenzied train-spotters

< removes conductor's cap, wipes brow >.

Or by using asterisks to *emphasize* words. Simply *wrap* the appropriate word: Hey everyone look at *me*.

l33t h4x0r d00dz

When your mouse misleads you into young and impressionable realms you might encounter language that looks like this: "l00k 4t ME. I'M @n L33t h4x0r dUD3." ("Look at me. I'm an elite hacker dude.") To translate see:

http://www.geocities.com/mnstr_2000/

Or better still, back-peddle out of there.

For more

If you come across an abbreviation you don't understand, ask its author. Don't worry about appearing stupid as these expressions aren't exactly common knowledge. Alternatively, consult one of the many online references such as:

Acronym Finder http://www.acronymfinder.com
Emoticon Universe http://emoticonuniverse.com
Jargon and Hacker style http://www.tuxedo.org/~esr/jargon/html/
Microsoft lexicon http://www.cinepad.com/mslex.htm
NetLingo http://www.netlingo.com
Slang Zone http://www.sabram.com/site/slang.html

Mailing lists

If you want email by the bucketload, join some mailing lists. This will involve giving your email address to someone and receiving whatever they send **until you beg them to stop**. Mailing lists fall into two categories: closed (one way) or open. **Closed lists** are set up by some sort of authority or publisher to keep you informed of news or changes. Anything from hourly weather updates to product release announcements. They're **one way only**: you don't contribute. What comes through an **open list**, however, is **sent by its members** – and yes, that could be you.

The purpose of most lists is to broadcast news or encourage discussion about a specific topic – anything from alien abductions to Zimbabwean zoos. In some cases, the list itself forms a group, like a social club, so don't be surprised if discussion drifts way off topic or into personal and indulgent rants. You'll see. But you'll also find lists are an easy way to keep up with news and to meet a few peers, maybe in person, too. People just like you:

Flame Warriors **http://www.winternet.com/~mikelr/flame1.html**

How it works

Each mailing list has two addresses: the **mailing address** used to contact its members; and the **administrative address** used to send commands to the server or maintainer of the list. Don't mix them up or everyone else on the list will think you're a dill.

Most lists are **unmoderated**, meaning they relay messages immediately. Messages on **moderated** lists, however, get screened first. This can amount to downright censorship, but more often it's welcome, as it can improve the quality of discussion and keep it on topic by pruning irrelevant and repetitive messages. It all depends on the moderator, who's rarely paid for the service. Certain other lists are moderated because they carry messages from one source, such as the US Travel Warnings. Such lists often have a parallel open list for discussion.

If you'd rather receive your mail in large batches than have it trickle through, request a **digest** where available. These are normally sent daily or weekly, depending on the traffic.

As discussions are conducted entirely by email, **the only software you need is your everyday mail program**.

Climbing aboard a list

Joining should be simple. In most cases, you **subscribe** by email or through a form on a Web page. It depends who's running the list. Once you're on an open list, you'll receive all the messages sent to the list's address, and everyone else on the list will receive whatever you send. Your first message will either welcome you to the list, or ask you to confirm your email address (to stop prank subscriptions). **Keep the welcome message**, as it should also tell you how to **unsubscribe**, and set other parameters, such as ordering it in **digest format**. You'll need to follow the instructions to the letter. Don't bother **writing a courtesy letter**, as it will only confuse the automated list manager.

Finding lists

Most busy sites publish newsletters (one way lists) to keep you up to date with what's happening in their world – just look for an option to provide your email address. To find open discussion lists, see p.171.

Starting your own list

If you'd like to **create your own public list, private list,** or **discussion group,** see:

Coollist **http://www.coollist.com**

Topica **http://www.topica.com**

Yahoo Groups **http://groups.yahoo.com**

They're free, and simple to manage from the Web. Or if you want to get serious, ask your provider or network manager to set you up a Listserv, Listproc or Majordomo account on their server.

Coping with the volume

Before you set off subscribing to every list that takes your fancy **consider using separate email addresses** for mailing lists and personal mail. Apart from the obvious benefits in managing traffic and filtering, it protects your personal account from **evil spammers** (p.131). If nothing else, you should at least **fil-**

ter your list messages (p.130) accordingly so your high-priority mail doesn't get buried amongst the junk. Remember when posting from your second identity, to ensure you switch mail accounts first. You can select whichever identity you want to post from through the drop-down window in the **From:** bar.

Vacation alert!

If you're trotting off from your mail for a while, consider unsubscribing from your high-volume lists. Otherwise you might face a serious mail jam when you return.

Newsgroups

Would you like a **deep and meaningful discussion** on the matters closest to your heart; an **answer to a question** that's been bugging you forever; to **share your expertise** with others; or just hook up with **people who think like you**? If so, the place for you is Usenet news, the Net's prime discussion area. Don't be confused by its name, it's not about delivering the news as you know it. In this context, news relates to the messages stored in more than 85,000 discussion groups. These groups are called "**newsgroups**", and each one is dedicated to a specific topic.

How it works

A **Usenet newsgroup** is a bit like a **free public notice board**. When you send (post) a message to a newsgroup, everyone who reads that group can see it. They can then **contribute to the discussion publicly** by posting a reply and/or **contact you privately** by email. Normally, however, it's like a public conversation that anyone can join. You can't tell who's reading your messages unless they post. It's possible to read any message, in any group, as long as it remains on your news provider's system. That could be anywhere from a few days to a month depending on the policy it has set for each group.

Web discussions

You'll also come across discussion groups in various guises on the Web. They might be called **message boards**, **guestbooks**, **bulletin boards**, **egroups**, **communities**, or **forums**, but they work in much the same way as newsgroups. That is, they allow you to post a message for other people to read. You shouldn't need help in figuring them out. If it's not immediately obvious, there'll normally be instructions somewhere nearby. You'll find thousands indexed at:

Forum One **http://www.forumone.com**

You can set up your own Web discussion group in minutes at:

Yahoo Clubs **http://clubs.yahoo.com**

What you'll need

Apart from an Internet connection, all you'll need to get Usenet happening on your machine is a **newsreader** (the program you use to view and post to newsgroups) and **access to a news server**. You'll already have a newsreader if you've installed

Outlook Express or Netscape. And, as **most ISPs maintain a news server** as part of the package, you should be ready to go. Just call your ISP's support line or refer to the support section on its homepage to find the address. If your ISP doesn't carry Usenet, you can access it through the Web, via **Google Groups** (http://groups.google.com), but you'll find it slow in comparison. Alternatively, you could seek an account with a specialist news provider (p.226).

Choosing a newsreader

If you're using **Outlook Express** for email, you might as well start with it as your newsreader. It's not the most powerful option, but you'll find it the easiest. **Netscape Messenger** is okay too, but a little more cumbersome and unstable. It's only worth considering if you browse with Netscape. If you're using **Outlook**, you'll need to install Outlook Express, or another newsreader.

Apart from these there are several **dedicated programs** that will give you a **little more control over your sessions**, in exchange for at least twenty minutes of **complete confusion** as you try to unravel their unique ways of doing things. You will definitely need to **spend some time in the help files**. For PCs, try **Agent** from Forté (http://www.forteinc.com). It has two versions: Free Agent, which is free; and Agent, the registered, full-featured, Swiss-army-knife edition.

On the **Mac**, go straight for **MT NewsWatcher** (http://www.best.com/~smfr/mtnw/)

Setting up your newsreader

To start out, you'll need to specify your **news server**, **identity**, and **email address**. It should be part of your initial set-up routine. If not, to add a new Usenet service in **Outlook Express**, open Accounts from under the Tools menu, select "Add News"

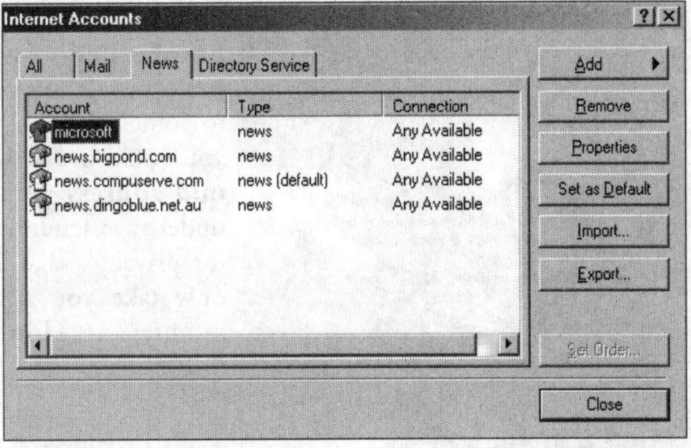

and follow the prompts. In **Netscape Messenger**, open "Preferences" from under the Edit menu, and add your Newsgroup server under Mail & Newsgroups.

Most newsreaders offer a whole bunch of options for how long you want to keep messages after you've read them, how much to retrieve, how to arrange your windows and so forth. Leave those in the default settings and go back when you understand the questions and know your demands. Right now, it's not so important.

Very important – mask your address!

Spammers regularly extract all the email addresses from Usenet to add to their bulk mail databases. Consequently, all savvy users doctor their addresses in an obvious way to fool bulk mailers, but not genuine respondents. For example, **henry@plasticfashions.com** might enter his address profile as **henry@die-spammer-die.plasticfashions.com** or **henry@remove-this-bit.plasticfashions.com**

It's essential to do the same, before you post your first message,

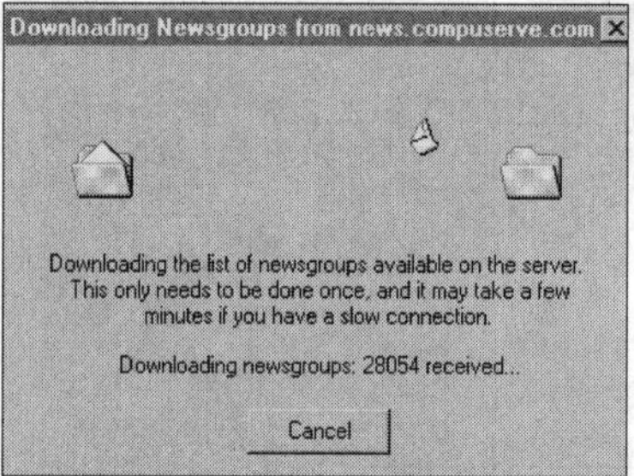

otherwise you'll be **bombarded with junk email** for years to come. Alternatively, you could **use a second address**, perhaps under a pseudonym, for privacy's sake. It'll only take you a few minutes at Hotmail (p.105).

Building a group list

Before you can jump in, you'll need to compile a list of the **newsgroups** available on your server. Your newsreader should do this automatically the very first time you connect to your news server. It's a big file, so expect to wait a few minutes.

As the newsgroups arrive on your list, they'll either appear in a window titled **New Groups** or go straight into the main list (commonly called All Groups). **To compile your newsgroup list** in Outlook Express, go online and click on your news server entry at the bottom of your mail folder list. In Messenger, go online, select the news server entry in your folder list and click on **Subscribe** under the File menu.

How to find a discussion

Newsgroups are divided into specific topics using a simple naming system. You can usually tell what a group's about by looking at its name. The first part is the **hierarchy** (broad category) under which it falls. Here are just some of the top-level and most popular (asterisked) hierarchies:

Hierarchy	Content
alt.	Alternative, anarchic, and freewheeling discussion*
aus.	Australian
bionet.	Biological
bit.	Bitnet LISTSERV mailing lists*
biz.	Commercial bulletins
can.	Canadian
comp.	Computing*
de.	German
k12.	Education through to grade 12
microsoft.	Microsoft product support
misc.	Miscellaneous*
news.	About Usenet itself*
rec.	Hobbies and recreational activities*
sci.	All strands of science*
soc.	Social, cultural, and religious*
talk.	The most controversial issues*
uk.	British

You'll notice **newsgroup names** contain dots, like domain names, however, they work differently. The name tells you what the group discusses, not its location.

The top of the hierarchy is at the far left. As you move right, you go down the tree and it becomes more specific. For instance, rec.sport.cricket.info is devoted to information about the compelling recreational sport that is cricket. Also, though several groups may discuss similar subjects, each will have its own angle. Thus while alt.games.gravy might have light and anarchic postings, biz.gravy.train would get right down to the business.

Browsing the groups

If your ISP has a decent newsfeed you should be faced with a list of at least 20,000 groups. Don't be put off by the volume;

your newsreader can sift through them in a flash. But before you start filtering, scroll down and see what's on offer.

In **Outlook Express**, click on your news server's entry in the folder list. Wait a few seconds for the buttons to appear, and then click on Newsgroups to bring up the **Newsgroup Subscriptions** box. To browse the groups, click inside the Newsgroups window and scroll up and down using your arrow keys or mouse wheel. To filter on the fly, click in the box marked "Display newsgroups which contain" and enter your search term. There's also a further check box option to search the brief descriptions that accompany some groups. You might as well check that box, although it's rarely useful.

In **Netscape Messenger**, select your news server's entry in the folder list and choose Subscribe, either from your right mouse button menu, or under the File menu. Messenger will then take a minute or two to download a message count for all the displayed groups. To browse through the groups, click on the hierarchy folders to reveal the tree below. To search through the newsgroup names, click on the Search tab, enter your query, and click on the Search Now button.

Find the right group

Unlike the Web, newsgroups aren't scattered across the Net in a chaotic mess. Your newsgroups list is effectively a complete directory of Usenet – or at least the part that your news provider carries.

By browsing and filtering, you should see a few groups that look interesting at first glance. However, you won't know whether they contain active discussions, or whether they're appropriate, until you subscribe and check them out. Although you can generally tell what groups are about just by looking at their names, sometimes it's not always so obvious.

There might also be several groups that appear to discuss the

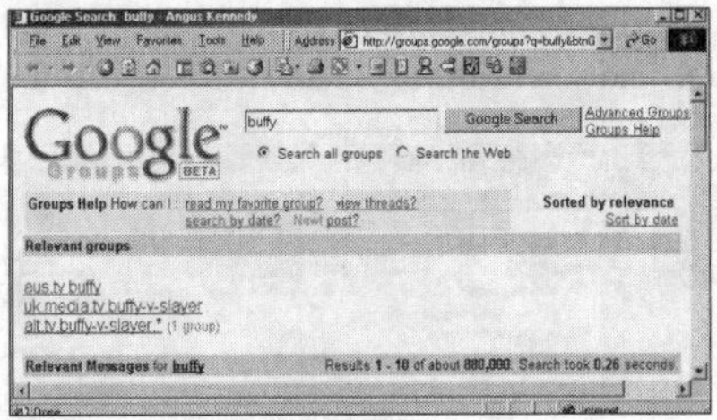

same thing. You'll find, though, there will always be some distinction, or if not, a dominant group. While filtering and browsing is fine for locating groups by their name, it's not always the quickest route. To fast-track the process, run a keyword search at **Google Groups**, take note of the "relevant groups" at the top of the page, and then locate them in your newsgroups list.

Don't overlook the local hierarchies (aus, can, uk, etc) for regional topics such as TV, politics, for sale, employment, and sport. For instance, if you want to find out what happened last week on Buffy in the UK, you might find uk.media.tv.buffy.v.slayer more in tune with your season than alt.tv.buffy.v.slayer

Subscribe to a group

The newsgroup list contains only the group names, not the actual messages. You have to **retrieve the messages** in a separate two-part process. But first you might need to **subscribe** to the group. This simply means putting a newsgroup into a special folder, or marking it in some way, so that it's away from the main list. You might be able to give it priorities, such as automatically updating headers or retrieving all message bodies upon connection, or it might just make it easier to locate. It differs between newsreaders.

To **subscribe to a group in Outlook Express**, click on the news server entry and choose "Newsgroups" from the Tools menu, toolbar or mouse menu. When the list appears, select a group, click **Subscribe**, and then **Goto** to commence downloading the message **headers**. The **headers** contain the message subject, posting date, and contributor's name. They can be threaded (bundled together) by subject, or sorted by date or contributor. Once all the headers have arrived, **clicking on a message will download its body**. You can then read it in the preview panel. If you wish to read the group again, just select it from under the news server folder and wait for the new headers to arrive. To **remove a newsgroup**, choose **Unsubscribe** from your mouse menu.

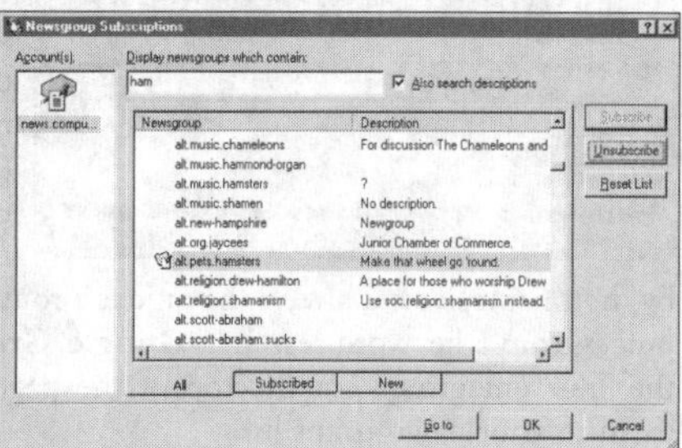

The process is almost identical in **Messenger**. Choose **Subscribe**, from the File menu, open the folders until you find your group, click on **Subscribe**, then close the window. Click on the group to start downloading headers. Selecting a message will download its body and display it in the preview panel.

Other newsreaders, and probably later versions of these, will use a different combination of menu choices to go through the same motions. Refer to the help file for instructions.

Download older messages

Your newsreader might not bring down all the headers from the news server, but only a preset amount. In Outlook Express the default is set to download the newest 300. To download older messages, select the newsgroup and repeatedly choose "**Get**

next 300 headers" from under the Tools menu, or click on the "**Get next headers**" button on the toolbar. You can change the setting to download more, or everything, under the Read tab in Options.

Bundle the threads

When someone posts a message with a new subject it's called "**starting a thread**". Replies to that initial message add to this thread. You'll find it a lot easier to follow discussions if you bundle these threads together. In Outlook Express, place a tick next to "**Group messages by conversation**" under Current View in the View menu.

Watch a thread

In Outlook Express, and most other newsreaders, **unread messages** will have bold headers like unread emails. Once you group the conversations, you'll know when someone's replied because the top message will appear bold. An even better way to tell is to "watch the thread (conversation)". Select any message in the thread, and click on the column to the immediate left with the glasses on top, or choose **Watch conversation** from under the Message menu. This will turn the headers red. When someone replies to your watched threads, the newsgroup entry will also appear **bold red** until you've read the messages. To **mark messages as read**, examine the options under the Edit and right mouse button menus.

You can also flag the threads, or sort by sender, date, subject and so forth, in the same way as email (p.130).

Posting

Posting is like sending email – and equally simple. You can start a new thread, follow up an existing one, and/or respond privately by email.

When you post, most programs automatically insert the newsgroup you're reading in the **Newsgroups**: line. When starting a thread, enter a **subject** that outlines the point of your message. That way it will catch the eye of anyone who's interested or can help. The subject line will then be used to identify the thread in future.

To post a new message in Outlook Express, enter a group and click on the **New Message** toolbar icon or select **New Message** from under the Message menu. The process is identical in Messenger.

To **crosspost** (post a message to more than one group), just add those groups after the first group, separated by a comma, and then a space. Replies to crosspostings are displayed in all the crossposted groups. Crosspost to the wrong groups, or too many groups, and you're sure to get abused or cancelled by one of the roving cancelbots.

Send a test post

Feel free to post whatever you like to any group with test in the name, such as alt.test, or misc.test, but remember not to use your real email address as it might generate a pile of responses, some unwelcome.

Replying

Replying (or responding) is even easier than posting. You can send your contribution to the relevant newsgroup(s) and/or email the poster directly.

It's sometimes appropriate **to reply by email as well as post**, so the original poster gets it instantly. It's also more personal and saves scanning the group for replies. Don't forget to edit the address if they've masked it. They'll normally provide some clue to their real address either in their signature, or within the address. But, of course, if they've used an obviously bogus address – which is very common – there's no point sending an email.

Like email, you also have the option of **including parts or the entire original message**. This can be quite a tricky choice. If you cut too much, the context could be lost when the original post is deleted. If everyone includes everything, it creates a lot of text to scan. Just try to leave the main points intact.

You'll find the various reply options beside or below your **New Message** menu entries in all newsreaders.

Reply above or below?

It used to be taboo to reply at the top of a message (called top posting) until Microsoft made it the default setting. Now only Usenet fundamentalists will chastise you for it. In some ways, it makes more sense to post on top as it saves having to scroll through lines of quoted text. On the other hand, it prevents you from replying to points within the message. Microsoft has also made replying messy by mucking up the indenting and wrapping so that **orphans are created through the replies**. Until it caves into the mounting pressure to rewrite the reply code, long threads will always look untidy. As a rule of thumb, **follow the format of the previous poster**. So if the previous reply is top posted, then likewise post your reply on top. Otherwise, you'll upset the logical thread of the conversation.

Canceling a message

If you've had second thoughts about something you've posted, select it in the newsgroup and choose **Cancel Message** from under the Message menu in Outlook Express or the mouse menu in Messenger. Unfortunately, it won't be instantly removed from every server worldwide so someone still might see it.

Blocking nuisances

If you don't like a certain person on Usenet, you can "plonk" them. If your newsreader has a **kill file**, just add their email address to that, or use your **Filters**. Then you'll never have to download messages they've posted again. You can also trash uninteresting threads in the same way, by setting a delete filter on the subject. But don't make it too broad or you might filter out interesting stuff as well. See:

http://www.kibo.com/kibokill/

Reading Offline

Reading articles one at a time online is convenient, but not if it's costing you to stay connected or you're tying up your only telephone line. Consider **downloading the article bodies along with the headers** to read offline at your leisure.

This is simple in Outlook Express. Before you go online, choose **Work Offline** from under the File menu, select the group, open its **Properties** from under the File or mouse menu, and make your selection under the **Synchronize** tab. Click on the group when you're next online, and choose **Synchronize** from under the Tools menu to retrieve whatever you've sent. Once you're offline, switch to **Work Offline** mode and browse through the articles as if you're online.

Decoding binaries (pictures, programs, audio, etc)

As with email, Usenet can carry more than plain text. Consequently, there are entire groups dedicated to the posting

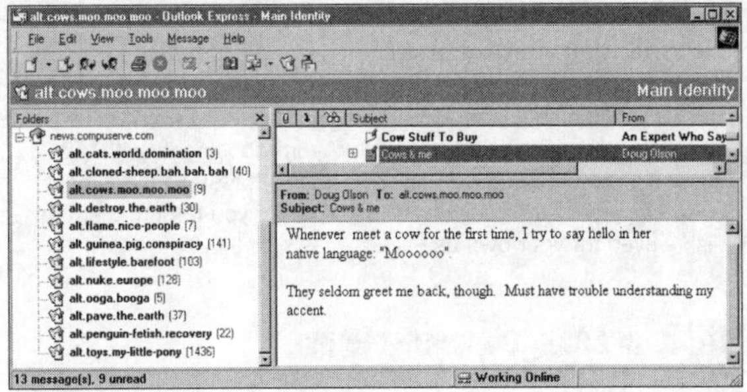

of **binary files** such as images, sounds, patches, and even full commercial programs. Such groups should have **.binaries** in their address.

Again like email, binary files must be processed, most commonly in UUencoding or MIME, before they can be posted or read. This is something you needn't think about, as your newsreader will do it automatically. Sometimes larger files, like movies, get chopped into several messages. Each part will have the same subject heading followed by its number. The problem is sometimes that parts go astray, which makes it impossible to reassemble the file.

Depending on your newsreader, to **retrieve a binary file** you might have to highlight all the parts and decode them in one go. Agent/Free Agent recognizes a set, just by clicking on one part. **Messenger** and **Outlook Express** both decode automatically within the window, but are very slow. You'd be better off with Agent or one of the many newsreaders dedicated to binary decoding.

To decode a multi-part attachment in Outlook Express, select the components and choose **Combine and Decode** from the Tools menu. With some newsreaders, you might need to retrieve the message body and decode in two stages. For other newsreaders, it's best to read your Help file to get it straight.

To **post a binary**, just attach it as in email and your newsreader will look after the rest.

> Warning: Virus check any programs you download from Usenet. Or better still, don't go near them, or Word documents with macros. And just because you can find full PlayStation CDs posted to *alt.binaries.cd* doesn't make it legal for you to burn them to disk – even for your own use.

Getting access to more groups

No news server carries every group. Some groups are restricted to a local geographical area or within one ISP's network. Other groups, which are deemed unpopular or irrelevant, might be cut to conserve disk space, or there might be a **policy to ban certain groups** and hierarchies. The decision on what you see and what you don't falls with whomever supplies your newsfeed.

This is not entirely a bad thing as it takes less bandwidth to keep the Usenet file up to date and thus reduces the general level of Net traffic. And **most providers are flexible**. If, say, your provider has arbitrarily decided to exclude all foreign-language and minor regional groups, and you're interested in Icelandic botany and Indian plumbing, you might be able to get the **groups added to the feed** simply by asking. However, sometimes omissions are due to **censorship**. Many providers remove groups on moral grounds, or to avoid controversy. The usual ones to get the chop are the alt.binaries.pictures.erotica (pornography), alt.sex and alt.warez (software hacking and piracy) hierarchies.

If you can't get the groups you want from your provider, your account doesn't come with a newsfeed (eg, at work), or you have privacy concerns, you needn't resort to another ISP. You could sign up for a **news-only account** with a Usenet specialist, such as:

http://www.newsguy.com

http://www.supernews.com

http://www.usenetserver.com

For help in choosing a **commercial newsfeed provider,** see:

http://www.newsreaders.com

http://www.exit109.com/~jeremy/news/providers/

http://members.tripod.com/~newscompare/

Publicly accessible news feeds are rare and short-lived:

http://www.newzbot.com

http://home1.gte.net/docthomp/servers.htm

Unless you're chasing binaries, you'd do better at **Google Groups**.

Searching Usenet

See (p.168).

How it gets from A to B

Although Usenet messages seem like email, they actually belong to a separate system called **NNTP** (Network News Transport Protocol). Your Usenet provider (eg, your ISP) maintains an independent database of Usenet messages, which it updates in periodic exchanges with neighboring news servers. It receives and dispatches messages anything from once a day to instantly. Due to this pass-the-ball procedure, messages might appear immediately on your screen as you post them, but propagate around the world at the mercy of whoever's in between. Exactly how much newsfeed you get, and what you see, depends on your provider's neighbors and how often they update their messages. Most of the time, these days, it's almost as fast as email.

No provider, however, can keep messages forever, as it needs the space for new ones, so it **expires postings** after a certain holding period. It's usual to delete messages after about four days and even sooner for large groups and **binaries**. Each provider has its own policy.

In addition, some newsgroups are **moderated** which means that postings are screened before they appear. Officially moderated groups are screened by whoever started the group or an appointee, but it's possible, though uncommon, that messages could be censored anywhere between you and the person who posted.

Starting your own newsgroup

With Usenet already buckling under the weight of 85,000+ newsgroups, you'll need fairly specialized tastes to get the urge to start another – plus a smattering of technical know-how. For instructions, see: *http://www.geocities.com/nnqweb/ncreate.html*

Further help

For beginners' guides, and more on Usenet in general, see:
http://www.geocities.com/nnqweb/nnqlinks.html
http://www.newsreaders.com

And for tips and hacks to **enhance Agent**:
http://www.skuz.net/madhat/agent/patch.html

Chat – join the party

You won't really feel the full impact of having instant access to a cast of millions until you jump into your first chat session. You might even find it a touch spooky at first. The way you can type something in, and within seconds, someone replies. Even if chat doesn't quite sound like your sort of thing, at least give it a go once or twice, just for fun.

You'll find Internet chat opportunities at almost every corner, particularly within the Online Services, and increasingly, on the **Web**. AOL and CompuServe are known for their **chat forums**, which often host interviews with notable **celebrities**. You have to be a member, though, to join in. But don't let that bother you because there are ample **chat forums on the Web (p.236)**, and way more again within an entirely separate system called **IRC (p.231)**. Or if you'd prefer to chat amongst your circle of friends, you might prefer to install an **instant messenger** (p.238) or even try your hand at **Internet telephony** and **videoconferencing** (p.241). The possibilities for communication are endless.

If you're only chatting in text, you won't need a particularly fast connection, nor a powerful computer. Voice and video are another matter: the more speed you throw at them, the better they work. Ideally, you don't want to be paying timed **online charges**, because once you're hooked, you'll end up squandering hours online.

How it works

Unlike Usenet and email, on Internet chat, **conversations are live**. Joining a **chat channel**, **chat room** or **chat forum** is like **arriving at a party**. It could be **full of people**, or you might be the first to arrive. Whatever you say in that channel is instantly broadcast to everybody else on the same channel, even if they're logged into a server on the other side of the world. And you can expect them to reply as instantly as if they were in the same room.

Some channels (chat rooms) are obviously dedicated to **specific topics** but most are merely **informal chat lines**. While chat might have business potential in areas such as customer support, it's overwhelmingly orientated to **social banter.** Such idle natter between **consenting strangers** can lead to the online equivalent of **seriously heavy petting**, and inevitably makes it particularly attractive to teens. It can also make it unnervingly confrontational, so tread with caution.

A caution

Of all the Net's corners, chat is the one most likely to trip up newbies – mainly because you can't hide your presence. For example, on Usenet, unless you jump in and post, no-one can tell you've been following the discussion. However, the second you arrive in an IRC channel **you'll be announced** to all and your nickname will remain in the names list for as long as you stay.

If you select someone's name in your channel, and click the right button, you'll be able to find out a little bit about them. Cross-reference that, and you might find out a little bit more. So bear in mind: others might be checking you out in the same way.

Whatever you do, **don't click on files sent to you** by a stranger. This is the most common way of spreading **Trojans** (p.144), which can do all sorts of damage such as hand over your PC to outsiders. While its file extension might say it's a harmless JPG image, it's possible that after the .JPG there's about one hundred spaces followed by an .EXE. In other words, it could be a program in disguise. And **don't rely on your virus checker** to pick them up. The kids on IRC are smarter than that.

As an extra precaution against attacks, install a personal fire-wall, such as **ZoneAlarm** (p.147). It will protect you from any-one trying to access your computer from outside, and alert you to any stealth programs trying to access the Internet from your machine.

For the same reasons, **don't enter any unfamiliar commands at the request of another person**. If someone is bothering you privately, protest publicly. If no-one defends you, change channels. If they persist, get them kicked out by an operator.

IRC

As **IRC** (**Internet Relay Chat**) predates the World Wide Web, up until recently, chatting online required specialized software. With the advent of the Web, and clever use of Java, new users seem to be overlooking the somewhat more arcane world of IRC in favor of the instant gratification of Webchat (p.236) and the instant messaging programs (p.238). Nonetheless, in many ways IRC is the technically superior system. The software gives you far greater control than you could ever expect from a simple Web interface. For this reason it's preferred by the more **techy types**, particularly file traders and Linux eggs. So, if you're hoping to meet your perfect match in IRC, expect them to be at one with computers. Perhaps even a little too much.

Choosing your chat software

Net software bundles often omit a standard IRC program. But that's no problem, you can download one in a few minutes. **mIRC** (http://www.mirc.co.uk) is by far the most popular under Windows, while **Ircle** (http://www.ircle.com) rules on the Mac. For more, check any of the major software archives (p.265).

Getting started

There's not much to configure. First, you'll need to think up a **nickname** for yourself. That's what will identify you in the channel. So if you make it something rude you can expect to be ignored or treated accordingly. Next, you'll have to decide what

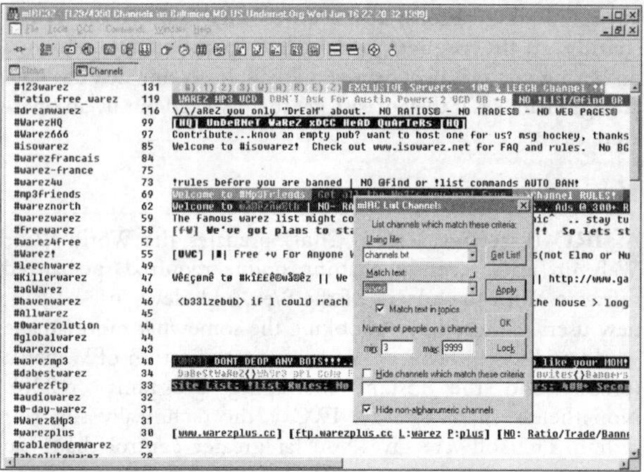

to enter as your **real name** and **email address**. For privacy's sake and to avoid potential embarrassment, stick to an alias. Finally, enter **a chat server address**. You'll probably be offered a choice from a drop-down menu, either within your user options or upon connecting. Experiment with a few and settle on whichever takes your fancy.

If it's not obvious where to enter your details refer to the program's Help files. In fact, it wouldn't hurt to run through any tutorials either. It might sound a bit pedestrian but it will pay off. Chat programs have an array of cryptic buttons and windows that are less intuitive than most Internet programs. And before you start randomly clicking on things to see what they do, **remember people are watching**.

The servers

There are hundreds of open IRC hosts worldwide; many of them linked together through networks such as **Undernet**,

DALnet, and **EFnet**. To ease the strain on network traffic, start with a **nearby host**. The best place to get a fresh list of servers, or indeed any information about IRC, is from the alt.irc newsgroup. But the quickest would be from: http://www.irchelp.org/irchelp/networks/

For starters, choose a host from your chat program's Connect Setup menu or try: us.undernet.org on port 6667.

IRC commands

IRC has **hundreds of commands**, but you can safely get by only knowing a few. However, the more you learn, the more you can strengthen your position. You can almost get away without learning any commands at all with modern programs, but it won't hurt to know the script behind the buttons, and you may even prefer it. Your client won't automate everything, so each time you're online test a few more. The Help file should contain a full list. If not, try any of the Chat help sites such as:

IRC Help http://www.irchelp.org

Chatcircuit http://www.chatcircuit.com

IRC-Chat.org http://www.irc-chat.org

There are far too many commands to list here, but those below will get you started. Note that **anything after a forward slash (/) is interpreted as a command**: if you leave off the slash, it will be transmitted to your active channel as a message and you'll look like a dork.

/AWAY <message> Leave message saying you're not available

/BYE Exit IRC session

/CLEAR Clear window contents

/HELP List available commands

/HELP <command> Return help on this command

/IGNORE <nickname><*><all> Ignore this nickname

/IGNORE <*><email address><all> Ignore this email address

/IGNORE <*><*><none> Delete ignorance list
/JOIN <#channel> Join this channel
/KICK <nickname> Boot this nickname off channel
/LEAVE <#channel> Exit this channel
/LIST <-MIN n> List channels with minimum of n users
/MOP Promote all to operator status
/MSG <nickname><message> Send private message to this nickname
/NICK <nickname> Change your nickname
/OP <nickname> Promote this nickname to operator
/PING <#channel> Check ping times to all users
/QUERY <nickname> Start a private conversation with this nickname
/TOPIC <new topic> Change channel topic
/WHO* List users in current channel
/WHOIS <nickname> Display nickname's identity
/WHOWAS <nickname> Display identity of exited nickname

Step by step through your first session

By now, you've configured your client, chosen a **nickname you'll never use again**, and are raring to go. The aim of your first session is to connect to a server, have a look around, get a list of channels, join one, see who's on, say something public, then something private, leave the channel, start a new channel, make yourself operator, change the topic, and then exit IRC. The whole process should take no more than about ten minutes. **Let's go**.

- ❒ Log on to a server and wait to be accepted. If you're not, keep trying others until you succeed. Once aboard, you'll be greeted with the MOTD (message of the day) in the server window. Read the message and see if it tells you anything interesting.
- ❒ You should have at least two windows available. One for input, the other to display server output. Generally, the two windows form part of a larger window, with the input box below the output box. Even

though your client's point and click interface will replace most of the basic commands, since you probably haven't read its manual yet, you won't know how to use it. So instead just use the commands.

- To see what channels are available, type: **/LIST** You'll have to wait a minute and then a window will pop up, or fill up, with thousands of channels, their topics, and the number of users on them. To narrow down the list to those channels with six or more users, type: **/LIST -MIN 6** Now you'll see the busiest channels.
- Pick a channel at random and join it. Channel names are always preceded by #, so to join the lard channel, type: **/JOIN #lard** and then wait for the channel window to appear. (Clicking on its name should have the same effect in most programs.) Once the channel window opens, you should get a list of the channel's occupants, in yet another window. If not, type: /WHO* for a full list including nicknames and email addresses.
- Now say something clever. Type: **Hi everyone, it's great to be back!** This should appear not only on the screen in your channel window, but on the screen in every other person's channel window. Wait for replies and answer any questions as you see fit.
- Now it's time to send something personal. Choose someone in the channel and find out what you can about them first, by typing: **/WHO** followed by their nickname. Your client might let you do this by just double-clicking on their nickname in the names window. Let's say their nickname is Tamster. To send a private message, just type: **/MSG Tamster Hey Tamster, I'm a clueless newbie, let me know if you get this so I won't feel so stupid.**
- If Tamster doesn't reply, keep trying until someone does. Once you're satisfied you know how that works, leave the channel by typing: **/LEAVE** Don't worry, next time you go into a channel, you'll feel more comfortable.
- Now to start your own channel. Pick any name that doesn't already exist. As soon as you leave, it will disappear. To start a channel called lancelink, just type: **/JOIN #lancelink** Once the window pops up, you'll find you're the only person on it. Now promote yourself to operator by typing: **/OP** followed by your nickname. Others can tell you have channel operator status because

your nickname will appear with an @ in front of it. Now you're an operator – you have the power to kick people off the channel, change the topic, and all sorts of other things that you can find out by reading the manual as recommended. To change the topic, type: **/TOPIC** followed by whatever you want to change the topic to. Wait for it to change on the top of your window and then type: **/BYE** to exit IRC.

That's it really; a whirlwind tour but enough to learn most things you'll need. Now before you can chat with other chatsters, you'll need to speak their lingo. See (p.205).

IRC games

Some chat channels are dedicated to **games**. You might play against other people, but more commonly you're up against programs called **bots.** Such programs are written to respond to requests in a particular way, and even learn from the experience. You'll also come across bots in standard chat channels. It might even take you some time to recognize you're not talking to a human.

For more about IRC games, see: http://dmoz.org/Games/Internet/Chat/IRC/

Webchat

Like almost every other aspect of the old world Internet, chat too has moved onto the Web. Webchat doesn't require a special IRC program. All you need is your Web browser. Because of this, it's becoming more popular than IRC, especially amongst the new arrivals.

Simple Webchat isn't as instant as IRC, as you have to wait a little while for the page to refresh to follow responses. However, most decent Webchat is done through Java, ActiveX or a small program download, which makes it just like a crippled, but foolproof, version of the real thing. And in some cases, you can circumvent the Web interface and log into the server directly with your normal chat program. You only need find out the server address, and then enter the channel name.

Just about all the top line portals, have strong chat facilities, divided by interest and region, coupled with planned events guides and links to chat elsewhere.

About.com **http://chatting.about.com**

Excite **http://chat.excite.com**

Lycos **http://chat.lycos.com**

MSN **http://chat.msn.com)**

Yahoo **http://chat.yahoo.com**

You'll also find chat (or at least a bulletin board) at any site that's attempting to create a community around their content, such as most investment, gaming, and newspaper sites. For more, browse the chat legs of the following directories:

LookSmart **http://www.looksmart.com**

Open Directory **http://dmoz.org/Computers/Internet/Chat/**

Yahoo **http://www.yahoo.com**

What's on

Although most of what goes on in chat rooms is spontaneous, they also play host to loads of organized events, including **celebrity interviews and topical debates**. The big ones tend to hide behind the Online Service curtain but

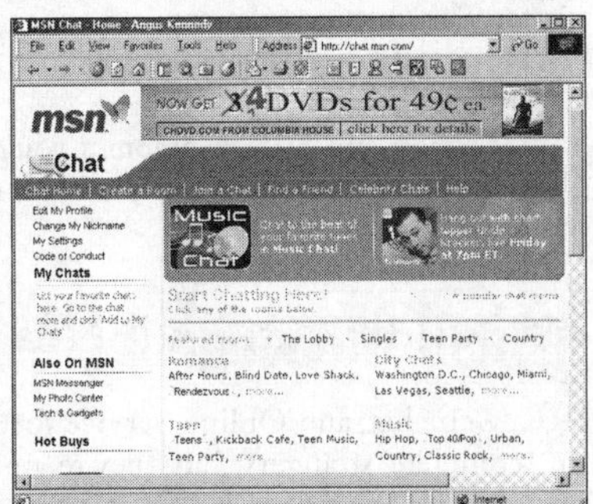

the Net still attracts its share. For a calendar of what's planned across all forms of Internet chat, including the structured Web-based alternatives, such as **Talk City** (http://www.talkcity.com), see **Yack** (http://www.yack.com). Also check the **events guides** at the various portals, such as http://guide.yahoo.com

For a directory of themed, regularly inhabited, and most popular channels across almost 30 networks, see: http://www.liszt. com/chat/

Chat worlds

There's no doubt virtual reality can look quite cute, but there's not much call for it. The best applications so far seem to be among the **chat worlds, virtual cities**, and **avatars**. These tend to work like IRC, but with an extra dimension or two. So rather than channels, you get rooms, playgrounds, swimming pools, and so forth. To switch channels, you might walk into another building or fly up into the clouds. You might be represented by an animated character rather than a text nickname and be able to do all sorts of multimedia things such as build 3D objects and play music.

This all sounds pretty futuristic and it's certainly impressive at first, but whether you'll want to become a regular is another matter. The most popular are:

The Palace http://www.thepalace.com

World's Chat http://www.worlds.com

If it's action and hi-tech graphics you're after, however, ditch chat, and head straight to the world of **Online Gaming**. See p.284.

Instant Messaging (IM)

IRC, Web chat, and Online Service forums are fine for meeting complete strangers, but they're not the best for talking privately amongst friends. If you'd like to corner your pals as soon as they pop online, consider an instant messaging (IM) program.

How they work

nstalling an IM program is a bit like joining a club. Once you're onboard you can **send messages, trade files** and set up **impromptu chat sessions** with other members. Although this sounds a bit like email, it goes a few steps further. For example, once you add someone to your contact (or buddy) list, you can instantly tell when they go online – unless they've chosen to hide their presence. So you can send them a quick note, and expect an immediate reply, or a text, voice or video chat session. If they're not online, you can send a note for them to receive the second they log on. While they're undoubtedly popular amongst the same gossipy set as other chat programs, Internet messengers are also beginning to find their place in the office as serious business tools.

Which one?

You're certainly not starved for choice when it comes to IM software. They are at least four worth investigating, all crammed with goodies beyond sending simple text messages. ICQ, for instance, can even send **SMS messages** to mobile phones. None will cost you any money either. They will, however, cost you plenty of time installing, figuring out how they work and,

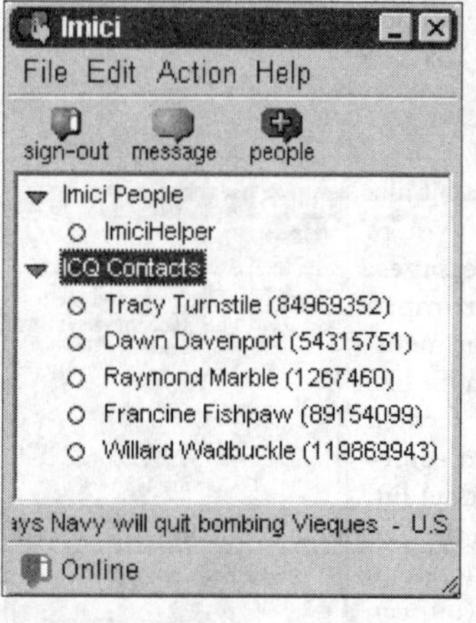

of course, playing message ping-pong. AOL commands the lion's share of the market with **AOL Instant Messenger (AIM)** and **ICQ**, the two most heavily featured, and popular, systems followed by MSN and Yahoo's respective messengers.

AOL Instant Messenger **http://www.aol.com/aim/**
ICQ **http://www.icq.com**
MSN Messenger **http://messenger.msn.com**
Yahoo Messenger **http://messenger.yahoo.com**

At the time of writing, none can communicate with the other, so if your friends have already taken the dive in one direction, you might as well go the same way. However, if your friends are split between two or more, you might prefer the pleasantly simple **Imici**. It can co-operate with all four major systems, without burdening you with any unnecessary bumfluff.

Imici **http://www.imici.com**

The downside

Once the **novelty subsides**, you might find instant messengers to be more of a **nuisance** than they're worth. AIM and ICQ would have to be two of the most notoriously buggy and meddlesome programs in mass circulation. If you find them crashing too often, popping up windows, interfering with your online activities, and/or slowing down your system, disable them from loading at startup. If you tire of being perpetually buzzed by your friends as you're trying to work, opt to hide your presence (invisible mode). And finally, when you're ready to give them the flick, be sure to completely uninstall them through Add/Remove programs in the Control Panel.

Apart from their nuisance potential, and drain on your system resources, they also introduce a new security risk. As with any other medium, never run any files sent to you by strangers, and preferably operate behind a firewall such as **ZoneAlarm.** If you install ICQ, at least read the following:

http://www.icq.com/features/security/

Internet telephony

The concept of using the **Internet as an alternative to the telephone network** is getting some quarters quite frisky – mainly because it can **cut the cost of calling long distance** to that of a local call plus Internet charges (at both ends). It works but don't expect the same fidelity, convenience, or reliability, as your local regular phone network. In other words, give it a go for curiosity's sake, but don't invest any money in it.

To place a Net call through your computer, you need a **soundcard, speakers**, and a **microphone** – standard multimedia fare. If your soundcard permits duplex transmission, you can hold a regular conversation, like an ordinary telephone; otherwise it's more like a walkie-talkie where you take turns to speak. A modem is generally ample for the task but the higher the bandwidths at each end the better your chance of decent sound quality.

Phone programs

You have plenty of choice in **Net phone programs**. Some, like **Internet Phone**, are similar to IRC – you log into a server and join a channel. Others, such as **WebPhone**, are more like an ordinary phone and start a point-to-point connection when you choose a name from a directory. Check into any software archive for a selection (p.265).

Most regard **Microsoft NetMeeting** as the pick of the pack. It has **real-time voice and video conferencing**, plus things like collaborative application sharing, document editing, background file transfer, and a whiteboard to draw and paste on. Plus, it's free. Grab the latest version through Windows Update or from:

http://www.microsoft.com/netmeeting/

Internet to telephone

It's also possible to initiate a call from your PC to a normal telephone at the other end. With **DialPad** (http://www.dialpad.com), you can talk as long as you like to any number in the US, from anywhere in the world, entirely free and call phones worldwide at a cut price rate. **Net2Phone** (http://www.net2phone.com) is similar, but charges within the US.

Calling a phone rather than a PC is a lot more convenient as it means you can call almost anyone worldwide, whether or not they're online. Of course, it's not as convenient as using a telephone at your end, so compare the price with a **discount calling card** and decide whether it's worth the added bother.

Alternatively, there's **Aplio Phone** (http://www.aplio.com), which looks like an ordinary telephone and works similarly except it automatically initiates a call through each end's ISP. The sound is passable, albeit with slight delay, but you'll need to tally the combined cost of both party's Internet access and local call charges, and factor in the cost of the units at each end, to tell whether its cheaper than a discount calling card. It seems unlikely.

Video conferencing

You might like the idea of seeing who you're talking to, but you'll need serious bandwidth to make **Internet video conferencing** any more than a slide show. But if it means seeing live footage of a loved one across the world, perhaps it's worth it. All you need's a relatively cheap video cam, and **Netmeeting**.

10

Download software

So many programs, so little time

Whether you need a browser upgrade, the latest Quake patch, or some obscure CD mastering software, the Internet is the very first place to look. Just about every program that's released nowadays finds its way on to the Net, and most of the time you can download a full working copy. If not, at the very least, you should be able to order it on disk by email direct from the publisher.

What you certainly will be able to find is all the **Internet software** you'll ever need. And the good news is you can download the pick of the crop, for free. Not only that, but you can often upgrade your system and existing software for free. So don't be afraid to replace your starter kit. Once you're online, you can use whatever you like.

File transfer – defined

The operation of copying a file – such as a program, image, movie, or even a Web page – from one machine to another is called a **file transfer**. When it's headed for your machine, it's called a **download**. Normally, downloading simply "**copies**" the file to your hard drive, leaving the original undisturbed. An **upload** is a transfer in the other direction. You need special permission from the server to delete, upload, or change files (p.253).

What you'll need

You won't need any special software to start downloading; you can do almost everything with your Web browser. However, as your demands increase, you might like to investigate the range of dedicated file transfer (**FTP**), sharing, archiving and download management utilities. We'll discuss these in the following pages.

Where to start

The very first thing to do once you've read what follows is to drop into Windows Update (p.58) and pick up the latest browser, mail software, drivers, and security patches (p.146). Next, peruse our list of recommended programs (p.259), and then hit the software guides for more (p.265).

Free and almost free

While the Internet might be a veritable clearinghouse of freely available software, it's not all genuinely free. There are five types of programs you're allowed to use, at least for a while, without paying. They're known as **freeware, adware, shareware, betas,** and **demo programs**.

Freeware

Freeware is provided by its author(s) at no cost to you. It could be a complete program, a demonstration sample with crippled features, a patch to enhance another program, or an interim upgrade. If you like the program, write and thank the developers. It's the least you can do in return.

Adware

Adware is freeware that serves you advertising banners. The banners themselves aren't usually a hindrance, but sometimes the mechanism of getting them to you can cause nasty crashes. Then there's the question of whether they're spying on you. See p.261.

Shareware

Shareware comes with strings attached, which you accept when you install or run the program. Commonly, these may include the condition that you must pay to continue to use it after an initial free trial period, or that you pay if you intend to use it commercially. Sometimes a shareware program, while adequate, is a short form of a more solid or better-featured registered version. You might upgrade to this if you like the shareware, usually by paying a registration fee, in return for which the author or software distributor will mail you a code to unlock the program or its upgrade.

Betas

Betas (and Platform Previews) are distributed as part of the testing process in commercial software development. You shouldn't pay for them as they're not finished products. But they're often good enough for the task, and usually right at the cutting edge of technology. Take Netscape and Internet Explorer betas, for example. They've been the most popular programs ever to hit the Net.

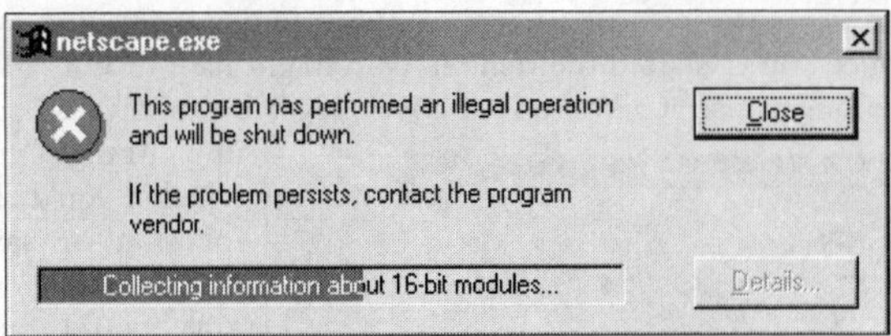

With all betas, expect to encounter **bugs and quirks** now and again and don't be too upset by having to restart the program (or your computer) occasionally – it's all part of the development process. Do report recurring faults to the developers; that's why they let you have it free. If you notice a pattern, email the distributors and ask for a fix. If it's just too buggy, get an alternative.

Demo programs

Demo software is crippled or stripped back to the point that you can see what it does, but if you want to use it, you'll need to order the full program.

Plunder the Web

Most of your downloads will come from the Web. For instance, if you were to read a review of a computer game you can bet your back door it will contain a link to download a demo. To retrieve it, all you should need to do is **click on the link and follow the prompts**. You might have to supply a bit of information, but it all should be self-explanatory. Your Web browser will take care of everything. Well, almost everything, as you'll soon find out.

The download process

Once you've started the transfer, (you might have to wait a little longer than it takes to load a Web page), a window will pop up asking you whether you'd like to **open or save the file**.

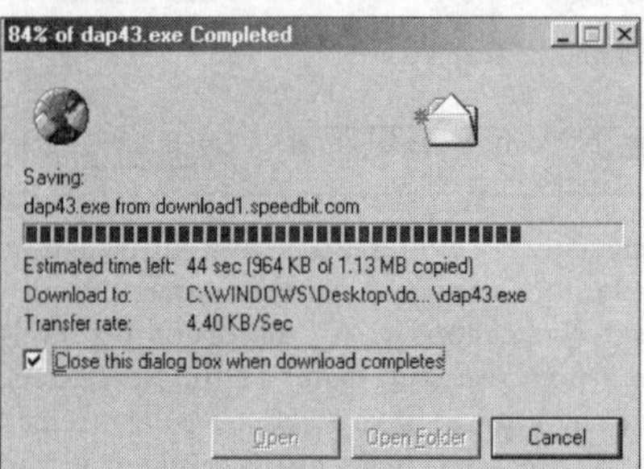

You would only choose open if you want to play or display the file as it downloads. For example, if you're downloading a movie or sound file over a high bandwidth connection.

Otherwise, choose "**Save**" and browse to where you'd like to put it on your computer. The Desktop is usually the most convenient location (see p.253). Once that's done a new window will appear with a running estimate of the transfer rate and time to completion.

The **Mac version of Internet Explorer** will automatically place all downloads in a **Download folder** unless you specify elsewhere within the Receiving Files section of Preferences. It also combines all concurrent downloads into a single **Download Manager** window.

Carry on surfing

There's no reason to down tools while you wait for the download to finish. You can continue to browse the Web, and even start more downloads. Bear in mind, however, that Web pages will take longer to load with a download going on in the background.

How it works

Web pages typically consist of several images laid out on a page of text. So when you load one, you're actually kicking off multiple file transfers – a separate transfer for each element of the page. Your Web browser recognizes the elements are parts of a Web page and displays them in your browser. Now let's say you click on a link to a file that's not normally an element of a Web page, such as a program. When your browser locates the file, it will examine its file type (p.149) and decide it's not meant to be displayed. Because it doesn't know what to do, it will ask you whether to open or save it.

What if it tries to open the file?

If you want to save a file to your hard drive but your browser insists on trying to open it, or display it as a page, rather than click on the link, right-click and choose "Save Target as" from the mouse menu. This often happens with movies and PDF (Adobe Acrobat) files. You can prevent it from happening in future by adjusting the offending program's settings.

FTP or HTTP – huh?

You don't need to understand the protocols used for transferring files on the Internet, but you're sure to bump into the terminology. The two most used for downloading are **HTTP** (HyperText Transfer Protocol) and **FTP** (File Transfer Protocol). About all you need to know is that HTTP is handled by a **Web server**, and FTP by an **FTP server** (see p.251). If you're presented with alternative links for either protocol, flip a coin.

Resume downloads

As downloads can take some time – hours, even, if it's a big program and your link is slow – it's helpful if your transfer program supports **resume downloads**. Then if you drop out, you can go back and pick up where you left off. That's a real lifesaver if you're 90 percent through downloading a 35 MB game demo. Netscape and Internet Explorer are supposed to support resume downloads, but it rarely works in practice. All the more reason to get a dedicated **download manager.**

Download managers

If you're serious about downloads, get a download manager, such as **Download Accelerator** (http://www.download accelerator.com), which is available free of charge, or **Mass Downloader** (http://www.metaproducts.com), which is shareware. Both integrate into your mouse button menu, but Mass Downloader is a little more powerful in that it can leech all the links in one action. You can assign them to take over whenever they detect a file download of a certain type such as .zip, .exe, or .mp3.

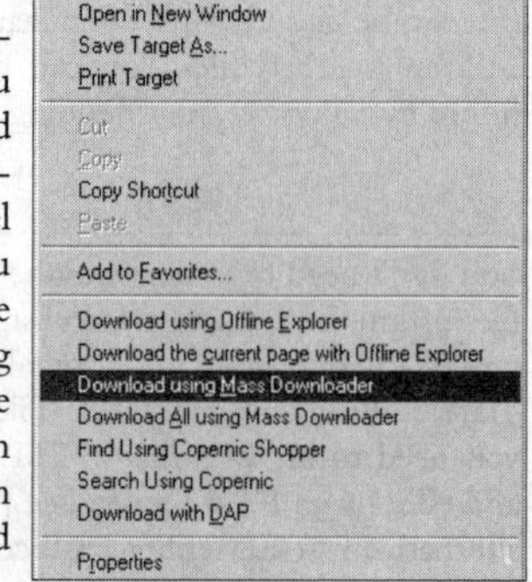

They can search for alternative locations and tell you which one is quickest, and speed up downloads considerably by setting up parallel transfer streams. And if you break the transfer it can take over where it left off (as long as the server supports resume downloads). Experiment with the option of letting them monitor your clipboard and browser clicks. But you might find they get in the way and prefer to just call them up as needed. There are plenty of similar products, but steer clear of Go!Zilla, which causes nasty crashes in Internet Explorer.

FTP Servers

Only a couple of years ago, most of your downloads would come from dedicated FTP servers. They still exist, but more and more files are being stored on the Web. Nonetheless, FTP still plays an important role in storing and moving files about the Internet.

FTP programs

While you can use your Web browser or download manager to handle your FTP downloads, serious FTP heads prefer dedicated FTP programs, especially if they're **uploading files** such as Web pages. You'll find a wide choice on offer at any of the major file archives (p.265). None are anywhere near as easy as using a Web browser. You'll definitely need to **read the Help file**.

FTP addresses

FTP domains are often prefixed by ftp. but that's not a rule. When you're supplied a file location it could be in the form ftp.fish.com/pub/dir/jane.zip That tells you that the file jane.zip is located in the directory pub/dir on the ftp.fish.com server. You can enter that address directly into your Web browser to start the download process. If the file isn't there, you'll see some kind of error message. You can try browsing the server to see if it's moved by removing the file's name (jane.zip) from the end of the address – in the same way you'd look for a missing Web page

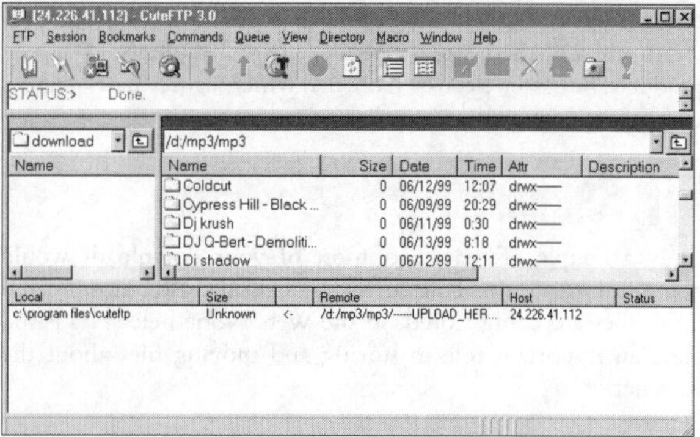

(p.172). However, not all servers will let you browse. You'll soon find out.

Logging into an FTP server

Unless you've been granted special permission to log into an FTP server to transfer files, you'll have to use one that permits **anonymous FTP**. Such sites follow a standard log-in. Once you're in, you can look through the contents of a limited number of directories and transfer files to, and sometimes from, your computer.

Many **Net servers** have areas set aside for anonymous FTP. Some even carry massive specialist **file archives**. And most **software houses** provide updates, patches, and interim releases on their own anonymous FTP sites. No single server will have everything you need, but you'll soon find favorites for each type of file. Your ISP should have an FTP area, too, where you can transfer files for updating Web pages, download access software, and exchange files with colleagues.

Browsing an FTP server

You can browse an FTP server in much the same way as your own hard drive, except under the restrictions set by the administrator. Once you're accepted onto the server, you'll see a listing of the initial directory's contents. Look for a contents file called **readme, index**, or the like. That should tell you what's in the folder.

Uploading files

Unless the owner has specifically granted you permission, you won't be able to upload, rename, delete, or move files on a remote server. This is called "**read only**" access. In essence, this means you can "read" but you can't "write" or delete. Site administrators can fine-tune these permissions in all sorts of ways. For instance, if you're building your own Web site, and you need to upload new pages, you'll have to enter a password to gain "write" access.

You can upload through your Web browser but it's simpler with a dedicated program. You'll need to log into the site, probably with a legitimate user name and password, switch to the directory and start the transfer. With most programs it's as simple as dragging and dropping the file. Check your Help file if it's not obvious.

Set up your folders

Before you start installing every Internet program you can find, sort out your **folders**. Otherwise, you'll make a jungle of your hard drive.

Hard drives are organized into tree-like structures. In DOS, UNIX and Windows 3.x, each level is called a **Directory**. In Macs and Windows 95/NT and later, it's called a **Folder** – they mean the same thing. For simplicity's sake we'll call them folders. The top level of a drive is called the **Root**. It's for system start-up files only, so don't lob anything in there. No matter what system you're running, you should use the following first-level folders:

Programs

Install all **programs** into their own separate subfolders under a first-level folder called **Program Files, Apps**, or similar. Most Windows programs will install themselves by default in the Program Files folder. It's wisest to take that choice if possible, as it's less likely to cause problems later.

Download

Configure your **browser, newsreader and download managers** to download to a common **Download folder** and create a shortcut (alias) on your desktop to open it. Think of it as an in-tray and clear it accordingly. Alternatively, save files onto your **Desktop**, but deal with them straight away.

Temporary

Once you've downloaded the installation program, extract it to an empty **Temporary folder** and then install it under the **Programs hierarchy**. Once done, delete the contents of the Temporary folder. If you have space, keep the original installation file in case you need to re-install it. Put it in your **Archive** folder.

Archive

Rather than clog up your Download folder, create a dedicated **Archive folder** with enough **subfolders** to make it easy to find things again. As you download new versions of programs, delete the old one.

You could open your archive to your peers through an FTP server or a file-sharing program like Gnutella. It should be the first place to delete files to make space.

Data

Put irreplaceable files, such as those you create, into a **Data folder** tree (such as My Documents) and regularly back it up onto another medium such as a floppy disk, Zip drive, CD, or onto the Web. If you're short of disk space, use WinZip or Stuffit to compress it all into manageable chunks.

Free storage online

Need somewhere to stash your most precious files for safekeeping, to free up some room on your hard drive or backup your iMac? Then, see:

FreeDrive http://www.freedrive.com
Xdrive http://www.xdrive.com

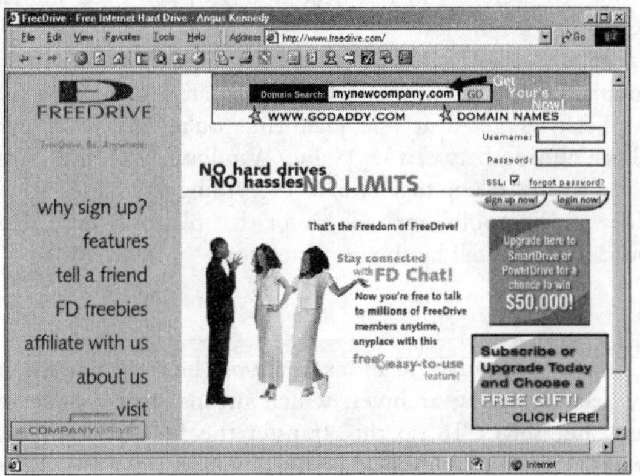

Send a file to a friend – alternatives to email

If you use an **instant messenger (p.238)** to stay in touch online, rather than attach files by email, try sending them point to point. It's more efficient. Look for the option under the right-click menu.

Alternatively, set up a file-sharing server on your system, or an online drive as mentioned above, and let them log in and grab it. **Whalemail** (http://www.whalemail.com) is another online drive with a twist. It's set up specifically for sharing files. Upload your file, submit your contacts, and it will send your friends the download address.

File types and compression

There are two good reasons to compress files. One is to decrease their storage demands, the other to reduce transfer times. After you download a compressed file, you must decompress it to get it to work. Before you can decompress it, you need the right program to do the job.

In general, it's easy to tell which technique has been used by looking at the file name or where it's located. Unless the site is specifically targeted at one platform, you're usually offered a **folder choice** between DOS, PC/Windows, Mac, and UNIX. Once you've taken that choice everything contained in that folder and its subfolders will be for that platform only. If not, you can usually tell by the file extensions.

PC archives

PC archives mostly end in .exe or .zip. The .exe files are usually self-extracting archives, which means they can decompress themselves. To do this, transfer the file to a temporary directory and double-click on it. If you're on a PC, get the latest copy of **WinZip** (http://www.winzip.com), and the latest **Aladdin Expander** (aka **Stuffit Expander**) for Windows (http://www.aladdinsys.com) and place their shortcut icons on your desktop. The great thing about this combination is that it will handle just about everything, including files compressed on Macs. And it's easily configurable to extract archived files automatically just by double-clicking on them in Explorer, or by dropping them onto the Stuffit or WinZip icons.

Mac files

Compressed **Macintosh files** usually end **.bin, .cpt, .sit, .sea,** or .hqx. The .sea files **self-extract** by clicking on them, the rest by dropping on, or opening with **Stuffit Expander**.

If you're **expanding a Mac file for PC use**, set the options under Cross Platform to "convert text files to Windows format when the file is known to contain text" and "never save files in MacBinary Format".

Internet Explorer will **automatically decode** MacBinary and Binhex files unless you specify otherwise within Download Options in Preferences.

Stock your toolbox

Don't expect your browser or operating system to be able to open every type of file you throw at it. You might need some more software. For our pick of the essentials, see (p.259).

File extensions and decompression programs

The following table shows some common **file extensions** and the **programs needed to decompress** or view them. For a list of every file format in the world, see:

http://whatis.techtarget.com/fileFormatA/

Extension	Filetype	Program to decompress or view
.ace	ACE	archiveWinAce, WinRAR
.asf	Advanced	Windows Media Player streaming format
.bin	MacBinary	MacBinary, usually automatic in Macs
.bmp	Bitmap	Graphics viewer
.cab	Cabinet file	Winzip
.cpt	Mac Compact	Compact Pro, Stuffit Expander Pro archive
.doc	MS Word	Word processor such as MS Word document or Wordpad
.exe	PC executable	Self executing from DOS or Windows
.gif	Graphic	Graphics viewer Interchange Format
.hqx	Mac BinHex	BinHex, Stuffit Expander
.jpg	Compressed graphic	Graphics viewer
.mov	Quicktime movie	Quicktime Player
.mp3	MP3 audio file	Media player
.mpg	Compressed video	Media player
.pls	MP3 playlist	Media player
.pdf	Portable Document File	Adobe Acrobat
.pit	Mac PackIt	PackIt
.ra,.ram	RealAudio	RealPlayer
.rar	RAR compressed archive	WinRAR, WinACE
.sea	Mac Self-extracting	Click on icon to extract archive
.sit	Stuffit compressed	Stuffit Expander archive
.txt	Plain text	Notepad, text editor, word processor
.wav	WAV audio file	Media player
.wma	Windows media file	Windows Media Player
.uu, .uue	UU-encoded	WinZip, Stuffit Expander
.zip	ZIP compressed archive	WinZip, Stuffit Expander

Watch out for viruses

Remember to always examine incoming files for bogus extensions (p.149) and scan for viruses before opening (p.147). You don't need to scan your whole system, just the file.

Software roundup

Now that Web browsers have become such Internet software lucky dips, it's no longer so important to scout around for accessories, and you certainly needn't pay for some "Internet made easy" kit. All the same, even though you can get by with the bare bones, there's no reason to rough it. One way to stack up with Net software is to install it from the free CDs given away with PC rags. A better way is to get the latest versions fresh from the Net. You could start by poking your snout into the software troughs listed on (p.265). But before you trot off there, read this section, and get set with the crucial downloads first. They're all free – at least for a limited time – though some have superior commercial versions.

Downloading, installing, and uninstalling

Downloading a program from the Net should be relatively painless. Just go to its developer's **Web page**, read about it first, decide whether it sounds useful, and if so, fill in any required details, and pick the appropriate version for your system.

It's good laboratory technique to download everything onto your **Desktop** or into a central folder called, say, "download". Once the program's downloaded, copy it to a temporary folder for installation. After it's installed, delete the contents of the temporary folder and either shift the original file into an archive or delete it. (See p.253).

Most files will **self-extract**, so installation should be as simple as following the prompts. If not, you'll need an archiving program such as **WinZip** or **Aladdin (Stuffit) Expander** (see p.256) to extract the installation files. Once extracted, read the accompanying text files for installation instructions. It's usually a matter of clicking on a file called "install.exe" or "setup.exe" in Windows, or on an install icon on the Mac. Try it for a few days. If it doesn't serve a purpose, remove it from your hard drive so you don't clog up your system with rubbish. In Windows, that means deleting it from within **Add/Remove Programs** in the Control Panel. If there's no entry in there, look for an uninstall icon in its Start menu folder. If neither exists, it will be safe to delete the file directly from its folder. Note that some programs will hijack your file associations, so to get file types to open automatically with a previous program you might have to go into that program's settings or simply reinstall it.

Most programs now offer the option to automatically check for updates. However, it's a common source of **mystery crashes** so switch it off and check manually.

Windows Update – browser update

Your first concern will be to make sure your system has what it takes to dial up, connect to your ISP and then jettison you onto the Web. Your next operation should be to **update your browser** to its latest version, bring your operating system up to date, and, if you like, gradually try some added extras. If you're running Windows with Internet Explorer, you can do it all through Windows Update (see also p.58). Check back at least once every couple of weeks:

Windows Update http://www.windowsupdate.com

Update your drivers

To get the best from your hardware, grab all the latest device drivers – especially for your video card and modem. You'll find the newest drivers at the component manufacturer's Web site, or sometimes at your PC maker's site. They're normally located in the support section. Look for "files", "downloads" or "drivers", and follow the prompts. Alternatively, try one of the driver guides (p.267).

What to avoid – protect your privacy

It seems few people will pay for software if they can avoid it. Run a search on "crack" or "serial no" in any search engine, or check into **AstaLaVista** (http://www.astalavista.com) and you'll soon see how rife pirating has become. As a result, Internet software developers have been forced to prostitute their programs to ad serving networks and marketing sharks. At first glance this free **"adware"** alternative to full-featured registered software might seem a happy marriage – the advertisers get exposure, the marketers get their stats, the programmers get paid and you get the product for nix. Unfortunately, it's rarely that clean cut, and those **pesky ad banners** are the least of your worries.

Gibson Research (http://grc.com/optout.htm), for example, has gone as far as labeling it **"spyware"** accusing the ad hustlers of all sorts of privacy infringements including tracking your online activities and calling home with the results. At the time of writing these allegations are a little on the wild side, with little concrete supporting evidence, but they're still plausible. And like all the best conspiracy theories, it's easier to prove guilt than innocence.

Invasion of privacy, however, is only half the story. Adware is also notorious for **crashing your system**. And some leave behind active remains after they're uninstalled, further adding to your woes.

On an even more cynical note, the adware concept has also sparked off a rash of **useless programs** that are little more than purpose-built ad servers or data collectors. You can usually spot them because they sound like "as seen on TV products" – that is, they're designed to sell, not to use. Don't even consider installing anything that claims to **accelerate your browser**, **optimize your modem**, enhance your **mouse cursor**, or **serve extra information on the sites you visit**. Your browser is touchy enough as it is, without adding more junk to it. You especially do not need **search aids that integrate into the browser**.

You'll find **RealNetworks** and **AOL/Netscape** will aggressively thrust third-party software your way during updates. Say no to it all. Read independent reviews before you download anything, and get it straight from the source.

If the prospect of browsing the Web entirely ad-free sounds appealing, try **Adfilter** (http://www.adfilter.co.uk) or **WebWasher** (http://www.webwasher.com). They can automatically cull ad banners and pop-ups, which might even speed up your session. The downside is they could also cut useful information, or disable critical tasks like Windows Update. Take care.

Detect and remove "spyware"

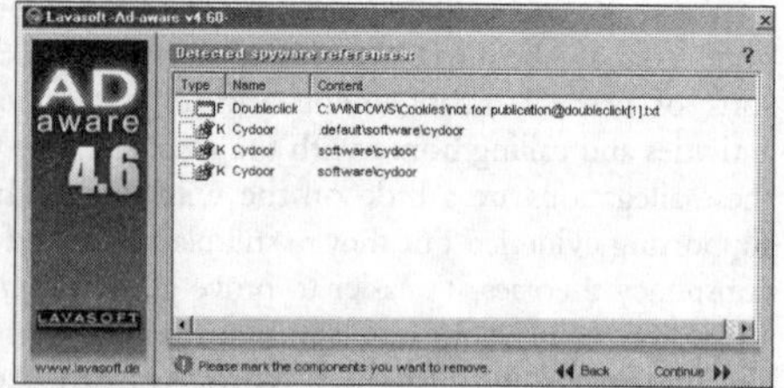

The nastiest side effect of so-called spyware is that their parasites often remain on your system even after you've uninstalled the overlying product. These often cause weird behavior such as crashes and improper shutdowns. If your system is playing up, it wouldn't hurt to clean out any spyware to see if it helps. Look no further than **Ad-aware** (http://www.lavasoft.de). It can scan your memory, registry, and hard drives for known spyware, and allow you to selectively remove the ad systems. Of course, removing the ad systems might disable the associated program, so before you remove them you'll have to weigh up the alternatives.

Wrap up in a security blanket

As mentioned tirelessly throughout this book, unless you want to expose yourself to a multitude of security risks, you'll need to keep your system up to date, run all incoming files through a fine toothed comb, and install a firewall (p.147). Just follow the instructions starting on p.142.

PDF – portable document files

You're sure to encounter the odd portable document file (PDF), particularly at government sites. These are like laid-out brochures, and can be viewed within your Web browser using **Adobe's Acrobat Reader** (http://www.adobe.com/products/acrobat/) plug-in. They're supposed to display inside your browser, but they're just as likely to crash it. Because PDFs can contain fonts and images, they're often quite bloated compared to their Word or Word Perfect equivalents. It's better to click on the link, choose "Save target as" from your mouse menu, save them to your Desktop and then click on the file to view. If you don't mind the Reader launching automatically, but not embedded within your browser, open Adobe Acrobat, choose General under Preferences in the File menu, and uncheck the box "Web browser integration". To launch the "Save as" dialog box instead (preferable), amend your Windows file settings. In Windows 98, open My Computer, click on Folder Options under the View menu and go to the File Types tab. Select Adobe Acrobat under the Registered File Types and then click the Edit button. Uncheck the option to Browse In Same Window. Under Windows ME, Folder Options is under the Tools menu. Select PDF under the File extensions, click on the Advanced button and check the box to "confirm open after download".

Sort out your media players

Next sort out your media players, image viewers, and plug-ins. For both PC and Macs, grab the latest versions of:

Shockwave http://www.macromedia.com/shockwave/

RealPlayer http://www.real.com

Windows Media Player http://www.windowsmedia.com

QuickTime http://www.quicktime.com

This will cover all the popular music and video formats, at least twice over, but you might still prefer to switch programs. You'll be able to assign what plays what within each program's settings. Alternatively, if you'd like a program to take over, just reinstall it. For a rundown on the various music players, see p.271.

It's also handy to have some **image viewing and editing software** so you can flick through saved pictures and fool around with them. Try **ACDSee** (http://www.acdsee.com) as a viewer and set it to associate with all image formats. The full release becomes inoperative after 30 days, whereas the Classic version merely nags you to register. **Irfanview** (http://www.irfanview.com) is a free alternative, but is not quite as polished. If your editing demands run a bit higher, try **Paint Shop Pro** (http://www.jasc.com), the next best thing to Adobe's professional, though somewhat overpriced, PhotoShop.

Manage your downloads

Although Internet Explorer will resume failed transfers (sometimes) it's not a feature that's either reliable or well implemented. If you find yourself downloading frequently, you'll soon appreciate the benefits of a trusty Download Manager that can queue up and schedule, set up multiple streams, and of course, recover dropped transfers. Oddly, there's one built into the Mac version of Internet Explorer, but not the PC version. There are plenty of PC options but none can be recommended without reservation, particularly those that fall into the adware category. Try **Download Accelerator** (http://www.downloadaccelerator.com) and **Mass Downloader** (http://www.metaproducts.com) first. (See p.250)

Other Internet software

Despite Microsoft, AOL, Netscape and Real Networks, there's still competition left in the boutique end of the Internet software trade. You'll find numerous standout programs mentioned within the relevant sections throughout this book, but of course, there are many more, and new strains appear daily. So don't take our word for it. If you become embroiled in Usenet, for instance, investigate several newsreaders and ruthlessly toss them out if they fail to meet your expectations. Check into any of the following software guides and you'll be sure to leave with a few downloads in progress!

Software guides

When it comes to software, your biggest problem won't be finding it, but **narrowing down the choices**. That's why you'll need to turn to a software guide for assistance. These sites **list, review** and **rate programs**, and sort them into various **categories**, to make it easier to find the best tool for each job.

So where do you start? Try one of the megasites such as **Download.com**. You might be best browsing through a different one every session to see what you can find. None of them will list every program, even within one category, nor can they hope to keep up with the features changed in every release. That means the reviews are prone to going out of date or being superceded by a more recent program. Nonetheless, they do make an effort, and usually, it's enough.

Megasites – All platforms

C|Net Download.com http://www.download.com

Jumbo http://www.jumbo.com

Software Vault http://www.softwarevault.com

ZDNet Hotfiles http://www.hotfiles.com

PC-only

Rocket Download http://www.rocketdownload.com

Simtel http://www.cdrom.com

Slaughterhouse http://www.slaughterhouse.com

Winfiles http://www.winfiles.com

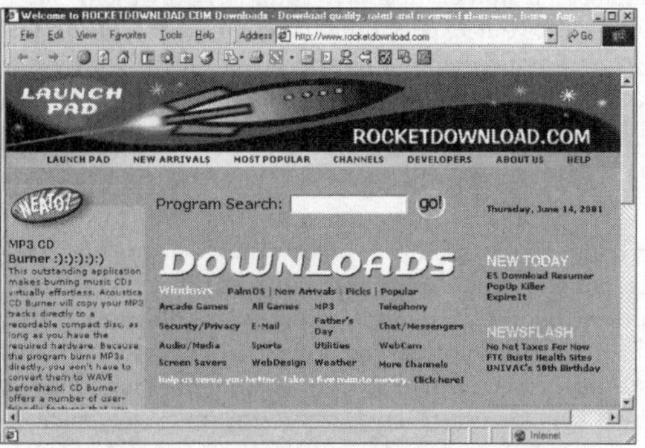

Mac-only

Chez Mark http://www.chezmark.com

Hyperarchive http://hyperarchive.lcs.mit.edu

Mac Orchard http://www.macorchard.com

Pure Mac http://www.pure-mac.com

Version Tracker http://www.versiontracker.com

Internet software

Dave Central **http://www.davecentral.com**

Stroud's **http://www.stroud.com**

Tucows **http://www.tucows.com**

Freeware

Freeware **http://www.freewarehome.org**

Moochers **http://www.moochers.com**

No Nags **http://www.nonags.com**

Son of Spy **http://www.homestead.com/sonofspy/files/**

Tweaking your system

Tweakfiles **http://www.tweakfiles.com**

Locating hardware drivers

http://www.windrivers.com

http://www.driverforum.com

http://www.drivershq.com

http://www.driverguide.com

Find an alternative site

If you know the name of the file, or you need an alternative download location, try searching:

Copernic **http://www.copernic.com**

FTPfind **http://www.ftpfind.com**

Lycos **http://ftpsearch.lycos.com**

Shareware.com **http://www.shareware.com**

11

Turn on the music

Listen live, or play it later

You can sometimes learn more about someone by rifling through their records than knowing how they paid for them. Which might explain why back in the early days of vanity home page publishing, when the Web was anarchistic and thoroughly geeky, listing your entire music collection was deemed cooler than posting your résumé.

Back then it wasn't practical to put audio samples online. Digitized music eats buckets of bytes, which makes it time consuming to download – especially with the old 14.4Kbps modems. But since then technology has advanced. Both in the speed at which we connect, and in the way we store music. As a result, people can now place their actual collections online, much to the anguish of the music biz.

How it works

Music as it's stored on a CD is too bulky to put online. A minute of sound needs roughly 10 megabytes of disk space. Which means a four-minute track could take more than three hours to download with a 56K modem. But thankfully, there are several techniques that can compress the music to eat less space, thus making it quicker to transfer. Which one you'd use would depend on whether you want to listen to the music live (**streaming**) or download it to your computer and play it later (**MP3**). For more, see: http://www.howstuffworks.com/mp3.htm

Stream it live

Getting music to play in real time over a modem connection takes some pretty clever footwork in the **audio compression** department. Put very simply, this involves stripping out the bits that matter least to your ears. The catch is the more you take out, the worse it sounds.

An online radio station can only work with as much data as it can transfer live across your connection. So **the slower the connection, the lower the fidelity**. But just because you have a nice clean fast connection doesn't mean you'll get better sound. The files are encoded at a fixed rate low enough to cater for the average connection speed.

Sometimes, though, there'll be separate choices for low and high bandwidth connections. If you choose high bandwidth over a modem you won't be able to download the data fast enough to play it live. It will take ages to load and then drop out constantly. The same will happen if you choose low bandwidth and there's too much traffic between you and the server. Because heavy traffic and packet loss is a way of life on the Net, most players "**buffer**" a small amount of data in advance to cover up intermittent hiccups. You can set the buffer in the player's options. But normally once you've entered your connection speed at setup, you shouldn't need to worry about it again.

As you can imagine, this amount of audio compression takes its toll on fidelity. So when you tune into Radio Nova (http://www.novaplanet.com) across the Net, it won't sound as good as straight off the radio in Paris. But you might be surprised that it doesn't sound too bad either. Somewhere **between AM and FM** is a fair comparison.

Play it again with MP3

Tinny sound might be okay for taste-testing CDs at Amazon, or when it's your only chance of hearing a foreign station, but there are better options if you have time to download the tracks. The one that's all the rage right now is **MP3**. It sounds much better than streaming audio because it's not as compressed. This compression level is called the **bitrate**. It tells you the average number of bits used to store one second of audio data. The more bits you use, the better it sounds, but the longer it takes to download.

Most MP3s on the Net are encoded at a bitrate of **128 Kbps**. This isn't far off **CD quality**. You won't be able to tell the difference over your PC speakers, but you might if you play it through your home stereo. A four-minute track recorded at 128 Kbps would need 3.8 megabytes. So with a 56K modem, this should take less than twenty minutes to download. MP3s can be encoded at a range of rates, depending on the quality required.

Here's the catch

While it's fine to rip MP3s from your own CDs and listen to them on your PC or portable MP3 player, unless the artist or publisher has granted you express permission, **it's illegal to distribute these copies or post them to your Web site.** That means most of what you find through file-sharing agents like **Napster** is in flagrant breach of copyright. In practice, if you're caught lobbing a few MP3s onto your Web site you might simply be told to pull them down. But if you're caught attempting to profit from them, you'll almost certainly be prosecuted. So irrespective of whether you believe exposure through illegal copying might increase sales to the benefit of all, beware that it could land you in the stew. If you need the point belted into you, see: **http://www.riaa.com** and **http://www.bpi.co.uk**

Load up with software

Before you can listen to anything, you'll need the right playing software. See what you already have and then build from there. Make sure your speakers work, and go online. The main formats in order of popularity are **RealMedia, MP3, Windows Media, QuickTime, Streaming MP3**, and **Liquid Audio**. The annoying part is the main players will happily take over playing all these formats (and more), but they most likely won't do them all properly. You're better off installing a few players and assigning the formats to whichever player handles them best. You might already have enough to get started, as most are optional add-ons with browser installations. While some of the following have commercial versions, you should download the free options first.

RealPlayer

Let's start with **RealMedia**. This incorporates both RealVideo and RealAudio, the formats most commonly used for live radio and television broadcasts, and music samples at online CD shops. Drop by the **Real.com Guide** (http://realguide.real.com) and click on one of the broadcasts. Does it call up the **RealPlayer**? If not, click on the link to download the player and install it. When it asks which formats it should play, let it take over everything for the time being. You can always change it back later. If you already have the player, click on the option under Help to update it to the latest version. Forgo investigating **RealJukebox**, its MP3/CD player and playlist organizer, until you've tried **MusicMatch Jukebox** (see p.274).

Windows Media

If you're running Windows, update **Windows Media Player**. It's the native player for a variety of new streaming formats. They should be supported by other programs such as the RealPlayer and **WinAmp**, but Media Player will do them better. Again, it can handle all sorts of other formats, including WAV, AU, and MP3, as well as play your CDs. However, **leave RealPlayer to handle Real Media**. You can get the latest version through **Windows Update**, by clicking the option under the Help

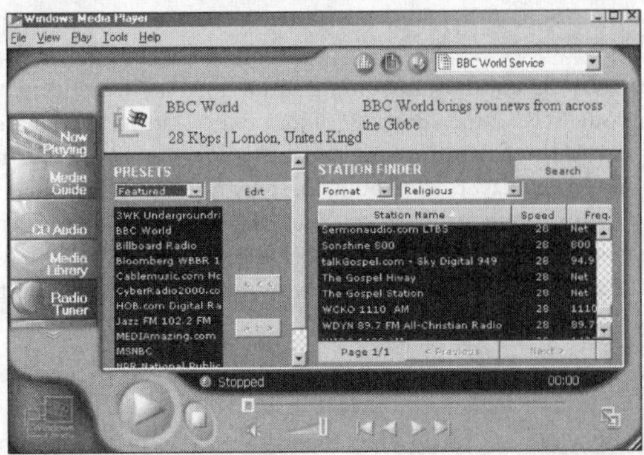

menu in Windows Media Player, or by downloading it from the **Windows Media guide** (http://www.windowsmedia.com). There's also a **version for the Mac** (http://www.mactopia.com). For help, try the Microsoft newsgroups (p.97) or this FAQ: http://www.nwlink.com/~zachd/pss/pss.html

QuickTime

Next, stop by Apple's **QuickTime** Guide (http://www.quicktime.com) and see if you can play what's on offer. Don't be surprised if Windows Media Player or RealPlayer attempts to open the file, but gives you a useless error message. If so, download the QuickTime player and assign it to **associate with only the native Macintosh file types** – under Preferences/Registration/File Type Associations. While the QuickTime player can also handle other types, it's pretty rustic compared to the competition, and persistently nags you to pay. Still, Apple's proprietary video technology is widely used to edit movies and distribute promos so it's worth having support for it, especially if you have a **high bandwidth connection**.

Shoutcast and streaming MP3

Shoutcast is another streaming audio format, which lets you turn your MP3 library into an online radio station within about half an hour of reading and tweaking. It's supported by most leading MP3 players – though best by WinAmp, the original force behind the technology. You can listen by logging into http://www.shoutcast.com and choosing a station. If you like what you hear, grab **RadioSpy** (http://www.radiospy.com) to help find stations.

Liquid Audio and other formats

By now you should be able to play everything that's thrown your way. Apart from the main formats, there are a few less popular alternatives such as **Liquid Audio** (http://www.liquidaudio.com). Generally, all you'll need to play them is to download a RealPlayer plug-in. You'll be offered a range of these when you check for new updates. But generally, if you strike an unsupported format somewhere, they'll usually provide a link to the player. You can safely do without most of them so stick with the basics for now.

Choose your MP3 jukebox

If you've been paying attention, you'll have at least one program that can play MP3s. But once you start to accumulate a large collection of MP3 files, you'll appreciate a full-blown MP3/CD jukebox – such as WinAmp, RealJukebox, Sonique, Windows Media Player or MusicMatch Jukebox – in that role. Typically, these all-in-one jukeboxes can play your music CDs, automatically look up the track listings at Gracenote's **CDDB database** (http://www.cddb.com), rip tracks from a CD and encode them into MP3s, play streaming broadcasts, search your hard drive for media files, and catalog your music library into **playlists**. Again, you can get by without paying, but you mightn't get the full product. Sometimes if you pay to upgrade to the full version you'll get more features such as being able to encode your own MP3s at a higher fidelity. You might like to try a few before you settle, but once you've made a choice, completely uninstall the rejects (except Windows Media Player) so they don't interfere. Alternatively, save yourself the bother, and just download the best:

MusicMatch Jukebox **http://www.musicmatch.com**

What plays what

The worst part of installing another media player is that it will try to hijack all your media settings. Once you've established a preferred player for a format, go through its Options/ Preferences/Settings and specify that you'd like it to be the default for that media type. It's something that's often well hidden. In RealPlayer, for example, it's under the Upgrade tab in Preferences. If you can't find the option, refer to the help file, try the publisher's support page, or ask in Usenet.

For more music software

You'll find hundreds of music players and utilities for free download through:

Download.com **http://www.download.com**

MP3.com **http://www.mp3.com**

MP3 for the Mac **http://www.mp3-mac.com**

Shareware Music Machine **http://www.hitsquad.com/smm/**

ZDnet **http://music.zdnet.com**

Find the music

Go to any search engine, type in MP3 and you'll get the impression they're taking over the Net. To a certain extent they are.

Music is the new pornography for consuming network bandwidth. Which means you won't have any trouble finding MP3s. Like any search, though, you might need to try a few places if you're after something very specific or obscure. And of course, it has to be put online in the first place.

MP3 hubs

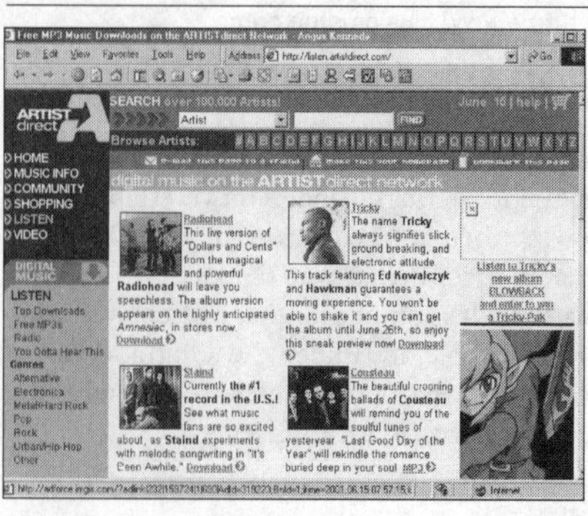

The MP3s you'll strike will fall into three main categories: **free previews** authorized by the artist or publisher; tracks you can **pay to download**; and illegal **bootlegs**. Free previews tend to be from acts that can't get radio airplay and are eager for exposure, but that's no rule. You can usually preview pay tracks in a low-fi format, such as RealAudio or streaming MP3, before purchasing. Here are a few commercial sites that have both free and pay-to-download **legal MP3s**:

Artists Direct **http://www.artistdirect.com**

AudioGalaxy **http://www.audiogalaxy.com**

ClickMusic **http://www.clickmusic.co.uk**

Dmusic **http://www.dmusic.com**

Emusic **http://www.emusic.com**

Epitonic http://www.epitonic.com

iCrunch http://www.icrunch.com

IUMA http://www.iuma.com

Launch.com http://www.launch.com

Liquid Audio http://www.liquidaudio.com

Listen.com http://www.listen.com

MP3.com http://www.mp3.com

MP3.com.au http://www.mp3.com.au

Peoplesound http://www.peoplesound.com

RioPort http://www.rioport.com

Vitaminic http://www.vitaminic.co.uk

Once you hit the search engines and file sharing agents you'll start seeing the contraband. That's not to say they only index bootleggers. They don't, but if you come across lots of songs you recognize you'll know you're in dodgy waters. Don't be impressed by an engine just because it returns hundreds of hits. You might find they're mostly dead links. To search using a Web page front end, try:

AudioFind http://www.audiofind.com

AudioGalaxy http://www.audiogalaxy.com

FindMP3 http://www.findmp3.org

Findsongs http://www.findsongs.com

Look4Mp3 http://www.look4mp3.com

Lycos http://music.lycos.com

Several software agents can also poll multiple search sites at once. They're okay, but not outstanding. Such as:

Copernic http://www.copernic.com

MP3Fiend http://www.mp3fiend.com

Finally, try using a normal search engine to find **fan pages**, which might lead you to all sorts of gems like outtakes, rare singles and live bootlegs.

File sharing networks

Much to the alarm of artists and labels, most of the activity in MP3 isn't happening at the commercial and official sites, but the underground **file-sharing** networks, made notorious by **Napster. File sharing programs** enable you to share your own library online, and of course, pick through everyone else's.

At the time of writing, however, Napster is close to dead. Continuous legal action has seen it bludgeoned into submission. A similar fate befell Scour, except in its case, it was because of movie rather than audio sharing. Both are likely to be reborn with commercial sensibilities.

As a result, serious MP3 hounds have migrated onto other networks. The best alternative at present is **WinMX**, which can search personal servers running its own Peer Networking Protocol, plus networks using the OpenNap and Napster protocols. What that means in English is that it's still open slather, despite the court cases.

Napster **http://www.napster.com**

Scour **mhttp://www.scour.com**

WinMX **http://www.winmx.com**

While most of the alternatives aren't as fast or heavily populated as WinMX, they might turn up something different:

Filetopia **http://www.filetopia.com**

Gnutella **http://www.gnutella.co.uk**

Kazaa **http://www.kazaa.com**

Limewire (Gnutella clone) **http://www.limewire.com**

The following are riddled with spyware (p.262) and, unless you're desperate, probably best avoided:

AudioGalaxy Satellite **http://www.audiogalaxy.com**

Bearshare (Gnutella clone) **http://www.bearshare.com**

iMesh **http://www.imesh.com**

Trading over Usenet and IRC

Set your **newsreader to filter on MP3** and you'll uncover a bevy of groups dedicated to posting music binaries, though again predominately bootlegs. As always, **read the FAQ** first: **http://www.mp3-faq.org**

IRC (p.231) isn't only used for idle chatter. It's also a hotbed of file trading, thanks to the **DCC** command and mIRC scripts like **Multimedia Jukebox** (http://spr.darkrealms.org). Log onto any server, and list the channels and topics that match MP3. But don't accept any programs – they'll be Trojans for sure.

Find streaming music

Real-time audio comes in two forms: **live** broadcasts and **on-demand** pre-recordings. Tapping into a live broadcast is like switching on a radio. Except you have a lot more choice. For starters, you're not restricted to your local reception area. That means you can tune into real world stations from right around the globe. And as anyone can set up a broadcast without a special license, there are also thousands of "stations" you won't hear anywhere else. On top of that there are loads of special events and concerts being piped online. All you need to know is where to look. To help you on your way, see the **Radio section** of our Web guide: p.414.

The difference with on-demand audio is the material is pre-recorded. So no matter when you join, the clip will start at the beginning. You might come across the odd archived radio broadcast, but its biggest use is for **previewing CDs** at online music stores like Amazon. There's no better way to shop for music – as long as your credit card can handle the pressure. For a guide to **CD shopping**, see p.390.

Listen

Unless you have a very fast connection, you'll need to download hi-fi MP3s to your machine in order to play them. The same goes if you want to save them to play later. If clicking on a Web link to an MP3, or other large media file, starts your player rather than a download, right-click and choose "**Save Target**

As" from the mouse menu. Adjust your player's settings to prevent it from happening in future.

Think about where you'd like your music to arrive. It makes the most sense to set up an incoming folder dedicated to audio downloads. Then once you've listened to them, transfer them into your main music library under sensible subfolder names. Still, your jukebox won't mind if you lump them all in together, as it should be able to separate them by their internal ID (naming) tags.

As MP3s are big files, it's wise to relegate transfers from the Web or an FTP server to a **download manager** (p.264) that supports resume downloads. However, if you're using a file-sharing program such as WinMX (p.277), this won't be necessary as they look after the entire download process.

Turn on the broadcast

Clicking on a streaming audio (or lo-fi MP3) link should call up the appropriate player. After a few seconds of buffering, you should hear the clip or broadcast. If you can't hear any sound, but it appears to be playing, check the player's volume control. If that's up full, try your master volume settings. You can reach these in Windows by clicking on the speaker in your system tray. If nothing opens when you click on the link, or a player opens but fails to recognize the format, you'll either need to reset the file associations in the preferred player, or reinstall it.

Roll your own MP3s

If your CD drive supports DAE (digital audio extraction), and it should, you can extract MP3s from your own CDs. Technically this is a two-step process that involves "ripping" an audio track from the CD into a WAV file, and then encoding it into an MP3. But most ripper/encoder programs can copy straight from the CD into MP3. The program you choose – and its associated compression algorithm – could make a difference to the sound quality, so read some reviews and try a few before coding up your entire CD collection.

Still, the bitrate will always be the **biggest determinant of sound quality**. Although 128 Kbps has become the defacto standard online, if you intend to convert them back to WAV files to create a **compilation CD**, encode them at upwards of 192 Kbps. Under that, you will definitely hear the artifacts on a decent sound system.

For better sound, also consider ripping your CDs into WAVs, before encoding into MP3.

If you can't seem to rip a crackle free copy, try

Exact Audio Copy **http://www.exactaudiocopy.de**

For more on encoding, see:

http://www.mp3-converter.com and

http://www.r3mix.net

Keep your CDs online

If you'd like access to your CD collection from any computer online, beam your CDs to **My MP3** (**http://www.mp3.com**). You simply insert your CD and it will look it up in its database. If it has the album in its library, it adds the tracks to your personal collection. You can then access them at any time without ever having to upload any MP3s. And any CDs bought from their online music store partners can be beamed across instantly. Incredible, but true.

MP3 hardware

Part of MP3's recent surge in popularity has been due to the proliferation of **portable players**. These are like a Walkman, but somewhat less convenient in that to "change a disk" you have to upload tracks from your computer. Being mainstream consumer items, you'll find them at any electrical outlet, or airport duty free. Things to look out for when shopping:

❑ **USB or Parallel Port uploads?** USB is faster, if your computer supports it.

❑ **Supports your system?** Check if you use a Mac or Windows 2000.

❑ **Memory?** Figure on about one-megabyte per minute of music. Is it expandable and how much to add extra storage?

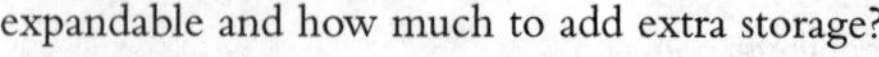

❑ **Power?** What's the battery life and does it come with a charger?

❑ **Upgradeable?** Not being able to upload software upgrades could render the unit obsolete before its time.

❑ **Display?** Does it display track names?

❑ **Size?** Smaller might mean a short battery life.

For opinions on the latest models, try the computer press, techno toy mags like *Stuff* and *T3*, or sites with consumer reviews (p.182) such as like Epinions, MP3.com and Amazon.

Burning to a CD

If you want to play your MP3s or Windows Media files on a regular CD player, you'll need to convert them to the WAV format and burn them to CD. For more on converting and burning, see:

CDR FAQ http://www.cdrfaq.org

CDR Info http://www.cdrinfo.com

CDRLabs http://www.cdrlabs.com

CDRW Central http://www.cdrwcentral.com

CMJ http://www.cmj.com/mp3/

For instructions on how to rip your vinyl collection, see:
http://homepages.nildram.co.uk/~abcomp/lp-cdr.htm

Rather buy the CD?

Then see our guide to buying music online (p.390).

For more

If the following FAQs:
http://webhome.idirect.com/~nuzhathl/mp3-faq.html
http://www.mp3-faq.org
http://www.askmp3.com
don't answer your questions, try the newsgroup:
alt.music.mp3

For the latest news and reviews on MP3 and streaming audio, drop by any of the MP3 supersites (p.276) or:

About.com http://mp3.about.com

MP3.com http://www.mp3.com

ZDNet http://music.zdnet.com

MP3 for Macs http://www.mp3-mac.com

DailyMP3 http://www.dailymp3.org

You'll find much more by searching Dmoz.org, or Yahoo, for MP3.

12

Play games

Rule the planet

Taking on the computer in games like Quake, Half-Life and Serious Sam isn't much of a challenge. But over the Internet, playing against real people – even strangers – such games take on a whole new dimension. And things become way more serious. In fact, once you've played in multi-player mode, you'll never want to play alone again.

Multi-player capability has become standard in most new games, and not just in the action genre. Almost any computer game that can be played by two or more people can be played online.

Finding opponents

To bring in another player to a computer game, you'll need to connect to their machine. The simplest way is via a **serial link**. Just run a null modem cable between your serial ports. It's a fast connection, and quick to set up, but restricts it to two players at

cable's length apart. The same can be done over a **telephone line**, using modems. Again it links only two players and is limited by modem speed.

To conscript more victims, you need a proper network. A **local area network (LAN)** is best. That's where you connect all the machines via network cards and cables. If you'd like to experience network gaming at its fastest and fairest, drop by a cybercafé (p.28) that caters for gamers. However, the most popular way to find an opponent, even at 4am, is via the **Internet**.

The problem with Internet gaming

Although it's the easiest way to meet other players, the Net has its drawbacks for games that require split-second reactions. **Latency** is the biggest issue. That's the length of time it takes data to reach its destination. If it takes too long, it makes a fast game such as Quake unplayable. Then there's **packet loss** – that's where segments of data fail to reach the other end and must be retransmitted. This has the same slowing effect as high latency.

Online games use latency correction algorithms that attempt to predict likely moves. However, players with lower latency (ping) times, usually those close to the server, will always be at a distinct advantage, giving the game an inbuilt bias.

What you'll need

And now for the really bad news: 3D games (and these are the most popular), appreciate every bit of speed you can throw at them. If you want to win, you'll need to be more than just a quick draw on the mouse. You'll need a fat connection, a fast processor, plenty of RAM, and most of all, **3D video acceleration**. In fact, serious gamers obsess about their video cards, the driver software associated with rendering the images, and overclocking their PC chips to melting point. If you'd like to improve your gaming frame rate (sometimes at the expense of stability), experiment with the latest video drivers. If you're running anything with an Nvidia chip, you'll find a whole assortment of official releases and "leaked" betas. For advice, consult the alt.comp.periphs.videocards newsgroup (p.212) that discusses your chipset.

Until recently, serious gamers shunned Macs, due to their **substandard 3D graphic support**. Consequently, games developers have been concentrating on the greater PC market. Mac versions often appear months after the PC release, if at all. In gaming terms, that makes the platform about as fashionable as last year's top 40.

PCs, however, are now being challenged by the new generation of console machines, which are not only cheaper but have superior graphics. **Sega Dreamcast** (http://www.dreamcast.

com), **Sony PlayStation 2** (http://www.playstation2.com), and **Microsoft XBox** (http://www.xbox.com) are all Net enabled. Dreamcast comes with a modem, PlayStation 2 can connect via a USB modem or broadband card, while the Xbox has both USB and Ethernet ports.

Let's rock!

Once you're armed, online and ready to duel, you'll need to track down some willing chumps. That's usually not too hard, but how you go about it depends on what game you're playing. If it won't let you start midway, you'll need to meet in some kind of lobby and wait for a new game to start. Otherwise, you only need find the nearest available game and jump aboard. Most recent games such as **Tribes II, Serious Sam** and the basic board games that come with **Windows ME** include inbuilt support for finding, and chatting to, opponents, but many still require a third-party program.

The best way to start is to download **GameSpy Arcade** (http://www.gamespy.com) and **Kali** (http://www.kali.net). They enable you to find the closest games, with the lowest lag times, and then automate the connections. **When you're shopping for an ISP ask if it runs gaming servers**. It would be quite a bonus if it does, as it will mean playing with little or no lag – a major advantage.

Quake

id Software's **Quake** was the first major game designed primarily for online play. Over a network, it's usual to switch off the "monsters" and fight with or against other players. Serious Quakers form clans, complete with their own custom-designed outfits, called skins. Clan members compete side by side against other clans or individuals.

Quake III comes with its own Netplay support. For more see http://www.bluesnews.com and http://www.quake.com

Team play

The most recent trend is not to pit you against the world, but to join a team. The first generation of team play arrived in Quake's Team Fortress add-on, where you had to choose a team, pick a character type, and battle against one or more opposing teams. But there are now many more mission types such as Capture The Flag, where the goal is to raid the other team's base and pinch their flag.

Breaker, breaker!

Want to chat with your teammates or opponents as you play? Try **Roger Wilco** (http://www.resounding.com). It works like an Internet telephone, but uses so few resources it shouldn't interfere with your game. Or if you'd like to step it up a notch, try

Microsoft's Game Voice (http://www.microsoft.com/sidewinder/) headset, which also enables voice activation of commands such as switching weapons.

Where to find the real eggs

Remember those ancient **text-based games** where you'd stumble through imaginary kingdoms looking for hidden objects, uttering magic words, and slaying trolls? Believe it or not, they're still going strong, and are now multiplayer, with some 100,000 players entwined in more than 3000 gaming worlds, like **Wheel of Time** (http://wotmud.org), **Lord of the Rings** (http://mume.pvv.org) and **Discworld** (http://discworld.imaginary.com).

What sets these apart from conventional arcade games is their community spirit, and the level of character involvement as players become absorbed in their alter-egos. This can make them especially addictive, and possible dangerous psychologically, as obsessive types can be prone to retreat to their fantasy worlds for comfort. Nonetheless, if it sounds your bag, see http://www.mudconnector.com and the newsgroup hierarchy rec.games.mud.

Somewhat up the evolutionary ladder graphically, but along similar lines, **Ultima Online** (http://www.uo.com), the latest in the Ultima fantasy series, throws you into a continually evolving virtual world, complete with day and night. The idea is to create not only a battleground, but a social community for thousands of players. As does **EverQuest** (http://www.everquest.com), creating a spectacular fantasy world in the process.

For games – and more info

Although you'll come across simple games such as chess, checkers, cards or backgammon that you can play through a Web interface the best games are way too big to download as a Java

applet. They're so big you might even balk at downloading demo versions from the Web. Check out the gaming magazines, such as **PC Gamer** (http://www.pcgamer.com), **Computer Gaming World** (http://www.zdnet.com/cgw/), and **PC Zone** (http://www.pczone.co.uk). They're often the best place to find out what's hot in online gaming. Not just because gaming companies send them software evaluations early, but because they invariably come with a **free CD-ROM full of games**. Although you can generally get demos off the Net sooner, with most decent games weighing in at over 50 MB, it's a worthy saving in download time. Especially when you'll flick most of them out after a few minutes.

On the Net, the best source of news and downloads are the main games Web sites (p.360).

13

Your first Web site

Stake your claim

It won't be long before you'll want a crack at your own Web page. You don't need to be anyone particularly important, or a company with something to sell. If you have something to say or display, there's plenty of room for you on the World Wide Web. As long as it's not against the law, you can publish whatever you like – anything from how to build a **psychotronic mind-control deflector** (http://zapatopi.net/afdb.html) to your **navel fluff collection** (http://www.feargod.net/fluff.html).

What's involved?

Publishing a Web page is a three-phase operation. You need to **create your site in HTML** (p.296), find somewhere to park it on the Web (p.303), and finally **transfer all the pages** from your computer to your newfound Web server (p.307). However, before you do anything, you should acquaint yourself with HTML, the Web's markup language.

HTML – a code for all browsers

The formatting commands used to style and position the images, text, and other components within a Web page belong to a relatively simple language called HTML (**H**yper**T**ext **M**arkup **L**anguage). The HTML tags (p.299) tell the Web browser how to display the contents of the page. In theory, any machine that can browse the Web should be able to display the page as intended by the author. Not always in practice, however, as the leading browser companies (Microsoft and Netscape) have done their own thing, rather than adhere to the **W3C**'s (http://www.w3c.org) standards. So a page that displays perfectly in IE6 for the PC, might look wonky in Netscape 4.7 on the Mac. Consequently, most professional developers test their pages on a number of browsers before setting them live.

Where do I start?

Even if you build your pages with a WYSIWYG (What-You-See-Is-What-You-Get) editor that hides all the code, at some point you'll probably need to go in and tweak the raw HTML. The best time to learn the basics behind HTML is right now, before you build your first page. Read on.

Prepare your images

As you know, Web pages can contain more than just text. In fact, placing and preparing graphics is half the art to Web design. If they're too big, for example, your pages will take too long to load. Here's how to get them right.

Getting an image onto your computer

There are three ways to produce a digital image. Talents permitting, you could create one on your computer with **drawing software**. You'll find various paint programs through the software guides (p.265), but they'll pale in comparison to professional level products such as:

Adobe Illustrator **http://www.adobe.com**

CorelDraw **http://www.corel.com**

Macromedia Fireworks **http://www.macromedia.com**

You could import a copy of a slide, photograph, magazine page, drawing, or just about anything two dimensional, into your computer with a computer peripheral called a **scanner**. It works a bit like a photocopier, except instead of printing, it sends a digital image directly to your hard drive.

Or, you could take a photograph with a **digital camera** – or still from a **digital video camera** – and import it into your computer. For advice on buying a scanner or digital camera, consult the consumer guides in our Shopping section (p.182).

Reduce its size for online consumption

Before you post your digital image on the Web, or attach it to an email, you might need to reduce its size in bytes, otherwise it will take too long to download. You can do this in three ways.

You can reduce the **dimensions of the image in pixels**, making the picture itself smaller. For example, if it measures 1024x768, you could reduce it to say, 800x600. This would reduce the file size, but not affect the quality of image.

You can convert it to a **compressed image format**. Images saved in formats such as **BMP** or **TIFF** are uncompressed, which means they take up more disk space. Converting (or saving) them to a compressed format such as **JPG, GIF** or **PNG** will reduce the byte size dramatically. However, this saving comes at the cost of quality. You can also adjust the quality of the image when you convert it.

Which brings us to the third method. The more you **reduce the quality** of an image, the less bytes it will need. So, ultimately it's a trade-off.

If the image is likely to wind up **in print**, then quality matters, so maybe you shouldn't touch it at all. The least you can do, if you're sending an uncompressed image by email is to drop it into a ZIP or Stuffit file (p.256). This will allow you to send a smaller file without affecting the image. Don't bother doing the same for JPGs or GIFs, as they're already compressed.

GIF or JPEG?

The two most popular image formats on the Web are **JPEG** (JPG) and **GIF**. The main difference is GIFs can only display 256 colors, while JPEGs can display 16 million. JPEG also permits a greater degree of compression, which makes for smaller images. As a result, most photographs and finely detailed images are best saved as JPEGs.

GIFs have their uses, though. If an image consists of only a few colors, or has large expanses of the same color, GIF is often more efficient. GIFs can also be animated like a slideshow, and have transparent backgrounds. Consequently, they're often used for bars, icons, banners, and backgrounds. Experiment for yourself and you'll soon get the picture.

Processing your images – tips

Remember, the fewer images you use on your Web page, and the smaller they are in bytes, the quicker your page will load. So if you're putting your entire photo album online, consider creating a gallery of thumbnails (small reduced quality images), with links to larger higher quality images. Dozens of programs can do this automatically.

Online photo galleries

Like to show off your happy snaps, and perhaps even sell the prints? Upload them here and wait for the orders to roll in:
Club Photo http://www.clubphoto.com
Kodak Ofoto http://www.ofoto.com
PhotoLoft http://www.photoloft.com
Photopoint http://www.photopoint.com
Yahoo! Photos http://photos.yahoo.com

However, no matter how many images you're displaying, operate first before sending them online. Start by planning your page. Decide what size image you'll need. You can reduce its size by cropping (chopping out a section), or resizing the entire image. Any basic image editor will offer these options. Just keep a copy of your original image, in case you make a mistake!

Whenever you save in a compressed format, you'll lose a little quality. So rather than make incremental changes to the compressed image, complete any touch-ups and cropping in the uncompressed format, and then experiment with different levels of compression until you're happy with the quality vs. size. You'll find the quality, or compression levels, offered as an option when you convert or save the image as a JPG.

Image processing software

Start by downloading an image viewer/editor (p.264) such as **Irfanview** so that you can flip through images quickly, convert between formats and make minor adjustments.
Irfanview http://www.irfanview.com

With practice, you can reduce byte size considerably without sacrificing quality. Almost any image viewer/editor can do the job, but you can skip all the trial and error, by using a dedicated file reduction program such as JPEG Optimizer.
JPEG Optimizer http://www.xat.com

For serious touching up, however, you'll need something more powerful such as **PaintShop Pro**, or the professional's choice, **Adobe PhotoShop**. Both also have a range of Web compression tools, such as automated gallery generators.

PaintShopPro **http://www.jasc.com**

PhotoShop **http://www.adobe.com**

You'll find an ample range of free Web graphics programs through the software guides listed on (p.265). For help using them, see:

About.com **http://graphicssoft.about.com**

Open Directory **http://dmoz.org/Computers/Graphics/**

Pinoy7 **http://www.pinoy7.com**

Build your site

Once you've worked out what to say on your site, the next thing to decide is how to convert your thoughts into HTML. Let's examine some of your options, starting with the easiest, first.

Nothing to pay – no need to learn HTML

If you need to get something online quickly, without learning HTML, and don't mind that it looks a bit pre-fabricated, head straight to one of the free Web hosting services. In most cases, you can build your entire site though a drag and drop site builder, step-by-step wizard, or by simply filling in a set of templates. You won't need any software, or to hunt around for a hosting service, as they provide the lot all rolled into one. Just read the instructions and follow the prompts. While it's almost impossible to go wrong, don't expect to create a work of art. See (p.303).

Grow your own HTML

HTML is simpler than computer programming in general, but

it's even more repetitive and tedious. Once you understand how it works, you'll probably prefer to do most of your work in a site editor that automates as much as possible. But if you need to tweak to the code, at least you'll know what you're doing. And trust us, you will need to tweak.

Dozens of programs can convert text to HTML in some fashion. Often in a **WYSIWYG** manner, meaning you don't have to look at any of the underlying code. This is not only restricted to the dedicated site editors. Microsoft Office programs such as Word, for example, can save your documents as HTML, ready for shipment onto the Web. Nonetheless, a dedicated Web site editor will do a far better job. These come in two main flavors: **WYSIWYG** or **HTML**.

A **WYSIWYG editor** is a little like a desktop publishing program. You work with objects and boxes, rather than raw code. Some also allow you to directly edit the code as well.

When you work with an **HTML editor**, on the other hand, you work directly on the code behind the page, either manually, or through automated shortcuts. While the editor itself can add all the appropriate code around your text, you'll still have to understand what you're doing. That means you'll definitely need to learn HTML, or at least the basics. The good news is **it shouldn't take you more than an afternoon** to get the gist of it.

Select your site editor

The quickest way to get familiar with HTML is to **create a simple page from scratch**. You won't even need a site editor – a simple text editor like **NotePad** or **SimpleText** will do. However, an **HTML editor** will make the process far less laborious.

There are plenty of editors to choose from, but your choices will narrow when you know what kind of Web site you want to create, and how much you're willing to spend on software. In the meantime, you might as well start with something free such as:

1st Page 2000 (HTML) http://www.evrsoft.com

AceHTML (HTML) http://www.visicommedia.com

Arachnophilia (HTML) http://www.arachnoid.com

Coolpage (WYSIWYG) http://www.3dize.com

HTML Kit (HTML) http://www.chami.com/html-kit/

The next best thing about these programs is they all come with helpful HTML tutorials. By the couple of evenings it will take you to figure them out, you'll be well and truly versed with the basics of building a Web site. For more options, along with ratings and reviews, see:

Builder.com http://www.builder.com

Dave Central http://www.davecentral.com/webauth.html

Tucows http://www.tucows.com

ZDnet http://www.zdnet.com/downloads/webauthor.html

If you don't mind paying, **Microsoft FrontPage 2000** (http://www.microsoft.com/frontpage/), which comes with Office 2000 Premium, or by itself, makes the transition from familiar Office products like Word and Excel relatively painless. It's capable of producing highly professional sites, but is often criticized for producing bulky code.

Serious projects, however, demand serious editors. These pack in full support for Cascading Style Sheets, DHTML, ASP and other curiosities you really don't need to know about unless you're intent on doing it for a living. If you do, you'll want nothing short of **DreamWeaver.** Download the free trial from:

Macromedia http://www.macromedia.com

Once you read around, you'll quickly discover that, whatever the price, not one WYSIWYG editor offers full control over HTML. So whether you like it or not, you'll eventually end up grappling with raw code. In other words, resign yourself to learning some HTML.

Play tag – the basis of HTML

Next time you're online, examine the HTML that makes up any Web page. Choose "**View Source**" from under your browser's right mouse button menu, or **Source** from under the View menu, to see the raw code. The first thing you'll notice is that the text is surrounded with comments enclosed between less-than and greater-than symbols, like this:

```
<BOLD> My head hurts </BOLD>
```

These comments are known as **tags**. This tag makes the text appear bold when displayed in a browser. Most tags come in pairs and apply to the text they enclose. A forward slash signals the end of their relevance, as in: </BOLD>.

Your first page

Let's dive straight in and make a simple page. Create a new blank page in a text editor like **Notepad** or **SimpleText**, and then type in the following:

```
<HTML>(identifies the document as an HTML file)
<HEAD><TITLE>My First Page</TITLE></HEAD>
<BODY> I am a genius</BODY>
</HTML>(defines the end of the document)
```

Bravo, you've finished! Now close your editor, save the page onto your Desktop with the name index.html, and then double-click on it to open it in your browser.

You'll see your page has two parts: a **head** and a **body**. The head contains the title, which is displayed in the top bar of your browser. The body defines what appears within the browser window. Everything else is a refinement.

Save your pages

When you call up a Web page by entering the domain name (such as http://www.roughguides.com) into your browser, it actually retrieves a file called index.html or index.htm that's stored on that host. It's the same as entering
http://www.roughguides.com/index.html

So when you save the front page to your site you should call it: index.html or index.htm – all in lowercase. That way you'll have a shorter Web address to hand out. Unless you have a very good reason, save all your filenames in lowercase, as it's less likely to cause confusion. The rest of your pages should also use the same extension (.htm or .html). Name your other pages in a way that relates to their contents. The file names shouldn't contain spaces (use dashes or underscores) or non-English language characters.

Take a tutorial in HTML

Rather than explain a smattering of HTML tags, we suggest you try an online tutorial or two, and perhaps print one out for later reference. Alternatively, consult the tutorials and help files that accompany your site editor. You'll find just about everything you need to know about site building at:

About.com http://html.about.com
Builder.com http://www.builder.com
HTML Goodies http://www.htmlgoodies.com
HTML Writers Guild http://www.hwg.org
W3C http://www.w3.org/MarkUp/Guide/

Web Developers Library http://www.stars.com

WebMonkey http://www.webmonkey.com

And the newsgroup: alt.html

Make it "usable"

If the point of your Web site is to convey some message about you, your business, or your clients, make sure it's not a bad one. The first step in that direction is to present your site in a way that's **easy to navigate**, and your pages in a way that's **easy to read**. So the further you move away from the tried and tested **black text on a white background**, the harder you'll make it for your readers. After all, how many **successful magazines** or newspapers have you seen use colored print over a patterned background? Or, make it hard to get past the front page? The same goes for the Web. Almost all the successful sites stick to a similar minimal structure. The buzzword for this is "**usability**". You can read all about it here:

Alertbox http://www.useit.com

SpiderPro StyleGuide http://www.spiderpro.com/pr/pri.html

Usable Web http://usableweb.com

Yale Style Guide http://info.med.yale.edu/caim/manual/

A more entertaining way to learn how to design a good Web site is to see examples of what not to do, and ensure you don't make the same mistakes:

Fork in the Head http://www.forkinthehead.com

Web Pages That Suck http://www.webpagesthatsuck.com

If, after all that, you're still considering a patterned background, at least spare a thought for the colorblind:

Vischeck http://vischeck.com

But wait, there's more than HTML

Once you're comfortable with the logic behind basic HTML, you can glean advanced techniques by analyzing other Web pages or plundering their code. Just find a page you like and call up "**View Source**". You can cut and paste selections into your own pages, or save the file and tweak it with a text or HTML editor.

There are almost no bounds to the things you can do with a Web page. As you move up the levels of sophistication, you'll start to move out of the basic HTML domain, into DHTML, XML and more complex scripting and programming languages such as JavaScript, ActiveX, Shockwave, Java, PERL, CGI, and Visual Basic. You may also need access to the special class of storage space reserved for Web programs, known as the **cgi-bin directory**.

If you see a feature you like, and you can't work out how it's done by looking at the source code, ask the site's Webmaster, or search the Web for a good DIY document. There are plenty of books on the subject, but beware, the technology's moving so fast that they date quickly.

Flash

Flash lets you create colorful interactive animations in very small files. For example, a 10 second clip might only take up 10KB. But beware; the greatest design crime online is the use of flatulent Flash animations to welcome you to a site. It's about as likely to impress your visitors as making them walk across broken glass to read your Mission Statement. Apart from the obvious blunder of putting an obstacle between your guest and where they want to go, it might even crash their browser and lock them out of your site altogether. For more appropriate applications, visit **Macromedia** (http://www.macromedia.com). Then check out http://www.skipintro.com if you still don't get why Flash welcome screens are the pits.

Java

Java is not a mark-up code like HTML, but a serious programming language designed to be interpreted by any computer. That makes it perfect for the Web as you can place an applet (Java program) on your site and activate it from your Web page. Most browsers have in-built Java interpreters, so visitors don't need any extra software to view it. Some useful online calculators, translators and interactive quizzes are powered by Java, but then so are countless useless applications that slow your browsing for no good reason. As for writing applets yourself; if you think C++ is a chuckle, it's probably right up your alley. Good luck.

JavaScript

JavaScript, a Netscape innovation, extends the Java concept to HTML. Because it sits entirely within the HTML of the Web page, you can pinch the code from other pages, just like regular HTML. It can add tricks, which, with the odd exception in form creation for example, are just that: tricks. But if you want to create personalized messages for each visitor to your site, display a clock, or spawn twenty pop-up windows, try:

Javascript Source **http://javascript.internet.com**

WebCoder **http://www.webcoder.com**

Just keep in mind that most of your visitors would rather you didn't.

Park your pages

Once your Web pages and images are ready to go live, you'll need to find a server to house your handicraft. While it might seem logical to use the free space that came with your ISP account, consider what might become of your site if you switch providers. You stand to lose not only the space, but the Web address as well. Not to worry, free Web space is plentiful.

Hundreds of sites will give you all the space you need, plus homebuilding tools to ease the process of editing and uploading pages. The big names include:

Freeservers http://www.freeservers.com

Moonfruit http://www.moonfruit.com

Tripod http://www.tripod.com

Yahoo Geocities http://www.geocities.com

There are even a few without the usual hindrances associated with free space such as pop-up windows and ad banners. For example:

Homestead http://www.homestead.com

For more options, and help in choosing, check out the reviews at:

Free Web space http://www.freewebspace.net

But before you settle on a server, whether free or otherwise, first decide if you should **register your own domain name**.

Master of your own domain

Say you run a shop called Top Clogs and you want to flog your clogs over the Web. Don't even consider an address like: http://members.tripod.com/~clogs/topclogs.htm
To be taken seriously; only http://www.topclogs.com will do.

Of course, if someone else has already taken the name, you'll have to think of another – or offer to buy it from them. Any domain registry will instantly confirm if it's available, and register it for you within a matter of minutes. Such as:

Domain Direct http://www.domaindirect.com

DomainMonger http://www.domainmonger.com

Register.com http://www.register.com

Part of the registration process involves allocating **two DNS servers** to direct traffic to the Web server where you will eventually put your pages. If you do it through the above mentioned, they will park your site, and supply the DNS servers until you choose a hosting service. Alternatively, flick through any Internet or computing magazine for hundreds of alternative registries.

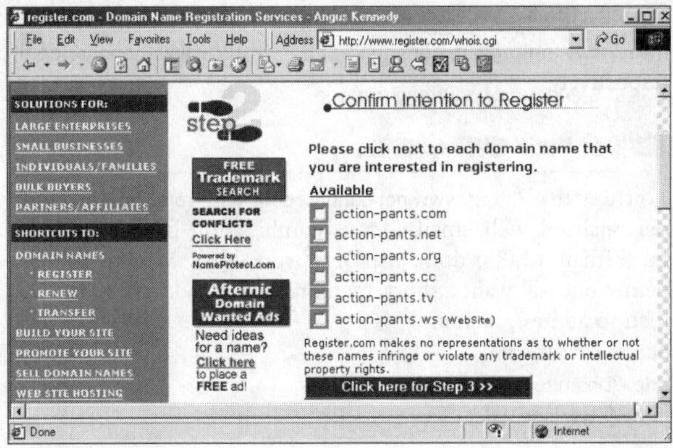

Once you've registered, you'll need to find some some permanent space. Compare prices and services listed at **Top Hosts, Find a Host**, or again, any computer magazine. **Internet Magazine**, for example, tests and ranks British hosts.

Check out the bandwidth and support thoroughly. You don't want to be stuck on a slow server. Generally, the best deals are in the US. However, it helps to locate close to your target audience, as your pages will load quicker.

Find a Host http://www.findahost.com

Internet Magazine http://www.internet-magazine.com

Top Hosts http://www.tophosts.com

Identify with your own country

If you would prefer an association with a country other than the USA, consider registering a regional domain ending in a country code. See the list of available codes and relevant contacts at: http://www.uninett.no/navn/domreg.html

You can register a wide range of countries at Register.com

Alternatively, to register Australian and UK names, try: http://www.netregistry.com.au and http://www.thename.co.uk respectively.

Almost your own domain

Netidentity (http://www.netidentity.com) will rent you a cheap personalized Web/email address combination from a range of more than 12,000 domains. Or, if you don't want to spend a penny but still want a short, memorable Web address, try a redirection address, such as:

http://www.v3.com
http://beam.to
http://www.iscool.net

Free domain hosts

A few operations will host your domain free, but don't expect the same level of service, speed, reliability, lifespan, support or credibility that you'd get from a good commercial service. They include:

Freeservers http://www.freeservers.com
Virtual Avenue http://www.virtualave.net
Webprovider http://www.webprovider.com

Warning – don't use your main address

Nothing will attract more junk email from scam merchants than registering a domain name. So rather than submit your main email address, set up an alternative account just for this purpose (p.105). Don't forget to check it occasionally for legitimate messages from your domain registrar, domain host, or perhaps even people wanting to buy your domain name.

Before you commit, read the reviews at:

Domain Hosting http://www.webweaver.nu/domain.htm

FreeWebSpace http://www.freewebspace.net

Uploading your site

The usual way to deliver files to a Web server is by FTP. This process requires a User ID, password and FTP address for your pages. Ask your hosting service if you're unsure.

Most HTML editing packages incorporate FTP software, or some kind of site uploading wizard. They can also synchronize the content to ensure you have the same files live and locally, as well as check for broken links and dead files. You'll find instructions in the Help menu.

But if you're building a serious site with a basic HTML editor and want a tool that caters to all servers and upload conditions, consider an easy drag-and-drop FTP client like **FTP Voyager**, and a **link validator**, such as **Linkrunner** or **SiteManager**, to scan your pages for broken links.

Alert Linkrunner http://www.alertbookmarks.com/lr/

Astra SiteManager http://www.mercuryinteractive.com

FTP Voyager http://www.ftpvoyager.com

You can check whether your site is compatible with various browsers at:

Web Site Garage http://www.websitegarage.com

Site tools

Once your site has settled on your server, you might like to enhance it with some free, or inexpensive, add-on accessories. For instant quizzes, polls, chat rooms, bulletin boards, guest books, visitor counters, tracking statistics, and much more, see:

Be Seen http://www.beseen.com

Extreme Tracking http://www.extremetracking.com

My Computer http://www.mycomputer.com

Free Site Tools http://www.freesitetools.com

Free Tools http://www.freetools.com

WebSite Toolbox http://www.websitetoolbox.net

To add a free search engine to your site, try:

Free Find http://www.freefind.com

Google http://www.google.com/services/

A Web or FTP server at home

Most people store their Web pages on a dedicated Web hosting service. However, once your computer's connected to the Net, it can also act as a Web or FTP server, just by running the right software. You can even run your own server on a regular dial-up account, though of course your pages or files will only be accessible while you're online – and you'll have a different IP address each time you log in, so you won't be able to pass it on until you're online. This is functional enough if you just want to demo a couple of Web pages to a colleague or friend. However, if you want a serious Web presence, you'll need a permanent connection to run your own server.

Servers are remarkably simple to install – read the Help file and you'll be up within half an hour. But take the time to set up your **security options** to allow only appropriate access to appropriate directories. That means things like making your Web pages read-only and your FTP incoming write-only. Otherwise you might get hacked.

Publicize your site

Once you've published your page and transferred it to your server, the real problems begin. How do you **get people to visit it?**

Before you crank up the publicity campaign, consider how you'd find such a site yourself and whether, if you stumbled across it, you'd bother stopping or returning. Most of all, decide whether it's ready for publicity before you take out full-page adverts in the ***Brisvegas Bugle.***

On a basic level, most people will arrive at your site by taking a link from another site or by typing in the address. That means if other pages link to yours, or people can find your address written somewhere, you'll stand a chance of getting traffic. Contact other sites like yours and suggest swapping links. Most will oblige, especially if you offer them useful content to put on their site. This sometimes starts a wonderful relationship. If you want to move up a step to sell or buy commercial syndicated material, visit

iSyndicate **http://www.isyndicate.com**

The best publicity machines, of course, are the search engines and directories. The biggest services should eventually find your site, but there's no need to wait. Visit each site in turn and look for a link to "**submit your site**", or similar, and follow the prompts. Alternatively, several services such as Addme! **http://www.addme.com** and Broadcaster **http://www.broadcaster.co.uk** can send your details to **multiple engines and directories** at once. You'll get better results if you do it yourself, though.

Next, generate some off-Web interest. Announce your site in relevant **newsgroups** and **mailing lists**. Make sure it's relevant, though; otherwise, you might only generate bad publicity.

Don't forget about the old world, either. **Include the address** on your stationery, business cards, Yellow Pages entry, and in all your regular advertising. Finally, if it's genuinely newsworthy, send a press release to whatever media might be interested, and throw a party with free food, drink and t-shirts for journalists.

Raise your ranking

When you enter keywords into a search engine, it will return a list of results in the order it deems most relevant. Different

engines work in different ways, so even if two engines find the same sites, they might present the results in a different order. Consequently, if you care about your site's **ranking**, you should go directly to each search engine and directory and find out **how it works**. Establish whether it accepts brief reviews, scans your page for key words, or indexes your site in full. If what you're doing is **new**, Yahoo might even create you a new category. For a list of the top referring search sites, see:
http://www.useit.com/about/searchreferrals.html

You can skew most search engines' results to rank in your favor by dotting appropriate words and phrases in key places in your HTML code. Most importantly, make sure your page titles are relevant. This is usually the main determinant of keyword ranking, followed by the contents of any "**meta tags**". It also doesn't hurt to add key words to the <alt> tags behind graphics. Here's an example of how the top of your page might look in HTML:

> <TITLE>Heavy Breathing Hamsters do Honolulu</TITLE>
>
> <META NAME="DESCRIPTION" CONTENT="Furry friends get fresh."> This will appear in search listing results.
>
> <META NAME="KEYWORDS" CONTENT="ham, pineapple, mozzarella, david attenborough"> Should increase your ranking when searching on these keywords.

Whatever you do, don't respond to spam that claims to be able to "raise your ranking". These schemes rarely work. Instead, do your own homework into the black art of search engines:

About.com http://html.about.com/cs/metatags/
Search Engine Tutorial http://www.northernwebs.com/set/
Search Engine Watch http://www.searchenginewatch.com

And finally, to measure your success, see:

Did It Detective http://www.did-it.com
LinkPopularity http://www.linkpopularity.com
Web Position Agent http://www.webposition.com

Part Two

The guide

World Wide Web
ISP Directory

14

World wide Web sites

No-one can tell exactly how many addresses are accessible from the Web. If you were to try to work it out you'd have to factor in not only every Web page, but all the off-Web links as well. That means every newsgroup on every news server, every chat room, every music sample, and potentially every computer hooked to the Internet in any way. The Web proper, though, is the most popular part, and it's what we'll deal with in this guide. As you'll see from the following listings, it's more than just the world's biggest library; it's something you'll have to experience for yourself to understand.

Technically, Web site addresses start with the prefix **http://** – anything else, although accessible from the

Web, really belongs to another system. What sets the Web apart is the way you can move around by clicking links. Most Web sites have links to other sites strewn throughout their pages. Plus, as a bonus, they might devote a section to listing similar sites (or simply ones they think might interest you). Just look for a section called "Links". Of course if you take such a link, you'll arrive at another site that could link to even more related sites. So although we only list a couple of thousand sites in the following pages, they'll lead you to millions more.

Finding what you want

The keys to finding your way around the Web are the **Internet search tools and directories**. See "Find It" (p.152), for how to use them.

How to get there

To reach a site, carefully enter its **address** (taking note of any capital letters) into your browser's **Address bar**. This is normally located directly underneath the menu. Although formal Web addresses start with **http://** you don't need to enter this bit unless you have a very old browser. **So if the address is listed as http://www.abc.com simply type www.abc.com**

An easier way to get there

You'll also find this entire listing on the Rough Guides' Web site. So rather than type these addresses individually, simply browse this chapter, get an idea of what you'd like to see, go online, type: **www.roughguides.com/internet/** and follow the links from there.

How to find a site again

When you see something you like, save its address to your **Favorites, Bookmarks**, or **Links bar**. To find it later, simply click on its name in the list. You could also read it offline by saving the page to disk or switching to Offline mode. For instructions, see p.78.

When it's not there

Some of the following sites will have moved or vanished altogether but don't let that deter you. For advice on how to track them down, see p.172.

Web sites directory

So far no-one has succeeded in creating a Dewey Decimal System for Web sites, and chances are they never will. Some Web sites sit across several categories, while others almost defy categorization. We've had a crack at shuffling them under sensible headings, but you still might need to use your lateral thinking a little. So check under a few categories, especially "Reference" before giving up hope. To search the Net by subject or keyword, try out some of the entries in Find it (p.152).

SUBJECTS

Web sites

Subject Guide

Amusement

Looking for a chuckle or perhaps to extend your lunch-break into the late afternoon? Click through the following directories to enter a whole new dimension of time wasting:

Humor Sites http://www.ranks.com/home/fun/top_humor_sites/
Open Directory http://dmoz.org/Recreation/Humor/
Yahoo http://dir.yahoo.com/Entertainment/Humor/

If you have a high bandwidth connection, or are blessed with abnormal patience, you might like to investigate the world of online animation. Offerings range from clones of old school arcade games to feature length Flash cartoons from renowned cartoonists such as the creators of Ren & Stimpy (**http://www.spumco.com**). Pursue the galleries and links from:

About Animation http://animation.about.com
Animation http://dmoz.org/Arts/Animation/

Flashkit http://www.flashkit.com
Flazoom http://www.flazoom.com
Shockwave http://www.shockwave.com

Assassin
http://www.newgrounds.com/assassin/
Toast a few excess celebrities.

Bert is Evil
http://www.fractalcow.com/bert/
Sesame Street star exposed in photo shocker.

Brain Candy
http://www.corsinet.com/braincandy/
Riddles, jokes, insults and general word play.

Burn Maker
http://toy.thespark.com/burn/
Convert weak platitudes into powerful vitriol.

Cartoon Bank
http://www.cartoonbank.com
Every cartoon ever published in The New Yorker.

Comedy Central
http://www.comedycentral.com
Download full South Park episodes, listen to comedy radio and see what's screening across the network. More of a station promo than a source of laughs.

Comic Book Resources
http://www.comicbookresources.com • http://www.bigpanda.net
http://www.zapcartoons.com • http://www.cartoon-links.com
http://www.geocities.com/Area51/Aurora/2510/greatest_comics/
Comic and cartoon sites, shops, fanfare – and the hundred greatest?

Complaint Letter Generator
http://www-csag.cs.uiuc.edu/individual/pakin/complaint/
Punch in a name for an instant dressing down.

Dean and Nigel Blend In

http://www.deanandnigel.co.uk
Witness the gentle art of urban camouflage.

Dobe's Punny Name Archive

http://www.eskimo.com/~dobe/
Thousands of unwise baby names.

Face Generator

http://www.facegenerator.com
Create your spitting image from a palette of human parts.

Funny Forwards

http://www.ilovebacon.com • http://humor.inept.net
http://www.collegehumor.com • http://www.mrjoker.net
http://www.millerinc.com • http://www.goofball.com
http://www.allfunnypictures.com
Most of the sight gags that arrive in your inbox courtesy of your caring friends will wind up in these, or similar, archives sooner or later. Usually, before your friends see them. Don't go near the galleries if you're a bit sensitive.

Horrorfind

http://www.horrorfind.com
A helpful hand into the darkness.

In the 70s/80s/90s

http://www.inthe70s.com
Re-enter the landscape that wallpapered your childhood memories.

Japanese Engrish

http://www.engrish.com
Copywriters wanted, English not a priority.

Jester: the Online Joke Recommender

http://shadow.ieor.berkeley.edu/humor/
It knows what makes you laugh.

Joke Jukebox

http://www.jokejukebox.com • http://www.uselessjokes.com
http://www.humordatabase.com • http://www.humournet.com
http://www.humor.com • http://www.jokeindex.com

http://www.looniebin.mb.ca • **http://www.jokecollection.com**
http://www.twistedhumor.com • **http://www.tastelessjokes.com**
So many jokes it's not funny.

National Lampoon

http://www.nationallampoon.com
Daily humor from the satire house that PJ built. Not what it was in the 70s as you'll see from the vault.

Newspaper Comic Strips

http://www.kingfeatures.com • **http://www.comics.com**
The entire works of the Phantom, Mandrake and friends.

The Onion

http://www.onion.com
Unquestionably, the finest news satire on or off the Net, and source of inspiration to:
http://www.satirewire.com • **http://www.herdofsheep.com (UK)**
http://www.chaser.com.au (AUS) • **http://www.strewth.org.au (AUS)**

Pocket Internet

http://www.thepocket.com
Gadgets, games, greeting cards, cartoons and more, updated daily.

Praksta's Paradise

http://www.ccil.org/~mika/
All the practical jokes from alt.shenanigans

Rec.humor.funny

http://www.netfunny.com/rhf/
Archives of the rec.humor.funny newsgroup, updated daily.

Sissyfight

http://www.sissyfight.com

Scratch, tease and tattle your way to playground supremacy.

Stick Figure Death Theater

http://www.sfdt.com
Stickcity citizens meet their sticky ends.

The Ultimate Suckup Machine

http://www.theschmoozer.com
Junk mail your quarry with weekly compliments. For something more surreal, try: http://www.geek-boy.com/scg/

UnderGround Online

http://www.ugo.com
Vigilante gang of counterculture sites that's close to the antithesis of AOL.

Art, Museums, and Photography

If you're an artist, photograph your work (preferably with a digital camera) and post it online. It's cheap gallery space that your disciples can visit at any time without leaving home. But don't expect them to stumble across it randomly. You'll need to hand out its address at every opportunity. And, don't forget to include news of your exhibitions and contact details.

Like the real world, finding art online is very much a click and miss (**http://www.badart.com**) affair, and of course entirely a matter of taste. Most major galleries are finding their feet online with limited exhibitions, and any artist who's at all switched on will have their work on the Web. If you're up for clicking, these link banks will locate just about everything that could be considered a bit arty:

ADAM http://adam.ac.uk
Art Planet http://www.artplanet.com
Artcyclopedia http://www.artcyclopedia.com
World Wide Arts Resources http://www.wwar.com

Or if the prospect of an art portal sounds more like your scene:

Artnet.com http://www.artnet.com

Artstar http://www.artstar.com

Art Advocate http://www.artadvocate.com

To find museums:

MuseumNetwork.com http://www.museumnetwork.com

Museums around the World http://www.icom.org/vlmp/world.html

24 Hour Museum (UK) http://www.24hourmuseum.org.uk

To set up your own free **online photo gallery**, (see p.295)

24 hours in Cyberspace
http://www.cyber24.com
One thousand photographers save the day.

3D Artists
http://www.raph.com/3dartists/
Art that looks too real to be real.

Aliens and UFO Art
http://www.wiolawa.com
Defy the Government by becoming as one with alien sculptures.

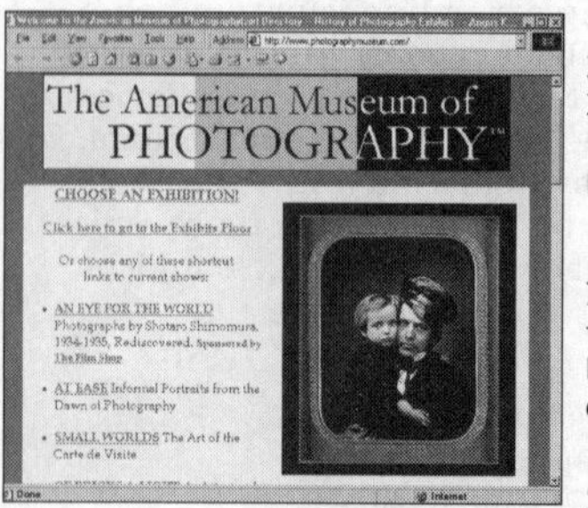

AllPosters.com
http://www.allposters.com • http://www.allaboutart.com
Plaster over the cracks in your bedroom walls.

American Museum of Photography
http://www.photographymuseum.com
Exhibitions from back when cameras were a novelty.

Amico.org
http://www.amico.org
Thumbnails from the top North American galleries.

Anime Pitstop

http://www.animepitstop.com • http://anime.about.com
Today Japan; tomorrow a schoolyard near you.

The Art Connection

http://www.art-connection.com
Buy British art.

Art Crimes: Writing on the Wall

http://www.graffiti.org
http://www.grafcafe.com
Spray for recognition, but don't call it art:
http://www.ci.eugene.or.us/nograffiti/

ArtMuseum

http://www.artmuseum.net
Infrequent exhibitions of modern US classics.

Artist's Exchange

http://artistexchange.about.com
Artists for artist's sake.

Core-Industrial Design Resources

http://www.core77.com
Get a hand with industrial design.

Dia Center for the Arts

http://www.diacenter.org
Web exclusives from "extraordinary" artists, plus the low-down on the NY Dia Center's upcoming escapades.

Digital Photography Review

http://www.dpreview.com
Considering a new camera? Read on. To learn how to use it, see:
http://www.photographytips.com

Elfwood

http://www.elfwood.com
Sketches and tales from a gaggle of junior fantasy and sci-fi buffs.

The Exploratorium

http://www.exploratorium.edu

Kid-friendly online exhibitions from San Francisco's Exploratorium.

Fine Art Lease
http://www.fineartlease.com
Borrow posh pictures to hang in your snooker room.

Great Buildings Collections
http://www.greatbuildings.com
Shuffle knowingly through 3D models of some 750 of the world's most notable structures.

Grove Dictionary of Art Online
http://www.groveart.com
Freeload on the definitive art reference for a day.

Interactive Collector
http://www.icollector.com
Bid on art and collectibles like celebrity cast-offs. Then, of course, there's always Ebay (p.186).

Labelcollector.com
http://www.labelcollector.com
Salute to the golden era of fruit crates and jars.

Library of Congress
http://www.loc.gov
Research tools, exhibitions, library services, current hot bills, and an unparalleled multimedia showcase of American history.

Life
http://www.lifemag.com
View Life magazine's picture of the day, then link through to some of the world's most arresting photographs. There's even more over at:

Australia's Newsphotos http://www.newsphotos.com.au
Time's Picture Collection http://www.thepicturecollection.com

Or for drunken celebrities:
Wire Image http://www.wireimage.com

Museum of Modern Art NY

http://www.moma.org
Not quite like being there in person, but a fair sampler of what's on show.

Photodisc

http://www.photodisc.com
Plunder these photos free, or pay for the hi-res versions.

Soda Connector

http://sodaplay.com/constructor/
Train ingenious spring models that obey the laws of physics and the whims of your idle mind.

Stelarc

http://www.stelarc.va.com.au
No artist has given his body to the Net like Prof Stelarc. More hanging around at:
http://www.suspension.org

Vincent Van Gogh Gallery

http://www.vangoghgallery.com
So, where else could you see his entire works in one place?

Year in the Life of Photojournalism

http://www.digitalstoryteller.com/YITL/
Tag along with voyeuristic pros and see what they do in their day to day.

Books and Literature

If a squillion Web pages aren't enough to satisfy your lust for the written word, then maybe you should use one to order a book. You'll be spoiled for choice with hundreds of shops offering millions of titles for delivery anywhere worldwide. That includes bumper showings from most of the major chains alongside exclusively online book havens such as Amazon and BOL. The superstores typically lay on all the trimmings, such as user ratings, reviews, recommendations, sample chapters, author interviews, bestseller lists, press clippings, publishing news, secure ordering, and usually gift-wrapping.

Major Chains

Barnes & Noble (US) http://www.bn.com
Blackwells (UK) http://bookshop.blackwell.co.uk
Book Passage (US) http://www.bookpassage.com
Borders (US) http://www.borders.com
Collins (AUS) http://www.collinsbooks.com.au
Dymocks (AUS) http://www.dymocks.com.au
Hammicks (UK) http://www.thebookplace.com
McGills (AUS) http://www.mcgills.com.au
Ottakars (UK) http://www.ottakars.co.uk
Waterstone's (UK) http://www.waterstones.co.uk
WHSmith (UK) http://www.bookshop.co.uk

Only on the Web

Alphabet Street (UK) http://www.alphabetstreet.com
Amazon (UK) http://www.amazon.co.uk
Amazon (US) http://www.amazon.com
BOL (UK, Europe, Asia) http://www.bol.com

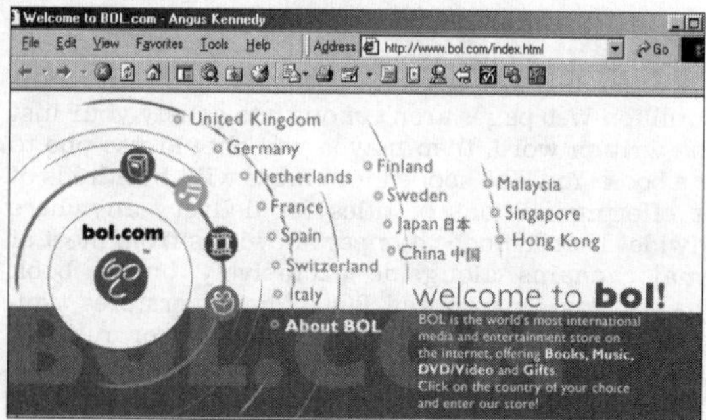

Buy.com (US, UK) http://www.buy.com
Fatbrain (US, Technical) http://www.fatbrain.com

Not listed here? Try browsing or subject-searching this directory of booksellers worldwide: **http://www.bookweb.org/bookstores/** For a rundown on **British merchants** see: **http://www.books.co.uk**

While Barnes & Noble and Amazon may rightly jostle over the title of "world's most ginormous bookstore", you'll find they all offer a staggering range, usually at substantial discounts. But because books are heavy, any savings could be offset by freight. And naturally, the further away you are, and the sooner you want it, the more it adds up. So, before you check out in a frenzy, see that you have the best deal:

AddAll (Worldwide) http://www.addall.com
Best Book Buys (US) http://www.bestbookbuys.com
BookBrain (UK) http://www.bookbrain.co.uk
BookFinder (US) http://www.bookfinder.com
Zoomit (UK, EUR, Latin America) http://www.zoomit.com

If the hype is to be believed, one day we might be downloading all our books into palm-sized electronic readers. You can already buy various brands of **eBook** (electronic book) readers at most electronic outlets, but as yet, they're not exactly sending the paper mills broke:

eBook Palace http://www.ebookpalace.com
Electronic Books http://www.electronic-books.com

Banned Books Online

http://digital.library.upenn.edu/books/banned-books.html
Extracts from books that riled the righteous.

Bibliofind

http://www.bibliofind.com • http://www.usedbooks.com
Millions of old, used, and rare books from sellers worldwide.

Book-A-Minute

http://www.rinkworks.com/bookaminute/
Knock over the classics in a lunch hour.

BookCloseouts

http://www.bookcloseouts.com
Lorry-loads of books slightly past their shelf life – including this one's first edition!

Bookwire

http://www.bookwire.com
US book trade news, bestseller lists, and author road schedules with content from the Publisher's Weekly and Library Journal. For UK publishing news, see: http://www.thebookseller.com

CrimeBoss

http://www.crimeboss.com
Shock comic covers from the mid-20th century.

Femaledetective

http://www.femaledetective.com
She always gets her man.

The Internet Public Library

http://www.ipl.org
Browse online books, magazines, journals, and newspapers.

January Magazine

http://www.januarymagazine.com
Dissecting books and authors.

JournalismNet

http://www.journalismnet.com
Tips and tools for tapping into the big cheat sheet. More facts for hacks at: http://www.facsnet.org • http://www.usus.org

MysteryNet

http://www.mysterynet.com
Hmm, now what could this be?

Poetry Society

http://www.poetrysoc.com (UK) • http://www.poets.org (US)

Halfway-houses for budding poets and their victims. You have to start somewhere: http://crappypoetry.com

Project Gutenberg

http://www.gutenberg.net
Copyrights don't live forever, they eventually expire. In the US, that's seventy-five years after first publication. In Europe, it's some seventy years after the author's death. With this in mind, Project Gutenberg is gradually bringing thousands of old texts online, along with some more recent donations. Sounds great but you might prefer the convenience of hard copy. See also: http://digital.library.upenn.edu/books/

Pure Fiction (US, UK)

http://www.purefiction.com
For pulp worms and writers alike. Not a word of it is true.

Shakespeare

http://the-tech.mit.edu/Shakespeare/
The Bard unbarred online.

The Slot: a Spot for Copy Editors

http://www.theslot.com
Soothing words of outrage for grammatical pedants.

Tech Classics Archive

http://classics.mit.edu
Hundreds of translated Greek and Roman classics. For more ancient and mediaeval literature, see: http://argos.evansville.edu

Text files

http://www.textfiles.com
Chunks of the junk that orbited the pre-Web Internet. For a slightly more modern slant, see: http://www.etext.org

Urban Legends

http://www.urbanlegends.com • http://www.snopes.com
Separate the amazing but true, from the popular myths.

Word Counter

http://www.wordcounter.com
Paste in your composition to rank your most overused words.

The Word Detective

http://www.word-detective.com • **http://www.quinion.com/words/**
Words never escape him.

The Yarn

http://www.theyarn.com
A story that offers you the choice of two paths at the end of each chapter. If one leads you to a dead end, you're asked to contribute.

Business

AccountingWeb

http://www.accountingweb.co.uk
Safe playpen for British beancounters.

Ad Critic

http://www.adcritic.com • **http://www.superbowl-ads.com**
Make a cuppa while you wait for this year's best US TV ads. For the best of the last twenty, see: **http://www.commercial-archive.com**
For UK and Australian ads going back to the fifties:
http://www.televisioncommercials.com • **http://www.tvc.com.au**

Ad Forum

http://www.adforum.com • **http://www.sourcetv.com**
http://www.portfolios.com
Gateway to thousands of agencies, their ads, and the humble creatives behind them.

Bizymoms

http://www.bizymoms.com
Crafty ways to cash up without missing the afternoon soaps.

Business.com

http://www.business.com
Attempting to become the Yahoo of business sites.
For more European sites and trade data, see:
http://www.dis.strath.ac.uk/business/

Business Magazines

Most business magazines archive their past editions online, break news throughout the day, and provide excellent starting points for company resource. For example:

Advertising Age ....http://www.adage.com
Adweek ....http://www.adweek.com
Barrons..http://www.barrons.com
Business Review Weekly (AUS) ..http://www.brw.com.au
Campaign (UK) ....http://www.campaignlive.com
Fast Company.................................http://www.fastcompany.com
Financial Review (AUS).................http://afr.com
Financial Times (UK) ....http://www.ft.com
Forbes ....http://www.forbes.com
Upside ....http://www.upside.com
Wall Street Journal ....http://www.wsj.com

See also Newspapers and Magazines (p.398), and Money (p.381)

Clickz

http://www.clickz.com
The Web as seen by the marketing biz.

Cluetrain Manifesto

http://www.cluetrain.org
Modern day translation of the "customer is always right". Read it or perish. Alternatively, if you'd prefer an update on "never give a sucker an even break" consult the Ferengi Rules of Acquisition:
http://www.psiphi.org/DS9/rules.html

Companies Online

http://www.companiesonline.com
Get the score on almost a million US companies.

Corporate Anthems

http://corporateanthems.raettig.org
What to whistle while you work.

Setting Up an Online Shop

When you're ready to put your business online, you should seek advice from – and probably the services of – someone who knows what they're doing. Setting up an online shop is a lot more involved than whipping up a simple Web page (p.291). Start by looking for "ecommerce" software and shop hosting service reviews in the computer, Internet, and business press so you know what's on offer. What's best for you will depend largely on the size of your inventory. You might find a quick solution in one of the hundreds of click and build stores, such as:

Amazon http://www.zshops.com
BigStep http://www.bigstep.com
Biz Infinity http://www.bizfinity.com
BT Ignite (UK) http://www.btignite.com
Click and Build http://www.clickandbuild.com
Demon (UK) http://www.demonpowertrader.com
Freemerchant http://www.freemerchant.com
Jumbostore http://www.jumbostore.com
Magic Moments (UK) http://www.magic-moments.com
Merchandizer http://www.merchandizer.com
Site America http://www.siteamerica.com
VirginBiz (UK) http://www.virginbiz.net/shop/
Yahoo US http://store.yahoo.com

If your bank won't give you a merchant account for online trading, try a specialist PSP (Payment Service Provider). Compare the transaction costs, annual fees, and International restrictions at:

BidPay http://www.bidpay.com
Checkfree http://www.checkfree.com
Datacash http://www.datacash.com
Netbanx http://www.netbanx.com
Secure Trading http://www.securetrading.com
WorldPay http://www.worldpay.com

Customers Suck!
http://www.customerssuck.com
Grumbly dispatches from the retail front.

Delphion Intellectual Property Network
http://www.delphion.com
Sift through a few decades of international patents, plus a gallery of obscurities. Ask the right questions and you might stumble across tomorrow's technology long before the media. For UK patents see: http://www.patent.gov.uk

Entrepreneur.com
http://www.entrepreneur.com
Get rich now, ask us how.

The Foundation Center
http://fdncenter.org
Companies who might happily spare you a fiver.

Fucked Company
http://fuckedcompany.com
Join the rush to gloat over startup shutdowns.

Garage.com
http://www.garage.com
Matchmaking agency for entrepreneurs and investors founded by Apple's Guy Kawasaki. For more help milking funds for your online white elephant, see: http://www.moneyhunter.com

Guerilla Marketing
http://www.gmarketing.com
Get ahead by metaphorically butchering your competitor's families and poisoning your customer's water supply.

InfoUSA
http://www.infousa.com
Find likely Americans to bug with your presentation.

International Trademark Association
http://inta.org
Protect your brand identity.

Killer Internet tactics

http://www.killertactics.com

How to murder brain-dead Web surfers with HTML.

Patent Café

http://www.patentcafe.com

Protect your crackpot schemes and see them through to fruition.

Planet Feedback

http://www.planetfeedback.com

http://www.thecomplaintstation.com

Let US companies know what you think of their service.

Super Marketing: Ads from the Comic Books

http://www.steveconley.com/supermarketing.htm

The ads that kept you lying awake at night wishing you had more money.

The Wonderful Wankometer

http://www.cynicalbastards.com/wankometer/

Measure corporate hyperbole. Couple with:

http://www.dack.com/web/bullshit.html

Computing and Tech News

Every decent PC brand has a site where you can download

the latest drivers, get support, and find out what's new. It won't be hard to find. Usually it's the company name or initials between a **www** and a **com.**

So you'll find Dell at: **http://www.dell.com**, Compaq at: **http://www.compaq.com**, Gateway at: **http://www.gateway.com**, and so forth. Most of the big names also have international branches, which will be linked from the main site. Consult Yahoo if that fails. If you're in the market for new computer bits, check out the best price across US online vendors:

AnandTech http://www.anandtech.com/guides.html
Price Watch http://www.pricewatch.com
Shopper.com http://www.shopper.com

Popular package software vendors include:

Buy.com (UK, US) http://www.buy.com
Chumbo.com http://www.chumbo.com
Jungle.com (UK) http://www.jungle.com

Bear in mind, if you live outside the US, any imports might be taxed upon arrival.

Apple

http://www.apple.com
Essential drop-in to update your Mac, pick up QuickTime, and be hard sold the latest hardware. To top up with news, software, and brand affirmations, see:
http://www.macaddict.com • http://www.appleinsider.com
http://www.tidbits.com • http://www.macintouch.com
http://www.macnn.com • http://www.macslash.com
Don't even think of looking at http://www.ihateapple.com It will only upset you.

Bastard Operator from Hell

http://bofh.ntk.net • http://www.theregister.co.uk
If you work in a big office, you know this man.

Troubleshooting

The best place to find an answer to your computer problems is usually on Usenet (p.212). Chances are it's already been answered, so before you rush in and post, search the archives through Google Groups.

Google Groups http://groups.google.com

That's not to say you won't find the answer on the Web. You probably will, so follow up with a Web search. You'll find a choice of engines at the very bottom of the results page. If you click on Google, for example, it will perform the same search in the Web database. Apart from Usenet, there are several very active computing forums on the Web, such as:

Computing.net http://www.computing.net
Tek Tips http://www.tektips.com

Along with hundreds of troubleshooting and Windows news sites, such as:

ActiveWin http://www.activewin.com
Annoyances http://www.annoyances.org
Common Problems
http://www.users.qwest.net/~careyh/fixes.htm
Help.com http://www.help.com
Virtual Dr http://virtualdr.com
WinOScentral http://www.winoscentral.com

Don't forget to keep your hardware installation drivers up to date. You'll find the latest files for download direct from the manufacturer's Web site, or at driver guides such as these:

Driver Forum http://www.driverforum.com
Drivers HQ http://www.drivershq.com
Driver Guide http://www.driverguide.com
Windrivers http://www.windrivers.com

For browser-related trouble, see (p.96).

Chankstore FreeFont Archive

http://www.chank.com/freefonts.htm

Download a wacky Chank Diesel display font free each week. If there's

still space in your font sack, arrive hat in hand at:
http://www.printerideas.com/fontfairy/
http://zapo.virtualave.net
http://www.fontface.com

Clip Art

http://webclipart.about.com
Bottomless cesspit of the soulless dross used to inject life into documents.

CNET

http://www.cnet.com
Daily technology news and features, plus reviews, shopping, games, and downloads, along with schedules, transcripts, and related stories from CNET's broadcasting network.

Desktop Publishing

http://desktoppub.about.com • http://desktoppublishing.com
Get off the ground in print.

Dingbats

http://dingbats.i-us.com
For when you just can't get enough symbol fonts.

Easter egg archive

http://www.eeggs.com
A racing game in Excel 2000, a basketball game in Windows 95, and a raygun-wielding alien in Quark Xpress? They're in there all right, but you'll never find them on your own. Here's how to unlock secrets in scores of programs.

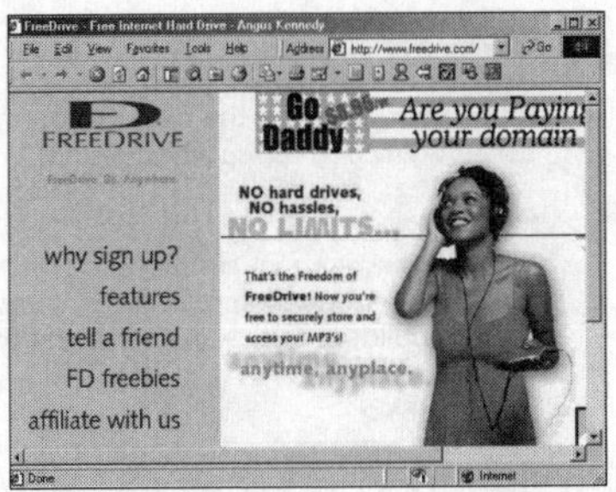

FreeDrive

http://www.freedrive.com
http://www.idrive.com
Free storage space on the Net that's perfect for backups and file transfers.

Happy Hacker

http://www.happyhacker.org
Crash course in l33td00dz 101.

MacFix-It

http://www.macfixit.com
Diagnose what's ailing your Mac.

Microsoft

http://www.microsoft.com
If you're running any Microsoft product, and the chance of that seems to be approaching 100 percent, drop by this disorganized scrapheap regularly for upgrades, news, support, and patches. That includes the latest free tweaks to Windows, Office, and all that falls under the Internet Explorer regime.

Modem Help

http://www.modemhelp.com • http://www.56k.com
http://www.modemhelp.org
Solve your dial-up dramas for modems of all persuasions including cable, ISDN, and DSL. And be sure to check your modem maker's page for driver and firmware upgrades, especially if it's X2 or K56flex.

Need to Know

http://www.ntk.net
Weekly high-tech wrap-up with a sarcastic bite.

Newslinx

http://www.newslinx.com
Have the top Net technology stories, aggregated from around 50 sources, delivered to your mailbox daily. Or for the highlights in a digest: http://classifieds.news.com.au/ni/netnews/

Palmgear

http://www.palmgear.com
Know your palm like the back of your hand. For the Pocket PC, see: http://www.pocketmatrix.com

PC Mechanic

http://www.pcmech.com/byopc/ • http://www.tweak3d.net
http://arstechnica.com/tweak/hardware.html
How to build, or upgrade, your own computer.

PC Tweaking

http://www.anandtech.com • http://www.arstechnica.com
http://www.pcextremist.com • http://www.pureperformance.com

http://www.sharkyextreme.com • http://www.shacknews.com
http://www.tomshardware.com • http://www.tweaktown.com
http://www.ugeek.com • http://www.mvps.org/serenitymacros/
How to overclock your processor into the next millennium, tweak your bios, and upgrade your storage capacity to attract members of the opposite sex.

PCWebopaedia

http://www.pcwebopedia.com
Superb illustrated encyclopedia of computer technology.

Programmers Heaven

http://www.programmersheaven.com
Code your way to eternal fulfilment, in almost any language.

The Register

http://www.theregister.co.uk
Punchy tech news that spins to its own tune.

Scantips

http://www.scantips.com
Become a scan-do type of dude.

Slashdot.org

http://slashdot.org
News for those who've entirely given up on the human race.

Techtales

http://www.techtales.com • http://www.helpdesktech.com
Customers – they might always be right but they sure do ask the darndest things.

Virus Myths

http://www.vmyths.com
If someone sends you an email insisting you forward it on to everyone you know, send them here instead. You won't catch a virus if you follow the advice on (p.142).

Wired News

http://www.wired.com
The Net's best source of breaking technology news plus archives of Wired magazine.

Woody's Office Portal

http://www.wopr.com
Beat some sense out of Microsoft Office. For Outlook, see:
http://www.slipstick.com/outlook/faq.htm

Yahoo Computing

http://www.yahoo.com/Computers/
The grandpappy of all computing directories.

ZDNet

http://www.zdnet.com
Computing info powerhouse from Ziff Davis, publisher of PC Magazine, MacUser, Computer Gaming World and scores of other IT titles. Each magazine donates content such as news, product reviews, and lab test results; plus, there's a ton of prime Net-exclusive technochow. The best place to start researching anything even vaguely computer-related.

Education

Just about every tertiary institution in the world should be online by now, so don't expect to find any listed here. Just drill down through Yahoo, the Open Directory (p.162), or About.com (**http://education.about.com**) to find their admission centers, staff listings, study guides and so forth. Most also place their lecture materials online, which makes the Net perfect for distance learning and of course, skipping classes. Homework sites are also plentiful, but questionably useful. You'd probably do better by keying your subject into a search engine. After all, the entire Internet is an education resource. Nevertheless, you might find a few shortcuts through the likes of:

About Homework http://homework.about.com
Bigchalk http://www.bigchalk.com
HighWired http://www.highwired.com
Homework Spot http://www.homeworkspot.com

Academic Info

http://www.academicinfo.net

Research directory for students and teachers.

Evil House of Cheat

http://www.cheathouse.com

Thousands of college essays, term papers, and reports.

SearchEdu

http://www.searchedu.com

Search millions of university and education pages.

Study Abroad

http://www.studyabroad.com

Hop grass that's greener.

Study Web

http://www.studyweb.com

Ideal school research aid with thousands of leads split by topic.

Web66: International School Web Site Directory

http://web66.coled.umn.edu/schools.html

Add your school's Web page if it's not already listed.

Employment

If you're looking to move on up, beware that if you post your résumé online your boss could find it – embarrassing at the very least. The same situation could also arise if you leave it online once you're hired. Most job agencies have sites these days, and the better ones update at least daily. Consequently, there are far too many to attempt to list here. What's best for you will depend on what field you're in and where you want to work. Bigger isn't always better, as you'll find yourself competing with more applicants. On the other hand, your prospective employer isn't likely to restrict their job search to a site that isn't well known.

So maybe you'd be better off searching the newspaper classifieds, or checking out the agencies that advertise in your vocation's trade mags. Better still, if you have a company in your sights check its Web site for vacancies, or write to its "Human Resources Officer". It should go without saying that you should never interview with any company without fully surveying its Web site, along with its main competitors and other industry voices. Whether you're looking for a job, or to fill a vacancy, try:

http://www.adecco.com (INT) • http://www.monster.com (INT) http://www.topjobs.com (INT) • http://www.drakeintl.com (INT) http://www.headhunter.net (INT) • http://www.seek.com.au (AUS, UK) http://www.ajb.dni.us (US) • http://www.flipdog.com (US) http://www.careerbuilder.com (US) • http://www.joboptions.com (US) http://www.futurestep.com (US) • http://www.hotjobs.com (US) http://www.gojobsite.com (EUR, UK) http://www.hotjobs.com.au (AUS) http://www.fish4jobs.co.uk (UK) • http://www.jobsearch.co.uk (UK) http://www.reed.co.uk (UK) http://www.jobsunlimited.co.uk (UK) http://www.peoplebank.com (UK)

Cool Works

http://www.coolworks.com

Seasonal jobs in US resorts, national parks, camps, ranches, and cruise lines.

Expat Network

http://www.expatnetwork.co.uk

Subscription placement and settling service for working globetrotters.

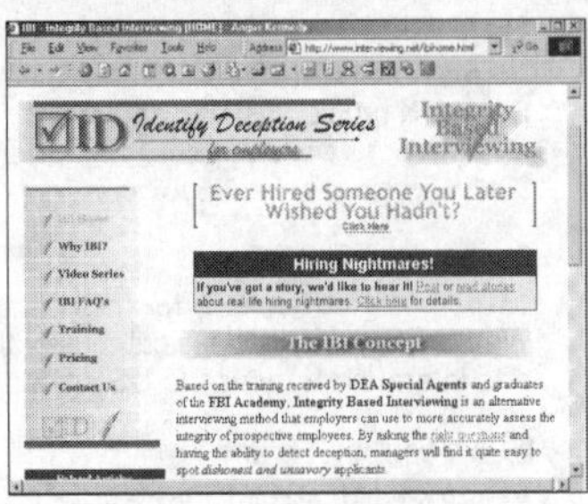

Integrity Based Interviewing

http://www.interviewing.net
Ex-federal agents show you how to get to the truth without drawing any blood.

I-resign.com

http://www.i-resign.com
Quit now, while you're ahead.

The Riley Guide

http://www.rileyguide.com
Messy, but massive, directory of job-hunting resources.

Salary Info

http://www.salary.com • http://jobsmart.org/tools/salary/
See what you're worth, and then how much you'd need in another town: http://www2.homefair.com/calc/salcalc.html

Yahoo Careers

http://careers.yahoo.com
As ever, Yahoo is in on the act, and as ever, does it superbly. This arm, however, handles only US placements. But key "employment" as a search term, or click on "international", and you'll be awash with options spanning the globe.

Entertainment and Events

Finding out what's on in town, and booking your perch, has never been easier – once you settle on a trusty online source. Your local newspaper's site would be the first logical port of call. Then see how these multi-city guides cater to your locale and interests:

CitySearch http://www.citysearch.com
Sidewalk (AU) http://www.sidewalk.com.au
Time Out http://www.timeout.com
Tribes http://www.tribe.com.au

Aloud (UK)

http://www.aloud.com
Book UK music, festival, and event tickets online. For theatre tickets, see: http://www.whatsonstage.com and for what's on listings see: http://www.eventselector.co.uk

CultureFinder (US)

http://www.culturefinder.com
What's on guide to classical music, theatre, opera, dance, and visual arts in around a thousand US cities.

Music Festival Finder

http://www.festivalfinder.com
Upcoming North American outdoor gigs of all persuasions. For the UK, see: http://www.timeout.com/festivals/

NME Ticketshop (UK)

http://www.nmetickets.com • http://www.tickets-online.co.uk
Reserve music tickets across the UK.

Operabase

http://www.operabase.com
What's on where in worldwide opera, plus details of past performances and reviews.

Ticketmaster/Ticketek

http://www.ticketmaster.com • http://www.ticketmaster.co.uk
http://www.ticketmaster.com.au • http://www.ticketek.com.au
Book event tickets online in the US, UK, and Australia.

Fashion

Unless it entirely erodes your reading time the Net isn't likely to cut your guilty expenditure on glossy mags. While there's a spree of fledgling style zines and something of sorts from nearly all the big rack names, none of it compares to getting it in print (see p.398 for more):

Conde Naste (UK) http://www.condenast.co.uk

Conde Naste (US) http://condenast.com

Cosmo http://www.cosmomag.com
Elle (INT) http://www.elle.com
Esquire http://www.esquire.com
FHM (INT) http://www.fhm.com/international/
Flare (CAN) http://www.flare.com
GQ (UK) http://www.gq-magazine.co.uk
Marie Claire http://www.marieclaire.com
Tatler http://www.tatler.co.uk
Vogue (INT) http://www.vogue.com/intl/
Wallpaper http://www.wallpaper.com

Nonetheless, they will certainly supplement your vice. What you will find the Net better for is researching products, checking out brands and saving money on consumables like cosmetics at stores such as:
http://www.drugstore.com • http://www.gloss.com
http://www.ibeauty.com • http://www.perfumania.com
http://www.reflect.com • http://www.sephora.com
http://www.theperfumeshop.com • http://www.hqhair.com
http://www.beu.co.uk • http://www.thinknatural.com

Buying clothes is tough, but popular nonetheless. They're out there, if you know what you're doing, but you'll soon see why Boo.com failed. The best place to find fashion sites is in your regular glossies and newspaper's style section – both in editorial and ads. Label sites are sometimes interesting for new season looks, stockists and sometimes, direct ordering.

Cosmetic.org
http://www.cosmetic.org

http://www.ienhance.com
Adjust your imperfection without pills or creams.

FashionBot

http://www.fashionbot.com
Search several UK high-street retailers' catalogs.

Fashion Information

http://www.fashioninformation.com
Pay for trend forecasting reports.

Fashion Net

http://www.fashion.net • http://www.efashion.com
Handy shortcut to the highest profile shopping, designer, magazine, modeling and fashion industry sites, with enough editorial to warrant an extended stopover.

Fashionmall.com

http://www.fashionmall.com • http://www.brandsforless.com
http://www.bluefly.com • http://www.designersdirect.com
Mail order familiar, and mostly American, labels.

Fashion UK

http://www.fuk.co.uk
Minimal, but fresh, vanity monthly out of London.

Firstview

http://www.firstview.com
See what's trotting the catwalks – sometimes at a price.

InShop (US)

http://www.inshop.com
Track shop sales and promotions in your area.

The Lipstick Page

http://www.thelipstickpage.com
Cosmetic appliances for fun and profit.

Moda Italia

http://www.modaitalia.net
Patch through to the Italian rag traders.

Mullets of the Gods

http://www.mulletgods.com • **http://www.mulletjunky.com**
Don't touch the back, or the sides: **http://www.badburns.com**

Solemates: The Century in Shoes

http://www.centuryinshoes.com
Stepping out in the 20th century.

Victoria's Secret

http://www.victoriassecret.com
Order online or request the catalog preferred by nine out of ten teenage boys.

Film, TV, and Stars

Most TV stations maintain excellent sites with all kinds of extras such as live sports coverage and documentary follow-ups. We won't need to give you their addresses because they'll be flashing them at you at every opportunity. In any case, you'll find them all at: **http://www.tvshow.com**

For personalized listings, perhaps delivered by email, try your local Yahoo, or:
http://www.sofcom.com.au/TV/ (AUS)
http://www.clicktv.com (CAN)
http://www.unmissabletv.com (UK)
http://www.radiotimes.beeb.com (UK)
http://www.digiguide.co.uk (UK)
http://www.ananova.com/tv/ (UK)
http://www.gist.com (US)
http://www.tvguide.com (US)
http://www.tvgrid.com (US)
http://tv.zap2it.com (US)

For more options, and other countries:
http://www.tvshow.com/tv/scheds/

To be notified when something's on:
Spyonit **http://www.spyonit.com**

Several sites specialize in TV episode guides:
Epguides.com http://epguides.com
Hu's Episode Guides http://www.episodeguides.com
Mighty Big TV http://www.mightybigtv.com

But if you want obsessive detail along with picture galleries, scripts, spoilers, and rumors, search Yahoo or the Open Directory for a site dedicated to that show. If it's current and popular, you'll be confronted with hundreds of choices. For the strictly nostalgic:
TV Cream (UK) http://tv.cream.org
Yesterdayland http://www.yesterdayland.com

Or if you'd prefer a video or DVD, you won't find a bigger range than:
Reel.com http://www.reel.com
Amazon http://www.amazon.com (.co.uk)
Black Star (UK) http://www.blackstar.co.uk

To compare prices:
http://www.dvdpricesearch.com • http://www.formovies.com

For more on DVD hardware and software:
http://www.7thzone.com • http://www.dvdfile.com

When it comes to movies, one site clearly rules:
The Internet Movie Database http://www.imdb.com

To say it's impressive is an understatement. You'll be hard pressed to find any work on or off the Net as comprehensive as this exceptional relational database of screen trivia from over 100,000 movies and a million actors. It's all tied together remarkably well – for example, within two clicks of finding your favorite movie, you can get full filmographies of anyone from the cast or crew, and then see what's in the cooker. Still, it's not perfect, or without competition. For example, you'll find a similar service with superior biographies and synopses at the colossal:

All Movie Guide http://www.allmovie.com

Or for more Chan, Li and Fat:

Hong Kong Movie Database http://www.hkmdb.com

They'll also direct you to external reviews, as will these search engines:

Cinemachine http://www.cinemachine.com
Movie Review Query Engine http://www.mrqe.com

But perhaps you'd prefer a summary:

Rotten Tomatoes http://www.rottentomatoes.com

Or a recommendation based on your tastes:

MovieLens http://movielens.umn.edu

While at least one site picks the all-time greats:

Greatest Films http://www.filmsite.org

Far more are content to trash:

Bad Movie Night http://www.hit-n-run.com
Filthy Critic http:/bigempire.com/filthy/
Mr Cranky http://www.mrcranky.com
The Stinkers http://www.thestinkers.com

Roll in it:

Astounding B Monster http://www.bmonster.com
Bad Movie Report http://www.stomptokyo.com/badmoviereport/
Badmovies.org http://www.badmovies.org
Oh the Humanity http://www.ohthehumanity.com
Shock Cinema http://members.aol.com/shockcin/
Trash City http://www.trshcity.demon.co.uk

Or just point out the blunders:
Movie Mistakes http://www.movie-mistakes.com

But none unveil box office evil like:
Childcare Action Project http://www.capalert.com
Movie Rat http://www.saunalahti.fi/~mitt/movierat.htm
Screen It! http://www.screenit.com

For whispers of what's in production:
Ain't It Cool News http://www.aint-it-cool-news.com
CHUD http://www.chud.com
Coming Attractions http://www.corona.bc.ca/films/
Dark Horizons http://www.darkhorizons.com
IMDB http://www.imdb.com/Sections/Inproduction/

You can even download films and TV shows to watch on your computer. And not only amateur shorts like:
Atom Films http://www.atomfilms.com
Pixelfest http://www.pixelfest.com

But even full-length box office hits, TV archives:
CinemaPop http://www.cinemapop.com
Cinema Now http://www.cinemanow.com
IFilm http://www.ifilm.com
LikeTelevision http://www.liketelevision.com
MovieFlix http://www.movieflix.com
Moviefly http://www.moviefly.com
New Gen Films http://www.newgenfilms.com
SightSound http://www.sightsound.com

And shoot-em-ups:
Westerns http://www.westerns.com

To reach out to a star:

CelebrityEmail.com http://www.celebrityemail.com
Celebrity Addresses http://www.writetoaceleb.com

Every celebrity has at least one obsessive fan site (**http://www.ggower.com/fans/**) in their honor. Finding them can sometimes be tricky. If they're not listed in Yahoo, try:
http://www.celebhoo.com • http://www.celebsites.com
http://www.webring.org • http://www.csotd.com
http://directory.google.com/Top/Arts/Celebrities/

Search engines tend to find porn scuttlers who've loaded their HTML metatags with celebrity names. Easy bait, when you consider that most fans could go a glimpse of their idol in various states of undress (**http://www.cndb.com**). If they succeed in catching your attention, at least have the sense not to pull out your credit card. Adding -naughty -naked -nude to your search term, or enabling an adult filter such as Google's SafeSearch (under preferences), might help weed them out.

asSeenonScreen

http://www.asseenonscreen.com
Buy stuff you've seen on TV or in movies.

Drew's Script-O-Rama

http://www.script-o-rama.com • **http://www.scriptshack.com**
Hundreds of entire film and TV scripts. Need help writing or selling your own? Try here: **http://www.celluloidmonkeys.com**

E! Online

http://www.eonline.com
Daily film and TV gossip, news, and reviews.

Empire Magazine

http://www.empireonline.co.uk
Reviews of every film showing in the UK.

Famous Birthdays

http://www.famousbirthdays.com
http://us.imdb.com/OnThisDay
See who shares your birthday.

Find a Grave

http://www.findagrave.com
See where celebrities are buried.

Friends Place

http://www.friendsplace.com
Every script of every episode ever. But, if you have that much spare time it might make you wish you had some of your own.

Gil*galad's Martian Theaethyr

http://www.televar.com/~gnostran/
Applying AstroTarotry to old movies makes them so much clearer.

Hollywood Reporter

http://www.hollywoodreporter.com
Tinseltown tattle, previews, and reviews daily, plus a flick biz directory.

Jump the Shark

http://www.jumptheshark.com
Nominate the point when a TV series plot loses it.

Live TV

http://www.comfm.fr/live/tv/
Tune into live video feeds from hundreds of real world television stations. To record US cable shows and play them back in Real Video (court case pending) see: http://www.recordtv.com

Melon Farmer's Video Hits

http://www.dtaylor.demon.co.uk
Challenges British screen censorship.

Movie Cliches

http://www.moviecliches.com
Nothing unfamiliar.

Moviemags.com

http://www.moviemags.com
Directory of film print and ezines.

Movies.com

http://www.movies.com • http://www.mca.com
http://www.film.com
Preview box office features and trailers direct from the major studios.

Satco DX Satellite Chart

http://www.satcodx.com
Where to point your dish and what you can expect to receive.

SciFi.com

http://www.scifi.com • http://scifi.ign.com •
http://www.fandom.com
Science fiction news, reviews, and short films.

Screen Network Australia

http://www.sna.net.au
Gateway to Australian film and TV sites. For news, reviews, and interviews, see: http://www.urbancinefile.com.au

Showbizwire

http://www.showbizwire.com
Entertainment newsbreaks from about 50 major sources.

The Smoking Gun
http://www.thesmokinggun.com
http://www.apbnews.com/media/gfiles/
Celebrity shame dug up from police records complete with the photocopied sources.

Soap City
http://www.soapcity.com
http://members.tripod.com/~TheSoapBox/
http://www.soapweb.co.uk (UK) • http://www.soapdigest.com
Keep up with who's doing what to whom, whom they told, and who shouldn't find out, in the surreal world of soap fiction.

TV Eyes
http://www.tveyes.com
Informs you when your search term is mentioned on TV.

TV Show
http://www.tvshow.com
Everything TV, from schedules of every station worldwide and links to just about every show ever made, to the technical aspects of production and broadcasting. Start all your TV-related searches here.

TV Tickets
http://www.tvtickets.com
Secure your chance to clap on cue.

Variety
http://www.variety.com
Screen news fresh off the PR gattling gun.

VCR Repair Instructions
http://www.fixer.com
How to take a VCR apart and then get all the little bits back in so it fits easier into the bin.

Who would you kill?
http://www.whowouldyoukill.com
So who would you toss into Dawson's Creek?

Food and Drink

Any decent search engine or recipe database will uncover more formulas for food than you could possibly cook in a lifetime. Start by casting your line into the Fish Finger king's collection:

Birdseye Recipe Search http://www.birdseye.com/search.html
Meals for You http://www.mealsforyou.com
Recipedia http://www.lycos.com/search/recipedia.html
Recipe Archives http://recipes.alastra.com

When following recipes, note where they're from so you don't mix up the measures. For example, an Australian tablespoon is four, not three, teaspoons.

Beershots

http://micro.magnet.fsu.edu/beershots/
Beers of the world put under a microscope.

Bevnet

http://www.bevnet.com
Know your new age beverages. Here's how to brew the "real thing":
http://www.sodafountain.com

Breworld.com

http://www.breworld.com
None of the usual beer yarns like waking up in a strange room stark naked with a throbbing head and a hazy recollection of pranging your car. Here, beer is treated with the same dewy-eyed respect usually reserved for wine and trains. Like to send your chum a virtual beer? Stumble over to: http://www.pubworld.co.uk

Chile-Heads

http://chileheads.netimages.com • http://www.ringoffire.net
Get 'em while they're hot.

Chocolate Lover's Page

http://chocolate.scream.org
The good gear: where to find recipes and dealers.

Cigar Aficionado

http://www.cigaraficionado.com

Archives, shopping guides, and tasting forums from the US glossy that sets the benchmark in cigar ratings. Modeled on: http://www.thethirdrail.com/crack/

Cocktails

http://www.cocktailtime.com • http://cocktails.about.com
http://www.webtender.com • http://www.barmeister.com
http://www.drinkboy.com

Guzzle your way to a happier home. Yes, do buy the book.

Cook's Thesaurus

http://www.foodsubs.com

Find substitutes for fatty, expensive, or hard-to-find ethnic ingredients.

Epicurious

http://www.epicurious.com

Online marriage of Condé Nast's Gourmet, Bon Appetit, and Traveler magazines, crammed with recipes, culinary forums, and advice on dining out worldwide.

The Espresso Index

http://www.espresso.com • http://www.espressotop50.com

Kickstart your morning with the FAQs on coffee.

Final Meal Requests

http://www.tdcj.state.tx.us/stat/finalmeals.htm

The prospect's enough to spoil your appetite.

Internet Chef

http://www.ichef.com

Over 30,000 recipes, cooking hints, kitchen talk, and more links than you could jab a fork in.

Kitchen Link

http://www.kitchenlink.com

Points to more than 10,000 galleries of gluttony.

Moonshine

http://moonshine.co.nz • http://www.geocities.com/kiwi_distiller/

Get blind (possibly literally) on homemade spirits.

Buying Groceries Online

Your chances of being able to order home-delivered groceries online will be much higher if you live in a big city. Expect to pay a premium for the convenience. Although most of the following have physical stores, they mightn't offer their full range online:

http://www.colesonline.com.au (AU)
http://www.greengrocer.com.au (AU)
http://www.shopfast.com.au (AU)
http://www.woolworths.com.au (AU)

http://www.telegrocer.com (CAN)
http://www.sainsbury.co.uk (UK)
http://www.somerfield.co.uk (UK)
http://www.tesco.co.uk (UK)
http://www.waitrose.com (UK)
http://www.iceland.co.uk (UK

http://www.egrocer.com (US)
http://www.ethnicgrocer.com (US)
http://www.webvan.com (US)
http://www.homeruns.com (US)
http://www.netgrocer.com (US)
http://www.peapod.com (US)

An Ode to Olives

http://www.emeraldworld.net/olive.html
You'll never look at an olive ambivalently again.

Restaurant Row

http://www.restaurantrow.com
Key in your dining preferences and find the perfect match from hundreds of thousands of food barns worldwide.

Spice Advice

http://www.spiceguide.com
Encyclopedia of spices covering their origins, purposes, recipes, and tips on what goes best with what.

Tasty Insect Recipes

http://www.ent.iastate.edu/misc/insectsasfood.html
http://www.eatbug.com
Dig in to such delights as Bug Blox, Banana Worm Bread, Rootworm Beetle Dip, and Chocolate Chirpie Chip Cookies (with crickets).

Tea & Sympathy

http://www.enteract.com/~robchr/tea/
Home of the Rec.Food.Tea FAQ.

Thai Recipes

http://www.importfood.com/recipes.html
Just click if you don't have an ingredient.

Tokyo Food Page

http://www.bento.com
Where and what to eat in Tokyo, plus recipes. More help packing sushi at: http://www.learn-sushi.com and http://www.sushi101.com

Top Secret Recipes

http://www.topsecretrecipes.com • http://www.copykat.com
At least one commercial recipe, such as KFC coleslaw, revealed each week. Many are surprisingly basic.

The Ultimate Cookbook

http://www.ucook.com
Pinch recipes from hundreds of popular cookbooks. More food porn unplugged at: http://www.cook-books.com

Vegetarian Society of the UK

http://www.vegsoc.org
Support for fussy eaters.

Wine Spectator

http://www.winespectator.com
Research your hangover.

Fortunes and Personality Tests

American Federation of Astrologers

http://www.astrologers.com
Impress your hairdresser by becoming a fully accredited seer by correspondence course.

Astrology – Atlas and Time Zone Database

http://www.astro.com/atlas/
Know exactly what was happening upstairs the second of your birth. Or if you prefer your cold readings (http://www.skepdic.com/coldread.html) with a touch less pseudo-scientific mumbo jumbo, try:
http://www.astrology.com • http://astrology.about.com
http://www.astrocenter.com • http://www.artcharts.com
Now see what old sensible shoes has to say:
http://www.skepdic.com/astrolgy.html

Biorhythm Generator

http://www.facade.com/attraction/biorhythm/
Generate a cyclical report that can double as a sick note.

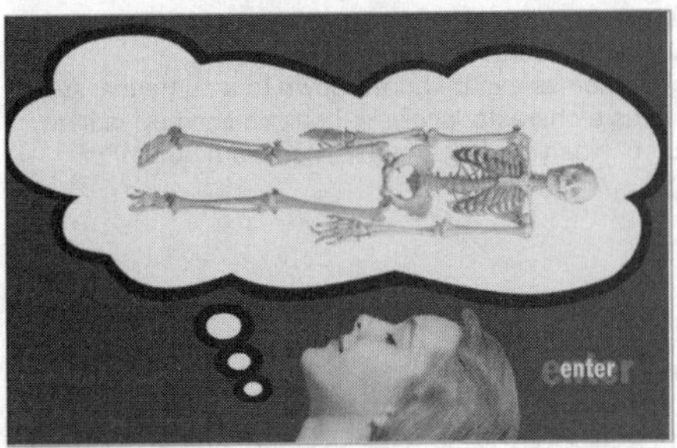

Dreamstop

http://www.dreamstop.com
Analyze your night visions, and jot them into a journal to share with your friends.

I Ching

http://www.facade.com/Occult/iching/
If the superior person is not happy with their fortune as told by this ancient Chinese oracle, one can always reload and get another one.

Psyche Tests

http://www.psychtests.com
http://www.keirsey.com • **http://www.queendom.com/tests.html**
http://www.emode.com • **http://buster.cs.yale.edu/implicit/**
So, what breed of dog are you? Smug skeptics (**http://www.skepdic.com/myersb.html**) say you'll get closer to the truth here: **http://www.learner.org/exhibits/personality/**

RealAge

http://www.realage.com
Compare your biological and chronological ages. Here's how long you can expect to live:
http://www.msnbc.com/modules/quizzes/lifex.asp

The Spark

http://www.thespark.com
Are you the bitch or bastard they say, or are you merely a bit pregnant? Take the tests to find out.

What's in your name?

http://www.kabalarians.com/gkh/your.htm
The Kabalarians claim names can be boiled down to a numerical stew and served back up as a character analysis. Look yourself up in here and see what a duff choice your folks made. Then blame them for everything that's gone wrong since.

Games

Most multiplayer games can be played across the Net. There are also thousands of simple table, word, arcade, and music games as diverse as Chess, Blackjack, Connect 4, and Frogger that can be played on the Web courtesy of Java and Shockwave. In some cases you can contest online opponents for prizes. Peruse the selection on offer at:

Flash Kit http://www.flashkit.com
Flazoom http://www.flazoom.com
Flipside http://www.flipside.com
FreeArcade.com http://www.freearcade.com
Gamesville http://www.gamesville.com
Playsite http://www.playsite.com
Pogo.com http://www.pogo.com
Real Arcade http://www.realarcade.com
Shockwave.com http://www.shockwave.com
The Riddler http://www.riddler.com
The Station http://www.station.sony.com
Yahoo Games http://games.yahoo.com
Web Games http://www.happypuppy.com/web/

Autolotto

http://memelog.com/autolotto/
Arrange to enter and compete in online lotteries automatically.

The Best Games Music in the World Ever

http://gamemusic.siliconcircus.co.uk
Put someone special in the mood.

Blues News

http://www.bluesnews.com
Keep up with what's Quakin'.

ContestGuide

http://www.contestguide.com • http://www.contestworld.com
http://www.iwon.com • http://www.loquax.co.uk (UK)
http://www.uggs-n-rugs.com.au/contests/ (AUS)
Get junk mailed for life by entering loads of competitions.

Game Downloads

http://www.fileplanet.com • http://www.freeloader.com
Stock up on gaming software.

GameFAQs

http://www.gamefaqs.com
Stuck on a level or just want to know more?

Grrl Gamer

http://www.grrlgamer.com
Team up with other game grrls and prepare to kick dweeb boy butt right across their own turf. More reinforcement at: http://www.gamegirlz.com and http://www.womengamers.com

Kasporov Chess

http://www.kasparovchess.com • http://chess.about.com
Take tips from the Russian master and then find an opponent.

PC Game Finder

http://www.pcgame.com
Search the leading game lairs for previews, reviews, cheats, and demos.

Vintage Gaming

http://www.vg-network.com • http://www.emux.com
http://www.download.net
Revive old school arcade games like Xevious on your home PC.

PC Games

For reviews, news, demos, hints, patches, cheats, downloads, and other PC game necessities try:

Adrenaline Vault http://www.avault.com

Gamers Ammo http://www.gamers-ammo.com
Gamers.com http://www.gamers.com
Games Domain http://www.gamesdomain.com
Gamespot http://www.gamespot.com
Gamespy http://www.gamespy.com
Happy Puppy http://www.happypuppy.com
Macintosh Gamer's Ledge http://www.macledge.com
Old Man Murray http://www.oldmanmurray.com

Console Games

Console Domain http://www.consoledomain.com
Hotgames.com http://www.hotgames.com
Psx Extreme http://www.psxextreme.com
Video Game Strategies http://vgstrategies.about.com

Genealogy

Trace your ancestry

Don't expect to enter your name and produce an instant family tree, but you should be able to fill in a few gaps or dig up some dirt on your ancestors:
http://www.genhomepage.com • http://www.genealogytoday.com
http://www.familytreemaker.com • http://www.cyndislist.com
http://www.ancestry.com • http://www.familysearch.org
http://www.rootsweb.com • http://www.surnameweb.org

Once you've found a name, put a face to it:
Ancient Faces http://www.ancientfaces.com

Greetings Cards and Invites

If stretching the bounds of good taste doesn't bother you,

you'll find thousands of sites that will gladly speckle your message with multimedia tutti-frutti. Rather than forward your "card" directly, your victim will generally receive an invitation to drop by and collect it from the site. And, of course, being masked by a third party makes it perfect for harassing valentines and sending ransom notes. For hundreds of virtual card dispensers, see:

Card Lady http://www.cardlady.com
Free Greeting Cards http://www.freegreetingcards.org
Postcard Heaven http://www.postcard-heaven.com
Postcards.com http://www.postcards.com

But, check out the most popular ones first:

Blue Mountain http://www.bluemountain.com
eGreetings http://www.egreetings.com
Hallmark http://www.hallmark.com
Pulp Cards http://www.pulpcards.com
Regards.com http://www.regards.com
Tackymail http:/www.tackymail.com
Virtual Insults http://www.virtualinsults.com
Yahoo Greetings http://greetings.yahoo.com

Digital Voodoo
http://www.pinstruck.com
Curse thy neighbor.

Hotpaper.com
http://www.hotpaper.com
Fill in the blanks to create handy everyday documents like greetings cards, references, eviction notices, and credit card disputes.

Interflora
http://www.interflora.com
Punch in your credit card number, apology, and delivery details, and land back in the good books before you get home. For thousands more flower vendors, drill down through your local Yahoo, or see:
http://dmoz.org/Shopping/Flowers/Florists/
For advice on floral etiquette, history, meanings, and choosing the right

florist, see: http://www.aboutflowers.com

Invites

http://invites.yahoo.com • http://www.regards.com
http://www.egreetings.com
Throwing a slide night? Here's an easy way to create an instant email invitation and manage the thousands of RSVPs. For help planning: http://www.theplunge.com

iPrint

http://www.iprint.com • http://www.cardcorp.co.uk (UK)
Need some business cards or invitations fast? Design them online for snappy delivery either via email or on the paper of your choice. Naturally, the latter option costs.

Postcardland

http://postcardland.com
Confuse your parole officer by sending them a postcard from the other side of the world.

Virtual Presents

http://www.virtualpresents.com • http://www.it3c.co.uk
Why waste money on real gifts when, after all, isn't it the thought that counts?

Health

While the Net's certainly an unrivaled medical library, it's also an unrivaled promulgator of the 21st-century equivalent of "old wives' tales". So by all means research your ailment and pick up fitness tips online, but like the pill bottles say, check with your doctor before putting it to work. While you're with your GP, ask if they use the Net for research and if so, which sites they recommend. While not being online by now doesn't necessarily make them a bad doctor, it does suggest they're a little complacent.

Don't expect to go online for first aid advice. If it's an emergency, you won't have time. The Net is better for in depth research and anecdotal advice. None of which comes quickly. But once you've spent a few sessions online studying your complaint, you'll be fully prepared to state your case. You'll know straight away whether your GP knows their stuff. To find a doctor, dentist or specialist, try: **http://www.medavenue.com** (US) or **http://www.netdoctor.co.uk** (UK).

WorldClinic (**http://www.worldclinic.com**) provides phone fax or email response that could save your life on the road.

It's hard to say where to start your research. Perhaps a directory: Yahoo et al have seriously stacked medical arms, or you could try one of the specialist health portals:

Achoo http://www.achoo.com
Hospitalweb UK http://www.hospitalweb.co.uk
MedExplorer http://www.medexplorer.com
Patient UK http://www.patient.co.uk
SearchBug http://www.searchbug.com/health/

Or a government gateway:

Healthfinder http://www.healthfinder.gov
HealthinSite (AUS) http://www.healthinsite.gov.au
Health on the Net http://www.hon.ch
NHS Direct (UK) http://www.nhsdirect.nhs.uk
US National Library of Medicine http://www.nlm.nih.gov
World Health Organization http://www.who.int

You'll find tons of excellent self-help megasites, though the presence of sponsors may raise ethical questions. Their features vary, but medical encyclopedias, personal health tests and Q&A services are fairly standard fare. Starting with the former US **Surgeon General's** site, try:

Dr Koop http://www.drkoop.com
HealthAtoZ.com http://www.healthatoz.com
HealthCentral http://www.healthcentral.com
HealthWorld http://www.healthy.net
Intellihealth http://www.intelihealth.com
Mayo Clinic http://www.mayoclinic.com
Netdoctor.co.uk http://www.netdoctor.co.uk
ThriveOnline http://www.thriveonline.com
24Dr.com (UK) http://www.24dr.com
WebMD (US, CA) http://www.webmd.com
WebMD (Lycos) http://webmd.lycos.com
Yahoo Health http://health.yahoo.com

Most of the above are fluent in the needs of mothers-to-be, but if you're at that stage of your life when you can't get too much information on babies and their descent into the light, try:

B4Baby (UK) http://www.b4baby.co.uk
Baby Center http://www.babycenter.com
Baby Centre (UK) http://www.babycentre.co.uk
Baby World (UK) http://www.babyworld.co.uk
Dr Greene http://www.drgreene.com
MotherChild (AUS) http://www.motherchild.com.au
National Childbirth Trust (UK) http://www.nct-online.org
Parent Soup http://www.parentsoup.com
Parenthood Web http://www.parenthoodweb.com
Pregnancy Calendar http://www.pregnancycalendar.com

But for serious research go straight to **Medline**, the US

National Library of Medicine's database. It archives, references, and abstracts thousands of medical journals and periodicals going back to 1966. You can get it free at PubMed, but the subscription services may have access to more material. These are aimed more at health pros and students:

BioMedNet http://www.bmn.com

Medscape http://www.medscape.com

Ovid http://www.ovid.com

PubMed http://www.ncbi.nlm.nih.gov/PubMed/

Despite first appearances, Martindale's maintains an outstanding directory of medical science links:

Martindale's Health Science guide
http://www-sci.lib.uci.edu/HSG/HSGuide.html

If you know what you have and you want to contact other sufferers, use a search engine (**http://www.google.com**) or directory (**http://dmoz.org**) to find organizations and personal home pages. They should direct you to useful mailing lists and discussion groups. If not, try Google Groups (**http://groups.google.com**) to find the right newsgroups, and PAML (**http://www.paml.org**) for mailing lists.

Alex Chiu's Eternal Life Device

http://www.alexchiu.com
Live forever or come back for your money.

All Nurses
http://www.allnurses.com
Springboard to chat groups, research data, professional bodies, jobs, and other nursing resources.

Alternative Medicine

http://altmedicine.about.com

http://www.alternativemedicine.com
http://www.wholehealthmd.com • http://www.alternativedr.com
http://dmoz.org/Health/Alternative/
Part of the Net's ongoing research function is the ability to contact people who've road-tested alternative remedies and can report on their efficacy. Start here and work your way to an answer. See also the entry for Quackwatch.

Aromatherapy

http://www.aromaweb.com
Psuedoscience it may be (http://skepdic.com/aroma.html), but you'll be on the way to smelling better. And, surely that can't be a bad thing.

Ask Dr Weil

http://www.drweil.com
Popdoctor Andrew Weil's eagerness to prescribe from a range of bewildering, and often conflicting, alternative therapies has seen him called a quack in some quarters, but not by Warner. TIME put him on the front cover and gave him a job peddling advice beside vitamin ads. Whether or not you believe in food cures, his daily Q&As are always a good read.

Cancer Research Project

http://www.ud.com
Use your computer to help find a cure for cancer.

Color Vision Test

http://www.umist.ac.uk/UMIST_OVS/UES/COLOUR0.HTM
Do you dress in the dark or are you merely color-blind?

Dr Squat

http://www.drsquat.com • http://www.weightsnet.com
Avoid getting sand kicked in your face through deep full squats.

Drugs

http://www.erowid.org • http://www.lycaeum.org
http://www.trashed.co.uk
http://www.perkel.com/politics/issues/pot.htm
http://www.neuropharmacology.com
http://www.druglibrary.org
Everything you ever wanted to know about the pleasure, pain and politics of psychoactive drugs and the cultures built around them.

GYN101

http://www.gyn101.com
Swot up for your next gynecological exam. But if you're after honors go straight to: http://www.obgyn.net

Gyro's Excellent Hernia Adventure

http://www.cryogenius.com/mesh/
Holiday snaps from under the knife.

HandHeldMed

http://www.handheldmed.com • http://medicalpocketpc.com
http://www.pdamd.com
Arm your pocket computer with medical software and references.

Medicinal Herb Faq

http://metalab.unc.edu/herbmed/mediherb.html
If it's in your garden and it doesn't kill you, it can only make you stronger. More leafy cures and love drugs at:
http://www.algy.com/herb/
http://www.botanical.com
http://www.herbal-ahp.org

Mental Health

http://www.mentalhealth.com
Guaranteed you'll come out of this site convinced there's something wrong with you. Worry your way along to:
http://www.anxietynetwork.com
http://www.onlinepsych.com

Museum of Questionable Medical Devices

http://www.mtn.org/quack/
Gallery of health-enhancing products where even breaks weren't bundled free.

Nutritional Supplements

http://www.nutritionalsupplements.com
First-hand experiences with vitamins, bodybuilding supplements, and other dubious health-shop fodder.

Quackwatch

http://www.quackwatch.com • http://www.ncahf.org
http://www.hcrc.org • http://nccam.nih.gov
Separating the docs from the ducks. Don't buy into any alternative remedies until you've read these pages.

Reuters Health

http://www.reutershealth.com
Medical newswires, reviews, opinion, and reference.

RxList

http://www.rxlist.com • http://www.virtualdrugstore.com
http://www.pharminfo.com
Look up your medication to ensure you're not being poisoned.

Spas Directory (UK)

http://www.thespasdirectory.com
Locate a British spa or health resort.

Talk Surgery

http://www.talksurgery.com
Discuss your operation with people who appear interested.

The Virtual Hospital

http://www.vh.org
Patient care and distance learning via online multimedia tools such as illustrated surgical walkthroughs.

The Visible Human Project

http://www.nlm.nih.gov/research/visible/
Whet your appetite by skimming through scans of a thinly filleted serial killer, and then top it off with a fly-through virtual colonoscopy. For higher production values, see the Virtual Body:
http://www.medtropolis.com

What Have I Got?

http://www.whathaveigot.net

Worry yourself sick through self-diagnosis.

Wing Hop Fung

http://www.winghopfung.com
Chinese cures by mail order.

World Sexual Records

http://www.sexualrecords.com
Go for gold in slap and tickle.

Yoga

http://www.timages.com/yoga.htm • http://www.yogasite.com
Stretch yourself back into shape with a personalized routine.

Home and Garden

Ask the Master Plumber

http://www.clickit.com/bizwiz/homepage/plumber.htm
Save a small fortune by unblocking your own toilet.

Australian Botanical Gardens

http://www.anbg.gov.au
Guide to Canberra's Botanical Garden and flora down under.

Buy.co.uk

http://www.buy.co.uk/Personal/
Clinch the best deal on British utilities and loans.

Carniverous Plants FAQ

http://www.sarracenia.com/cp.html
Erect your first line of defense.

Feng Shui

http://www.qi-whiz.com • http://www.fengshui-fanzine.co.uk
Recreate the ambience of a Chinese restaurant.

GardenWeb

http://www.gardenweb.com
Hosts a multitude of gardening forums both here and on its European and Australian sister sites, plus a gardening glossary, plant database,

calendar of garden events, plant exchange, and plenty of meaty articles. Here's more:
http://www.gardensonline.com.au
http://www.gardenbed.com.au
http://www.gardenguides.com • http://gardening.about.com
http://www.gardening.com
http://www.gardening365.co.uk (UK)
http://www.e-garden.co.uk (UK)
http://www.expertgardener.com (UK)
For even more gardening sites, try the following arms of the Open Directory:
http://dmoz.org/Home/Gardens/
http://dmoz.org/Science/Biology/Botany/

Gothic Gardening

http://www.gothic.net/~malice/
Grow a little greenhouse of horrors.

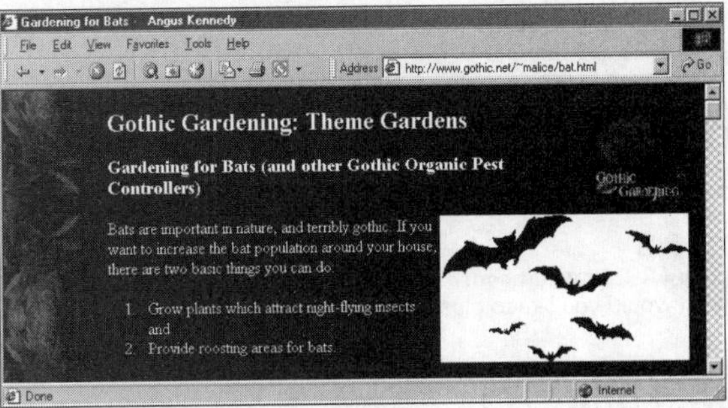

Home Improvement Network

http://www.improvenet.com (US)
http://www.improveline.com (UK)
http://www.homepro.com (UK)
http://www.myspace.com.au (AUS)
Peruse the latest design ideas and find someone to do the job. You can even screen your local builders against public records and find the one least likely to quaff all your home brew and sell your nude holiday snaps to the National Enquirer.

Home Sewing Association
http://www.sewing.org
Pick up hints from a bunch of sew and sews.

Home Tips
http://www.hometips.com • http://www.homestore.com
http://www.doityourself.com • http://www.naturalhandyman.com
http://www.askthebuilder.com
Load your toolbox, roll up your sleeves, and prepare to go in.

How to Clean Anything
http://www.howtocleananything.com
Just add elbow grease.

Internet Directory for Botany
http://www.botany.net/IDB/ • http://botany.about.com
Starting points for serious plantlife research.

The Kitchen Garden Online
http://www.taunton.com/kg/
For cooks who love to garden, or perhaps vice versa.

Postcode Plants Database (UK)
http://fff.nhm.ac.uk/fff/
Find the right native trees, shrubs, and flowers for your area.

This to That
http://www.thistothat.com
So what would you like to glue today?

Kids (mostly)

It's your choice whether you want to let them at it headlong or bridle their experience through rose-colored filters. But if you need guidance, or pointers towards the most kidtastic chowder, set sail into these realms:

About.com (Kids) http://kids.about.com

American Libraries Assoc
http://www.ala.org/parentspage/greatsites/

Australian Families Guide http://www.aba.gov.au/family/
Kids Click http://www.worldsofsearching.org
Kids Domain http://www.kidsdomain.com
Kids Identifying and Discovering Sites http://kids.library.wisc.edu
Lightspan http://www.lightspan.com
Open Directory: Kids http://dmoz.org/Home/Kids/
Scholastic International http://www.scholastic.com
Surfing the Net with Kids http://www.surfnetkids.com
Yahooligans (Yahoo for kids) http://www.yahooligans.com

The search engines Google, AltaVista, and All the Web can also be set to filter out adult content. For encyclopedias and dictionaries, see p.418.

Adolescent Adulthood

http://www.adolescentadulthood.com
How to flirt, date, kiss, and ultimately dump, so you won't spend the rest of the year being teased at the bus stop.

Beakman & Jax

http://www.beakman.com
Answers to typical kid questions from the likes of "why poop is brown" and "why farts smell" to "why your voice sounds different on a tape recorder" and "why the TV goes crazy while the mixer is on".

Bizarre Things You Can Make In Your Kitchen

http://freeweb.pdq.net/headstrong/
Rainy-day science projects and general mischief such as volcanoes, stink bombs, cosmic ray detectors, fake blood, and hurricane machines.

The Bug Club

http://www.ex.ac.uk/bugclub/
Creepy-crawly fan club with e-pal page, newsletters, and pet care sheets on how to keep your newly bottled tarantulas, cockroaches, and stick insects alive.

Bullying Online

http://www.bullying.co.uk
Advice and support channels for bullied children and their parents.

Perhaps a few sessions of self-defense might be a good place to start: http://www.blackbeltmag.com/bbkids/

Children's Literature Web Guide

http://www.ucalgary.ca/~dkbrown/
Critical roundup of recent kids' books, and links to texts.

Club Girl Tech

http://www.girltech.com
Encourages smart girls to get interested in technology without coming across all geeky.

Cyberteens

http://www.cyberteens.com
Submit your music, art, or writing to a public gallery. You might even win a prize.

Decoding Nazi Secrets

http://www.pbs.org/wgbh/nova/decoding/ • http://www.thunk.com
Use World War II weaponry to exchange secret messages with your clued-in pals.

Disney.com

http://www.disney.com
Guided catalog of Disney's real world movies, books, theme parks, records, interactive CD-ROMs and such, plus a squeaky-clean Net directory. For an unofficial Disney chaperon, see: http://laughingplace.com

eHobbies

http://www.ehobbies.com
Separating junior hobbyists from their pocket money.

Funbrain

http://www.funbrain.com
Tons of mind-building quizzes, games, and puzzles for all ages.

Funschool

http://www.funschool.com
Educational games for preschoolers.

The History Net

http://www.thehistorynet.com • http://www.historybuff.com
Bites of world history, with an emphasis on the tough guys going in with guns.

Kids' Games

http://kidsnetgames.about.com
http://dmoz.org/Home/Kids/Games/
http://www.wicked4kids.com
http://www.kidsdomain.com/games/
http://www.randomhouse.com/seussville/games/
http://games.yahoo.com/games/yahooligans.html
Give the babysitter a break.

Kids' Jokes

http://www.kidsjokes.co.uk
http://www.users.bigpond.com/lander/default.htm
Reams of clean jokes, riddles, and knock-knocks.

Kids' Space

http://www.kids-space.org
Hideout for kids to swap art, music, and stories with new friends across the world.

Learn2

http://learn2.com
Figure out how to do all sorts of things from fixing a zipper to spinning a basketball. While the interests aren't strictly for kids, there's nothing here that's too hard for a whippersnapper.

The Little Animals Activity Centre

http://www.bbc.co.uk/education/laac/
The second the music starts and the critters start jiggling you'll know you're in for a treat. Let your youngest heir loose here after breakfast and expect no mercy until morning tea. As cute as it gets.

Magic Tricks

http://www.magictricks.com • http://www.trickshop.com
http://www.magicweek.co.uk
Never believe it's not so.

Neopets

http://www.neopets.com
Nurture a "virtual pet" until it dies.

Roper's Knots

http://www.realknots.com
It's not what you know; it's what knots you know.

Sing Along Midis and Lyrics

http://www.niehs.nih.gov/kids/musicchild.htm
Gather round for a spot of keyboard karaoke.

StarChild

http://starchild.gsfc.nasa.gov
Nasa's educational funhouse for junior astronomers. See also:
http://www.earthsky.com • http://www.starport.com

Starwars Origami

http://ftmax.com/ArtLife/Origami/SW/sw.htm
Graduate from flapping birds onto Destroyer Droids and Tie Fighters. Prefer something that will actually fly? See: http://www.aricraft.com
For more paperfolding, see: http://www.origami.com

Toy Stores

http://www.faoschwartz.com • http://www.toysrus.com (.co.uk)
It's just like Xmas all year round.

The Unnatural Museum

http://www.unmuseum.org
Lost worlds, dinosaurs, UFOs, pyramids and other mysterious exhibits from the outer bounds of space and time.

The Yuckiest Site on the Internet

http://www.yucky.com
Fun science with a leaning towards the icky-sticky and the creepy-crawly. But if you want to get thoroughly engrossed in the gross, slither right along to: http://www.grossology.org

Law and Crime

For legal primers, lawyer directories, legislation and self-help:

Australian Legal Info Inst http://www.austlii.edu.au
Delia Venables (UK) http://www.venables.co.uk
FindLaw (INT) http://www.findlaw.com
Free Advice (US) http://www.freeadvice.com
InfoLaw (UK) http://www.infolaw.co.uk
Law.com (US) http://www.law.com
Lawoffice.com (US) http://www.lawoffice.com
Lawrights (UK) http://www.lawrights.co.uk
'Lectric Law (US) http://www.lectlaw.com
Nolo.com (US) http://www.nolo.com
UKLegal (UK) http://www.uklegal.com

For more on criminal activities, trends, arrests and law enforcement, rustle through the following guides:

About Crime http://crime.about.com
Crime.com http://www.crime.com
Crime Spider http://www.crimespider.com
Open Directory http://dmoz.org/Society/Crime/

APBnews.com

http://www.apbonline.com
Highly acclaimed network news service focusing on crime, justice, and safety.

Brutal.com

http://www.brutal.com

Bad news from around the world, as it breaks.

Burglar.com

http://www.theburglar.com
Profit from stolen goods that somehow happened into your possession.

Copyright Myths

http://whatiscopyright.org
http://www.templetons.com/brad/copyright.html
Just because it's online doesn't make it yours.

Crime Magazine

http://www.crimemagazine.com
Encyclopedic collection of outlaw tales.

CrimeNet (AU)

http://www.crimenet.com.au
Pay to search a database of Aussie crims.

Cybercrime

http://www.cybercrime.gov
How to report online crooks.

Desktop Lawyer (UK)

http://www.desktoplawyer.net
Cut legal costs by doing it online.

Dumb Laws

http://www.dumblaws.com
Foreign legislation with limited appeal.

ECLS

http://www.e-commercelawsource.com
Global monitor and directory of online business law.

Police Officer's Directory

http://www.officer.com • http://www.cops.aust.com (AUS)
http://www.crimespider.com
Top of the pops cop directory with more than 1500 baddy-nabbing

bureaus snuggled in with law libraries, wanted listings, investigative tools, hate groups, special ops branches, and off-duty home pages. To see who's in Scotland Yard's bad books: http://www.met.police.uk

PursuitWatch

http://www.pursuitwatch.com
Get paged when there's a live police chase on TV.

Rate your risk

http://www.nashville.net/~police/risk/
See if you're likely to be raped, robbed, stabbed, shot, or beaten to death in the near future.

Money

If your bank's on the ball it will offer an online facility to check your balances, pay your bills, transfer funds, and export your transaction records into a bean counting program such as Quicken or Money. If that sounds appealing, and your bank isn't already on the case, start looking for a replacement. Favor one you can access via the Internet rather than by dialing direct. That way you can manage your cash through a Web browser whether you're at home, work, or in the cybercafé on top of Pik Kommunisma. For help finding a true online bank:

MyBank http://www.mybank.com
Online Banking Report http://www.netbanker.com
Qualisteam http://www.qualisteam.com

As long as you can resist the urge to daytrade away your inheritance, the Net should give you greater control over your financial future. You can research firms, plot trends, check live quotes, join tip lists and stock forums, track your portfolio live, trade shares, and access more news than is fit to read in a lifetime. By all means investigate a subscription service or two – at least for the free trial period – but unless you need split second data feeds or "expert" timing advice you should be able to get by without paying. Start here:

Yahoo Finance http://quote.yahoo.com

or local counterpart such as

Yahoo Australia http://quote.yahoo.com.au
Yahoo UK http://quote.yahoo.co.uk

Apart from housing the Net's most exhaustive finance directory, Yahoo pillages data from a bunch of the top finance sources and presents it all in a seamless, friendly format. Enter a stock code, for example, and you'll get all the beef from the latest ticker price to a summary of insider trades. In some markets stocks have their own forums, which, let's face it, are only there to spread rumors. In other words, be very skeptical of anything you read or that's sent to you in unsolicited email. For more, see:

Investment Scams
http://www.sec.gov/investor/pubs/cyberfraud.htm

Yahoo is by no means complete nor necessarily the best in every area, so try a few of these as well:

ABC (AU) http://www.abc.net.au/news/business/
Asia Gateway http://www.asiagateway.com
Bloomberg (INT) http://www.bloomberg.com
CBS MarketWatch http://cbs.marketwatch.com
Egoli (AU) http://www.egoli.com.au
FinancialWeb http://www.financialweb.com
Free Real Time Quotes http://www.freerealtime.com
Gay Financial Network http://www.gfn.com
Interactive Investor (UK, SA, Asia) http://www.iii.co.uk
Investorama http://www.investorama.com
Market Eye (UK) http://www.market-eye.co.uk
MetaMarkets http://www.metamarkets.com

Microsoft MoneyCentral http://moneycentral.msn.com
Money Extra (UK) http://www.moneyextra.com
Muslim Investor http://www.muslim-investor.com
Quicken (US, AU) http://www.quicken.com (.au)
Raging Bull http://www.ragingbull.com
The Street http://www.thestreet.com
Wall Street City http://www.wallstreetcity.com
Wall Street Research Net http://www.wsrn.com

You'll no doubt be after a broker next. As with banking, any broker or fund manager who's not setting up online probably doesn't deserve your business. In fact, many traders are dumping traditional brokers in favor of the exclusively online houses. E*Trade (**http://www.etrade.com**), for example, offers discount brokerage in at least nine countries (click on "International" to find your local branch). But traditional brokers are catching on. Many have cut their commissions, and offer online services in line with the Internet competition. So it pays to shop around. You might find you prefer to research online and trade by phone. To compare US brokers:

Gomez.com http://www.gomez.com
Ms Money http://www.msmoney.com
Smart Money http://www.smartmoney.com

If you're outside the US, try your local Yahoo for leads. A word of warning, though: some online brokers have experienced outages where they were unable to trade. So if the market crashes in a big way, it mightn't hurt to play safe and use the phone instead.

BigCharts
http://www.bigcharts.com • http://www.stockcharts.com
http://www.tradesignals.com • http://www.livecharts.com
Whip up family-sized graphs of US stocks, mutual funds, and market indices.

Clearstation

http://www.clearstation.com

Run your stock picks through a succession of grueling obstacle courses to weed out the weaklings or simply copy someone else's portfolio.

Earnings Whispers

http://www.earningswhispers.com

When a stock price falls upon the release of higher than expected earnings, chances are the expectations being "whispered" amongst traders prior to open were higher than those circulated publicly. Here's where to find out what's being said behind your back. For the biggest surprises, see: **http://biz.yahoo.com/z/extreme.html**

Financial Times

http://www.ft.com

Business news, commentary, delayed quotes, and closing prices from London. It's free until you hit the archives.

Foreign Exchange Rates

http://quote.yahoo.com • http://www.xe.net/ucc/full.shtml

Round-the-clock rates, conversion calculators, and intraday charts on pretty close to the full set of currencies.

To chart further back, see:

http://pacific.commerce.ubc.ca/xr/plot.html

Hoovers

http://www.hoovers.com

Research US, UK, and European companies.

ICreditReport

http://www.icreditreport.com

Dig up any US citizen's credit ratings.

IExchange.com

http://www.iexchange.com

Tracks and ranks market prophets.

Insider Scores

http://www.insiderscores.com

Get the inside on US and Asian directors' trades.

Investment FAQ

http://www.invest-faq.com

Learn the ropes from old hands.

InvestorWords

http://www.investorwords.com

Can't tell your hedge rate from your asking price? Brush up on your finance-speak here.

Island

http://www.island.com

See US equity orders queued up on dealers' screens.

Missing Money

http://www.missingmoney.com • http://www.findcash.com

Reclaim those US dollars you're owed.

MoneyChimp

http://www.moneychimp.com

Plain English primer in the mechanics of financial maths.

Money Origami

http://www.umva.com/~clay/money/

It's much more fun when you can make something out of it.

Motley Fool

http://www.fool.com • http://www.fool.co.uk

Forums, tips, quotes, and sound advice.

Paypal

http://www.paypal.com

Arrange online payments through a third party.

RateNet

http://www.rate.net • http://www.bankrate.com

Tracks and ranks finance rates across over 11,000 US institutions in 175 markets. Also links to thousands of banking sites and investment products. For UK and Australian rates, see:

http://www.blays.co.uk • http://www.buy.co.uk

http://www.bankchoice.com.au

Tax & Accounting Sites Directory

http://www.taxsites.com

Links to everything you need to know about doling out your annual pound of flesh.

Technical Analysis Tutorials

http://www.e-analytics.com/techdir.htm

Beginners guide to fortune-telling the markets using charts and indicators.

Wall Street Journal Interactive

http://www.wsj.com

Not only is this online edition equal to the print, its charts and data archives give it an edge. That's why you shouldn't complain that it's not free. After all, if it's your type of paper, you should be able to afford it, bigshot.

Where's George?

http://www.wheresgeorge.com

Put a tail on your greenback.

Music

If you're at all into music you've certainly come to the right place. Whether you want to hear it, read about it, or watch it being performed, you'll be swamped with options. If you're after a specific band, label, or music genre, the Ultimate Band List on Artists Direct should be your first port of call:

Ultimate Band List http://www.ubl.com

Followed by these directories:

About.com http://home.about.com/musicperform/
Open Directory http://dmoz.org/Arts/Music/
SonicNet http://www.sonicnet.com/allmusic/
Yahoo http://music.yahoo.com

As ever, if these fail to satisfy, try:

Google http://www.google.com

For an astoundingly complete music database spanning most popular genres, with bios, reviews, ratings, and keyword crosslinks to related sounds, sites, and online ordering, see:

All Music Guide http://www.allmusic.com

But for searching through discographies of practically every album ever released on CD, nothing comes close to Gracenote's CDDB database, which provides the track listings in most computer CD players. It's fantastic for finding out who performed a certain song, or what album it was on. Okay, maybe Amazon comes close.

Amazon.com http://www.amazon.com
Gracenote http://www.gracenote.com

And don't overlook our own compilations and printed guides to Rock, Reggae, Drum & Bass, Jazz, Classical, House, Techno, Soul, World, and Opera:

Rough Guides to Music
http://www.roughguides.com
World Music Network
http://www.worldmusic.net

Feel like singing along but don't know the words? Try tapping the song, performer, or author into SongFile for a hyperconnected rundown on everyone concerned with the tune, and often the lyrics, sheet music, and a link to buy it on CD. If it doesn't stock the sheet music, try Yahoo for another dealer.

Songfile http://www.songfile.com

Or for rapping rhymes:

Original Hip Hop Lyrics Archive http://www.ohhla.com

Much of the mainstream music press is already well established online. For the latest music news:

Artists Direct http://artistsdirect.com

You'll find thousands of archived reviews, charts, gig guides, band bios, selected features, shopping links, news, and various sound artifacts courtesy of these familiar beacons:

Billboard http://www.billboard-online.com
Blues and Soul http://www.bluesandsoul.co.uk
Dirty Linen http://kiwi.futuris.net/linen/
Folk Roots http://www.froots.demon.co.uk
NME http://nme.com
Q http://www.q4music.com
Rolling Stone http://www.rollingstone.com
The Source http://www.thesource.com
Spin http://www.spin.com
Vibe http://www.vibe.com

And if your concentration is up to it, MTV:

Americas http://www.mtv.com • http://www.mtvla.com
Asia Pacific http://www.mtvasia.com
Europe http://www.mtveurope.com
UK http://www.mtv.co.uk • http://www.mtv2.co.uk

Don't buy a stereo component until you've consulted the world's biggest audio opinionbases:

AudioReview.com http://www.audioreview.com

AudioWeb http://www.audioweb.com

eCoustics http://www.ecoustics.com

What Hi-Fi http://www.whathifi.com

Or if you wouldn't settle for less than a single-ended triode amp:

Audiophilia http://www.audiophilia.com

GlassWare http://www.glass-ware.com

Stereophile http://www.stereophile.com

Triode Guild http://www.meta-gizmo.com

Consult these directories for manufacturers, shops, and other audio sites:

AudioWorld http://www.audioworld.com

Hifiheaven.com http://www.hifiheaven.com

UK Hi-Fi Dealers http://hifi.dealers.co.uk

Addicted to Noise

http://www.addict.com • http://www.addict.com.au

Monthly news and reviews with a heavy bias towards the rowdy end of the pop rock spectrum.

Art of the Mixed Tape

http://www.artofthemix.org

"If you have ever killed an afternoon making a mix, spent the evening making a cover, and then mailed a copy off to a friend after having made a copy for yourself, well, this is the site for you". Kind of says it all.

Band Names Registry

http://www.bandname.com

Register your bandname, post some press releases, find a soundtrack deal, and then look for someone to play all the instruments.

Buying Records Online

Shopping for music is another area where the Net not only equals, but outshines, its terrestrial counterparts. Apart from the convenience of not having to tramp across town, you can find almost anything on current issue, whether or not it's released locally, and in many cases preview album tracks in RealAudio. You might save money, too, depending on where you buy, whether you're hit with tax, and how the freight stacks up. Consider splitting your order if duty becomes an issue.

The biggest hitch you'll strike is when stock is put on back order. Web operators can boast a huge catalog simply because they order everything on the fly. This puts you at the mercy of their distributors. The trouble is your entire order might be held up by one item. The better shops check their stock levels before confirming your order, and follow its progress until delivery.

As far as where to shop goes, that depends on your taste. In terms of sheer innovation, Tunes.com stands out by profiling your preferences, recommending selections, linking to reviews, and serving up ample samples. Amazon is also impressive – but then you can't go too far wrong with most of the blockbusters:

Amazon (US, UK) **http://www.amazon.com (.co.uk)**
AudioStreet (UK) **http://www.audiostreet.co.uk**
BOL (INT) **http://www.bol.com**
Book, Music, Video Store **http://www.bmvs.com**
Borders **http://www.borders.com**
CDNow **http://www.cdnow.com**
CD Universe **http://www.cduniverse.com**
Chaos (AUS) **http://www.chaosmusic.com**
HMV (AUS, JP, UK, US) **http://www.hmv.com**
Sam Goody **http://www.samgoody.com**
Tower Records **http://www.towerrecords.com**
Tunes.com **http://www.tunes.com**
Virgin Megastore **http://www.virginmega.com**

Or, if you're after something more obscure, you'll find no shortage of options under the appropriate Yahoo categories or at: **http://www.offitsface.com/links.html**

Like these, for example:

CyberCD

http://www.cybercd.de • **http://www.musicexpress.com**

German outfits with enormous catalogs, though not so cheap.

Dusty Groove

http://www.dustygroove.com

Soul, jazz, Latin, Brazil, and funk on vinyl and CD.

Funk45

http://www.funk45.com

Rare 70s funk and soul.

dusty groove america

Global Electronic Music Market

http://gemm.com

One-point access to over two million new and used records from almost two thousand sources. See also: http://www.secondspin.com

Hard to find records

http://www.htfr.com

Record-finding agency that specializes in house, hip-hop, soul, and disco vinyl.

Penny Black

http://www.pennyblackmusic.com

Indie pop, punk and electronica.

Record Finder

http://www.recordfinders.com

Deleted vinyl, including over 200,000 45s.

Rockinghorse Records (AU)

http://www.rockinghorse.net

Indie, dance, and Australian obscurities.

For a listing of price comparison agents see Shopping (p.195).

Canonical List of Weird Band Names

http://www.geminiweb.net/bandnames/
Just be thankful your parents weren't so creative. Here's the story behind a few: http://www.heathenworld.com/bandname/

Classical Music on the Net

http://www.musdoc.com/classical/
http://www.gmn.com/classical/
Gateway to the timeless.

The Dance Music Resource

http://www.juno.co.uk
New and forthcoming dance releases for mail order, UK radio slots, and a stacked directory.

Dancetech

http://www.dancetech.com
One-stop shop for techno toys and recording tips. For more on synths: http://www.synthzone.com and http://www.sonicstate.com

Dial-the-Truth Ministries

http://www.av1611.org
So why does Satan get all the good music?

DJ University

http://dju.prodj.com
Become a wedding spinner.

dotmusic

http://www.dotmusic.com
Top source of UK and global music news, weekly charts, and new releases in RealAudio. See also: http://www.music3w.com

Getoutthere.bt.com

http://www.getoutthere.bt.com
Expose your unsung talents or listen to other unsigned acts.

Harmony Central

http://www.harmonycentral.com
Directory and headspace for musicians of all persuasions.

Independent Underground Music Archive

http://www.iuma.com
Full-length tracks and bios from thousands of unsigned and indie-label underground musicians.

Jazz

http://www.jazzreview.com • http://www.allaboutjazz.com
http://www.downbeat.com
Bottomless drawer of beard-stroking delights.

Kareoke.com

http://www.kareoke.com
Sing along in the privacy of your own home.

Large Hot Pipe Organ

http://www.lhpo.org
Thrill to the throb of the world's first MIDI controlled, propane powered, explosion organ.

Launch.com

http://www.launch.com
Thousands of music videos, audio channels, record reviews, and chat forums.

Live Concerts

http://www.liveconcerts.com
Major gigs live in RealAudio.

MIDI Farm

http://www.midifarm.com
Synthesized debasements of pop tunes, TV themes, and film scores. Cheesy listening at its finest.

Minidisc.org

http://www.minidisc.org
Keep in tune with Sony's troubled Minidisc format.

Mr Lucky

http://www.mrlucky.com
Get smooth with rhythm 'n' booze.

Rap Network

http://www.rapnetwork.com • http://www.hiphopsite.com
http://www.scratch.dk • http://www.rebirthmag.com
http://www.360hiphop.com
Fresh phrases rhymed daily. All gesticulating hands on deck report to: http://www.turntablism.com

Scorchin' Soul

http://www.scorchinsoul.co.uk • http://www.soulcity.ndo.co.uk
Listen to hundreds of 60s and Northern Soul clips.

Shareware Music Machine

http://www.hitsquad.com/smm/
Tons of shareware music players, editors, and composition tools for every platform.

Show and Tell Music

http://www.showandtellmusic.com
Albums much cooler than anything you own.

Sonic Net

http://www.sonicnet.com
Big-name live cybercasts, streaming audio and video channels, chats, news, and reviews.

Sony

http://www.sony.com
Think about everything that Sony flogs. Now imagine it all squeezed under one roof.

Sounds Online

http://www.soundsonline.com
Preview loops and samples, free in RealAudio. Pay to download studio quality. If it's effects you're after: http://www.sounddogs.com

SS7x7 Sound System

http://www.ss7x7.com
http://www.jotto.com/bubblesoap/mixer.html

Mix your own tracks in Shockwave. Or, have a bit of a scratch:
http://www.turntables.de

Taxi

http://www.taxi.com
Online music A&R service. And guess what? You and your plastic kazoo are just what they're looking for.

Whammo (AUS)

http://www.whammo.com.au
Directory of Australian music news, releases, tours, and acts.

WholeNote

http://www.wholenote.com
Guitar resources and chat boards. For live lessons, see:
http://www.riffinteractive.com

For more music of the live streaming variety, fast forward to Radio (p.414) and for MP3s see: (p.270).

3D Insects

http://www.ento.vt.edu/~sharov/3d/3dinsect.html
Whiz around a selection of 3D bugs. They're not real insects but at

least they don't have pins through their backs. For a bigger range of bug bios see: http://insects.org

Bad Pets

http://www.geocities.com/bad_pets/
Animal owners speak out.

Birding

http://birding.about.com
http://www.camacdonald.com/birding/
http://dmoz.org/Recreation/Birdwatching/
Birds are such regional critters no one site could hope to cover them all. Use these to find the chirpiest one on your block.

The Complete Hamster site

http://www.hamsters.co.uk • http://www.direct.ca./hamster/
Definitive guides to online hamsters and their inevitable obituaries.

Dog of the Day

http://www.dogoftheday.com
Submit a shot of that drooling retard that adores you unconditionally. Or if it has its own Web page enter it in Dog Site of the Day: www.dogmark.net
No prize for guessing what's at http://www.catoftheday.com and http://www.petoftheday.com

eNature.com

http://www.enature.com
Vibrant field guides to North American flora and fauna.

Environmental Organization Directory

http://www.webdirectory.com • http://www.eco-portal.com
Find primary production and green-minded sites.

F@rming Online

http://www.rpl.com.au/farming/ • http://www.farmwide.com.au
Gateways to predominantly Australian agricultural resources.

ForestWorld

http://www.forestworld.com • http://forests.org
Timber tales from both sides of the dozer.

Interspecies Telepathic Communication

http://www.cyberark.com/animal/telepath.htm
Relax, you're not hearing voices. It's merely your pets playing mind games.

Mr Winkle

http://www.mrwinkle.com
Okay, so how cute is Mr Winkle? But is he really real?

Pet Shops

http://www.petsmart.com • **http://www.dogtoys.com**
http://www.petsonthe-brain.com (UK)
http://www.pets-pyjamas.co.uk (UK)
Seduce your mate with a rubber love-toy.

Planet Ark

http://www.planetark.org
Daily environmental news from Reuters. For more eco-news, try the Environmental News Network: **http://enn.com**

Predator Urines

http://www.predatorpee.com
Bewitch neighboring Jack Russells with a dab of bobcat balm or true blue roo poo: **http://www.roopooco.com**

Sea turtle migration-tracking

http://www.cccturtle.org/satwelc.htm
Adopt a bugged sea reptile and follow its trail.

Veterinary Medicine

http://vetmedicine.about.com • **http://netvet.wustl.edu**
Take good care of your little buddy.

World Society for the Protection of Animals

http://www.wspa.org.au (INT) • **http://www.rspca.org.au (AUS)**

http://www.rspca.org (UK)
Help protect animals from cruelty, and possible extinction. See also:
Australian Conservation Foundation http://www.acfonline.org.au
World Wildlife Fund http://www.wwf.org

News, Newspapers, and Magazines

Now that almost every magazine and newspaper in the world from Ringing World (**http://www.ringingworld.co.uk**) to the Falkland Island News (**http://www.sartma.com**) is discharging daily content onto the Net, it's beyond this guide to do much more than list a few of the notables and then point you in the right direction for more. The simplest way to find your favorite read would be to look for its address in a recent issue. Failing that try entering its name into a subject guide or search engine. If you don't have a title name and would prefer to browse by subject or region, try:
Open Directory http://dmoz.org/News/
Yahoo http://dir.yahoo.com/News_and_Media/

Or a specialist directory:
AJR NewsLink http://ajr.newslink.org/news.html
Editor & Publisher http://www.mediainfo.com
Metagrid http://www.metagrid.com

NewsDirectory http://www.newsdirectory.com
Online Newspapers http://www.onlinenewspapers.com
Publist http://www.publist.com

Newspapers rarely replicate themselves word for word online, but they often provide enough for you to live without the paper edition. Not bad considering they're generally free online before the paper hits the stands. Apart from whatever proportion of their print they choose to put online, they also tend to delve deeper into their less newsy areas, such as travel, IT, entertainment, and culture. Plus they often bolster this with exclusive content such as breaking news, live sports coverage, online shopping, opinion polls, and discussion groups. In most cases they'll also provide a way to search and retrieve archives, though it might incur a charge. There are also a few sites that index multiple news archives, again, usually at a price. Such as:
Electric Library http://www.elibrary.com
FindArticles.com http://www.findarticles.com
NewsLibrary (US) http://www.newslibrary.com
Northern Light http://www.nlsearch.com

The best free services for searching current or recent stories across hundreds of international news sources are:
Moreover http://www.moreover.com
News Index http://www.newsindex.com

Like someone to monitor the Web and assorted newswires for mention of your product or misdeeds? Try:
Webclipping.com http://www.webclipping.com

A few of the more popular news bugles, to get you started:

Australia

The Age http://www.theage.com.au
The Australian http://www.news.com.au
Sydney Morning Herald http://www.smh.com.au

UK

Economist http://www.economist.com
Evening Standard http://www.thisislondon.co.uk
Express http://www.express.co.uk
Guardian http://www.guardian.co.uk
Independent http://www.independent.co.uk
Mirror http://www.mirror.co.uk
News of the World http://www.newsoftheworld.co.uk
Observer http://www.observer.co.uk
The Sun http://www.the-sun.co.uk
Telegraph http://www.telegraph.co.uk
Times http://www.thetimes.co.uk

USA

The Atlantic http://www.theatlantic.com
Boston Globe http://www.globe.com
Brill's Content http://www.brillscontent.com
Chicago Sun Times http://www.suntimes.com
Christian Science Monitor http://www.csmonitor.com
Detroit News http://www.detroitnews.com
Houston Chronicle http://www.chron.com
LA Times http://www.latimes.com
National Enquirer http://www.nationalenquirer.com
National Geographic News http://www.ngnews.com
New Republic http://www.tnr.com
Newsweek http://www.newsweek.com

NY Post http://www.nypost.com
New York Press http://www.nypress.com
NY Times http://www.nytimes.com
The Onion http://www.theonion.com
Philadelphia Newspapers http://www.philly.com
San Francisco Gate http://www.sfgate.com
San Jose Mercury http://www.sjmercury.com
Seattle Times http://www.seattletimes.com
Time Daily http://www.time.com
USA Today http://www.usatoday.com
Village Voice http://www.villagevoice.com
Washington Post http://www.washingtonpost.com
Weekly World News http://www.weeklyworldnews.com

World

Arab News http://www.arabnews.com
Bangkok Post http://www.bangkokpost.net
Daily Mail & Guardian http://www.mg.co.za
El País http://www.elpais.es
Frankfurter Allgemeine http://www.faz.de
The Hindu http://www.hinduonline.com
Independent Media Center http://www.indymedia.org
Irish Times http://www.ireland.com
Jerusalem Post http://www.jpost.com
La Repubblica http://www.repubblica.it
La Stampa http://www.lastampa.it
Le Monde http://www.lemonde.fr
South China Morning Post http://www.scmp.com
Straights Times http://www.asia1.com
St Petersburg Times http://www.sptimes.ru
Tehelka http://www.tehelka.com
Times of India http://www.timesofindia.com

Toronto Star http://www.thestar.com

Like much you do online, reading news is addictive. You'll know you're hooked when you find yourself checking into newswires throughout the day to monitor moving stories. Try these for a fix:

Breaking news

ABC (Aus) http://www.abc.net.au/news/
ABC http://www.abcnews.com
Ananova (UK) http://www.ananova.com
Associated Press http://wire.ap.org
BBC (UK) http://news.bbc.co.uk
CBS http://www.cbsnews.com
CNN http://www.cnn.com
Fox http://www.foxnews.com
ITN (UK) http://www.itn.co.uk
NBC http://www.msnbc.com
News24 (SA) http://www.news24.co.za
Paknews (Pak) http://www.paknews.org
Reuters http://www.reuters.com
Satayam (Ind) http://www.news.satyamonline.com
Sky (UK) http://www.sky.com
Sydney Morning Herald (Aus) http://www.smh.com.au/breaking/
Wired News http://www.wired.com

To tap into several sources simultaneously:

News aggregators

Arts & Letters Daily http://www.cybereditions.com/aldaily/
Asia Observer http://www.asiaobserver.com
Excite Newstracker http://nt.excite.com
FastAsia (Asia) http://www.fastasia.com

Moreover (World) http://www.moreover.com
NewsHub http://www.newshub.com
NewsNow (UK) http://www.newsnow.co.uk
Russian Story http://www.russianstory.com
TotalNews http://www.totalnews.com
Yahoo News http://dailynews.yahoo.com

Most of the major portals such as Excite, Yahoo and MSN, also allow you to create a custom news page that draws from several sources, though none do it quite so thoroughly as Crayon. Infobeat does similar but delivers by email.

Crayon http://www.crayon.net
Infobeat http://www.infobeat.com

While most magazines maintain a site, they're typically more of an adjunct to the print than a substitute. Still, they're worth checking out, especially if they archive features and reviews, or break news between issues. Again, check a recent issue or one of the directories for an address. If you'd rather subscribe to the paper edition try:

http://enews.com • http://www.mmnews.com

http://www.britishmagazines.com (UK)

http://www.magsuk.com (UK)

http://www.acp.com.au (AUS)

http://www.universalmagazines.com.au (AUS)

Then there are the "ezines" – magazines that exist only online, or are delivered by email. However, as almost any regularly updated Web page fits this description, the term has lost much of its currency. Although most ezines burn out as quickly as they appear, a few of the pioneers are still kicking on. The best known, or at least the most controversial, would be the Drudge Report, the shock bulletin that set off the Lewinsky avalanche. A one-hit wonder perhaps, but still a bona-fide tourist attraction on the info goat track. Salon, however, is the real success story. It spans the arts, business, politics, lifestyle, and technology in a style that's both smart and breezy. Microsoft's long-suffering Slate marks similar territory, but succeeds more in being terribly dull. While Suck, arguably the only ezine that ever mattered, sits in a smug class all by itself. Worth reading daily, if not for its cocked eye on all that's wired and painfully modern, then at least for Terry Colon's cartoons.

Drudge Report http://www.drudgereport.com
Salon http://www.salon.com
Slate http://slate.msn.com
Suck http://www.suck.com

While most ezines operate independently, there are two networks that will connect you to a slew of quality underground productions of almost opposite persuasions. You'll know instantly whether they're your scene:
Chick Click http://www.chickclick.com
UGO http://www.ugo.com

IGN (Internet Gaming Network) treads similar, though generally tamer, ground to UGO, partnering mostly with high quality gaming, sci-fi, wrestling, and comic sites.

IGN http://www.ign.com/affiliates/

For more, try browsing one of the directories listed at:
http://dmoz.org/News/Ezines/Directories/

People, Advice, and Support

Adoption.com

http://www.adoption.com • http://www.adopting.org
http://www.bastards.org
Find a child or your original parents. Or if you suspect Screaming Jay put a spell on your Momma: http://www.jayskids.com

Alien Implant Removal and Deactivation

http://www.abduct.com/irm.htm
Discover, within a free three-minute phone call, how many times you've been abducted and which implants you're carrying. Then it's just a matter of surgically removing them: http://www.alienscalpel.com and sorting out your mental health. Perhaps the latter is all that's needed.

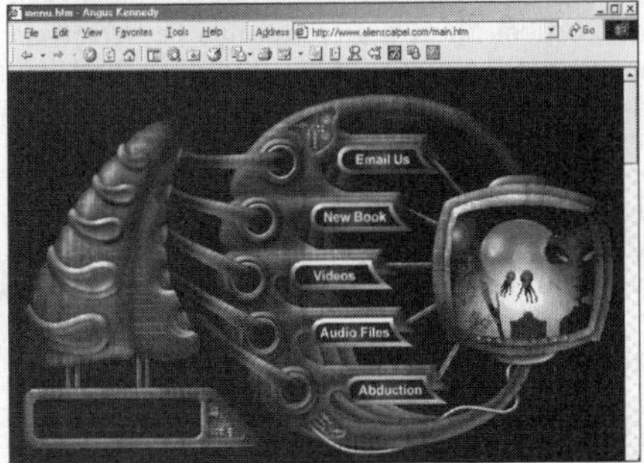

Final Thoughts

http://www.finalthoughts.com • http://www.mydeath.net
Plot your legacy.

Guy's Rules
http://www.guyrules.com
Learn to conceal your latent femininity.

Miss Abigail's Time Warp Advice
http://www.missabigail.com
Solve modern dilemmas with old school logic.

National Center for Missing and Exploited Children
http://www.missingkids.com
Help locate missing children and nail abductors.

Random Access Memory
http://www.randomaccessmemory.org
Store your treasured memories in a safe place.

Politics and Government

Most government departments, politicians, political aspirants, and causes maintain Web sites to spread the word and further their various interests. To find your local rep or candidate, start at their party's home page. These typically lay dormant unless there's a campaign in progress but can still be a good source of contacts to badger. Government departments, on the other hand, tirelessly belch out all sorts of trivia right down to the transcripts of ministerial radio interviews. So if you'd like to know about impending legislation, tax rulings, budget details and so forth, skip the party pages and go straight to the department. If you can't find its address through what's listed below, try:

Yahoo http://dir.yahoo.com/Government/
Open Directory http://dmoz.org/Society/Government/
or better still, jump on the phone.

For the latest counts from the tally room check the breaking news sites (p.402) on election night. Below is a selection of the most useful starting points in Australia, Britain, and the US.

Australia

Democrats http://www.democrats.org.au
Electoral Commission http://www.aec.gov.au
Federal Government http://www.fed.gov.au
Labour http://www.alp.org.au
Liberals http://www.liberal.org.au
Nationals http://www.npa.org.au
Prime Minister http://www.pm.gov.au
State & Local entry point http://www.nla.gov.au/oz/gov/

UK

British Politics Links http://www.ukpol.co.uk
Government Portal http://www.open.gov.uk
Labour http://www.labour.org.uk
Liberal Democrats http://www.libdems.org.uk
National Assembly for Wales http://www.wales.gov.uk
Natural Law http://www.natural-law-party.org.uk
Northern Ireland Assembly http://www.ni-assembly.gov.uk
Prime Minister http://www.pm.gov.uk
Republican National Committee http://www.rnc.org
Scottish Parliament http://www.scottish-parliament.com
Sinn Féin http://www.sinnfein.ie
Socialist Party http://www.socialistparty.org.uk
Tories http://www.conservatives.com
Ulster Unionist Party http://www.uup.org

USA

Democratic National Committee http://www.democratics.org

Federal Consumer Info Center http://www.info.gov
FedWorld http://www.fedworld.gov
GovSpot http://www.govspot.com
Greens http://www.greenparty.org
House of Reps http://www.house.gov
National Security Agency http://www.nsa.gov
Political Index http://www.politicalindex.com
Political Resources http://www.politicalresources.com
SearchGov http://www.searchgov.com
Senate http://www.senate.gov
Thomas (search Congress) http://thomas.loc.gov
WebActive Directory http://www.webactive.com/directory/
The Whitehouse http://www.whitehouse.gov

Amnesty International
http://www.amnesty.org
Join the battle against brutal regimes and injustice.

Antiwar
http://www.antiwar.com • http://www.iacenter.org
Challenges US intervention in foreign affairs, especially the Balkans and Middle East.

The Big Breach
http://www.thebigbreach.com
Download a free copy of the British MI6 spy and tell book.

The British Monarchy
http://www.royal.gov.uk
Tune into the world's best-loved soap opera.

Center for the Moral Defense of Capitalism
http://www.moraldefense.com • http://www.aynrand.org
Is greed still good in the Y2Ks? Maybe not good, but legal, says Microsoft's last bastion of sympathy.

Central Intelligence Agency
http://www.cia.gov

Want the inside on political assassinations, arms deals, Colombian drug trades, spy satellites, phone tapping, covert operations, government-sponsored alien sex cults, and the X-files. Well, guess what? Never mind, you won't go home without a prize:
http://www.copvcia.com
http://www.magnet.ch/serendipity/cia.html

The Chairman Smiles

http://www.iisg.nl/exhibitions/chairman/
Stunning exhibition of communist propaganda posters.

Communist Internet List

http://www.cominternet.org • http://www.yclusa.org
Angry intellectuals and workers unite.

Conspiracies

http://www.conspire.com • http://www.conspiracy-net.com
Certain people are up to something and what's worse they're probably all in it together. If these exposés of the biggest cover-ups of all time aren't proof enough, then do your bit and create one that's more convincing: http://www.turnleft.com/conspiracy.html

Council for Aboriginal Reconciliation

http://www.reconciliation.org.au
Unfinished business in the Lucky (for some) Country.

Disinformation

http://www.disinfo.com
The dark side of politics, religious fervor, new science, and current affairs you won't find in the papers.

Fax Your MP (UK)

http://www.faxyourmp.com
Pester your local member through an Internet to fax gateway.

FBI FOIA Reading Room

http://foia.fbi.gov
FBI documents released as part of the Freedom of Information Act. Includes a few files on such celebrities as John Wayne, Elvis, Marilyn, and the British Royals. Check out who's most wanted now at:
http://www.fbi.gov

Federation of American Scientists

http://www.fas.org

Heavyweight analysis of science, technology, and public policy, including national security, nuclear weapons, arms sales, biological hazards, secrecy, and space policy.

Foreign Report

http://www.foreignreport.com

Compact subscription newsletter with a track record of predicting international flashpoints well before the dailies.

The Gallup Organization

http://www.gallup.com • http://www.pollingreport.com (US)

Keep track of opinion trends and ratings.

Gates Foundation

http://www.gatesfoundation.org

See where the world's richest man is spreading it around.

Gay and Lesbian Alliance against Defamation

http://www.glaad.org

Stand up against media stereotyping, and discrimination, of those deviating from the heterosexual norm.

Gendercide

http://www.gendercide.org

Investigates mass killings were a single gender is singled out.

German Propaganda Archives

http://www.calvin.edu/cas/gpa/

Who did you think you were kidding, Mr Hitler?

Global Ideas Bank

http://www.globalideasbank.org
Suggest and rate schemes to improve our standard of life.

Grassroots.com (US)

http://www.grassroots.com
Tracks political action and election policies across the board, aided by TV Nation champ Michael Moore: (http://www.michaelmoore.com).

Greenpeace International

http://www.greenpeace.org
Rebels with many a good cause.

Hate Monitor

http://www.hatemonitor.org • http://www.splcenter.org
http://www.publiceye.org • http://www.paragraph175.org
Shining the public flashlight on hate groups and political forces that threaten to undermine democracy and diversity.

Hindu Holocaust Museum

http://www.mantra.com/holocaust/
Contends that the massacre of Hindus during Muslim rule in India was of a scale unparalleled in history, yet has largely gone undocumented.

InfoWar

http://www.infowar.com
Warfare issues from prank hacking to industrial espionage and military propaganda.

Jane's IntelWeb

http://intelweb.janes.com
Brief updates on political disturbances, terrorism, intelligence agencies, and subterfuge worldwide. For a full directory of covert operations, see: http://www.virtualfreesites.com/covert.html

Liberty

http://www.liberty-human-rights.org.uk
Championing human rights in England and Wales.

MediaAttack

http://www.mediaattack.com
Video clips of talking heads and their celebrity guests put on the spot with awkward questions.

National Charities Information Bureau
http://www.ncib.org • http://www.charity-commission.gov.uk
Investigate before you donate.

National Forum on People's Differences
http://www.yforum.com
Toss around touchy topics such as race, religion, and sexuality, with a sincerity that is normally tabooed by political politeness.

One World
http://www.oneworld.org
Collates news from over 350 global justice organizations.

Open Secrets
http://www.opensecrets.org
Track whose money is oiling the wheels of US politics.
More keeping 'em honest at: http://www.commoncause.org

Oxfam
http://www.oxfam.org
Pitch in to fight poverty and inequality.

The Progressive Review
www.prorev.com
Washington dirt dug up from all sides of the fence. For darker soil, try: http://www.realchange.org

Protest.net – A Calendar of Protest Worldwide
http://protest.net
Find a nearby riot you can call your own.

Revolutionary Association of the Women of Afghanistan
http://www.rawa.org
And you think you have problems with men: http://www.taleban.com.

Spunk Press
http://www.spunk.org
http://www.infoshop.org
All the anarchy you'll ever need organized neatly and with reassuring authority.

Trinity Atomic Web Site

http://www.fas.org/nuke/trinity/
See what went on, and what went off, fifty-odd years ago, then file into the archives of high-energy weapon testing, and see who else has been sharpening the tools of world peace.

US Census Bureau

http://www.census.gov
More statistics on the US and its citizens than you'd care to know. For UK and Australian stats, see: http://www.statistics.gov.uk and http://www.abs.gov.au

US Presidential Candidates and their Evil Genes

http://www.nenavadno.com/usaelections2000.html
Biocybernetic criminals from the 33rd dimension take America.

Property

Australian Real Estate

http://www.propertiesaustralia.com.au
http://propertyweb.com.au
Combines listings from hundreds of Australian brokers.

FinanCenter

http://www.financenter.com
Figure out your monthly payments or what you can't afford.

HomeAdvisor (US)

http://homeadvisor.msn.com
Slick one-stop shop for finding homes and loans.

Home Scout (US)

http://www.homescout.com
Scan hundreds of US and Canadian real estate listings.

HouseWeb (UK)

http://www.houseweb.co.uk • http://www.findaproperty.com
http://www.propertylive.co.uk • http://www.propertyfinder.co.uk
http://www.propertyfile.co.uk

http://www.property-sight.co.uk
Rent, buy, or sell property within the UK.

Ihavemoved.com (UK)
http://www.ihavemoved.com
Bulk notify UK companies of your new address.

International Real Estate Digest
http://www.ired.com
Locate real estate listings, guides, and property-related services worldwide.

Realtor.com (US)
http://www.realtor.com
Lists over a million US properties.

Spring Street
http://www.springstreet.com • http://www.apartments.com
Rent or buy a US apartment.

UpMyStreet
http://www.upmystreet.com
Astounding wealth of house price, health, crime, schools, tax, and other statistics on UK neighborhoods. Mighty useful if you're shifting base.

Radio and Webcasts

While almost all radio stations have a Web site, only a fraction pipe their transmissions online. The ever-increasing percentage that do, usually broadcast (Webcast) in RealAudio and/or Windows Media Format (see p.272), so grab the latest copies of both before setting out. Both players come with inbuilt station directories along with Web-based event guides which are fine for starting out but nowhere near complete. Yahoo and Voquette also run services that keep tabs on notable audiovisual happenings:

RealGuide http://realguide.real.com
Voquette http://www.voquette.com
Windows Media Guide http://windowsmedia.com

Yahoo Events http://www.broadcast.com

Not enough? Then try one of the specialist radio directories. These list physical radio stations with Web sites along with full-time stations that only exist online, normally lumped together by country or genre. If they don't provide a direct link to the live feed, visit the station's site and look for a button or link that says "live" or "listen". For a more complete listing of directories, see: **http://radiodirectory.com/Stations/Web_Directories/**

Internet Radio Directories

ComFM http://www.comfm.fr/live/radio/
Internet Radio List http://www.internetradiolist.com
Listen http://www.listen.com/home_rdir.jsp
Live Radio http://www.live-radio.net
Radio Locator http://www.radio-locator.com
RadioNow (UK) http://www.radionow.co.uk
RadioWise http://www.radiowise.com.au/stations_live.htm
Sunset radio http://sunsetradio.com
Virtual Tuner http://www.virtualtuner.com

Apart from the traditional single stream broadcasters, dozens of sites host multiple feeds. These might be live, on demand, on rotation, archived, or once-off events. They tend to work more like inflight entertainment than radio.

Multistream Webcasters

113 Audio http://www.113audio.com
Anime Hardcore http://www.animehardcoreradio.net
Betalounge http://www.betalounge.com
CD Now http://www.cdnow.com/radio/
GoGaGa http://www.gogaga.com

House of Blues http://www.hob.com
Interface http://interface.pirate-radio.co.uk
Listen Radio http://radio.listen.com
LiveConcerts http://www.liveconcerts.com
NetRadio http://www.netradio.net
Online Classics http://www.onlineclassics.net
Radio SonicNet http://radio.sonicnet.com
Spinner http://www.spinner.com
The Womb http://www.thewomb.com
Yahoo! Radio http://radio.yahoo.com

If you fancy setting up your own station or listening to the online equivalent of pirate radio, try:

DIY Stations

GiveMeTalk (Talk only) http://www.givemetalk.com
Icecast.org http://www.icecast.org
Live365 http://www.live365.com
MyPlay http://www.myplay.com

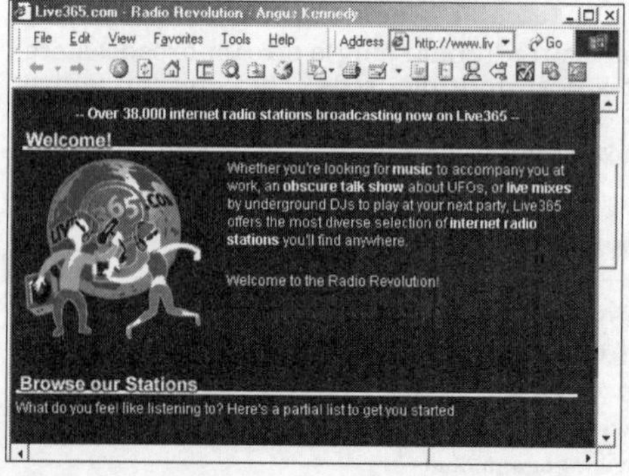

Radio SonicNet http://radio.sonicnet.com
Shoutcast http://www.shoutcast.com
Spotlife http://www.spotlife.com

To promote your own station or search for a song or artist currently playing across thousands of others:
RadioSpy http://www.radiospy.com

Or, to see, hear, and link to buy what's playing, or played recently, on hundreds of US FM stations
Emarker http://www.emarker.com
StarCD http://www.starcd.com

For everything else related to professional or amateur radio broadcasting:
Radio Directory http://www.radiodirectory.com

Crystal Radio
http://www.midnightscience.com
Build a simple wireless that needs no battery.

Phil's Old Radios
http://www.antiqueradio.org
If you ever drifted to sleep bathed in the soft glow of a crackling Bakelite wireless, Phil's collection of vacuum-era portables may instantly flood you with childhood memories.

Pirate Radio
http://pirateradio.about.com
Stake your claim on the airwaves.

Police Scanner
http://www.policescanner.com
http://www.apbnews.com/scanner/
http://www.javaradio.com
Live emergency scanner feeds piped into RealAudio. Eavesdrop on busts in progress. More on scanners at:
http://www.strongsignals.net

Reference

With the Net threatening the very foundations of the encyclopedia industry, it should come as no surprise to find most of the household names well entrenched online. While they're not all entirely free, they're certainly cheaper and more up to date than their bulky paper equivalents.

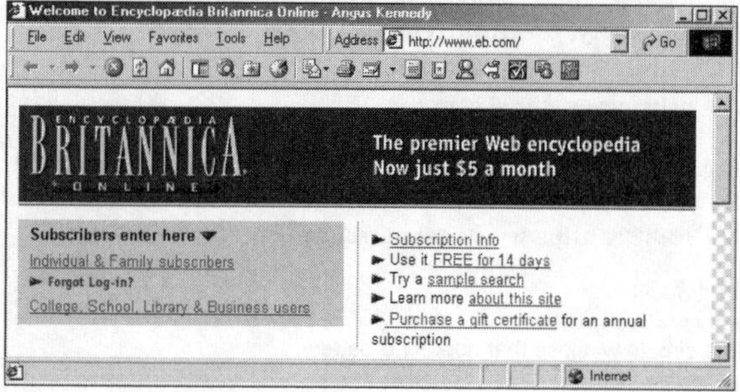

Britannica http://www.eb.com
Columbia http://www.bartleby.com/65/
Comptons http://www.comptons.com
Encarta http://www.encarta.com
Macquarie http://www.macnet.mq.edu.au
World Book http://www.worldbook.com

Nupedia is a new open content encyclopedia project collated by volunteers. You're invited to contribute:
Nupedia http://www.nupedia.com

For one-point access to over a thousand dictionaries across almost every language:
Dictionary.com http://www.dictionary.com

One Look http://www.onelook.com
YourDictionary.com http://www.yourdictionary.com

To query a broad selection of prominent reference works from Oxford University, Houghton Mifflin, Penguin, Macmillan, Bloomsbury, and Market House Books, consult:

Xrefer http://www.xrefer.com

Naturally, there are oodles of reference portals brimming with helpful reference tools. For instance:

Librarian's Index http://www.lii.org
LibrarySpot http://www.libraryspot.com
Open Directory http://dmoz.org/Reference/
Refdesk.com http://www.refdesk.com
Yahoo http://dir.yahoo.com/reference/

Acronym Finder

http://www.acronymfinder.com
http://www.ucc.ie/info/net/acronyms/acro.html
Before you follow IBM, TNT, and HMV in initializing your company's name, make sure it doesn't mean something blue.

All Experts

http://www.allexperts.com • http://www.askme.com
http://www.abuzz.com
Ask any question and let unpaid experts do the thinking.

Altavista Translations

http://world.altavista.com
Translate text, including Web pages, in seconds. Run some text back and forth a few times (http://www.telalink.net/~carl/multibabel/) and you'll end up with something that wouldn't look out of place on a Japanese T-shirt. If you can't pick the language, try: http://www.dougb.com/ident.html

alt.culture

http://www.altculture.com
Witty, digital A-Z of 90s pop culture. Fun to browse, maybe even enlightening, but don't blow your cool by admitting it.

Alternative Dictionary

http://www.notam.uio.no/~hcholm/altlang/
Bucket your foreign chums in their mother tongue.

American ASL Dictionary

http://www.handspeak.com
http://www.bconnex.net/~randys/
Learn sign language through simple animations.

Anagram Genius

http://www.anagramgenius.com
Recycle used letters.

Aphorisms Galore

http://www.aphorismsgalore.com
Sound clever by repeating someone else's lines.

Bartleby Reference

http://www.bartleby.com/reference/
Free access to several contemporary and classic reference works such as the American Heritage dictionaries, Columbia Encyclopedia, King's English, Emily Post's Etiquette, Cambridge History of English & American Literature, and the Anatomy of the Human Body.

Biography

http://www.biography.com
Recounting more than 25,000 lives.

Calculators Online

http://www-sci.lib.uci.edu/~martindale/RefCalculators.html
Awesome directory of some 10,000 online tools to calculate everything from how much sump oil to put in soap, to the burden of bringing up brats.

Cliché Finder

http://www.westegg.com/cliche/
Submit a word or phrase to find out how not to use it.

Earthstation1

http://www.earthstation1.com
The 20th century captured in sound and vision.

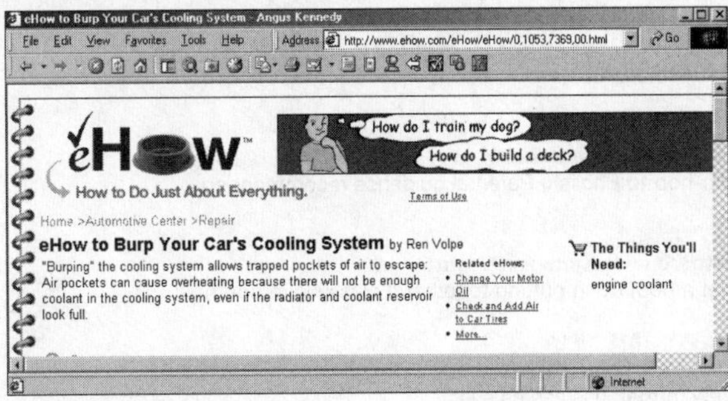

eHow

http://www.ehow.com

Make yourself useful through step-by-step tutorials.

Encyclopedia Mythica

http://pantheon.org/mythica/

Hefty album of mythology, folklore, and legend.

How to Speak to an Extraterrestrial

http://adrr.com/lingua/alien.htm

Crash course in ET101.

InfoPlease

http://www.infoplease.com

Handy, all-purpose almanac for stats and trivia.

Ka-BOOM! A Dictionary of Comic Book words

http://www.geocities.com/Athens/Marathon/5150/dictionary/

Become fluent in the language favored by leading superheroes.

Megaconverter

http://www.megaconverter.com

Calculate everything from your height in angstroms, to the pellets of lead per ounce of buckshot needed to bring down an overcharging consultant.

Princeton Review

http://www.review.com • http://www.collegeboard.org
Crack the SATs.

Rap Dictionary

http://www.rapdict.org
Hip-hop to English. Parental guidance recommended.

RhymeZone

http://www.rhymezone.com
Get a hoof up in putting together a classy love poem.

Roget's Thesaurus

http://www.thesaurus.com
New format: useless as ever.

Skeptic's Dictionary

http://www.skepdic.com
Punch holes in mass media funk and pseudo-sciences such as homeopathy, astrology, and iridology.

Spellweb

http://www.spellweb.com • http://bodin.org/altameter/
Compare two words or phrases and see which gets more hits in a search engine. If it demonstrates anything, it's that the Web is strung together with a lot of bad spelling.

The Straight Dope

http://www.straightdope.com
Cecil Adams's answers to hard questions. Find out how to renounce your US citizenship, what Kemosabe means, and the difference between a warm smell of colitas and colitis.

Strunk's Elements of Style

http://www.bartleby.com/141/
The complete classic of English usage in a nutshell, though unfortunately, not the latest edition. For more on grammar and style:
alt.usage.English FAQ http://homepages.tcp.co.uk/~laker/faq/
Education Finder http://www.edunet.com/english/grammar/
Garbl's Writing Resources http://www.garbl.com

Montreal Gazette Style Guide

http://www.montrealgazette.com/styleguide/

Symbols

http://www.symbols.com
Ever woken up with a strange sign tattooed on your buttocks? Here's where to find what it means without calling Agent Mulder.

What is?

http://www.whatis.com • http://www.webopedia.com
Unravel cumbersome computer and Internet jargon without having even more thrown at you.

Relationships and Friendship

Ask-a-Chick

http://www.ask-a-chick.com
Boys ask girls to set them straight.

Breakup Girl

http://www.breakupgirl.com
How to mend a broken heart and get on with your life. Here's how not to do it: http://www.crazy-bitch.com

ClassMates.com

http://www.classmates.com
You haven't forgotten. Now track them down one by one.

Cyberspace Inmates

http://www.cyberspace-inmates.com • http://www.jailbabes.com
Strike up an email romance with a prison inmate; maybe even one on death row.

Hot or Not?

http://www.hotornot.com • http://www.ratemyface.com
Submit a flattering photo and have it rated by passing chumps. So popular it has spawned a string of spoofs, such as:
http://www.amigothornot.com • http://www.amigeekornot.com
http://www.amifuglyornot.com • http://www.amipotornot.com

http://www.amiallyourbaseornot.com
To sort by rating, see: http://log.waxy.org/hot/
To instantly create your own custom Am I page:
http://www.iamcal.com/ami/

Love Calculator

http://www.lovecalculator.com
Enter your respective names to see if you're compatible.

Matchmaking Directories

http://www.cupidnet.com • http://www.singlesites.com
http://dmoz.org/Society/Relationships/
Come aboard, they're expecting you.

Pen Pal Directory

http://www.yahoo.com/Society_and_Culture/Relationships/Pen_Pals/
Exchange email with strangers.

PlanetOut

http://www.planetout.com
http://www.rainbownetwork.com (UK)
http://www.qrd.org • http://www.datalounge.com
http://www.queertheory.com
Directories to all that's that way inclined.

Secret Admirer

http://www.secretadmirer.com • http://www.ecrush.com
Find out whether your most secret crushed one digs you back.

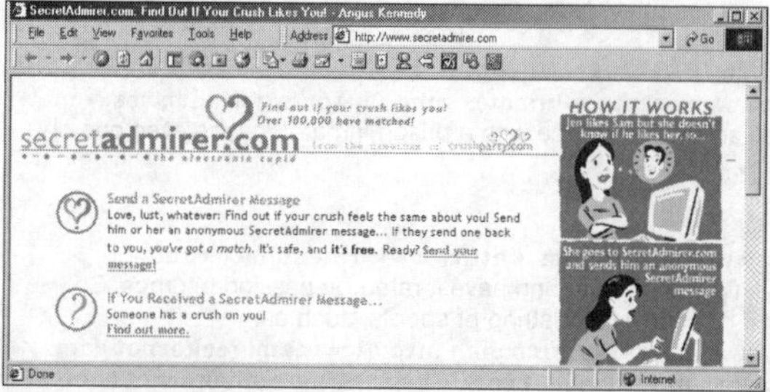

So There
http://www.sothere.com
A place to post your parting shots.

Swoon
http://www.swoon.com
Dating, mating, and relating. Courtesy of Condé Nast's Details, GQ, Glamour, and Mademoiselle. For dessert, try: http://dating.about.com

Vampire Exchange
http://www.vein-europe.demon.co.uk
http://www.sanguinarius.org
Give blood as an act of love.

Weddings in the Real World
http://www.theknot.com • http://www.nearlywed.com
Prepare to jump the broom, or untie the knot:
http://www.divorcesource.com

Religion

So many answers, so little time. If you haven't yet signed up with a religious sect, or are unhappy with the one passed down by your folks, here's your opportunity to survey the field at your own pace. Most are open to newcomers, though certain rules and conditions may apply. For a reasonably complete and unbiased breakdown of faith dealerships, try:

BeliefNet http://www.beliefnet.com
Comparative Religion http://www.academicinfo.net/religindex.html
Religious Tolerance http://www.religioustolerance.org

But don't expect such an easy ride from those demanding proof:

Atheism http://atheism.miningco.com
Christian Burner http://www.christianburner.com
The Secular Web http://www.infidels.org

Anglicans Online
http://anglicansonline.org
Gentle catapult into the Church of England worldwide.

Avatar Search
http://www.AvatarSearch.com
Search the occult Net for spiritual guidance and lottery tips.

The Bible Gateway
http://bible.gospelcom.net
Set your table with the Good Book.

Catholic Church – God's One and Only Church
http://www.truecatholic.org
Yet more troops armed with the truth.

Catholic Online
http://www.catholic.org
Saints, Angels, shopping, discussion and a portal to the online territory occupied by Catholics.

Celebrity Atheist List
http://www.celebatheists.com
Big names you won't spot in Heaven.

Cheesy Jesus
http://www.cheesyjesus.com
http://www.ship-of-fools.com/Gadgets/
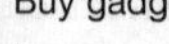
Buy gadgets to bring you closer to God.

Chick
http://chick.com
Hard-core Christian pornography.

Christian Answers
http://christiananswers.net
Movies and computer games reviewed, and hard questions answered, by Christians who know what's good for you and your family.

Christians v Muslims

http://debate.org.uk • http://www.rim.org/muslim/islam.htm
http://members.aol.com/AllahIslam/
http://www.answering-islam.org
http://www.muslim-answers.org
http://www.biblicalchristianity.freeserve.co.uk
Put your faith on the line.

Christian Naturists

http://home.vistapnt.com/markm/
Frolic with other Christian fun-seekers, the way God intended.

CrossSearch

http://www.crosssearch.com
Set sail through safe waters to find Christian groups of all denominations.

Crosswalk

http://www.crosswalk.com
Catch up with the latest on Jesus.

Demon Possession Handbook

http://diskbooks.org/hs.html
Train for a job with the Watcher's Council.

The Greatest Truth Ever Revealed

http://www.sevenseals.com
Revelations from survivors of the Waco siege.

The Hindu Universe

http://www.hindunet.org
Hindu dharma – the philosophy, culture, and customs.

The Holy See

http://www.vatican.va
Official hideout of the Pope and his posse.

Islamic Gateway

http://www.ummah.net • http://www.musalman.com
http://www.fatwa-online.com
Get down with Muhammed (sallallahu `alaihi wa sallam).

Jesus of the Week

http://www.jesusoftheweek.com

The original Mr Nice Guy in 52 coy poses per year. Catch him wink at: http://www.winkingjesus.com

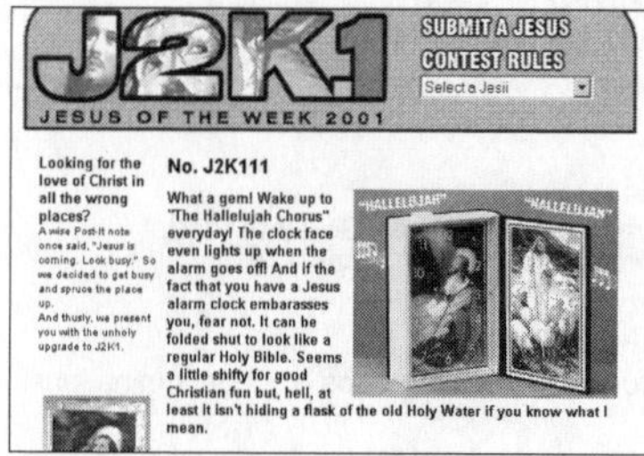

Jesus Puzzle – Was there no Historical Jesus?

http://human.st/jesuspuzzle/ http://jesuspuzzlerings.com
http://www.jesusdance.com

Solve the riddle; buy the ring; do the dance.

Miracles Page

http://www.mcn.org/1/miracles/

Spooky signs that point towards a cosmic conspiracy.

Not Proud

http://www.notproud.com

Confess your most entertaining sins.

Peyote Way Church of God

http://www.peyoteway.org

Unless you're Native American, or live in select southern US states, you stand to be locked up for finding God through the psychedelic cactus. Otherwise, feel free to fry your brain; just don't drive home from church.

Prophecy and Current Events

http://www.aplus-software.com/thglory/
http://www.prophezine.com

You'll never guess who's coming to dinner. Don't bother cooking, though; he's supposed to be a real whiz with food.

Religious Frauds

http://religiousfrauds.50megs.com
Esteemed reptile slayer David Icke sniffs out Christian cons.

Satinism 101

http://www.satanism101.com
Enter this address and go straight to Hell:
http://www.what-the-hell-is-hell.com • http://www.virtualhell.org

Ship of Fools: the Magazine of Christian Unrest

http://ship-of-fools.com
The lighter side of Christianity.

Skeptics Annotated Bible

http://www.skepticsannotatedbible.com
Contends that the Good Book is a misnomer.

Stories of the Dreaming

http://www.dreamtime.net.au
Selection of enchanting bedtime stories in text, video, and audio that explain creation from an Aboriginal perspective. Don't believe in creation? Go tell it to the jury: http://www.talkorigins.org

Totally Jewish

http://www.totallyjewish.com • http://www.maven.co.il
http://judaism.about.com
http://aish.com
Spiritual guidance and community portals for the chosen people (http://www.chosen-people.com) and curious goyim.

Universal Life Church

http://ulc.org
Become a self-ordained minister.

The Witches' Voice

http://www.witchvox.com
http://www.witchesweb.com
Expresses a burning desire to correct misinformation about witchcraft, a legally recognized religion in the US since 1985.

Zen
http://www.do-not-zzz.com
Take a five-minute course in meditation.

Science

To keep abreast of science news and developments stop by Scitech, which aggregates stories from the leading scientific media, and New Scientist's Site of the Day:
Scitech Daily Review http://www.scitechdaily.com
Site of the Day http://www.newscientist.com/weblinks/

Or go straight to one of the many science journals:
Archeology http://www.archaeology.org
BBC http://news.bbc.co.uk
Beyond 2000 http://www.beyond2000.com
British Medical Journal http://www.bmj.com
Bulletin of Atomic Scientists http://www.bullatomsci.org
Discover http://www.discover.com
Discovery Channel http://www.discovery.com
Earth Times http://www.earthtimes.org
Edge http://www.edge.org
Highwire Press http://highwire.stanford.edu
The Lancet http://www.thelancet.com
National Geographic http://www.nationalgeographic.com
New Scientist http://www.newscientist.com
Popular Mechanics http://www.popularmechanics.com
Popular Science http://www.popsci.com
Science à GoGo http://www.scienceagogo.com
Science Magazine http://www.sciencemag.org
Science News http://www.sciencenews.org
Scientific American http://www.scientificamerican.com
The Scientist http://www.the-scientist.com

SciQuest http://www.sciquest.com
Skeptical Inquirer http://www.csicop.org/si/
Technology Review http://www.techreview.com

Looking for a something specific, or a range of sites within a strand? Try browsing or searching a directory:

About Science http://home.about.com/science/
Hypography http://www.hypography.com
Open Directory http://dmoz.org/Science/
SciSeek http://www.sciseek.com
Treasure Troves of Science http://www.treasure-troves.com
Yahoo http://dir.yahoo.com/science/

The Braintainment Center

http://www.brain.com • http://www.mensa.org
http://www.iqtest.com • http://www.mind-gear.com
http://www.mindmedia.com
Start with a test that says you're not so bright, then prove it by buying loads of self-improvement gear. Short on brains? Try:
http://www.brains4zombies.com

Cool Robot of the Week

http://ranier.hq.nasa.gov/telerobotics_page/coolrobots.html
Clever ways to get machines to do our dirty work. For a directory of simulators, combat comps, clubs, and DIY bots, direct your agent to:
http://www.robotcafe.com

Documentation and Diagrams of the Atomic Bomb

http://serendipity.magnet.ch/more/atomic.html
Let's hope this doesn't fall into the wrong hands. Imagine the effect on your neighborhood:
http://www.pbs.org/wgbh/amex/bomb/sfeature/mapablast.html

History of Mathematics

http://www-groups.dcs.st-andrews.ac.uk/~history/
The life and times of various bright sparks with numbers.

HotAir – Annals of Improbable Research

http://www.improbable.com

Science gone too far, or around the bend. Includes the Ig Nobel awards for achievements that cannot, or should not, be reproduced.

How Stuff Works

http://www.howstuffworks.com
Unravel the mysterious machinations behind all sorts of stuff from Xmas to cruise missiles.

Interactive Frog Dissection

http://teach.virginia.edu/go/frog/
Pin down a frog, grab your scalpel, and follow the pictures.

The Lab (AU)

http://www.abc.net.au/science/
ABC science news and program info with Q&As from Aussie pop-science superstar, Dr Karl Kruszelnicki.

MadSciNet: 24-hour Exploding Laboratory

http://www.madsci.org
Collective of more than a hundred scientific smarty-pantses set up specifically to answer your dumb questions. More geniuses for hire at:
http://www.ducksbreath.com • http://www.wsu.edu/DrUniverse/
http://www.sciam.com/askexpert/ • http://www.sciencenet.org.uk

MIT Media Labs

http://www.media.mit.edu
If you've read Being Digital or any of Nicholas Negroponte's Wired columns, you'll know he has some pretty tall ideas about our electronic future. Here's where he gets them.

Museum of Dirt

http://www.planet.com/dirtweb/dirt.html
Celebrity dirt of an entirely different nature.

Netsurfer Science

http://www.netsurf.com/nss/
Subscribe to receive weekly bulletins on science and technology sites.

Nobel e-Museum

http://www.nobel.se
Read all about Nobel Prize winners.

Rocketry Online

http://www.rocketryonline.com
Take on NASA at its own game.

Skeptics Society

http://www.skeptic.com • http://www.csicop.org
Don't try to pull a swifty on this crowd.

USGS National Earthquake Info Center

http://gldss7.cr.usgs.gov
http://www.gps.caltech.edu/~polet/recofd.html
Stats and maps of most recent quakes worldwide.

Volcano World

http://volcano.und.nodak.edu
Monitor the latest eruptions, see photos of every major volcano in the world, and virtually tour a Hawaiian smoky without choking on sulfur fumes.

Web-Elements

http://www.webelements.com
http://www.chemsoc.org/viselements/
Click on an element in the periodic table and suss it out in depth. Now cross check its comic book reference:
http://www.uky.edu/Projects/Chemcomics/
and recite its poem:
http://www.superdeluxe.com/elemental/

Weird Science and Mad Scientists

http://www.eskimo.com/~billb/weird.html
http://www.student.nada.kth.se/~nv91-asa/mad.html
Free energy, Tesla, anti-gravity, aura, cold fusion, parapsychology, and other strange scientific projects and theories.

Why Files

http://whyfiles.news.wisc.edu
Entertaining reports on the science behind current news.

Space

If you have more than a passing interest in space, skip the popular science mags (p.430) and newswires (p.402), and go straight to the source:
NASA http://www.nasa.gov

Or any of these specialist space ports:
About Space http://space.about.com
Amateur Astronomy Magazine http://www.amateurastronomy.com
Astronomy.com http://www.astronomy.com
Astronomy Now http://www.astronomynow.com
Explorezone http://explorezone.com
Human Spaceflight http://spaceflight.nasa.gov
Jet Propulsion Lab http://www.jpl.nasa.gov
Planetary Society http://planetary.org
Sky & Telescope Magazine http://www.skypub.com
Space.com http://www.space.com
SpaceRef http://www.spaceref.com
SpaceScience http://www.spacescience.com
Universe Today http://www.universetoday.com

Alien Bases on Earth
http://www.earth-today.com
See, in great detail, where the Gods have parked their chariots.

Area 51
http://www.terraserver.com/Area51.asp
Inspect the first public satellite photos of the infamous no-fly zone.

Artemis Project
http://www.asi.org
Join a queue to go to the moon.

Astronomy Picture of the Day
http://antwrp.gsfc.nasa.gov/apod/astropix.html

Enjoy a daily helping of outer space served up by a gourmet astrochef.

Auroral Activity

http://www.sec.noaa.gov/pmap/

Instantly see the current extent and position of the auroral oval above each pole.

Auroras: Paintings in the Sky

http://www.exploratorium.edu/learning_studio/auroras/

http://www.alaskascience.com/aurora.htm

If you're ever lucky enough to see the Aurora during a solar storm, you'll never take the night sky for granted again. The Exploratorium does a commendable job in explaining a polar phenomenon that very few people understand. Except maybe these champs:

http://www.haarp.alaska.edu

Bad Astronomy

http://www.badastronomy.com

Ditch your lifetime's supply of space misconceptions and clichés.

Clickworkers

http://clickworkers.arc.nasa.gov

Wangle a NASA job onto your résumé by counting craters on Mars.

Comets & Meteor Showers

http://comets.amsmeteors.org

Be on the lookout for falling rocks.

Darksky

http://www.darksky.org

Join the campaign against wanton street lighting. You'll see why in the gallery.

Deep Cold

http://www.deepcold.com

Artistic mockups of chic space racers that never left the hangar.

Earth Viewer

http://www.fourmilab.ch/earthview/

View the Earth in space and time.

Heavens Above

http://www.heavens-above.com
Correctly identify nearby satellites and space stations.

Hubblesite

http://hubble.stsci.edu
Intergalactic snapshots fresh off the Hubble telescope.

Inconstant Moon

http://www.inconstantmoon.com • http://www.spacescience.co.uk
Click on a date and see what's showing on the Moon.

International Star Registry

http://www.starregistry.co.uk
Raise your flag in outer space.

Mars Home Page

http://mpfwww.jpl.nasa.gov
Get a bit more red dirt live from NASA's space safari before you stake out your first plot at: http://www.marsshop.com For the latest news, see: http://www.marsnews.com

MrEclipse

http://www.mreclipse.com
Dabble in the occultations.

Net Telescopes

http://www.telescope.org/rti/ • http://denali.physics.uiowa.edu/
Probe deep space by sending requests to remote telescopes.

Scope Reviews

http://www.scopereviews.com
Read first, buy later – or maybe build your own: http://www.atmjournal.com

Seti@home

http://setiathome.ssl.berkeley.edu • http://setifaq.org
Donate your processing resources to the non-lunatic end of the search for extraterrestrial intelligence by downloading a screensaver that analyzes data from the Arecibo Radio Telescope. Progress reports at:

http://www.seti.org • http://planetary.org
http://seti.uws.edu.au

Solar System Simulator

http://space.jpl.nasa.gov
Shift camp around the solar system until you find the best view.

Space Calendar

http://www.jpl.nasa.gov/calendar/
Guide to upcoming anniversaries, rocket launches, meteor showers, eclipses, asteroid and planet viewings, and happenings in the inter-galactic calendar.

Space Weather

http://www.spaceweather.com
http://www.windows.ucar.edu/spaceweather/
Monitor the influence of solar activity on the Earth's magnetic field.

Sport

For live calls, scores, tables, draws, teams, injuries, and corruption inquiries across major sports, try the newspaper sites (p.398), breaking news services (p.402) or sporting specialists like:

CBS Sportsline http://www.sportsline.com
ESPN Sportzone http://espnet.go.com
SkySports (UK) http://www.skysports.com
Slam Sports (Can) http://www.canoe.ca/slam/
Sport365 http://www.sport365.com
Sportal (INT) http://www.sportal.com
Sporting Life (UK) http://www.sporting-life.com
Sports.com (Euro) http://sports.com
Sports Illustrated http://sportsillustrated.cnn.com
SportsToday (Aus) http://www.sportstoday.com.au
Total Sports http://www.totalsports.com

Wide World of Sports (Aus) http://sports.ninemsn.com.au

But if your interest even slightly borders on an obsession, you'll find far more satisfaction on the pages of something more one-eyed. For clubs and fan sites, drill down through Yahoo and the Open Directory. They won't carry everything, but what you'll find will lead you to the forces that understand you better than your partner:

Open Directory http://dmoz.org/Sports/
Yahoo Sports http://dir.yahoo.com/recreation/sports/

Abdominal Training
http://www.timbomb.net/ab/
Build "abs ripped liked ravioli".

Adventure Sports Directory
http://www.adventuredirectory.com
http://dmoz.org/Sports/Extreme_Sports/
For all that falls under the banner of "extreme sports", from taking your pushbike offroad to the sort of sheer recklessness that would get you cut from a will. For something more flashy, check out:
http://www.pie.com and http://expn.go.com

Asimba
http://www.asimba.com
Log your training and nutrition regime online.

Australian Football League
http://www.afl.com.au
Men in tight shorts play aerial ping-pong.

The Bladder (AUS)
http://www.thebladder.com.au
Australian sport meets The Onion.

Cric Info – the Home of Cricket on the Internet
http://www.cricket.org
Because every ball matters.

Fishing Directories

http://www.thefishfinder.com • http://fishsearch.com

Trade tips and generally exaggerate about aquatic bloodsports.

Goals – Global Online Adventure Learning Site

http://www.goals.com

Chase adventurous lunatics like Mick Bird, who's circling the globe in a canoe.

NBA.com

http://www.nba.com

Pro basketball news, picks, player profiles, analyses, results, schedules, and highlight videos. See also Major League Baseball: http://www.mlb.com

NFL

http://www.nfl.com • http://www.nfluth.com

Media schedules, chats, news, player profiles, stats, and streaming highlight videos from the National Football League's past and current seasons.

Rugby League/Union

http://www.rleague.com • http://www.ozleague.com
http://www.scrum.com • http://www.rugbyheaven.com

Up to the minute coverage of hard men trotting in and out of the blood bin.

Sailing Index

http://www.smartguide.com • http://www.madforsailing.com
Everything seaworthy: from swapping yachts to choosing a GPS.

SkiCentral

http://www.skicentral.com • http://www.skiclub.co.uk
Indexes thousands of ski-related sites, such as snow reports, resort cams, snowboard gear, accommodation, and coming events in resorts across the world. For snowboarding, see:
http://www.soltv.com • http://www.boardtheworld.com.au
http://www.twsnow.com • http://www.board-it.com

SoccerNet

http://www.soccernet.com

ESPN's shrine to football in England and beyond. Not enough news? Try:

FA Premier http://www.fa-premier.com
Football365 http://www.football365.co.uk
Nationwide http://www.football.nationwide.co.uk
When Saturday Comes http://www.wsc.co.uk

For game, club, and player stats, see:

Soccerbase http://www.soccerbase.com
Teamtalk http://www.teamtalk.com

Stats

http://www.stats.com
Pig in to an overflowing trough of US sport statistics.

World Motorsport Index

http://www.worldmotorsport.com
Start here for your gasoline-induced pleasure.

World Surfing

http://www.goan.com/surflink.html
Every day's like big Wednesday. For daily breaks and Aussie seaboard cams, see: http://www.coastalwatch.com

Wrestling

http://www.wrestlezone.com • http://www.wrestlingdotcom.com
Vent the frustration of helplessly watching your boofhead heroes being piledriven, suplexed, and moonsplashed, by spilling some hardway juice virtually. If you'd prefer seeing them smack each other in the scone, see: http://www.secondsout.com

Telecommunications

Compare Phone Charges

http://www.magsys.co.uk/telecom/ (UK)
http://www.uswitch.com (UK)
http://www.buy.co.uk (UK)
http://www.phonechoice.com.au (AUS)
http://lowestphone.com (US) • http://www.getconnected.com (US)
http://www.ccmi.com (US) • http://www.phonesaver.com (US)
http://10-10phonerates.com (US)
http://www.lowermybills.com (US)
Shop around for the best phone rates.

Efax

http://www.efax.com • http://www.j2.com
Free up a phone line by receiving your faxes by email.

Free Fax Services

http://www.tpc.int
Transmit faxes via the Internet free.

Letterpost

http://www.letterpost.com

Buy a stamp. Type a message. Have it posted.

Mail2Wap

http://www.mail2wap.com

Collect your POP3 mail on a WAP phone.

MobileWorld

http://www.mobileworld.org

http://www.unwin.co.uk/phonez.html

Assorted info on mobile phones and cellular networks.

Postcode Pages

http://www.grcdi.nl/linkspc.htm

Find a postcode in almost any country.

Reverse Phone Directory

http://www.reversephonedirectory.com

Key in a US phone number to find its owner. To find a UK location see: **http://www.warwick.ac.uk/cgi-bin-Phones/nng/**

SMS Text Messages

http://www.quios.com • **http://www.mtnsms.com**

Send free text messages to mobile phones worldwide.

Stamps.com (US)

http://www.stamps.com • **http://www.estamp.com**

Buy your US stamps online.

The Telegraph Office

http://fohnix.metronet.com/~nmcewen/tel_off.html

http://www.navyrelics.com/tribute/bellsys/

Trip through the history of wired communications from Morse telegraphy to the Bell System.

UK.Telecom FAQ

http://www.gbnet.net/net/uk-telecom/

Satisfy your curiosity about the British phone network.

US Postal Services

http://www.usps.com

Look up a Zip code, track express mail, sort out your vehicle registration, or just get down and philatelic.

What does your phone number spell?

http://www.phonespell.org

Enter your phone number to see what it spells. The reverse lookup might help you choose a number.

World Time & Dialing Codes

http://www.whitepages.com.au/wp/search/time.html

International dialing info from anywhere to anywhere, including current times and area codes.

Time

Calendarzone

http://www.calendarzone.com

Calendar links and, believe it or not, calzone recipes.

DateReminder

http://www.datereminder.co.uk • http://www.cvp.com/freemind/

Remind yourself by email.

The Death Clock

http://www.deathclock.com

Get ready to book your final taxi.

International Earth Rotation Service

http://hpiers.obspm.fr
Ever felt like your bed's spinning? The truth is even scarier.

iPing (US)

http://www.iping.com
Arrange free telephone reminders for one or many.

Online Planners

http://www.dailydrill.com • http://www.appoint.net
http://www.when.com • http://www.visto.com
Maintain your planner online. Excite, Yahoo, MSN, and Netscape offer similar.

Time and Date

http://www.timeanddate.com
http://www.smh.com.au/media/wtc/smhwtc.html
Instantly tell the time in your choice of cities.
Keep your PC clock aligned with a time synchronizer:
http://www.eecis.udel.edu/~ntp/software.html

Time Cave

http://www.timecave.com
Schedule an email to be sent at a specific time in the future.

Time Cube

http://www.timecube.com
Disprove God through the simultaneous 4-day Time Cube.

Transport

Buying a Car

Before you're sharked into signing on a new or used vehicle, go online and check out a few road tests and price guides. You can complete the entire exercise while you're there, but it mightn't hurt to drive one first. Start here, and then search Google for enthusiast sites and forums.

Autobytel (INT) http://www.autobytel.com
Auto Channel http://www.theautochannel.com
Autohit (UK) http://www.autohit.co.uk
Autolocate (UK) http://www.autolocate.co.uk
Autotrader (UK, IE, EUR, SA) http://www.autotrader.co.uk
AutoWeb http://www.autoweb.com
BBC Top Gear (UK) http://www.topgear.beeb.com
CarClub http://www.carclub.com
Car Importing (UK) http://www.carimporting.co.uk
Carnet (Aus) http://www.car.net.au
CarPrice http://www.carprice.com
CarsDirect http://www.carsdirect.com
Carseekers (UK) http://www.carseekers.co.uk
Carstreet (IND) http://www.carstreet.com

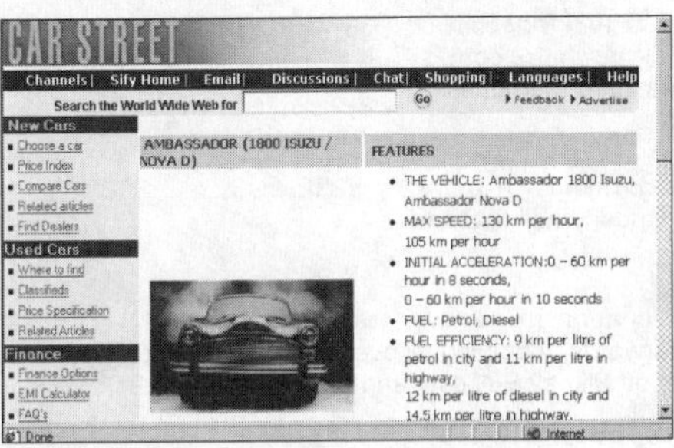

DealerNet http://www.dealernet.com
Drivers Seat http://www.driversseat.com
Edmunds http://www.edmunds.com
Exchange & Mart (UK) http://www.ixm.co.uk
Kelly Blue Book http://www.kbb.com
Microsoft CarPoint (Aus) http://carpoint.ninemsn.com
Microsoft CarPoint http://carpoint.msn.com

Oneswoop (UK) http://www.oneswoop.com
What Car? (UK) http://www.whatcar.co.uk

Am I going down?

http://www.amigoingdown.com
Enter your flight details to rate your chance of survival.

Airdisaster.com

http://www.airdisaster.com • http://come.to/crashes/
http://www.aviationnewsweb.com • http://planecrashinfo.com
Way more goes wrong up in the air than you realize. Here's why you should be terrified to fly. For first-hand tales of terror, see: http://www.pprune.com

Airsafe

http://www.airsafe.com
Overcome your fear of plummeting.

Air Sickness Bag Virtual Museum

http://www.airsicknessbags.com
Bring up some treasured memories.

Aviation

http://aviation.about.com • http://www.airliners.net
If it takes off and lands, you'll find it here.

Breath Testing

http://copsonline.com/online_breath_test.htm
Slurring your swearwords, wobbling all over the road, mounting gutters and knocking kids off bikes? Pull over and blow into this site.

FedEx

http://www.fedex.com
Book shipping, track parcels, or compare rates with UPS: http://www.ups.com and TNT: http://www.tnt.com

Layover

http://www.layover.com
Long, wide loads of truckin' stuff for prime movers and shakers.

License Plates of the World

http://danshiki.oit.gatech.edu/~iadt3mk/

Ring in sick, cancel your date, unplug the phone and don't even think about sleep until you've seen EVERY LICENSE PLATE IN THE WORLD.

NMRA Directory of Worldwide Rail Sites

http://www.ribbonrail.com/nmra/ • **http://www.trainorders.com**
Locophilial banquet of online railway shunts.

Radar Test

http://www.radartest.com
Outsmart the law through consumer electronics.

US Submarines

http:/www.ussubs.com
Scare the fish in your own custom-built U-boat.

Woman Motorist

http://www.womanmotorist.com
The demographic group motor vehicle insurers prefer.

Travel

Whether you're seeking inspiration, planning an itinerary, shopping for a ticket, or already mobile, there'll be a tool online worth throwing in your box. You can book flights, reserve hotels, research your destination, monitor the weather, convert currencies, learn the lingo, locate an ATM, scan local newspapers, collect your mail from abroad, find a restaurant that suits your fussy tastes, and plenty more. If you'd like to find first-hand experiences or traveling companions, hit the Usenet discussion archives at **Google** (**http://groups.google.com**) and join the appropriate newsgroup under the **rec.travel** or **soc.culture** hierarchies. As with all newsgroups, before you post a question, skim through the FAQs first:

Air Travel Handbook

http://www.cs.cmu.edu/afs/cs/user/mkant/Public/Travel/airfare.html

Rec.Travel Library **http://www.travel-library.com**

You could also try consulting a volunteer " expert":

Abuzz http://www.abuzz.com/category/travel/
All Experts http://www.allexperts.com/travel/
Ask Me http://www.askme.com

Then see what the major guidebook publishers have to offer:

Fodors http://www.fodors.com
Frommers http://www.frommers.com
Insiders http://www.insiders.com
Let's Go http://www.letsgo.com
Lonely Planet http://www.lonelyplanet.com
Moon Travel http://www.moon.com
Robert Young Pelton http://www.comebackalive.com
Rough Guides http://www.roughguides.com
Routard http://www.club-internet.fr/routard/

While it might seem like commercial suicide for the Rough Guides to give away the full text of its guides to more than 10,000 destinations, the reality is books are still more convenient, especially on the road when you need them most. If you'd like to order a guide or map online you'll also find plenty of opportunities either from the above publishers, the online bookshops (p.326), or from travel bookshops such as:

Adventurous Traveler http://www.atbook.com
Literate Traveler http://www.literatetraveller.com
Stanfords (UK) http://www.stanfords.co.uk

Many online travel agents also provide destination guides, which might include exclusive editorial peppered with chunks licensed from guidebooks linked out to further material on the Web. For example:

Away.com http://away.com
Escaperoutes (UK) http://www.escaperoutes.net

Travel Vision (UK) http://www.travelvision.com

The biggest problem with browsing the Web for regional information and travel tools is not in finding the sites, but wading through them. Take the following directories for example:

About Travel http://travel.about.com
Budget Travel http://www.budgetravel.com
Excite Travel http://travel.excite.com
Lycos Travel http://travel.lycos.com
My Travel Guide http://www.mytravelguide.com
Open Directory http://dmoz.org/Recreation/Travel/
Traveller Online http://www.travelleronline.com
Trip Advisor (US) http://www.tripadvisor.com
Virtual Tourist http://www.vtourist.com
World Travel Guide http://www.travel-guide.com
World Travel Net http://www.world-travel-net.com
Yahoo Directory http://www.yahoo.com/Recreation/Travel/
Yahoo Travel http://travel.yahoo.com

These are perfect if you want to browse through regions looking for ideas, or to find a range of sites on one topic – health, for example. But if you're after something very specific, you might find it more efficient to use a search engine, such as Google. Keep adding search terms until you restrict the number of results to something manageable. If you'd like to coincide your vacation with a festival or event, go straight to:

What's Going On http://www.whatsgoingon.com
What's on When http://www.whatsonwhen.com

Or for entertainment, eating, and cultural events, a city guide:

Citysearch http://www.citysearch.com
Sidewalk (Aus) http://www.sidewalk.com.au

Time Out http://www.timeout.co.uk
Wcities.com http://www.wcities.com
Yahoo Local (US) http://local.yahoo.com
Zagat (Dining) http://www.zagat.com

Is **Vindigo** the future of travel guides? Download its Palm Pilot or AvantGo city guides and decide for yourself:
Vindigo http://www.vindigo

If you're flexible and/or willing to leave soon, you might find a **last-minute special**. These Net exclusives are normally offered directly from the airline, hotel, and travel operator sites, which you'll find through **Airlines.com** (**http://www.airlines.com**) or Yahoo. There are also a few Web operators that specialize in late-notice and special Internet deals on flights, hotels, events, and so forth, such as:
Bargain Holidays (UK) http://www.bargainholidays.com
Best Fares http://www.bestfares.com
Lastminute.com (UK) http://www.lastminute.com
Lastminutetravel.com http://www.lastminutetravel.com
Smarter Living http://www.smarterliving.com
Travel Zoo http://www.travelzoo.com

Then there are the reverse-auction sites such as **Priceline.com** where you bid on a destination and wait for a bite. You might strike up a good deal if you bid shrewdly and don't mind the somewhat draconian restrictions (see: **http://www.angelfire.com/nt/priceline/**). **Hotwire** offers similar discounts on undisclosed airlines but names the price up front. If you're super flexible, you could try **Airhitch** or a courier:
Air Courier Assoc. http://www.aircourier.org
Airhitch http://www.airhitch.org
Hotwire http://www.hotwire.com

IAATC Air Courier http://www.courier.org
Priceline.com http://www.priceline.com

Booking a flight through one of the broad online ticketing systems isn't too hard either, but bargains are scarce. For example, unless you're spending someone else's money you'll want to sidestep the full fares offered on these major services:

Biztravel (US) http://www.biztravel.com
Expedia (UK) http://www.expedia.co.uk
Expedia (US) http://www.expedia.com
Travel.com.au (AUS) http://www.travel.com.au
Travelocity (Worldwide) http://www.travelocity.com
Travel Select (Worldwide) http://www.travelselect.co.uk
Travelshop (AUS) http://www.travelshop.com.au

Although they list hundreds of airlines and millions of fares, the general consensus is that they're usually better for research, accommodation, and travel tips than cheap fares and customer service. So if you think it's worth the effort, drop in and check which carriers haul your route, offer the best deals, and still have seats available. You can then use their rates as a benchmark. Compare them with the fares on the airline sites and discount specialists such as:

Bargain Holidays (UK) http://www.bargainholidays.com
Cheap Flights (UK) http://www.cheapflights.com
Deckchair (UK) http://www.deckchair.com
Ebookers.com (UK, EUR) http://www.ebookers.com
Flight Centre (Worldwide) http://www.flightcentre.com
Internet Air Fares (US) http://www.air-fare.com
1Travel.com (Worldwide) http://www.1travel.com
Lowestfare.com (US) http://www.lowestfare.com

Or compare the prices across several agencies simultaneously using a comparision:

Farechase http://www.farechase.com
Hotwire http://www.hotwire.com
Infochoice (AUS) http://www.flightchoice.com.au
Orbitz (US) http://www.orbitz.com
QIXO http://www.qixo.com
Sidestep http://www.sidestep.com
TravelHub (US) http://www.travelhub.com

Finally, see if your travel agent can better the price. If the difference is only marginal, favor your agent. Then at least you'll have a human contact if something goes wrong. See how the online bookers rate at:

Gomez.com http://www.gomez.com

12Degrees

http://www.12degrees.com
Rope in a guidebook author to plan your adventure holiday.

A2Btravel.com (UK)

http://www.a2btravel.com • http://www.ferrybooker.com
http://www.ukonline.co.uk/content/travel.html
Resources for getting into, around, and out of the UK, such as car-hire comparison, airport guides, train timetables, and ferry booking.

Africam

http://www.africam.com
Sneak a peek at wild beasts going about their business.

Art of Travel

http://www.artoftravel.com
How to see the world on $25 a day.

ATM Locators

http://www.visa.com/pd/atm/ • http://www.mastercard.com/atm/
Locate a bowser willing to replenish your wallet.

Get a Map

You can generate road and airport maps for most cities worldwide, driving directions for North America and Europe, US traffic reports, world maps and more at:

Expedia http://maps.expedia.com
MapBlast http://www.mapblast.com
MapQuest http://www.mapquest.com
Multimap (UK, EUR) http://www.multimap.com

To create UK or Australian street and road maps from postcodes or addresses, see:

Streetmap (UK) http://www.streetmap.co.uk
Whereis (AUS) http://www.whereis.com.au

If you require highly-detailed US topographic maps, try:

TopoZone http://www.topozone.com

For more maps, geographical and GPS resources see:

http://geography.about.com
http://dmoz.org/Reference/Maps/

Bed & Breakfast.com

http://www.bedandbreakfast.com • http://www.babs.com.au (AUS)
http://www.innsite.com
Secure your night's sleep worldwide.

CIA World Factbook

http://www.odci.gov/cia/publications/pubs.html
Vital stats on every country. For the score on living standards:
http://www.undp.org

Concierge.com

http://www.concierge.com
Get packing with advice from Traveler magazine.

Danger Finder

http://www.comebackalive.com/df/
Adventure holidays that could last a lifetime.

Digistreets

http://www.digistreets.com
Enter a London postcode in return for an instant photo of the address.

Electronic Embassy

http://www.embassy.org
Directory of foreign embassies in DC plus Web links where available. Search Yahoo for representation in other cities.

Eurotrip

http://www.eurotrip.com • http://www.ricksteves.com
Look out Europe, here you come.

Flight Arrivals and Departures

http://www.flightarrivals.com
Stay on top of takeoffs and touchdowns across North America.

Global Freeloaders

http://www.globalfreeloaders.com
Take in a globetrotting dosser in exchange for some return hospitality.

Hotel Discount

http://www.hoteldiscount.com • http://www.hotelnet.co.uk
http://www.hotelwiz.com
Book hotels around the world. For backpacker rates, try:
http://www.hostels.com

How far is it?

http://www.indo.com/distance/
Calculate the distance between any two cities.

IgoUgo

http://www.igougo.com
Packed full of travellers' photos and journals, this roughguides.com partner-site offers candid firsthand information.

Incredible Adventures

http://www.incredible-adventures.com
Convert your cash into adrenaline.

Infiltration

http://www.infiltration.org
Confessions of a serial trespasser.

International Home Exchange

http://www.homexchange.com • http://www.sunswap.com
http://www.homebase-hols.com
Swap hideouts with a foreigner until the heat dies down.

International Student Travel Confederation

http://www.istc.org
Save money with an authentic international student card.

Journeywoman

http://www.journeywoman.com
Reporting in from the sister beaten track.

Mail2Web

http://www.mail2web.com
Collect and send your POP3 mail instantly from any Web browser. Faster than Hotmail.

Mungo Park

http://www.mungopark.com
If you'd rather New Year in Timbuktu than Times Square.

My Travel Rights

http://mytravelrights.com
Disgruntled? Maybe you'll be reimbursed.

No Shitting in the Toilet

http://www.noshit.com.au
Delighting in the oddities of low-budget travel.

Roadside America

http://www.roadsideamerica.com
Strange attractions that loom between squished animals on US highways.

Sahara Overland

http://www.sahara-overland.com
Leave the city in a cloud of dust.

Satellite and Aerial Imaging

http://www.terraserver.com • http://terra.nasa.gov
http://www.crworld.co.uk • http://www.photolib.noaa.gov
http://www.globexplorer.com • http://www.multimap.com (UK)
See why nine out of ten Martian honeymooners prefer your planet.

Subway Navigator

http://www.subwaynavigator.com
http://www.manhattanaddress.com
Estimate the traveling times between city stations worldwide, or find the right stop in NY.

TNT Live!

http://www.tntmagazine.com
Survive London and venture onward with aid from expat streetmags, TNT, and Southern Cross

Tourism Offices Worldwide

http://www.towd.com
Write to the local tourist office. They might send you a brochure.

Traffic and Road Conditions

http://www.accutraffic.com • http://traffic.yahoo.com
Live traffic and weather updates across the US.

Travel and Health Warnings

http://www.dfat.gov.au (Aus) • http://www.fco.gov.uk (UK)
http://travel.state.gov (US)
Don't ignore these bulletins if you're planning to visit a potential hot-spot or health risk, but seek a second opinion before postponing your adventure. If you're off on business, try a professional advisory such as Kroll: http://www.krollworldwide.com

Travel Doctor

http://www.tmvc.com.au • http://www.cdc.gov/travel/
http://www.masta.org • http://www.travelhealth.co.uk
http://www.who.int
Brace yourself against the bugs eagerly awaiting your arrival. For a list

of travel medicine clinics worldwide, see: http://www.tripprep.com

Travelmag

http://www.travelmag.co.uk
Several intimate travel reflections monthly.

Travel Paperwork

http://www.travelpaperwork.com
Sort out the red tape before you hit the border.

Travlang

http://www.travlang.com
Add another language to your repertoire.

Unclaimed Baggage

http://www.unclaimedbaggage.com
You lose it; they sell it.

Visit Britain

http://www.visitbritain.com • http://www.uktravel.com
Understand the British way of doing things.

Walkabout

http://www.walkabout.com.au
Get the lowdown on the land down under.

WebFlyer

http://www.webflyer.com
Keep tabs on frequent flyer schemes.

Whats on When?

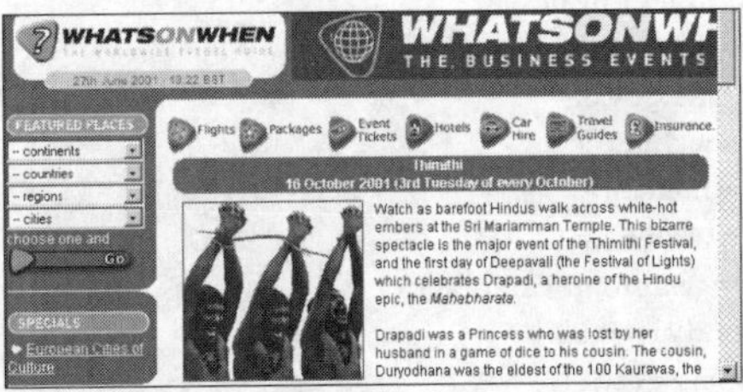

http://www.whatsonwhen.com • **http://www.whatsgoingon.com**
Annoyed you've missed Thaipusam or the Turning of the Bones yet again? Get your dates right here.

World Heritage Listing
http://www.unesco.org/whc/
Plan your itinerary around international treasures.

Weather

Most news sites report the weather but it's rarely up to the minute. For that you need to go directly to your local weather bureau or a specialist weather reporting service. For five-day forecasts, charts, storm warnings, allergy reports, and satellite photos for thousands of cities worldwide, try:

Accuweather http://www.accuweather.com
CNN Weather http://www.cnn.com/WEATHER/
Intellicast http://www.intellicast.com
Weather Channel http://www.weather.com
Weather Underground http://www.wunderground.com
Yahoo Weather http://weather.yahoo.com

For more intricate and timely detail, particularly outside the USA, drop by the local meteorological bureau:

Australia http://www.bom.gov.au
Brazil http://www.inmet.gov.br
Canada http://www.msc-smc.ec.gc.ca
China http://www.cma.gov.cn
Denmark http://www.dmi.dk
France http://www.meteo.fr
Germany http://www.dwd.de
Hong Kong http://www.info.gov.hk/hko/
India http://www.imd.ernet.in
Israel http://www.ims.gov.il

Italy http://www.meteoitalia.it
Latvia http://www.meteo.lv
Netherlands http://www.knmi.nl
New Zealand http://www.metservice.co.nz
Poland http://www.imgw.pl
Portugal http://www.meteo.pt
South Africa http://www.weathersa.co.za
Spain http://www.inm.es
Sweden http://www.smhi.se
UK http://www.metoffice.gov.uk
USA http://www.nws.noaa.gov

For other countries, amateur observations, and the fanatical extremes of weather watching, scan these specialist portals:

About Weather http://weather.about.com
Open Directory http://dmoz.org/News/Weather/
UM Weather http://cirrus.sprl.umich.edu/wxnet/
The Weather Resource http://www.nxdc.com/weather/
WMO Members http://www.wmo.ch/web-en/member.html

Climate Ark
http://www.climateark.org

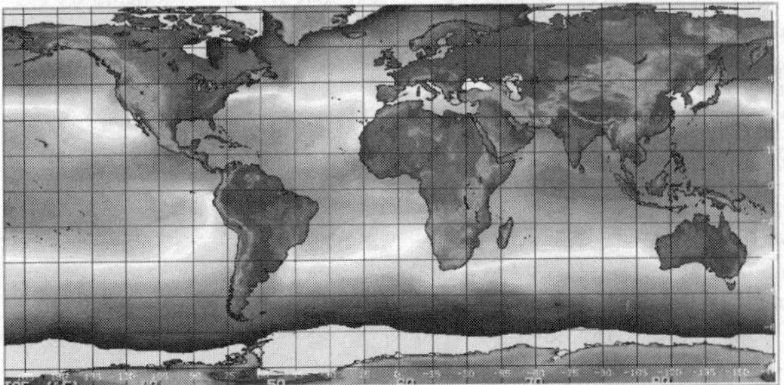

Fret about coming changes in the weather.

Ocean Weather

http://www.oceanweather.com
http://www.ssec.wisc.edu/data/sst.html
Chart the swells and temperatures across the seven seas.

Snoweye

http://www.snoweye.com • http://www.snow-forecast.com
Spy on thousands of ski resorts worldwide through strategically hidden cameras, or simply have the forecasts beamed directly to your WAP phone.

WeatherPlanner

http://www.weatherplanner.com
Plan your washing around a long-term forecast.

Weather Software

http://weather.hypermart.net/software.html
Stick out a wet thumb from the safety of your swivel chair.

Wild Weather

http://www.wildweather.com
http://australiasevereweather.com
http://www.storm-track.org • http://www.nssl.noaa.gov
Set your course into the eye of the storm.

World Climate

http://www.worldclimate.com • http://www.weatherbase.com
Off to Irkutzk next August? Here's what weather to expect.

World Meteorological Organization

http://www.wmo.ch
UN division that monitors global climate.

Absurd.org

http://www.absurd.org
Please do not adjust your set.

Aetherius Society

http://www.aetherius.org
Continue the legacy of the late Sir Dr George King, Primary Terrestrial Mental Channel of the Interplanetary Council.

Aliens and Soul Abduction

http://www.cia.com.au/brough/
Fact: spooky space dudes are stealing our souls. The Bible wouldn't lie: **http://aliensinthebible.com**

Brother Ellis Society

http://www.freespeech.org/besna/besna.html
Appease God by eating unwanted pets. No details spared. In complete contrast to: **http://www.jesusveg.com**

Christian Guide to Small Arms

http://www.frii.com/~gosplow/cgsa.html
"He that hath no sword, let him sell his garment, and buy one" – Luke 22:36. It's not just your right, it's your duty!

Circlemakers

http://www.circlemakers.org
Create crop circles to amuse New Agers and the press.

A Citizen from Hell

http://www.amightywind.com/hell/citizenhell.htm
If Hell sounds this bad, you don't want to go there.

Clonaid

http://www.clonaid.com
Thanks to the Raelians, we now know all life on earth was created in extraterrestrial laboratories. Here's where you can buy genuine cloned human livestock for the kitchen table. Ready as soon as the lab's finished.

The Darwin Awards

http://www.officialdarwinawards.com
http://www.darwinawards.com
Each year the Darwin Award goes to the person who drops off the census register in the most spectacular fashion. Here's where to read about the runners-up and er ... winners.

Derm Cinema
http://www.skinema.com
Know your celebrity skin conditions. But would you recognize them under a gas mask?
http://www.geocities.com/TimesSquare/Alley/8207/

Dolphin Society
http://www.dolphinsociety.org
Driftnet-eating submarines rescue humans who've shape-shifted into dolphins.

Dr MegaVolt
http://www.drmegavolt.com
The Doc sure sparked right up when they switched on the power, but could he cut in the big league?
http://www3.bc.sympatico.ca/lightningsurvivor/

English Rose Press
http://www.englishrosepress.com
Diana sends her love from Heaven.

Flatulence Filter
http://flatulence-filter.com
Because life wasn't meant to be a gas.

Fortean Times
http://www.forteantimes.com
Updates from the print monthly that takes the investigation of strange phenomena more seriously than itself. See also:
http://www.parascope.com and **http://www.bizarremag.com**

Freaks, Geeks, & Weirdness on the Web
http://www.rosemarywest.com/guide/
http://www.the-strange.com
http://www.student.nada.kth.se/~nv91-asa/
Make that three big sacks of assorted nuts, please.

Future Horizons
http://www.futurehorizons.net
Snap off more than your fair share through solid-state circuitry.

Gallery of the Absurd

http://www.absurdgallery.com
Strange ways to sell strange stuff.

God Channel

http://www.godchannel.com
Relay requests to God via His official Internet channel.

Great Joy In Great Tribulation

http://www.dccsa.com/greatjoy/
Biblical proof that Prince Chuck is the Antichrist and key dates leading to the end of the world. For more enlightenment, including how to debug the pyramids, see:
http://members.aol.com/larrypahl/lpahl.htm

I Can Eat Glass Project

http://hcs.harvard.edu/~igp/glass.html
Deter excess foreign suitors and carpet dealers with the only words you know in their language.

Illuminati News

http://www.illuminati-news.com
Storm into secret societies and thump your fist on the table.

International Ghost Hunters Society

http://www.ghostweb.com • http://www.ghostresearch.org
They never give up the ghost. Nab your own with:
http://www.maui.net/~emf/TriFieldNat.html

Itz Fun Tew Be Dat Kandie Kid

http://www.angelfire.com/ma/talulaQ/kandie.html
Mamas don't let your babies grow up to be ravers.

Kaol's Ol' Sinkin' Hole

http://www.geocities.com/SoHo/8090/
What's sexier than sinking in quicksand? Nothing says Kaol, except perhaps being gassed, drowned, strangled or blown out into space:
http://www.fortunecity.com/lavendar/mockingbird/472/

A Mathematical Survey of the English Language

http://www.geocities.com/garywaterbury/

Plot your future through simple arithmetic. Why didn't it occur to you sooner?

Mind Control Forum

http://mindcontrolforum.com
http://www.mindcontrolmanual.com
http://www.psychops.com • http://www.raven1.net
Unpick Big Brother's evil scheme and then put it to work on the dance-floor.

Mozart's Musikalisches Würfelspell

http://sunsite.univie.ac.at/Mozart/dice/
Compose a minuet as you play Monopoly.

Museum of Non-Primate Art

http://www.monpa.com
Become an aficionado of moggy masterpieces.

Myrla's Korner

http://myrla.tripod.com
Thank goodness the ancient felinoid Ka'ats from planet Zimmorrah have Myrna. Otherwise no-one would take them seriously.

News of the Weird

http://www.nine.org/notw/ • http://www.thisistrue.com
http://www.weirdlist.com
Dotty clippings from the world press.

Nibiruan Council

http://www.nibiruancouncil.com
Stock your bar to welcome the heroic Starseeds, Walkins, and Lightworkers from the Battlestar Nibiru, who will finally usher in the fifth dimensional reality.

Non-escalating Verbal Self Defence

http://www.taxi1010.com
Fight insults by acting insane.

Planetary Activation Organization

http://www.paoweb.com
Prevent inter-dimensional dark forces from dominating our galaxy by ganging up with the Galactic Federation of Light.

Reincarnation.org

http://www.reincarnation-org.com
Stash your loot with this crowd, then come back to collect it in your next life.

Reptoids

http://www.reptoids.com
Was that an alien or merely the subterranean descendant of a dinosaur?

Rocket Guy

http://www.rocketguy.com
Brian's about to launch himself into space. Bye-bye, Brian.

The Sacred Geometry Stories of Jesus Christ

http://www.jesus8880.com
How to decode the big J's mathematical word puzzle.

Sensoterapia

http://www.sensoterapia.com.co
Master the sex secret you'll never see revealed in this month's Cleo.

Sightings

http://www.sightings.com
Fishy newsbreaks from talk radio truthferret, Jeff Rense. For more real life X-file blather tune into: http://www.artbell.com

Sulabh International Museum of Toilets

http://www.sulabhtoiletmuseum.org
Follow the evolution of the ablution at the world's leading exhibition of bathroom businessware. No need to take it sitting down:
http://www.restrooms.org

Things My Girlfriend and I Have Argued About

http://homepage.ntlworld.com/mil.millington/things.html
Add this page to that list.

Time Travel Devices

http://home.inreach.com/dov/tt.htm
Step back to a time that common sense forgot.

Toe Amputation Project

http://www.bme.freeq.com/spc/toecutter.htm
No big deal. He still has a couple left.

Toilet-train Your Cat

http://www.karawynn.net/mishacat/ • **http://susandennis.com**
How to point pusskins at the porcelain.

Xenophobic Persecution in the UK

http://www.five.org.uk
If you're below British standards the MI5 will punish you by TV.

ZetaTalk

http://www.zetatalk.com
Nancy's guests today are those elusive aliens that frolic in the autumn mist at the bottom of her garden.

15

Internet Service Providers

The following directory lists some major Internet Service Providers (ISPs) in Britain, North America, Australia and New Zealand. It's by no means complete and inclusion shouldn't be taken as an endorsement. We've selected the larger, established providers with multiple dial-in access points, as these are the most versatile. Still, if you only access from home, it's possible you might get a better deal from a smaller, local operator.

Your first priority is to find a provider with **local call access**, preferably without paying a higher tariff for the

convenience. If our list doesn't help, ask around locally, or sign up temporarily, get online, and consult one of these **Net directories**:
http://www.thelist.com (global)
http://www.cynosure.com.au/isp/ (Australia)
http://www.internet-magazine.com/isp/ (UK)
http://www.net4nowt.com (UK)
http://www.ispcheck.com (USA)
http://www.isps.com (USA)

Unfortunately, these lists aren't so comprehensive either. Nor do they all offer advice. For something more subjective, read your local **computer/Internet publications**; in the UK, for example, *Internet* magazine (**http://www.internet-magazine.com**) runs monthly performance charts.

You'll also find ISP reviews in most of the **consumer opinion sites**, and the odd specialist ISP review site such as:
ISPreview (UK) http://www.ispreview.co.uk

What to ask

It's important to pick the right ISP. You want a reliable, fast connection; good customer support; and a company who'll stay in the game, so you won't need to change account or (worse) email address. The best approach is to **ask around, read magazine reviews, and see what others recommend**. If someone swears by an ISP, and they seem to know what they're talking about, give it a go. That's about the best research you can do.

So if you know someone who's hooked up, ask: Is it fast and reliable? Does it ever get so slow you feel like giving up? Is it ever difficult collecting or sending mail? Do you often strike a busy tone when dialing in? What's its support like? Have you ever been overcharged?

If you're not in that boat, and have to do your own research, look for answers to the following questions – maybe by calling a few of the Freecall numbers listed in the sections following and asking for their information packs and access software. It might seem laborious but it's not as painful as being stuck with poor access.

Broadband or modem?

The leap in speed between modem and broadband, such as ADSL, cable, apartment networks and satellite, can be astonishing. If broadband is offered in your area check it out, especially if it's reasonably priced. If you're lucky enough to have a selection of broadband options, weigh up their limitations before pouncing. The most notable issues are:

- **Cable** and **apartment networks** have to share bandwidth between neighbors, which can result in bottlenecks during peak hours.
- **Satellite** access comes either one-way or bi-directional. If you're offered the former you'll still need to uplink through a modem. Although it's fast, the packets have to travel lost distances through space, which increases latency making it unsuitable for gaming.
- **ADSL**, cable, and satellite are normally asynchronous services, meaning that they'll download much faster than upload. So if you intend to run a server or share large files, make sure you understand what you're buying.

Still, pricing is likely to be the biggest determinant, in which regard they can be appraised like any other ISP.

Free and ISPs

No-one gives away free Internet accounts without a catch. **In the UK**, it's quite simple – they take a cut of your phone bill. This scam can only exist because of the UK's archaic metered local call system. So the longer you stay online, the more you pay. On top of this, they normally fleece by the minute for support.

However, all of this should be rendered obsolete by the new **unmetered (freecall) accounts**, where you pay a fixed monthly fee for both Internet and phone charges. Unfortunately, as the metered call system remains in place, there are still usually **strings attached**. For instance, you can't use the account from another phone line. You can read all about them here:

http://www.net4nowt.com
http://www.ispreview.co.uk

Where local phone calls are unmetered or free such as in the **US**, **Canada** and **Australia**, the only way to turn a profit is to charge, or take commissions from, advertisers and market data hounds. To exchange your privacy for Internet access, scan the lists at:

http://www.emailaddresses.com/email_internet.htm

Costs

If you do have to pay a fee, you'll need to break it down to see that there are no hidden charges. Consider the following:

Can you access for the price of a local call?

Remember while you're online with a modem you're also on the phone.

Is there a free trial?

If you can trial a service without having to install any special software you've little to lose bar the email address if you decide not to proceed.

If not, is there a start-up cost?

You'll lose that money if you switch after the first month.

Do they offer unlimited access for a fixed fee? If not, what's the price structure?

A no limitations, all you can eat account is preferable for moderate to high users. That way you'll know your bill in advance and won't have to keep watching the clock. Otherwise, you could be up for all sorts of permutations usually based around a monthly minimum, followed by usage charges.

Is there a download limit?

Some, mainly broadband, ISPs charge a flat fee, with a megabyte transfer restriction. Once you hit the ceiling, you're billed extra per megabyte. Avoid this plan like the plague.

Is it cheaper during off-peak?

Dropping rates over the weekends and nights might sound like a good deal, but with everyone scrambling online at once, you'll face busy lines and sluggish networks.

Does it have or offer national or global roaming and how is it charged?

If you travel a lot it's handy to know you can still get connected, though if it comes at a high price it may not be worth it.

The basics

Does it offer free phone support? What are the hours?

Free phone support until the mid-evenings is standard fare. But a few ISPs, most notably the free UK outfits, charge by the minute for their pleasure. Chances are you will strike problems, you will be on the phone to them, and you won't want to wait until Monday morning. Factor that into your calculations.

Will you get one or more POP3 email addresses?

A recent trend amongst cheapskate providers is to issue a Webmail account in lieu of a proper POP3 address. This is rarely a satisfactory alternative. Sure, you can collect Webmail from any computer, but you can do the same with POP3 through free services like Mail2Web (**http://www.mail2web.com**). You'd even be better off with a free third party Webmail account (p.105) – one you won't lose if you switch providers. But a POP3 account is preferable, or even better, multiple POP3 addresses. Then you can keep separate addresses for different types of mail, and dish out an address or two to family and friends.

Is your name available?

You always have the option to choose the first part of your email address. You might like to use your first name or nickname. This will then be attached to the provider's host name. Check if your name's available and what the host name would be. The trouble with bigger providers is that most common names will already be taken. You really don't want an address like: **John3434@aol.com**

Does it run a Usenet server? If so, how many groups?

Usenet has more than 60,000 groups and it's still growing. That's 95 percent more than you'll ever want to look at in your lifetime. Most providers carry only a portion, but it's still usually over 15,000. The first ones to be axed are often foreign language, country specific, provider specific, and the adult (**alt.sex** and **alt.binaries**) series. If you particularly want certain groups, your provider can usually add them, but it may have a policy against certain material. If it says no to Usenet, keep shopping.

Does it throw in some free Web space?

Most ISPs include a few megabytes of storage free so you can publish your own Web page. In general, if you go over that megabyte limit there'll be an excess charge. Again like Webmail, you might be better off with one of the free Webspace providers (p.304), so you don't lose your home page if you switch. That said, if the ISP offers a page free of pop-up banners or adverts with an attractive address it might be worth considering. Don't make it a decider though.

Does it go on about its content?

Your priority is to get fast reliable Internet access. Forget about local content such as news and chat rooms. There's more than enough on the greater Net.

What else does it offer?

While your first priority should be to get fast reliable Internet access, see what else you can get with the deal, either as part of the bundle or as an added extra.

Is it fast and reliable?

What's its background?

Big names may offer certain advantages such as national

and even global dial-up points, security, guaranteed access, stability, and close proximity to the high-speed backbone. However, they can be slow to upgrade because of high overheads and may have dim support staff. Small, younger providers can be more flexible, have newer equipment, more in-tune staff, cheaper rates, and faster access, but conversely may lack the capital to make future critical upgrades. There aren't any rules; it's a new industry and all a bit of a long-term gamble.

Which backbones does it connect to, and at what speed?

Backbones are the high-speed longhaul connections that carry Internet traffic between ISPs and around the globe. A good ISP should tell you which backbone it uses and how big its connections are – or even provide a map of its backbone links around the world. Be suspicious of any ISP that can't answer this question. Better ISPs connect to more than one ISP – a practice called multi-homing. This means they're not bound to one route and can thus choose the fastest connection per request.

For more about backbones including the current state of traffic, see: **http://www.cybergeography.org** and **http://www.mids.org/weather/**

What is its maximum user to modem ratio?

The lower this ratio, the less chance you'll strike a busy tone when you call. As a yardstick, anything over 10:1 should start sounding warning bells that they're under-equipped.

Getting started

Can they supply you with a sheet of clear setup instructions for your system?

If you're running Windows 98+/NT/2000, an iMac or a Mac running OS 8.5, you already have the software, you only need the configuration settings and a little guidance filling them out. **Unless you're running an older system, or hooking up broadband, avoid any provider that insists you have to install their special connection software.** Nothing will muck up your system faster than meddlesome ISP-ware. Assure them that as soon as you get online you intend to download the latest version of Internet Explorer. If they have a problem with that, take a hike.

Britain

Provider	Telephone number	Web Address
BT Internet*	0800 800 001	http://www.btinternet.com
Claranet*	0800 358 2828	http://www.clara.net
Demon Internet*	020 8371 1234	http://www.demon.net
Easynet*	020 7681 4444	http://www.easynet.co.uk
Freeserve*	0870 550 0049	http://www.freeserve.com
Madasafish*	0800 0273 373	http://www.madasafish.co.uk
Netcom	0870 980 9107	http://www.netcom.net.uk
Nextra*	020 8255 5050	http://www.nextra.co.uk
NTL Internet*	0800 183 1234	http://www.ntl.com
Pipex*	0500 567 000	http://www.pipex.net
Virgin Net	0500 558 800	http://www.virgin.net

* Dialup and broadband.

North America

Provider Web address	Telephone number Points of Presence
@Home (Cable)	See Web page
http://www.home.com	USA, Canada, Netherlands, Australia
AT&T Canada	1 888 655 7671
http://www.attcanada.ca	Canada
AT&T WorldNet*	1 800 967 5363
http://www.att.net	USA

Bell Atlantic*	1 800 422 3555
http://www.bellatlantic.net	USA
EarthLink*	1 800 EARTH LINK
http://www.earthlink.com	USA, Canada
Inter.net	1 866 468 3736
http://www.us.inter.net	USA
Inter.net*	1 800 920 SURF
http://www.ca.inter.net	Canada
MSN	1 800 FREE MSN
http://free.msn.com	USA
NetZero (Free)	1800 333 3633
http://www.netzero.com	USA
Prodigy*	1 800 213 0992
http://www.prodigy.com	USA
XO*	1 888 699 6398
http://www.xo.net	USA, UK, Netherlands

* Dialup and broadband.

Australia and New Zealand

Provider	Telephone number	Web address
AAPT	138 888	http://www.smartchat.net.au
Austar*	132 432	http://www.austar.com.au
Connect	1800 818 262	http://www.connect.com.au
Dingo Blue	1300 551 455	http://www.dingoblue.com.au
iPrimus*	1300 303 081	http://www.primus.com.au
Optus Internet*	1300 301 325	http://www.optusnet.com.au
Ozemail	132 884	http://www.ozemail.com.au
Telecom XTRA (NZ)	0800 22 55 98	http://www.xtra.co.nz

Telstra Big Pond* ...... 1800 804 282 .... http://www.bigpond.com.au

Voyager (NZ) .... 0800 869 243 .... http://www.voyager.co.nz

* Dialup and broadband.

Roman

If you travel with a notebook, look for an account with instant local call access in your destination cities. **Nationally**, isn't hard to find. Most of the larger ISPs, for example all those we've listed, offer local dial up access across the country, or at least in the major cities. All the same, you should double-check first as there might be restrictions.

Internationally, is another story. While a handful of Online Services and ISPs have a genuinely international presence, the convenience often attracts steep premiums away from home, depending on the countries concerned. So before you sign up and head off, check the fine print first. Compare the rates at:

AOL **http://www.aol.com**

AT&T **http://www.attbusiness.net**

CompuServe **http://www.cis.com**

Inter.net **http://www.inter.net**

UUdial **http://www.uu.net/products/uudial/**

Alternatively, you could join an ISP that belongs to a **global roaming** group such as:

GRIC **http://www.gric.com**

IPass **http://www.ipass.com**

This means you can dial into any ISP in the group. Again, you'll be handsomely charged by the minute for the convenience, which is fine for email. If you plan to spend long hours on the Web it might be worth signing up with a local.

Be sure to test the foreign numbers before you leave – better to risk the expense of an international call than wait until you have to wrestle the hotel's system and a directory enquiries that can't understand your accent.

contexts

A brief history

Glossary

16

A brief history of the Internet

The Internet may be a recent media phenomenon but as a concept it's actually older than most of its users; it was born in the 1960s – a long time before anyone coined the buzzwords "Information SuperHighway". Of course, there's no question that the Net deserves its current level of attention. It really is a quantum leap in global communications, though – right now – it's still more of a prototype than a finished product. While Bill Gates and Al Gore rhapsodize about such household services as video-on-demand, most Netizens would be happy with a system fast enough to view stills-on-demand. Nonetheless, it's getting there.

The online bomb shelter

The concept of the Net might not have been hatched in Microsoft's cabinet war rooms, but it did play a role in a previous contest for world domination. It was 1957, at the height of the Cold War. The Soviets had just launched the first Sputnik, thus beating the USA into space. The race was on. In response, the US Department of Defense formed the **Advanced Research Projects Agency (ARPA)** to bump up its technological prowess. Twelve years later, this spawned **ARPAnet** – a project to develop a military research network, or specifically, the world's first decentralized computer network.

In those days, no-one had PCs. The computer world was based on mainframe computers and dumb terminals. These usually involved a gigantic, fragile box in a climate-controlled room, which acted as a hub, with a mass of cables spoking out to keyboard/monitor ensembles. The concept of independent intelligent processors pooling resources through a network was brave new territory that would require the development of new hardware, software, and connectivity methods.

The driving force behind decentralization, ironically, was the bomb-proofing factor. Nuke a mainframe and the system goes down. But bombing a network would, at worst, remove only a few nodes. The remainder could route around it unharmed. Or so the theory went.

Wiring the world

Over the next decade, **research agencies** and **universities** flocked to join the network. US institutions such as UCLA, MIT, Stanford, and Harvard led the way, and in 1973, the network crossed the Atlantic to include University College London and Norway's Royal Radar Establishment.

The 1970s also saw the introduction of **electronic mail,**

FTP, **Telnet**, and what would become the **Usenet newsgroups**. The early 1980s brought **TCP/IP**, the **Domain Name System**, **Network News Transfer Protocol**, and the European networks **EUnet** (European UNIX Network), **MiniTel** (the widely adopted French consumer network), and **JANET** (Joint Academic Network), as well as the Japanese **UNIX** Network. **ARPA** evolved to handle the research traffic, while a second network, MILnet, took over the US military intelligence.

An important development took place in 1986, when the US National Science Foundation established **NSFnet** by linking five university super-computers at a backbone speed of 56 Kbps. This opened the gateway for external universities to tap in to superior processing power and share resources. In the three years between 1984 and 1988, the number of host computers on the **Internet** (as it was now being called) grew from about 1000 to over 60,000. NSFnet, meanwhile, increased its capacity to T1 (1544 Kbps). Over the next few years, more and more countries joined the network, spanning the globe from Australia and New Zealand, to Iceland, Israel, Brazil, India, and Argentina.

It was at this time too, that **Internet Relay Chat** (IRC) burst onto the scene providing an alternative to CNN's incessant, but censored, Gulf War coverage. By this stage, the Net had grown far beyond its original charter. Although ARPA had succeeded in creating the basis for decentralized computing, whether it was actually a military success was debatable. It might have been bombproof, but it also opened new doors to espionage. It was never particularly secure, and it is suspected that Soviet agents routinely hacked in to forage for research data. In 1990, ARPAnet folded, and NSFnet took over administering the Net.

Coming in from the cold

Global electronic communication was far too useful and versatile to stay confined to academics. Big business was starting to notice. The Cold War looked over and world economies were regaining confidence after the 1987 stock market savaging. In most places, market trading moved from the pits and blackboards onto computer screens. The financial sector expected fingertip real-time data and that feeling was spreading. The world was ready for a people's network. And since the Net was already in place, funded by taxpayers, there was really no excuse not to open it to the public.

In 1991, the NSF lifted its restrictions on enterprise. During the Net's early years, its "**Acceptable Use Policy**" specifically prohibited using the network for profit. Changing that policy opened the floodgates to commerce with the greater public close behind.

However, before anyone could connect to the Net, someone had to sell them a connection. The **Commercial Internet eXchange (CIX)**, a network of major commercial access providers, formed to create a commercial backbone and divert traffic from the NSFnet. Before long, dozens of budding ISPs began rigging up points of presence in their bedrooms. Meanwhile, NSFnet upgraded its backbone to T3 (44,736 Kbps).

By this time, the Net had established itself as a viable medium for transferring data, but with one major problem. You had to know where to look. That process involved knowing a lot more about computers, and the UNIX computing language, than most punters would relish. The next few years saw an explosion in navigation protocols, such as WAIS, Gopher, Veronica, and, most importantly, the now-dominant World Wide Web.

The gold rush begins

In 1989, Tim Berners-Lee of **CERN**, the Swiss particle physics institute, proposed the basis of the World Wide Web, initially as a means of sharing physics research. His goal was a seamless network in which data from any source could be accessed in a simple, consistent way with one program, on any type of computer. The Web did this, encompassing all existing infosystems such as FTP, Gopher, and Usenet, without alteration. It remains an unqualified success.

As the number of Internet hosts exceeded one million, the **Internet Society** was formed to brainstorm protocols and attempt to co-ordinate and direct the Net's escalating expansion. **Mosaic** – the first graphical **Web browser** – was released, and declared to be the "killer application of the 1990s". It made navigating the Internet as simple as pointing and clicking, and took away the need to know UNIX. The Web's traffic increased by 25-fold in the year up to June 1994, and domain names for **commercial organizations (.com)** began to outnumber those of educational institutions **(.edu).**

As the Web grew, so too did the global village. The media began to notice, slowly realizing that the Internet was something that went way beyond propeller heads and students. Almost every country in the world had joined the Net. Even the White House was online.

Of course, as word of a captive market got around, entrepreneurial brains went into overdrive. Canter & Seigel, an Arizona law firm, notoriously "**spammed**" Usenet with **advertisements** for the US green card lottery. Although the Net was tentatively open for business, crossposting advertisements to every newsgroup was decidedly bad form. Such was the ensuing wrath that C&S had no chance of filtering out genuine responses from the server-breaking level of hate mail they received. A precedent was thus established for **how not to do business on the Net**. Pizza Hut, by contrast, showed how to do it subtly by setting up a trial service on the Web. Although it generated wads of positive publicity, it too was doomed by impracticalities. Nevertheless, the ball had begun to roll.

The homesteaders

As individuals arrived to stake out Web territory, businesses followed. Most had no idea what to do once they got their brand online. Too many arrived with a bang, only to peter out in a perpetuity of "under construction signs". Soon business cards not only sported email addresses, but Web addresses as well. And rather than send a CV and stiff letter, job aspirants could now send a brief email accompanied with a "see my Web page" for further details.

The Internet moved out of the realm of luxury into an elite necessity, verging toward a commodity. Some early business sites gathered such a following that by 1995 they were able to charge high rates for advertising banners. A few, including Web **portals** such as **InfoSeek** and **Yahoo**, made it to the

Stock Exchange boards, while others, like **GNN**, attracted buyers.

But it wasn't all success stories. Copyright lawyers arrived in droves. Well-meaning devotees, cheeky opportunists, and info-terrorists alike felt the iron fists of Lego, McDonald's, MTV, the Louvre, Fox, Sony, the Church of Scientology and others clamp down on their "unofficial Web sites" or newsgroups. It wasn't always a case of corporate right but of might, as small players couldn't foot the expenses to test **new legal boundaries**. The honeymoon was officially over.

Point of no return

By the beginning of 1995, the Net was well and truly within the public realm. It was impossible to escape. The media became bored with extolling its virtues, so it turned to **sensationalism**. The Net reached the status of an Oprah Winfrey issue. New tales of hacking, porn, bombmaking, terrorist handbooks, homebreaking, and sexual harassment began to tarnish the Internet's iconic position as the great international equalizer. But that didn't stop businesses, schools, banks, government bodies, politicians, and consumers from swarming online, nor the major **Online Services** – such as CompuServe, America Online, and Prodigy, which had been developing in parallel since the late 1980s – from adding Internet access as a sideline to their existing private networks.

As 1995 progressed, Mosaic, the previous year's killer application, lost its footing to a superior browser, **Netscape**. Not such big news, you might imagine, but after a half-year of rigorous beta-testing, Netscape went public with the third largest ever NASDAQ IPO share value – around $2.4bn.

Meantime, Microsoft, which had formerly disregarded the Internet, released **Windows 95**, a PC operating platform incorporating access to the controversial **Microsoft Network**. Although **IBM** had done a similar thing six months earlier with **OS/2 Warp** and its **IBM Global Network**, Microsoft's was an altogether different scheme. It offered full Net access but its real product was its own separate network, which many people feared might supersede the Net, giving Microsoft an unholy reign over information distribution. But that never happened. Within months, Microsoft, smarting from bad press, and finding the Net a larger animal even than itself, about-turned and declared a full commitment to furthering the Internet.

Browser wars

As Microsoft advanced on the horizon, Netscape continued pushing the envelope, driving the Web into new territory with each beta release. New enhancements arrived at such a rate that competitors began to drop out as quickly as they appeared. This was the era of "This page looks best if viewed with Netscape". Of course, it wasn't just Netscape since much of the new activity stemmed from the innovative products of third-party developers such as **MacroMedia** (**Shockwave**), **Progressive Networks** (**RealAudio**), **Apple** (**QuickTime**), and **Sun** (**Java**). The Web began to spring to life with animations, music, 3D worlds, and all sorts of new tricks.

While Netscape's market dominance gave developers the confidence to accept it as the de facto standard, treating it as a kind of Internet operating system into which to "plug" their products, Microsoft, an old hand at taking possession of cleared territory, began to launch a whole series of free Net tools. These included **Internet Explorer**, a browser with enhancements of its own, including **ActiveX**, a Web-centric programming environment more powerful than the much-lauded **Java**, but without the same platform independence, and clearly geared toward advancing Microsoft's software dominance. Not only was Internet Explorer suddenly the only other browser in the race, unlike Netscape, it was genuinely free. And many were not only rating it as the better product, but also crediting Microsoft with a broader vision of the Net's direction.

By mid-1997, every Online Service and almost every major ISP had signed deals with Microsoft to distribute its browser. Even intervention by the US Department of Justice over Microsoft's (logical but monopolistic) bundling of Internet Explorer as an integral part of Windows 98 couldn't impede its progress. Netscape looked bruised. While it continued shipping minor upgrades it no longer led either in market share or innovation. In desperation, it handed over the project of completely reworking the code to the general programming public at Mozilla.org. When AOL bought Netscape in early 1999, little doubt remained. Netscape had given up the fight.

Found on the Internet

Skipping back to late 1995, the backlash against Internet freedom had moved into full flight. The expression "**found on the Internet**", became the news tag of the minute, depicting the Net as the source of everything evil from bomb recipes to child pornography. While editors and commentators, often with little direct experience of the Net, urged that "children" be protected, the Net's own media and opinion shakers pushed the **freedom of speech** barrow. It became apparent that this uncensored, uncontrollable new media could shake the very foundations of democracy.

At first politicians didn't take much notice. Few could even grasp the concept of what the Net was about, let alone figure out a way to regulate its activities. The first, and easiest, target was **porn**, resulting in raids on hundreds of **private bulletin boards** worldwide and a few much-publicized convictions for the possession of child porn. BBSs were sitting ducks, being mostly self-contained and run by someone who could take the rap. Net activists, however, feared that the primary objective was to send a ripple of fear through a Net community that believed it was bigger than the law, and to soften the public to the notion that the Internet, as it stood, posed a threat to national wellbeing.

In December 1995, at the request of German authorities, **CompuServe** cut its newsfeed to exclude the bulk of newsgroups carrying sexual material. But the groups cut weren't just pornographers, some were dedicated to gay and abortion issues. This brought to light the difficulty in drawing the lines of obscenity, and the problems with publishing across foreign boundaries. Next came the **US Communications Decency Act**, a proposed legislation to forbid the online publication of "obscene" material. It was poorly conceived, however, and, following opposition from a very broad range of groups (including such mainstream bodies as the American Libraries Association), was overturned, and the decision later upheld in the Supreme Court.

Outside the US, meanwhile, more authorities reacted. In **France**, three ISP chiefs were temporarily jailed for supplying obscene newsgroups, while in **Australia** police prosecuted several users for downloading child porn. NSW courts introduced legislation banning obscene material with such loose wording that the Internet itself could be deemed illegal – if the law is ever tested. In **Britain**, in mid-1996, the police tried a "voluntary" approach, identifying newsgroups that carried pornography beyond the pale, and requesting that providers remove them from their feed. Most complied, but there was unease within the Internet industry that this was the wrong approach – the same groups would migrate elsewhere and the root of the problem would remain.

But the debate was, or is, about far more than porn, despite the huffing and puffing. For **Net fundamentalists**, the issue is about holding ground against any compromises in liberty, and retaining the global village as a political force – potentially capable of bringing down governments and large corporations. Indeed, they argue that these battles over publishing freedom have shown governments to be out of touch with both technology and the social undercurrent, and that in the long run the balance of power will shift toward the people, toward a new democracy.

Wiretapping

Another slow-news-day story of the mid-1990s depicted **hackers** ruling networks, stealing money, and creating havoc. Great reading, but the reality was less alarming. Although the US Department of Defense reported hundreds of thousands of network break-ins, they claimed it was more annoying than damaging. While in the commercial world, little went astray except the odd credit card file. (Bear in mind that every time you hand your credit card to a shop assistant they get the same information.) In fact, by and large, for an online population greater than the combined size of New York,

Moscow, London, Calcutta, and Tokyo, there were surprisingly few noteworthy crimes. Yet the perception remained that the Net was too unsafe for the exchange of sensitive information such as payment details.

Libertarians raged at the US Government's refusal to lift export bans on crack-proof **encryption algorithms**. But cryptography, the science of message coding, has traditionally been classified as a weapon and thus export of encryption falls under the Arms Control acts.

Encryption requires a secret key to open the contents of a message and often another public key to code the message. These keys can be generated for regular use by individuals or, in the case of Web transactions, simply for one session upon agreement between the server and client. Several governments proposed to employ official escrow authorities to keep a register of all secret keys and surrender them upon warrant – an unpopular proposal, to put it mildly, among a Net community who regard invasion of privacy as an issue equal in importance to censorship, and government monitors as instruments of repression.

However, authorities were so used to being able to tap phones, intercept mail, and install listening devices to aid investigations, that they didn't relish giving up their freedom either. Government officials made a lot of noise about needing to monitor data to protect national security, though their true motives probably involve monitoring internal insurgence and catching tax cheats – stuff they're not really supposed to do but we put up with anyway because if we're law-abiding it's mostly in our best interests.

The implications of such obstinacy went far beyond personal privacy. Business awaited browsers that could talk to commerce servers using totally snooper-proof encryption. Strong encryption technology had already been built into browsers, but was illegal to export them from the US. **The law was finally relaxed in mid 2000**.

The entertainment arrives

While politicians, big business, bankers, telcos, and online action groups such as **CommerceNet** and the **Electronic**

Frontier Foundation fretted the future of privacy and its impact on digital commerce, the online world partied on regardless. If 1996 was the year of the Web, then 1997 was the year the **games** began. Netizens had been swapping chess moves, playing dress-up, and struggling with the odd network game over the Net for years, but it took id Software's **Quake** to lure the gaming masses online. Not to miss out, Online Services and ISPs took steps to prioritize game traffic, while hard-core corporate data moved further back on the shelves.

Music took off, too. **Bands** and **DJs** routinely simulcast, or exclusively played, concerts over the Net while celebrities such as Michael Jackson, Joe Dolce, and Paul McCartney bared their souls in public chat rooms. Web pages came alive with the sound of music, from cheesy synthesized backgrounds to live radio feeds. Many online music stores like **CDNow** reported profits, while **Amazon** became a major force in bookselling.

And then there was the Net as a prime news medium. As **Pathfinder** touched down on Mars, back on Earth millions logged into NASA sites to scour the Martian landscape for traces of life. China marched into Hong Kong, Tiger Woods rewrote golfing history, Australia regained the Ashes, and Mike Tyson fell from grace, all live on the Net. In response to this breaking of news on Web sites and newsgroups, an increasing number of **print newspapers** began delivering online versions before their hard copies hit the stands. In 1997, if you weren't on the Net, you weren't in the media.

The casualties

Not everyone had reason to party in 1997. **Cybercafés** – the height of touted cool in 1995 – tended to flop as quickly as they appeared, as did many small **Internet Service Providers**, if they weren't swallowed by larger fish. From over thirty **browsers** in early 1996, less than a year later, only two real players – Netscape and Microsoft – remained in the game. The also-ran software houses that initially thrived on the Net's avenue for distribution and promotion faded from view as the two browser giants ruthlessly crammed more features into their plug-and-play Web desktops. Microsoft, and scores of other software developers, declared that their future products would be able to update themselves online, either automatically or by clicking in the right place. So much for the software dealer.

Meanwhile, **Web TV** arrived delivering Web pages and email onto home TV screens. It offered a cheap, simple alternative to PCs, but found its way to a smaller niche market than its fanfare predicted.

The whole **Web design industry** was due for a shakeout. Overnight Web cowboys – lacking the programming skills to code, the artistic merit to design, or the spelling standards to edit, yet who'd charged through the teeth for cornering the home-page design scam – were left exposed by the emerging professionalism. New media had come of age. The top Web chimps reworked their résumés and pitched in with online design houses. Major ad agencies formed new media departments, and splashed Web addresses over everything from milk cartons to toothpaste tubes.

Bizarrely though, 1997's best-known Web design team, **Higher Source**, will be remembered not for HTML handiwork, but for publishing their cult's agenda to top themselves in conjunction with the passing of the Hale Bopp comet. This was the Internet as major news story. Within hours of the mass suicide, several sites appeared spoofing both its corporate pages as well as its cult, **Heaven's Gate**. Days later, there were enough to spawn four new Yahoo subdirectories.

Back in the real world of **business and money**, major companies have played surprisingly by the book, observing netiquette – the Net's informal code of conduct. The marriage has been awkward but generally happy. Even the absurd court cases between blockbuster sites such as **Microsoft Sidewalk v. TicketMaster** and **Amazon v. Barnes & Noble** (over the "biggest bookstore in the world" claim) did little to convince Netizens that they were witnessing anything more than carefully orchestrated publicity stunts. Indeed, many felt launching a Web site without some kind of legal suit was a waste of free publicity. It seemed like just a bit of fun. And as big money flowed in, **bandwidths** increased, content improved, ma and pa scuttled aboard, and the online experience richened.

Alas, the same couldn't be said for the new school entrepreneurs. Low advertising costs saw **Usenet newsgroups and email in-trays** choked with crossposted get-rich schemes, network marketing plans, and porno adverts. Further, unprecedented **banks of email** broke servers at AOL, MSN, and scores of smaller providers. Temporarily, Netcom was forced to bar all mail originating from Hotmail, the most popular free Web email service, and consequent safe haven for fly-by-night operators due to the level of spam originating from its domain. At the same time, in July 1997, a mislaid backhoe ripped up a vital US backbone artery darkening large parts of the Net – something many had presumed impossible – and reducing the worldwide network to a crawl. The Net was nuclear-proof maybe, but certainly not invulnerable.

The world's biggest playground

By the end of 1997, the Net's population had skyrocketed to well over a hundred million. The media increasingly relied on it for research and, in the process, began to understand it. It could no longer be written off as geek-land when it was thrust this far into mainstream consciousness. Notable among the most recent arrivals were the so-called "grey surfers", predominantly retirees, who in some cases found it the difference between having few interests and few friends, and suddenly finding a reason to live. Indeed, the Net was looking not only useful, but essential, and those without it had good reason to feel left behind.

This new maturity arrived on the back of email, with the Web hot on its heels. As toner sales plummeted, surveys indicated that email had not only overtaken the fax, but possibly even the telephone, as the business communication tool of choice. However, at the same time, it could also lay claim to being the greatest time waster ever introduced into an office with staff spending large chunks of their days reading circulars, forwarding curios, and flirting with their online pals.

Email's speed, and the ease in carbon copying an entire address book, brought new implications to the six degrees of separation. Something with universal appeal, like the infernal dancing baby animation, could be disseminated to millions within a matter of hours, potentially reaching everyone on the Net within days. And, as most journalists were by this stage hooked in, whatever circulated on the Net often found its way into other media formats. Not surprisingly, the fastest-moving chain emails were often hoaxes. One such prank, an address of sensible old-timer advice, supposedly delivered by Kurt Vonnegut to MIT graduates (but actually taken from Mary Schmick's Chicago Tribune column) saturated the Net within a week. "Romeo and Juliet" director, Baz Lurhman, was so taken he put it to music resulting in the cult hit "Sunscreen", which even more incredibly was re-spoofed into a XXXX beer advert. All within six months.

On a more annoying note, almost everyone received virus hoaxes that warned not to open email with certain subject headings. Millions took them seriously, earnestly forwarding them to their entire address books. An email campaign kicked off by Howard Stern propelled "Hank, the ugly drunken dwarf" to the top of People's 100 Most Beautiful People poll as voted on the Net. Meanwhile the Chinese community rallied to push Michelle Kwan into second place. But the biggest coup of all was Matt Drudge's email leaking Bill Clinton's inappropriate affair with Monica Lewinsky, which sent the old world media into the biggest feeding frenzy since the OJ trial. Although it might not have brought down the most powerful man in the world, it showed how in 1998, almost anyone, anywhere, could be heard.

The show must go on

In May 1998, the blossoming media romance with hackers as urban folk heroes turned sour when a consortium of good-fairy hackers, known as the **L0pht**, assured a US Senate Government Affairs Committee that they, or someone less benevolent, could render the Net entirely unusable within half an hour. It wasn't meant as a threat, but a call to arms against the apathy of those who'd designed, sold, and administered the systems. The Pentagon had already been penetrated (by a young Israeli hacker), and though most reported attacks amounted to little more than vandalism, with an increasing number of essential services tapped in, the probability of major disaster veered toward looking possible.

Undeterred, Net commerce continued to break into new territories. **Music**, in particular, looked right at home with the arrival of DIY CD compilation shops and several major artists such as Massive Attack, Willie Nelson and the Beach Boys airing their new releases on the Net in MP3, before unleashing them on CD. However, these exclusive previews weren't always intentional. For instance, Swervedriver's beleaguered "99th Dream" found its way onto Net bootleg almost a year before its official release.

By now, celebrity chat appearances hardly raised an eyebrow. Even major powerbrokers like Clinton and Yeltsin had appeared before an online inquisition. To top it off, in April 1998, Koko, a 300-pound gorilla, fronted up to confess to some 20,000 chatsters that she'd rather be playing with Smokey, her pet kitten.

The red-light district

Despite the bottomless reserves of free Web space, personal vanity pages and Web diaries took a downturn in 1998. The novelty was passing, a sign perhaps that the Web was growing up. This didn't, however, prevent live Web cameras, better known as **Webcams**, from enjoying a popularity resurgence. But this time around they weren't so much being pointed at lizards, fish, ski slopes or intersections, but at whoever connected them to the Net – a fad which resulted in numerous bizarre excursions in exhibitionism from some very ordinary folk. Leading the fray was the entirely unremarkable Jennifer Ringley, who became a Web household name simply for letting the world see her move about her college room, clothed and, very occasionally, otherwise. She might have only been famous for being famous, but it was fame enough to land her a syndicated newspaper column about showing off and, of course, a tidy packet from the thousands of subscribers who paid real money to access Jennicam.

But this was the tame end of the Net's trade in voyeurism. And these were boom times for pornographers. Research suggested as high as 90 percent of network traffic was consumed by porn images. That's not to suggest that anywhere near 90 percent of users were involved, only that the images consume so much bandwidth. The story in Usenet was even more dire with more than 80 percent of the non-binary traffic hogged by spam and spam cancel messages. Meanwhile, the three top Web search aids, HotBot, Altavista and Yahoo, served click-through banners on suggestive keywords. However you felt about pornography from a moral standpoint, it had definitely become a nuisance.

The bottleneck

As 1998 progressed, **cable Internet access** became increasingly available, and even affordable in the USA. New subscribers could suddenly jump from download speeds of, at best, 56 Kbps to as high as 10 Mbps. Meanwhile several telcos, such as PacBell and GTE, began rolling out ADSL, another broadband technology capable of megabit access, this time over plain copper telephone wires. However, even at these speeds, users still had to deal with the same old bottleneck. Namely the Internet's backbone, which had been struggling to cope with even the low-speed dial-up traffic.

The power to **upgrade the backbone**, or more correctly backbones, lies in the hands of those who own the major cables and thus effectively control the Internet. It's always seemed inevitable that the global telecommunication superpowers would starve the smaller players out of the market. And the emergence of Internet telephony has forced telcos to look further down the track at the broader scenario where whoever controls the Internet not only controls data, but voice traffic as well. They recognize that their core business could be eroded by satellite and cable companies. To survive, telcos need to compete on the same level, provide an alternative, or join forces with their rivals. At the moment all three seem viable options.

The dust clears but the fog remains

As we packed up shop for the millennium, fretting over double-digit date blunders, the Internet settled into a consolidation phase. For the most part, what was hot got hotter while the remainder atrophied. Broadband cable, ADSL, and satellite access forged ahead, particularly in the US and Australia. Meanwhile in the UK, British Telecom stooped to an eleventh-hour exploit on its unpopular metered local call system, weaseling deals with local ISPs to enable free access by divvying up its phone bill booty. Surprisingly, instead of torching 10 Downing St for allowing the situation to exist in the first place, browbeaten Brits snapped it up, propelling free access pioneer Freeserve to the top of the ISP pops within months. At the time of writing, the situation is thickening with **budget all-you-can-eat ADSL** and **unmetered Internet calls** about to hit the UK streets.

Interest in online commerce surged with explosive growth in stock trading, auctions, travel booking, and mail order computers. Big-budget empire builders such as AOL, Amazon, Cisco, Disney, Excite, Microsoft, and Real Networks hit overdrive announcing intertwined strategic mergers and continued swallowing and stomping on smaller talent. Most notably AOL, with little more than a dip into petty cash, wolfed down Netscape. Not, as many assumed, for its revolutionary browser but for the sizable userbase still buzzing its browser's default home page. This, however, wasn't the Netscape of the mid-1990s, but a defeated relic that had lost its way, ceased innovating, and appeared unable to ship products. Its legacy had been passed over to Microsoft, which remained in court squabbling over Internet Explorer, Windows 98, and its success in cornering all but some 5 percent of the operating system market share. Apart from whatever voyeuristic pleasure could be gained from king-hitting computing's tallest poppy, the Department of Justice's case grew increasingly meaningless against the broader backdrop. No matter what the outcome, the computer-wielding public had arrived well before their dinner bell and their problem was not lack of choice, but lack of quality. Even Apple's allegedly foolproof iMac fell way short of a sturdy carriage to traverse the Net, play games, and make life generally more pushbutton computerized.

By this stage the Internet was ready to become a public utility, but both the computing and access provision industry remained rooted within a hobbyist mindset. As PC dealers shamelessly crammed their systems with interfering utilities, ISPs continued to supply inadequate bandwidth, unreliable software and irresponsible advice. Yet no alternative existed, and governments appeared incapable of intelligent input. As the 20th century bit the dirt, you didn't have to be a geek to get on the Net, but it sure didn't hurt.

The American dream

Doomsday was not televised live as daylight broke across the year 2000. Planes did not crash, Washington was not nuked, and ATMs did not randomly eject crisp dollar bills. Instead, attentions turned to cast fresh aspersions on the ever-inflating Internet stock bubble. The new tech stocks were driving the biggest speculative frenzy since Tulipmania. Every grandmother and her cabbie wanted in on the **Dot Com** action. **Cisco Systems**, a network hardware supplier and hardly a household name, celebrated its tenth birthday by briefly becoming the world's biggest company (in terms of market cap). To add further insult to the old world order, AOL, foster home to twenty million chirpy AOLers, offered its hand to the **TIME Warner** cross media conglomerate. Meanwhile billionaire playboy **Bill Gates**, the very essence of the American dream, continued defiantly delivering his own brand of truth, justice and the Microsoft way to the desktops of 19 out of 20 computers. What could possibly go wrong?

Too much gold for one gringo

Enter US District **Judge Thomas Penfield Jackson** who declared that Microsoft had maintained its monopoly by anti-competitive means, and that it should sever both physical and corporate ties between its Internet software and Windows. This ruling, he assured, would result in higher quality products due to increased competition. Which raised the question why software standards weren't directly on trial instead. But Microsoft had made few friends outside the fans of Ayn Rand, particularly within the ironically Mac monopolized media. Any public spanking was welcomed, so this was as good as a win. Yet, in reality, it was an unsatisfying outcome for all concerned. Not least for investors, whose tech share portfolios crumbled. And so that was it for the speculative Dot Com start-ups. As the house of Gates fell, so too did the bricks around it. By the time Flash riddled **Boo.com** folded in May 2000, Dot Com was already a dirty word.

With an appeal pending in the Supreme Court, Microsoft brazenly released **ME**, yet another version of Windows with Internet Explorer inside, and furthermore announced its future applications would be delivered on demand across the Net. What little sympathy remained for Bill and his merry cast of outlaws was almost completely eroded.

Nobody can stop the music

As wave after wave of email borne viruses sneezed from Outlook address books, it seemed clear that most office workers lacked basic computer training. Overlooked in the endless blather of mass media hysteria was the simple truth that **Melissa**, **Happy 99**, **I Love you**, and similar Internet worms could only be propagated by the grossly incompetent. It also seemed certain that it would happen again.

But viruses weren't the only source of mischief. A 15-year old Canadian, going by the name of Mafiaboy, unleashed a bevy of **Denial of Service** attacks temporarily knocking out several high profile Web sites such as Yahoo, Amazon and eTrade. Despite his relatively low level of technical expertise he was able to outwit the FBI for almost three months. Even then it was only his chat room confession that triggered the arrest.

With pirate **MP3 music tracks** hogging the bulk of college network bandwidth, legal action inevitably followed. **Napster** faced the music against stadium rockers Metallica, and the Recording Industry Association of America sued MP3.com over its ingenious Beam-It service. While the holders of copyright won in the courts of law, back in the real world it was not only business as usual, but the publicity drew millions of new music lovers into the trading loop. As mounting legal pressure pummeled Napster into the commercial reality of blocking copyrighted material from its servers, traders merely migrated to decentralized networks such as **WinMX** and **Gnutella**.

Dumb money

As the **new economy** lay gutted on the screens of the NASDAQ and beyond, many predicted a global meltdown in 2001. Yet, despite 90 percent falls in dotcom blue chips like Cisco, Amazon, and Yahoo, the broader economy remained surprisingly intact. So too did Microsoft, with the DC Court of Appeals overruling Judge Jackson's remedy to split the company. The appropriate sentence for its browser war crimes remains to be decided by the new look Bush DOJ.

Hard cash failures ushered in hard cold facts, and one of those was no secret to those who'd been online since the BBS days. The Net's popularity had been largely driven by the lure of something for nothing. Few wanted to pay when so much was free. Few wanted to click on banner ads. And even fewer could profit from advertising in someone's diary. As we waved goodbye to the dumber dotcoms, we also bid farewell to a romantic delusion called cyberspace. The Internet was no longer an exotic frontier, but a ubiquitous utility like the telephone.

And it certainly was everywhere. Suddenly it seemed mandatory to cast anything online that could be cast online. From inane Coke vending machines to inane reality TV experiments like Big Brother. So, of course, it seemed logical that celebrity bomber Timothy McVeigh should exit the jeering hordes live via RealVideo. When a federal judge refused the Entertainment Network's request to Webcast the execution in April 2001, it was the surest sign we'd entered a brave new era. One where common sense still stood a chance.

A brighter tomorrow

Now that the **people's network** has the globe in an irreversible stranglehold, you might assume the wired revolution is as good as over. Perhaps it is, but for those in the dark, the reality can be less comforting. A passable knowledge of the Internet in 1997 was enough to land you a job. Today, in many fields, it's becoming a prerequisite. It's a case of get online or get left behind. But the most worrisome aspect is not the difficulty in getting online, but the time involved in keeping up to date, and its stress on our physical, mental, and social wellbeing.

Still, like it or not, the Net is the closest thing yet to an all-encompassing snapshot of the human race. Never before have our words and actions been so immediately accountable in front of such a far-reaching audience. If we're scammed, we can instantly warn others. If we believe there's a government cover-up, we can expose it through the Net. If we want to be heard, no matter what it is we have to say, we can tell it to the Net. And, in the same way, if we need to know more, or we need to find numbers, we can turn to it for help.

What's most apparent all up, is that humanity looks in pretty okay shape. That's kind of ironic, because it didn't necessarily look that way before. But we've now been able to see that for every extreme there appears to be many more moderates; for every hate group, a thousand peace-makers; and for every conspiracy theory, if not some sensible explanation, then at least a few attentive ears. We've been able to examine the weirdest and the worst the world has to offer and contrast it against a greater global theme. Now that our boundaries are so much easier to explore, the future of not only the Net, but the planet itself, surely looks brighter.

The problem with such rapid improvement is that our expectations grow to meet it. But the Net, even at age thirty-something, is still only in its infancy. So be patient, enjoy it for what it is today, and complain, but not too much. One day you'll look back and get all nostalgic about the times you logged into the world through old copper telephone wires. It's amazing it works at all.

17

Glossary

A

ActiveX Microsoft concept that allows a program to run inside a Web page.

Add/Remove Programs Correct place to uninstall programs from Windows. Found in the Control Panel.

ADSL (**A**synchronous **D**igital **S**ubscriber **L**ine). Broadband over the phone line.

Anonymous FTP server Remote computer, with a publicly accessible file archive, that accepts "anonymous" as the log-in name and an email address as the password.

Antivirus scanner Program that detects, and sometimes removes, computer viruses.

AOL (**A**merica **O**nline). Last surviving Online Service. Loved by all.

Applet A small program.

Archive File that bundles a set of other files together under a single name for transfer or backup. Often compressed to reduce size, or encrypted for privacy.

Attachment File included with email or other form of message.

B

Backbone Set of paths that carry longhaul Net traffic.

Bandwidth Size of the data pipeline. Increase bandwidth and more data can flow at once.

Binary file Any file that contains more than plain text such as a program or image.

Binhex Method of encoding, used on Macs.

Bookmarks Netscape file used to store Web addresses.

Bounced mail Email returned to sender.

Bps (**B**its **p**er **s**econd). Basic measure of data transfer.

Broadband High-speed Internet access.

Browser Web viewing program such as Internet Explorer.

Buffer Temporary data storage.

Bug Logical, physical or programming error in software or hardware that causes a recurring malfunction.

C

Cache Temporary storage space.

Client Program that accesses information across a network, such as a Web browser or newsreader.

COM port See Serial port

Context menu See Mouse menu

Crack Break a program's security, integrity, or registration system, or fake a user ID.

Crash When a program or operating system fails to respond or causes other programs to malfunction.

Cyber In IRC, may be short for cybersex, that is the online equivalent of phone sex.

Cyberspace Coined by science-fiction writer William Gibson, to describe the virtual world that exists within the marriage of computers, telecommunication networks, and digital media.

D

Default The standard settings.

Dialog box Window that appears on the screen to ask or tell you something.

Dial-Up connection Temporary network connection between two computers via a telephone line.

Digital signing Encrypted data appended to a message to identify the sender.

DNS Domain Name System. The system that locates the numerical IP address corresponding to a host name.

Domain Part of the DNS name that specifies details about the host, such as its location and whether it is part of a commercial (**.com**), government (**.gov**), or educational (**.edu**) entity.

Download To copy files from a remote computer to your own.

Driver Small program that acts like a translator between a device and programs that use that device.

DSL (**D**igital **S**ubscriber **L**ine). Encompasses all forms including ADSL. Sometimes called xDSL.

E

Email Electronic mail carried on the Net.

Email address The unique private Internet address to which email is sent. Takes the form **user@host**

F

FAQ (**F**requently **A**sked **Q**uestions). Document that answers the most commonly asked questions on a particular topic.

File Anything stored on a computer, such as a program, image, or document.

File compression Reducing a file's size for transfer or storage.

File extension Set of characters added to the end of a filename (after a period) intended to identify the file as a member of a category (file type). For example, the extension .TXT identifies a text file.

Finger A program that can return stored data on UNIX users or other information such as weather updates. Often disabled for security reasons.

Firewall Network security system used to restrict external and internal traffic.

Firmware Software routines stored in the read only memory of a hardware device.

Frag Network gaming term meaning to destroy or fragment. Came from DOOM.

FTP File Transfer Protocol. Standard method of moving files across the Internet.

G

GIF (**G**raphic **I**mage **F**ile format). Compressed graphics format prefered for use in small Web images such as buttons and icons.

Google Popular Web search engine located at **http://www.google.com**

Gopher Defunct menu-based system for retrieving Internet archives, usually organized by subject.

Hacker Someone who gets off on breaking through computer security and limitations. A cracker is a criminal hacker.

Header Pre-data part of a packet, containing source and destination addresses, error checking, and other fields. Also the first part of an email or news posting which contains, among other things, the sender's details and time sent.

Home page Either the first page loaded by your browser at start-up, or the main Web document for a particular group, organization, or person.

Host Computer that offers some sort of services to networked users.

HTML (**H**yper**T**ext **M**arkup **L**anguage.) The language used to create Web documents.

HyperText links The "clickable" links or "hot-spots" that interconnect pages on the Web.

I

ICQ Popular Instant messaging program. **http://www.icq.com**

Image map A Web image that contains multiple links. Which link you take depends on where you click.

IMAP Internet Message Access Protocol. Standard email access protocol that's superior to POP3 in that you can selectively retrieve messages or parts thereof as well as manage folders on the server.

Infinite loop See loop.

Install To place a program's working files onto a computer so that it's ready to be set up and used. Normally done by clicking on a setup file (often called setup.exe).

Instant Messaging Point to point chat such as ICQ.

Internet Co-operatively run global collection of computer networks with a common addressing scheme.

Internet connection sharing (ICS) Allows a networked computer to access the Internet through another's connection. A feature of Windows 98 SE and later.

Internet Explorer Microsoft's Web browser bundled with the operating system since Windows 98. Download from: **http://www.microsoft.com/ie/**

Internet Favorites Internet Explorer folder for filing Web addresses.

Internet Shortcut Microsoft's terminology for a Web address or URL.

IP (**I**nternet **P**rotocol). The most important protocol upon which the Internet is based. Defines how packets of data get from source to destination.

IP address Every computer connected to the Internet has an **IP address** (written in dotted numerical notation), which corresponds to its domain name. Domain Name Servers convert one to the other.

IRC (Internet **R**elay **C**hat). Internet system where you can send text, or audio, to others in real time, like an online version of CB radio.

ISDN (**I**ntegrated **S**ervices **D**igital **N**etwork). International standard for digital communications over telephone lines. Allows data transmission at 64 or 128 Kbps.

ISP (Internet **S**ervice **P**rovider.) Company that sells access to the Internet.

J

Java Platform-independent programming language designed by Sun Microsystems. **http://www.sun.com**

JPG/JPEG Graphic file format preferred online because its high compression reduces file size, and thus the time it takes to transfer.

K

Kbps (**K**ilobits per second). Standard measure of data transfer speed.

Kill file Newsreader file into which you can enter keywords and email addresses to stop unwanted articles.

L

LAN (**L**ocal **A**rea **N**etwork). Computer network that spans a relatively small area such as an office.

Latency Length of time it takes data to reach its destination.

Leased line Dedicated telecommunications link between two points.

Link In hypertext, as in a Web page, a link is a reference to another document. When you click on a link in a browser, that document will be retrieved and displayed, played or downloaded depending on its nature.

Linux Freely distributed implementation of the UNIX operating system.

Log on / Log in Connect to a computer network.

Loop See infinite loop.

M

MIME (**M**ultipurpose **I**nternet **M**ail **E**xtensions). Standard for the transfer of binary email attachments.

Mirror Replica FTP or Web site set up to share traffic.

Modem (**Mo**dulator/**Dem**odulator). Device that allows a computer to communicate with another over a standard telephone line, by converting the digital data into analog signals and vice versa.

Mouse menu Useful custom menu that pops up when you right-click (by default) on screen items such as icons, Web links, and taskbars.

Mouse wheel Rolling wheel positioned between the right and left mouse buttons on suitably equipped mice. Invaluable for scrolling pages and selecting weapons in first person shooters.

MP3 A compressed music format.

MPEG/MPG A compressed video file format.

Multithreaded Able to process multiple requests at once.

N

Name server Host that translates domain names into IP addresses.

The Net The Internet.

Netscape Web browser – and the company that produces it, now owned by AOL.

Newbie Newcomer to the Net, discussion, or area.

Newsgroups Usenet message areas, or discussion groups, organized by subject hierarchies.

NNTP Network News Transfer Protocol. Standard for the exchange of Usenet articles across the Internet.

Node Any device connected to a network.

O

Online 1.The state of being connected to a network, typically the Internet. 2. Describes a resource that is located on the Internet.

Outlook Microsoft's business email program incorporated into MS Office. Includes scheduling and contact tools, but no Usenet reader.

Outlook Express Leaner version of the above that's bundled free with Internet Explorer, and Windows 98 and later. Smarter choice for home use.

P

Packet Unit of data. In data transfer, information is broken into packets, which then travel independently through the Net. An Internet packet contains the source and destination addresses, an identifier, and the data segment.

Packet loss Failure to transfer units of data between network nodes. A high percentage makes transfer slow or impossible.

Patch Temporary or interim add-on to fix or upgrade software.

Ping Echo-like trace that tests if a host is available.

Platform Computer operating system, such as Mac OS, Windows, or Linux.

Plug-in Program that fits into another.

POP3 (Post Office Protocol). Email protocol that allows you to pick up your mail from anywhere on the Net, even if you're connected through someone else's account.

POPs Points of Presence. An ISP's range of local dial-in points.

Port number The numerical address of a process running on a computer attached to the Internet.

Portal Web site that specializes in leading you to others.

Post To send a public message to a Usenet newsgroup.

Protocol Agreed way for two network devices to talk to each other.

Proxy server Sits between a client, such as a Web browser, and a real server. Most often used to improve performance by delivering stored pages like browser cache and to filter out undesirable material.

QuickTime Apple's proprietary multimedia standard. Commonly used to preview movies online. Download the Windows player from **http://www.quicktime.com**

README file A last-minute document, included with program setup files, that gives installation instructions and other messages from the developers. Sometimes useful when things go wrong.

RealAudio A standard for streaming compressed audio over the Internet. See: **http://www.real.com**

Registry Windows database for system and software configuration settings. Edit (at your own risk) by typing Regedit at the Run command in the Start menu.

Robot Program that automates Net tasks such as collating search engine databases or automatically responding in IRC. Also called a Bot.

S

Search engine Database of Web page extracts that can be queried to find reference to something on the Net. Example: Google (**http://www.google.com**)

Server Computer that makes services available on a network.

Shareware Software with a free trial period, sometimes with reduced features.

Signature file 1. Personal footer that can be attached automatically to email and Usenet postings. 2. Database used by virus scanners to keep track of strains. Update regularly.

Spam (n & v). Junk email or Usenet postings.

Streaming Delivered in real time instead of waiting for the whole file to arrive, eg RealAudio.

Stuffit Common Macintosh file compression format and program.

Surf Skip from page to page around the Web by following links.

T

TCP/IP (Transmission Control Protocol/Internet Protocol). The protocols that drive the Internet.

Telnet Internet protocol that allows you to log on to a remote computer and act as a dumb terminal.

Temporary Internet Files Special system folder used by Internet Explorer to store Web pages contents for quick recall when backtracking. Wise to empty contents regularly through Internet Properties, General tab.

Trojan (horse) Program that hides its true (usually sinister) intention.

Troll Prank newsgroup posting intended to invoke an irate response.

U

Update (v) Bring a program, program version, operating system, or data file (such as a virus scanner signature) up to date by installing a patch, revision or complete new version.

Upgrade A newer, and presumably improved version of a hardware or software system, or the process of installing it.

Upload Send files to a remote computer.

UNIX Operating system used by most ISPs and colleges. So long as you stick to graphic interfaces, you'll never notice it.

URL (Uniform Resource Locator). Formal name for a Web address.

USB (Universal Serial Bus). High speed serial bus standard that allows for the connection of up to 127 devices and offers advanced plug and play features. Gradually replacing the serial, parallel, keyboard, and mouse ports.

Usenet User's Network. A collection of networks and computer systems that exchange messages, organized by subject into newsgroups.

Utility program A small program which extends, supplements or enhances the functionality of the operating system.

UUencode Method of encoding binary files into text so that they can be attached to mail or posted to Usenet. They must be UUdecoded to convert them back. Most mail and news programs do it automatically. Alternative to MIME.

V

Vaporware Rumored or announced, but non-existent, software or hardware. Often used as a competitive marketing ploy.

Version Number Unique code used to distinguish between product releases.

W

Warez Slang for software, usually pirated.

The Web The World Wide Web or WWW. Graphic and text documents published on the Internet that are interconnected through clickable "hypertext" links. A Web page is a single document. A Web site is a collection of related documents.

Web authoring Designing and publishing Web pages using HTML.

Webmaster Person who maintains a Web site.

World Wide Web See Web, above.

WYSIWYG What You See Is What You Get. What you type is the way it comes out.

Y

Yahoo The Web's most popular Web portal: **http://www.yahoo.com**

Z

Zip PC file compression format that creates files with the extension .zip, usually using the WinZip program (**http://www.winzip.com**). Frequently used to reduce file size for transfer or storage on floppy disks.

Still confused . . .

Then try:

PC Webopedia **http://www.webopedia.com**
What is? **http://www.whatis.com**
Netlingo **http://www.netlingo.com**

18

51 things to do with this book

You're on the Net, so where now? Has it all been worth the effort? Here, in no particular order, are 51 ways to idle away your online time. Just key in the Web address or go to the page in this book for instructions.

1. **Look yourself up on the Web**
   http://www.google.com

2. **Re-ignite an old flame**
   See p.124

3. **Deactivate an alien implant**
   See p.405

4. **Get fresh with the US President**
   http://www.whitehouse.gov

5. **Go undercover**
   See p.138 and p.215

6. **Dig up dirt on a movie star**
   See p.347

7. **Flirt with a stranger**
   See p.197

8. **Land a cushy job**
   See p.341

9. **Cast a voodoo spell**
   http://www.vudutuu.com

10. **Join a kooky cult**
    See p.425 and p.460

11. **Kick butt**
    See p.284

12. **Tune in to foreign radio**
    See p.414

13. **Find out if you're "hot" or "not"**
    See p.423

14. **Rekindle your childhood interests**
    See p.152 and p.197

15. **Make your first billion**
    See p.381

16. **Get fanatical about football**
See p.437

17. **Relocate to Mars**
http://www.marsshop.com

18. **Confirm you're mad**
http://www.mentalhealth.com

19. **Plot an exotic adventure**
See p.447

20. **Cast no doubt on your ancestry**
See p.363

21. **Become a whiz with nuclear arms**
See p.431

22. **Cheat your way through college**
See p.341

23. **Stock up on frilly bras**
See p.177

24. **Keep up with your hometown gossip**
See p.398

25. **Stare into deep space**
See p.434

26. **Cook up a treat**
See p.355

27. **Toilet-train your cat**
See p.466

28. **Secretly watch sport at work**
See p.437

29. Nab your crushed one
http://www.secretadmirer.com

30. Never lose an argument
See p.152 and p.197

31. Track down a killer novel
See p.325

32. Build your own computer
See p.338

33. Seek legal advice
See p.379

34. Obey the Interplanetary Council
See p.461

35. Eavesdrop on a drug bust
http://www.policescanner.com

36. Clone a companion
http://www.clonaid.com

37. Start your own magazine
See p.291

38. Sort out your weeds
See p.372

39. Show off your baby snaps
See p.126 and p.295

40. Consult a mad scientist
http://www.madsci.org

41. Become a minister of the Universal Life Church
See p.429

42. **Indulge in hypochondria**
http://www.whathaveigot.net

43. **Learn how to be cool**
http://www.geocities.com/SunsetStrip/4160/big.html

44. **Work from the Bahamas**
See p.342

45. **Start an argument**
See p.197

46. **Sit in on a live gig**
http://www.liveconcerts.com

47. **Master your own music compilation CD**
See p.282

48. **Disappear with the Foreign Legion**
http://www.foreignlegionlife.com

49. **Strike up a bargain**
See p.185

50. **Email a smoochy tune**
See p.128

51. **Admit you now have a problem**
http://www.internetaddiction.com

Got a favorite site or activity on the Net?
Then let us know by email at:
angus@easynet.co.uk

a

c

f

g

h

i

m

n

o

p

q

r

t

u

w

Feedback

This guide has already helped more than 3 million people online since 1995, many of whom have written back with suggestions. I'm grateful for this feedback as it makes the job of keeping it up to date and useful so much easier.

You're now holding the seventh edition. That means it's been written seven times – each time undergoing a major overhaul. That's how much the Internet changes each year. Sites disappear, addresses change, and things that are hot suddenly go cold. So don't be too alarmed if the sands have shifted slightly since this was written. Nonetheless, if you find errors I'd like to know.

Being such a popular book means it's spawned many imitators, which you'll no doubt see in the shelves beside it. Please compare this guide to those, and if you feel they do a better job, then write to me and tell me where I've gone wrong.

If you feel we've cheated you out of your money, you can get even by giving this book a scathing review at one of the online bookstores (p.326).

Angus Kennedy
angus@easynet.co.uk

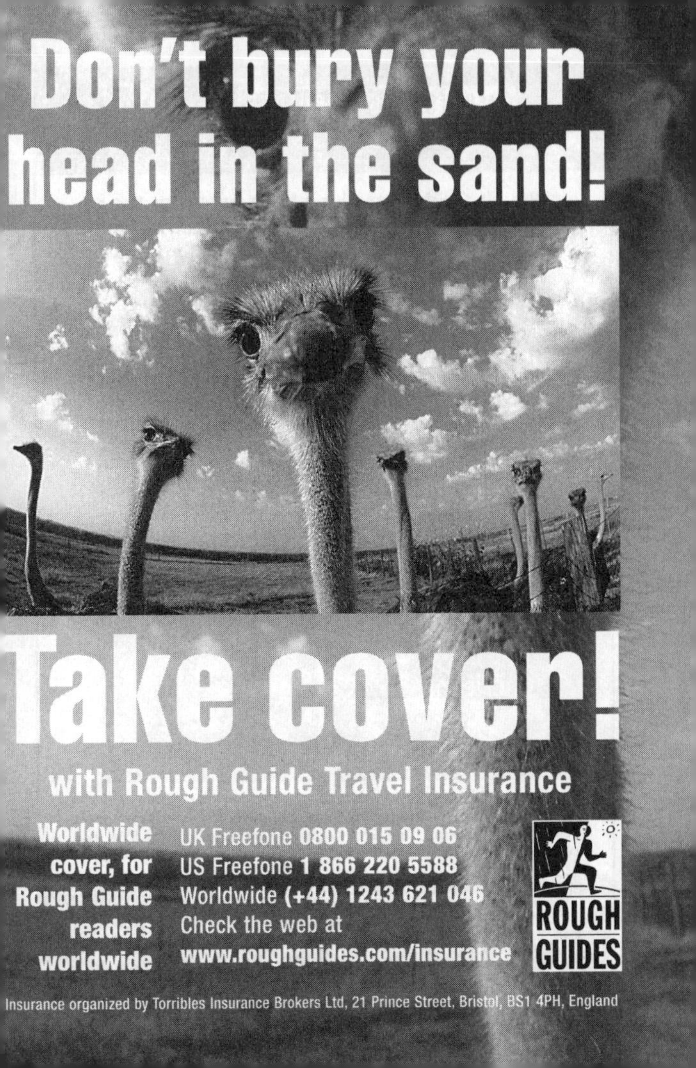
Don't bury your head in the sand!
Take cover!
with Rough Guide Travel Insurance
Worldwide cover, for Rough Guide readers worldwide
UK Freefone 0800 015 09 06
US Freefone 1 866 220 5588
Worldwide (+44) 1243 621 046
Check the web at
www.roughguides.com/insurance
ROUGH GUIDES
Insurance organized by Torribles Insurance Brokers Ltd, 21 Prince Street, Bristol, BS1 4PH, England

notes

notes

notes